PRIMARY PHILOSOPHY

MICHAEL SCRIVEN

D.Phil (Oxford), M.A. (Melbourne)
Professor of the History and Philosophy of Science
Indiana University

McGRAW-HILL BOOK COMPANY

New York   St. Louis   San Francisco   Toronto   London   Sydney

Primary Philosophy

Library of Congress Catalog Card Number 65–28826
1234567890 MP 7321069876

*To the students who have been my friends
and the friends whose student I have been.*

"What is the use of studying philosophy if all that it does for you is to enable you to talk with some plausibility about some abstruse questions of logic, etc., and if it does not improve your thinking about the important questions of everyday life . . . ?"

—*Wittgenstein to Malcolm*
(Ludwig Wittgenstein: A
Memoir, *by Norman
Malcolm*)

PREFACE

This book discusses the great philosophical problems of our day; not the technical ones, but the ones whose answers directly bear on our lives, the ones that everyone thinks philosophy should answer. And the discussion in this book arrives at answers; it isn't just an intellectual juggling exhibition of the on-the-one-hand-this-but-on-the-other-hand-that variety. This commitment to answers may turn out to be mistaken, if the questions cannot be answered, but it must be tried. It is said that every age must rewrite its histories; it is clear that every age must do its own philosophy. Some of today's philosophical problems are old problems, but some of them are new; and even the old problems have new twists, and new answers to them have appeared or old answers decayed. We cannot assume that the complexion of philosophy is best determined through the eyes of dead philosophers. We must look for ourselves.

It is often said that contemporary philosophy has turned its back on the great problems. The short comment is that astronomy, physics and mathematics have done the same. The problems occupying these subjects today are rarely classical, popular, or practical. Yet there are few complaints about this state of affairs, because we know that consequences of great everyday interest spring from these abstract speculations. Armies of applied scientists and engineers exist to extract these consequences, but the economic and social pressures that create such armies are rarely found for philosophy. Yet it should not be concluded that contemporary research in philosophy has no applications to the philosophy of everyday life. On the contrary, it implies important changes in the complexion of that philosophy. This book is intended to convey those changes. Perhaps that means it is a journeyman's book and not a scholar's; it is rather to be hoped that in philosophy one can still combine the noble aims of both professions. At any rate, the questions discussed and the length of the discussions reflect not only academic judgments of importance and difficulty but the reactions of many thousands of students at nearly a hundred schools, colleges and universities where earlier versions of these discussions were aired.

In passing, one might note that any reluctance among professional philosophers to take stands about or even discuss the issues of everyday philosophy is amply justified by the reactions of society when they do. The philosopher engaged in public controversy lives dangerously; he escapes derision for irrelevance only by risking doom for subversion. For every Marx there are many martyrs; gibes are never so bitter as hemlock.

Of course, there are many ways to explore the country of philosophy. This book is for the mountain climbers. It is designed to take you from the foothills to the main peaks by the shortest path a healthy novice can handle. Not all guides think these peaks can be scaled at all, let alone by a novice, and they will recommend other itineraries, in which the great vistas from lesser hills are studied more carefully and the many trails and tricks worked out by our predecessors are thoroughly learned. Others feel more optimistic about your eventual success but nevertheless believe that such activities are the best preliminary training. For those with the time and the inclination to undertake a longer apprenticeship, this book may be usefully supplemented with readings from an historical anthology, of which the outstanding example is Pap and Edwards, *A Modern Introduction to Philosophy* (Free Press), or from a less directive and more methodology-centered single-author treatment, of which the best example is John Hospers' *Introduction to Philosophical Analysis* (Prentice-Hall). But if you are here only for the views, we are not the guides you want.

Michael Scriven

ACKNOWLEDGMENTS

This book has benefited greatly from the criticisms of a number of philosophers who read drafts of parts or all of it. It is probable that the names of others should appear below, for this has been a long task and one's memory is not so long. I hope that any such critic and many new ones will give me the chance to acknowledge their help if good fortune provides a future occasion. Good criticism is by far the most valuable condiment in the philosopher's diet, even if not the most palatable, and it has been and will be very greatly appreciated.

Tony Flew performed, in a truly noble and characteristically meticulous way, the colossal task of line-by-line criticism of what would have been the complete final draft. Arthur Danto commented on an early draft of almost every chapter, and various drafts of one or more chapters were criticized by Kurt Baier, Gerald Barnes, Monroe Beardsley, Richard Brandt, Paul Dietl, Paul Edwards, Albert Elsen, Gilbert Harman, Herbert Hart, Charles Hartshorne, Sidney Hook, Blair Knight, Mernet Larsen, Robert McLaughlin, Jack Rawls, Jerome Shaffer, Morris Weitz, Georg Henrik von Wright, Gabrielle Yablonsky and the Free Philosophy group at Indiana University.

On the production side, I have been especially fortunate not only in the secretary who carried the main burden, Ida Darsow, but in those who assisted her so intelligently and so faithfully, and in the truly exceptional cooperation of my editor and his assistants; Carolyn Crow bore the main burden of the index magnificently.

Finally, I am indebted to Professor John Wisdom, the Aristotelian Society, and Basil Blackwell & Mott, Ltd., for permission to reprint the extract from "Gods" on page 67, first published in the *Proceedings of the Aristotelian Society*, Vol. 45, 1944, and reprinted in *Philosophy and Psychoanalysis*; and to Professor Norman Malcolm and the Oxford University Press for permission to reprint the extract from *Ludwig Wittgenstein: A Memoir* which appears as the inscription to this book.

CONTENTS

CHAPTER V   MAN   168

CHAPTER VI   RESPONSIBILITY   198

CHAPTER VII   MORALITY   229

I

PHILOSOPHY

0. THE AIM OF THE BOOK

This book is devoted to a discussion of certain fundamental philosophical problems which are here called the primary problems of philosophy. The primary problems of philosophy are those to which everyone has an answer, whether he knows it or not, and which everyone can understand whether he has tried to or not. A man's private behavior makes clear whether he believes morality to be just a system of conventions, art a matter of taste, and God a myth; and the questions whether he is right in these beliefs are three of the primary problems of philosophy. Although he may never discuss these issues in his lifetime, he does not hereby avoid them; and they are the first questions he raises if he has an inquiring mind and a desire to justify his behavior or understand the most penetrating puzzles about his world. Even for those who dismiss philosophical speculation with disdain for many years, there often comes a day when they are tormented by deep questions: Why did this terrible thing have to happen? How can you be so *sure* this is the right thing to do? What have I done to deserve this? Why are any of us here at all? Such questions—not themselves primary problems—exhibit vast philosophical assumptions which are answers to the primary problems, answers of the kind we shall examine here. And they illustrate the sense in which the primary problems of philosophy are the primary problems of life. We cannot choose whether to answer them, for to live requires that we answer them in our lives. We can only choose whether to think about them.

Fifty years ago Bertrand Russell wrote a book called *The Problems of Philosophy*, in which he said that philosophy should not be studied "for the sake of definite answers to its questions, since no definite answer can, as a rule, be known to be true, but rather for the sake of the questions themselves . . . ." The primary problems of philosophy are usually raised by those with an urgent need for definite answers, and for them Russell's view is a discouraging one. But he was writing in part of other problems and at another time. For the *primary* problems, at *this* time, it seems possible to give and justify definite answers. Certainly the attempt should be made; and if it fails, it must be made again and again.

Primary philosophy is the study of these problems and the answers to them. It is here discussed in the language of the layman. Technical language and technical references are therefore avoided or relegated to footnotes; but technical *skill* cannot be thus dismissed. The arguments may use simple language, may even—it is to be hoped—involve simple steps, but they will not make casual reading for those unused to discussion of abstract questions.

There is no discussion of the answers given by great men from past and present ages unless they were clearly right or temptingly wrong, and then the discussion is not of their views as their views but as answers to problems. This is not a history, although it is indebted to history. It makes no claims of originality and thereby avoids the need to untangle the origin of the views discussed. That is a separate task, and to combine it with discussing the problems does no service to either. To *introduce* philosophy by means of its history all too often requires that one disgrace scholarship or bore the reader, for to master the language and thought of another age is essential for proper understanding and impossible for the beginner. The history of philosophy is a subject for the advanced worker, and the usual historical tour through philosophy is as interesting and superficial as "Europe in Ten Days."

1. THE FORM OF THE BOOK

Each chapter has the same simple structure. It begins with a list of questions of the kind to be discussed: the list is not exhaustive but offers a sample of the questions to be answered. The material from which the answers will be constructed is then introduced in an orderly way, and the questions are further analyzed to show how they can be answered by means of it. Summaries of the more complicated answers are given in conclusion, where condensation does not introduce excessive distortion. The unorganized list of questions with which chapters begin is indigestible for the would-be fast reader. It is meant to be. Put in a natural order, these questions *would* read too fast. Each of them should bring one up short and make one look at it hard. The list might have been replaced by a discursive introduction to the problems, but this would have necessitated relating the questions to each other, and the proper way of doing that depends on answering the questions; so it should not be done at the beginning. The questions are what we really do begin with.

By contrast, the development of the answers will sometimes seem too easy (the footnotes are used for more difficult material that is relevant but unessential). For those familiar with the great debates that have gone on through the centuries about some of them, it may seem sacrilegious, arrogant, or naïve to ignore some of the famous alternative answers. The newcomer, on the other hand, will sometimes wonder why anyone could ever have argued about such obvious points. The procedure adopted is governed by a single consideration. It is designed to avoid an insidious temptation in the treatment of philosophical problems: the temptation to throw the student into a succession of swamps, from each of which in turn he is proudly rescued only to be pushed into the next. That procedure gives the teacher the wonderfully comforting feeling of doing important rescue work, a feeling whose glow quite over- whelms the chill of conscience. The aim here is to point out what seems to be the best path through the swamps and only explain how to win the struggle with the crocodiles that actually inhabit this path. Many of the ancient diffi- culties in philosophy should be avoided rather than conquered, if you believe that getting through to the primary answers is more important than getting exercise.

2. PHILOSOPHICAL ARGUMENT

Philosophical argument proceeds at a level of abstraction and by means of inferences that are often difficult for the novice to grasp. When stripped of its technical jargon, as it is here, it sometimes appears to be entirely without substance to those more familiar with the rigid moves and elaborate vocabu- lary of formal sciences. Yet subtlety should not be mistaken for sterility. Philosophical argument is no more a feeble form of mathematics than is sci- ence, no more a feeble form of science than is jurisprudence.

The elusive nature of philosophical argument is forced upon it by its high aims. Philosophy is the one subject in which no unquestioned assumptions are allowed, in which every premise and every principle of reasoning must themselves be justified. It is this that makes its challenge the greatest of all intellectual challenges, and the legitimate procedures of philosophical proof the most elusive. Of course the proofs in mathematics are more conclusive than philosophical proofs *for someone who accepts the axioms from which they begin.* But those axioms are continually being challenged, though not within the context of everyday mathematical activities. Now if the *axioms* of mathematics are to be justified, we must turn to the philosophy of mathematics, to the great debates between the formalists, the intuitionists, and the platonists. And that debate cannot be settled by a mathematical proof, because it concerns what counts as a proof. So the certainty of mathematics and, similarly, of science is merely conditional; it rests upon assumptions that cannot themselves be proved within mathematics and science. These assumptions can be supported only within the *philosophy* of mathematics or of science. If one feels that mathematical and scientific proofs are really satisfactory, one is taking a stand on a particular position in the philosophy of that subject. One must believe that that stand could be justified, shown to be superior to the many alternatives which great thinkers have preferred. So one is committed to the view that some philosophical positions *can* be established beyond reasonable doubt. Indeed, exactly the same argument applies with respect to the primary problems of philosophy. We can easily give practical arguments of one kind or another that seem very convincing. But the question whether they really should be convincing is itself a philosophical question, and when we get behind the scenes to settle it, of course we find that the simple conventions of ordinary argument can no longer be regarded as adequate. But if ordinary argument is practically valuable, there must surely be some kind of rules for the game behind the scenes in terms of which we can show this. Perhaps the rule is simply that whatever works best is right. In short, non-philosophy rests on philosophical assumptions, and if, as we firmly believe, there are sound procedures of argument in science, mathematics, or practical contexts, we should be able to show that they are sound; i.e., there should be sound procedures for philosophical demonstration.

In a field in which no starting points are beyond criticism, proofs will at first be only conditional: at first they will say, "From *this* assumption we are forced to this conclusion." Then we must develop similar "conditional proofs" that begin from other assumptions, the other possible starting points, and show that the end point is the same. When this can be done for a set of starting points that exhausts the possibilities, we shall have a proof of much greater absolute power than proofs within mathematics or science, each of which begins from a particular set of assumptions not shown to be the best within the subject. And this is the goal of philosophical argument.

Even when we cannot show that *all* roads lead to Rome, a great deal is still possible. The man who raises a particular primary problem, who asks whether aesthetic judgments have true objectivity, perhaps, or whether any of us can really be blamed for what we do, is normally willing to grant that there are other people and real objects—that the critics and paintings and people he praises or despises are not figments of his imagination. And granted that assumption, we can often satisfy him with a conditional proof beginning with such premises, the ones that he is willing to accept. In this respect the philosopher is like a mathematician who offers a proof within a particular system.

Yet even the conditional philosophical proof may still strike a mathematician or a scientist as unconvincing for another reason. He will be struck by the relative imprecision of the terms of ordinary discourse in comparison with mathematical terms. He may even make the naïve blunder of supposing that philosophical disputes are simply due to the confusion arising from this imprecision. Of course he would not object to the language of probability theory or statistics on the ground it does not give precise information about every member of the ensembles it discusses: this feature, which is a kind of imprecision, is its value, not its weakness. In exactly the same way, everyday language could not perform the tasks for which it is needed if it were precise in the way appropriate to mathematics; in particular it would lack the flexibility that allows it to adapt itself to novel objects and circumstances. And it is this possibility of extending the use of a common term that makes poetry, good reporting, scientific theorizing, and logical analysis not only possible but matters of skill. The skills required are not those of mathematical deduction, but then nor are the skills of statistical inference of that kind. Logical and philosophical analysis using ordinary language requires a different skill; in return it can handle problems that cannot be handled, and sometimes cannot even be expressed, in a precise language. And the impossibility of expressing problems in a precise language does not show them to be a by-product of confusion; they are an essential outcome of serious thought about complex features of the world in which we live that cannot be described in a rigid vocabulary. It must be noted that the more general questions in science often require for their formulation a language which cannot be precisely defined in the present sense, the language of space and time and mass and temperature and quantity and measurement. In short, only the divorce between mathematics and reality makes exact definition possible in that field. It is *because* the primary problems concern issues central to our lives that they cannot be solved by moving to an abstract language.

In practical terms, it is easy enough to see that decisive proof is still possible even with language whose terms have imprecise boundaries. Such proof must proceed by steps that do not exploit this borderline vagueness. Again, it is important to remember that the total meaning of a sentence may be clear, even though some of the words in it are extremely difficult to define in the abstract. For example, no one has any difficulty in understanding the sentence, "It is true that Socrates could have escaped from Athens, but he chose not to";

but it is difficult or impossible to give a truly precise definition of "truth" or "choice" in the abstract, i.e., one that will cover all proper uses. So this sentence can be used as a premise in an argument without risk, as long as conclusions which use these terms in a different sense are not drawn from it.

In philosophy, we lift ourselves up by our bootstraps: we begin with problems which we think of, state, and discuss in ordinary language, but we eventually reach a better understanding of the very concepts used in the original question, an understanding which may even lead us to improve or abandon them. We develop our instinct for the sense of words just as a physician develops his instinct for the significance of symptoms. That we can do this is as interesting as, but no more nearly impossible than, the fact that we can use imprecise instruments to make more precise ones, proceeding thus from the stone ax to the scalpel. That we sometimes change or abandon our starting language is no reason for thinking that we should, or even that we could, always do so. That philosophy is much concerned with the messy meanings of the terms of ordinary language is just a sign that it is concerned with the complex problems of a life which that language was tailored to describe.

Thus, philosophical proof requires more consideration of the alternatives to the assumptions with which proofs begin than mathematical proof, it requires special skills and techniques for handling its imprecise starting language, and it deals with questions for which conceptual analysis and not experimental testing is the primary tool. If you read these conditions carefully, you will see they also describe the procedures of judges of the highest courts, the most theoretical physicists, the purest of pure mathematicians, and many of the most original writers. What these men do is not sharply distinct from philosophy. Philosophy surrounds us on all sides, and only the use of its name can be escaped.

3. THE TEMPTATION OF ABSTRACT ANSWERS

The first question we take up in Chapter II is: Why should we be reasonable or rational? [1]

It is a mark of someone with a philosophical turn of mind that he finds questions such as this peculiarly fascinating. This question calls into court one of the great tools of inquiry, the reason, and hence is important; it raises two of the great debates in current and ancient thought, those between reason and faith and between reason and intuition, and hence is exciting; and, moreover, it is awesomely simple to ask and painfully awkward to answer and hence is intensely challenging. It demands of us: Are there reasons for the use of reasons?

[1] There are certain subtle and interesting distinctions between the terms "rational" and "reasonable," but they need not be distinguished for present purposes.

There is a special fascination about simple-to-ask but hard-to-answer questions like this wherever they occur. In physics, examples are the search for the ultimate constituents of matter or the ultimate relationship of space and mass; in mathematics, the attempts to provide logical foundations for arithmetic, arithmetical foundations for geometry and analysis, or to prove Goldbach's hypothesis (that every even number can be expressed as the sum of two primes) or the four-color theorem (that a map maker could never need more than four colors to distinguish adjoining countries); and in astronomy, the estimation of the age and size of the Universe.

The seductive power of such questions in philosophy is sufficiently strong to tempt us into an immediate and general reply. We try to meet the challenge head on; we try to answer with a single, necessarily very abstract sentence or system. It is a crucial part of the aim of this book to show that this temptation must be resisted if we are to be successful. There is another and better way. We must sink test holes before designing a skyscraper, for sometimes we find that a simple shed is all the site will stand and all the shelter that we need.

4. ANALYSIS BY EXAMPLES AND CONTRASTS

Before we answer any question, we must make sure we understand it thoroughly. This is obvious enough; what is less obvious is how we are to tell whether we understand. Usually, no one would try to answer a question unless he felt that he understood it, and what other indication could he possibly have besides his feelings? So we usually judge our understanding by our feeling of understanding or perhaps by formulating and checking a definition of any term that puzzles us. There is a simple way of checking one's feeling of understanding or one's definitions; it is not a guarantee, but it is of the greatest value. It consists in carefully applying one's presumed understanding or proposed answers to a number of very concrete examples. With the question "Why be reasonable?" for instance, one might have a feeling of understanding the question and yet lack actual understanding because one had no real idea of the *alternatives* to being reasonable. It can hardly make sense to defend or attack reasonable behavior or the rational method if no other behavior or method is conceivable. Now there are at least two entirely different kinds of alternatives to reason, and they require quite different treatments. If one were to react to the question by immediately attempting to describe exactly what it would be like not to use reason, this distinction (between intuitive and irrational behavior) would promptly emerge. Consideration of examples not only reveals this difference but suggests methods of handling the problem itself. Examples also help to give the philosophical problem impact on those who find its general form too abstract to be interesting, those with a nonphilosophical or an antiphilosophical turn of mind. So in this case, instead of answering immediately, we ask, "What is it to be rational or reasonable *in a particular case* (which we specify) and what *else* can one be?" Then we may see a way of giving general reasons for or against being rational rather than whatever the alternatives are. The meaning of a term in isolation is often unclear, although its meaning by contrast with another is clear, in the same way that its general meaning may be unclear even when its meaning in a particular sentence is perfectly clear.

Just as observations are the foundation of scientific theories, so examples are the foundation of philosophical analyses. And just as the use of scales of measurement in science is fruitful because it increases the number of distinctions one can make and hence the informativeness of any particular description, so the study of contrasts and comparisons in conceptual analysis refines one's understanding of the concept in its uncontrasted use. There is an obvious psycholinguistic basis for the use of examples and contrasts. We learn to use a language in contexts; we become exceedingly sensitive to the subtle differences in the contextual cues that suggest the use of, for example, the term "suggest" instead of "indicate." Most people are very good at spotting an ungrammatical expression, but they cannot formulate the definitions or rules of grammar which express their knowledge; indeed, this is in general impossible. Skills are usually not describable in terms that make it possible to duplicate them by following the description carefully, and verbal skills are no exception. Consequently, when it is particularly important to clarify the meaning of a term, the best procedure is the one which most effectively evokes the relevant linguistic skill, and that procedure is the presentation of a whole context, not the weak substitute of definition. Definitions are useful as reminders, rarely as real translations; and when a precise definition *is* possible, one may be sure the term defined is either a new technical term or one not of great importance for scientific or philosophical issues, or that the definition contains terms exactly as hard to understand as the original term.

The use of contrasts is partly a special case of using context, but it is also founded on the central fact in the psychology of perception that sensory perception of differences is enormously more sensitive than absolute discrimination.[2] A subject can distinguish two tones, colors, or forms that are presented simultaneously or in close succession even when he cannot recognize either of them among others at a later date or distinguish them if they are widely separated. Analogously, we can refine our procedures of logical analysis by asking for discrimination between similar terms rather than for explicit defini-

[2] It is easy to see why discrimination is a more precise process than recognition from a consideration of the perceptual processes of matching and labeling. Reflection on these processes also leads us to increased understanding of the reason for the success of the ingenious and sensitive "semantic-differential" instruments, the extraordinary feats of memory by stage mentalists, and the distinction between the art and the science of clinical diagnosis.

tions of a term. We say, "Do you mean 'certain' rather than 'chancy' or 'certain' rather than 'conceivably wrong'?" or "Do you mean 'rational' in the sense in which it is opposed to 'irrational' or 'rational' in the sense in which it is opposed to 'instinctive'?"

It is partly for these reasons that dialogue is so important in philosophy. When considerable precision about the sense in which someone is using a term is important, even the extended context of a paragraph or a page is not enough, for it may contain only one or two uses of the term. We need to be able to check our interpretive hypothesis by firing some test examples and contrasts at the language user, and it is important to do this before he builds too much upon what may be a loose foundation. So the author as well as the student of a philosophical viewpoint often benefits more from a short dialogue than from extensive prose or preaching. Wittgenstein, like Socrates earlier, appears to have felt at times that this consideration makes written philosophy almost pointless, certainly relatively valueless by contrast with verbal exchange. Clearly the best procedure varies from topic to topic and depends on the aims and needs of particular expositors and listeners. Once again the contrast with other subjects is clear. The finished product of the mathematician's labors is the polished proof, clear and convincing to those with the proper training. But the philosopher is often interested in a problem whose precise nature it is a large part of his task to determine; the form of words in which it expressed (Are we really free? . . . to blame? . . . mortal? . . . alone?) can have many meanings. So a dialogue is *necessary*. It is a process of successive approximation, first to the problem and then to the solution, and, done well, it can be an elegant demonstration of the process of clarification *cum* connection which is the essence of philosophical proof.

II

KNOWLEDGE

0. THE PROBLEMS

Why should we bother to be reasonable or rational at all? Is it possible or even desirable to be wholly rational? May there not be alternative routes to truth, besides reason: perhaps faith, or insight, or intuition? Is it appropriate to judge faith by the standards of reason? Since we know our senses can mislead us, how can we be certain of anything? Since all knowledge comes ultimately from experience and not from reading or listening, doesn't this make much of it inexpressible? Aren't concepts like knowledge, truth, and freedom indefinable and hence impossible to discuss precisely? Isn't truth eventually a matter of agreement and hence a matter of convention rather than something absolute? Can we be sure that the rules of reason or logic we use are the right ones?

1. RATIONAL VERSUS IRRATIONAL

If you want to buy a car, you can go about it in two ways. You might stop next time you see a car for sale, when you are feeling in the mood to buy one, and offer the owner whatever money you happen to have in the bank that day. Or you might first sit down and set out (1) a list of special features that are important to you, perhaps including high speed and small size or large trunk and seating capacity combined with economy; (2) your bank balance, assets, commitments, and actual borrowing power; (3) models of cars that fit (1) and (2) from tables of dimensions and performance; (4) cars now available of these models, from the classified advertising columns and telephone calls to dealers; and (5) a procedure for testing a fair selection of the candidates that pass (4), to see which suits you best in practice without committing yourself too early. Then, after testing, you buy the car that seems to do best. We would ordinarily say that the first procedure is impulsive, foolish, shortsighted, imprudent, irrational; the second, sensible, thorough, intelligent, prudent, rational. Notice that even the first procedure involves extensive use of reason and experience: it is much *more* reasonable, given that you want a car, than offering your money to a gas station attendant or a shoeshine boy or offering more money than you have. This kind of contrast suggests that rational behavior involves carefully selecting the most satisfactory available means to whatever ends one has in mind.

But this is not all there is to rationality, because the ends or goals are themselves open to rational criticism. The most efficient way to reduce weight is to eat less, but this does not show that every girl who eats less in order to reduce is rational: she may already be too thin.

We judge the rationality of the end or goal (e.g., to reduce weight) by looking for other goals to which it is a means. In this case, the further goal is perhaps to become a fashion model. But another further aim is to remain in good health, and this is generally a more important aim for the individual. If further dieting is necessary to achieve a model's dimensions but will seriously affect health, it would be irrational for someone to diet who valued health above that particular career (or who wanted to continue the career for long). Hence, even though a girl diets in the most rational way, which is by eating less of a balanced diet, it does not follow that she is rational to diet.

So a more accurate definition of rationality would be *selecting the most efficient available means to achieving a rationally acceptable end.* This appears circular: we are defining rationality in terms of "a rationally acceptable end." But we can give an independent definition of this phrase. Notice how we showed that the aim of losing weight might not be rational; we brought up another, more valued goal that was inconsistent with it. In general, an aim is rationally acceptable as long as it cannot be shown to be irrational in this way.

Suppose Mr. Summer wants to spend the rainy season in Yucatán and mortgages his house to do it. Is this a rational thing to do? The first question is, Is mortgaging the best way to raise funds (that is, "best" in terms of his present and future needs and preferences, e.g., not to borrow from friends)? If it is not, mortgaging is not rational. If it is, we next turn to the end mentioned. Why does Summer want to go to Yucatán in the steamy season? Perhaps he can get what he wants from steam baths and Sun Valley. If he can and knows this, he is being irrational. If he does not know it, we tell him, and if he is rational, he changes his plans. But suppose he wants to collect the rare Yucatán swallow-tailed butterflies. We might now look into such questions as the effect of the trip on his health, his finances, domestic arrangements, and so on. Suppose he passes every test—he is single, well-paid, and healthy and has tremendous interest in the Lepidoptera. Then the case for the rationality of his action has been made, because the case for showing his ends to be irrational—or the means recognizably inappropriate—has failed. Of course, one might still have lingering puritanical doubts about the morality of such trips while millions starve in Asia, but even such doubts might be countered by showing the need for a really satisfying vacation in order to lead a life of good works while on the job. Moral pangs like these are discussed later in the book.

So rationality is rather like legality; it requires that certain rules be obeyed where relevant, rules which form a hierarchy to which successive appeal is made, but apart from that it lays down no requirements about people's ultimate interests. A choice, act, or belief is rational if it is the best-supported available means to one's ends—unless the ends are not the best-supported available means to any further ends one might have. Hence the concept of rationality makes sense only when we already have ends and have started thinking about the best means to them or their relative importance. So *some* tastes and desires must already exist for reason to operate at all and they do not have to be justified—until we develop other ends in the light of these, which become independent, or until we discover conflicts between these and the original set. In the field of ethics we shall try to demonstrate a similar point: morality places no restrictions on people's values unless they produce (or are likely to produce) conflicts with those values of others that do not themselves produce such conflicts. In politics and law there are similar principles about the noninterference of the state or the law in affairs that have no effect on the state or the public, respectively.

There are of course borderline cases concerning which we cannot really say that one alternative is better supported or more rational than another, but the definition given above has some application in most instances. If our car buyer left out even one step—perhaps failing to take a trial run in the kind of car he selected *after its advantages had been pointed out*—we would unhesitatingly say his behavior was not sensible, was less than rational. The italicized qualification is important, and we must now focus on it. To be rational requires only that one use the best method one knows of to attain one's ends, and when the truly best method could only be recognized if one had very technical knowledge or training, one would not be held irrational for not knowing it. Still, one would not have to possess technical knowledge to make use of it, and to fail to seek technical advice where it was obviously relevant would be irrational. In fact, the notion of irrational behavior extends even further, for even if we did not in fact know a better method or know that we should ask someone else whether such a method existed, we might still be called irrational. It might be that we could easily have foreseen being in a situation of the kind that has appeared (indeed, did foresee this) and have neglected to provide ourselves with the kind of training that is obviously appropriate for the case which has arisen. For example, it is irrational for an insurance agent to insure a man heavily without checking his background just because he likes the man's looks, even if he does not realize the extent to which looks are a bad guide, because he should have read widely enough to have found this out. Thus irrationality comes closer to being a matter of using the wrong methods (and moves further from being a matter of using what the agent *knows* are wrong methods). But the two are never quite the same: only extreme and not all examples of irrationality involve ignoring one's own known-to-be-best alternatives. (Or, if it is argued that irrationality really has this narrower sense, we can simply limit our claim to the quality of making maximum use of reason—the approach which is sometimes loosely referred to as scientific, though it extends far beyond science).

Up to a point we make a distinction between being careless (or not thorough) and being irrational, but when it is clear that carelessness is extremely costly, then it is a sign of irrationality to be careless—for this is recklessness, that is, lack of reckoning or reasoning, which is irrational. The stronger terms are normally applied only when the stakes are rather high. A man rarely lives a day without behaving unreasonably or in a less-than-fully-rational way; he may speak sharply to someone else because he is annoyed with himself, forget which pocket his keys are in because he does not always put them in the same one, give the wrong change at the market, believe an advertisement of the prestige type for buying annuities from a life insurance company, feel that he's a better person than a man who did not go to Harvard simply for that reason, and eat more than he should for lunch. Given that none of us is entirely rational, the question arises, Should we—and if so, *why* should we—try to be *more* rational? The answers are simple to state, harder to prove.

We should try to be more rational simply because we want certain things and being more rational is *by definition* a better way to go about getting them. Hence, if anything is of importance to us, being rational is automatically important to us, because it is the best means to the ends we think important.

Why be rational about buying a car? Because we want a car that meets certain conditions, without beggaring ourselves, and so we should pay attention to various test reports and banking arrangements which tell us how to get such a car in such a way; i.e., we should proceed rationally. To proceed less rationally here is to leave out of account something which is of considerable importance to us [1] or to allot it less than or more than that importance. Hence the justification for being rational here is that it is the only way to give due weight, in estimation and in action, to the considerations that should get it: it is the only way because any way that does this is *automatically* called rational. If someone agreed that a certain procedure gave just the right weight to all the relevant considerations but wasn't the rational one to use, we would say he didn't understand the term. So we can say this is part of the meaning of "rational," i.e., it is true by definition.[2] Hence, if one accepts the legitimacy of anyone's wanting anything, one must concede the legitimacy, indeed the supremacy, of rationality. As a special case, if what we want is knowledge or truth, we must believe those claims which are best—and are well supported by the evidence.

Might not someone simply want to be irrational, have irrationality as his dominant goal? If he wanted to continue to enjoy being irrational, which is part of what is meant by saying that irrationality is his dominant goal, he would have to plan rationally for his continued existence. This would show rationality was still a necessity, or at least desirable, for him. If irrationality were *all* he wanted, he could not have it, because it can exist only with respect to other aims. Unless there is some course of action or belief which would be rational, there could not be one which is irrational. And, by definition, there could not be a rational course of action unless there are some ends already given so that one can judge which means most efficiently lead to them. So, for him to have irrationality as a goal he must have *other* goals.

In fact he must act so as *not* to achieve them, in which case it might be hard to make sense of the claim that they were his goals. In fact, we might argue that he was acting rationally but with the *opposite* goals, although not fully aware of this. In general, just as one cannot have chess strategies without chess pieces, so irrationality is impossible without other wants or needs, for irrationality is a way of acting with respect to one's wants or needs.[3]

Conversely, it would be foolish to suggest that one might have rationality

[1] Or to others when they are (or rationally should be) important to us. (See *Morality* chapter.)

[2] Statements that are true or false by definition can be identified without having to give the definition; one need only be sure that to deny or assert them would be a sure sign of lack of comprehension of terms or constructions in them. *True by definition* usually means, and is here taken to mean, "true by virtue of the meanings of the terms."

[3] There are some cases in which it can be rational to adopt an irrational belief or to act irrationally (examples are discussed later), but one does this just because it is the only way to survive or to attain some other overriding end.

as one's only aim. For rationality is a quality of certain ways to achieve aims and so could not exist unless other aims existed. Of course, it can be an aim as soon as one has other aims, but it can never be the only aim, any more than "obey the law" can be the only law.

2. THE COST OF RATIONALITY

Don't we *lose* something by the rational approach? To get down to cases, someone may say, "Isn't impulse buying more *fun* than comparison shopping?" For some people it is. As long as the increase in fun derived from spontaneity outweighs the probable loss caused by such factors as lack of durability, excessive interest payments, and subsequent dissatisfactions, it is not irrational to buy on impulse. But we have all learned from experience that the more important the purchase, the more likely it is that "Decide in haste, repent at leisure" will apply. In those cases, it is irrational to buy on impulse. The methodical, logical, analytic approach is not always rationally required; so in certain cases, snap judgments or impulse buying may be perfectly reasonable, perhaps because time is short or because it's more fun. This leads us to a second distinction which is often confused with the rational-irrational distinction: the distinction between coming to a conclusion by reasoning and by an immediate jump. The method of reasoning is not the same as the reasonable method. If you can judge pitch by ear, it is perfectly reasonable to do so, rather than by calculating it from the readings on acoustical instruments. Of course a process of reasoning must be involved in deciding whether a nonreasoning process is reliable, i.e., whether it is reasonable to employ it, for intuition or judgment does not carry built-in guarantees any more than it is a condensed reasoning process. Once it has passed its qualifying examination, however, a new judgment skill is just as respectable a part of the armory of reason as any well-tested instrument is part of the apparatus of science.

In general, we may say that rationality is the best *policy* in the sense that it is the one most likely to achieve our ends and least likely to "cost us" too much—by comparison with irrationality. This follows from its definition, for "the best *available* means" to an end is clearly the one with the best chance of success.[4]

Of course, on a particular occasion or even on a series of occasions, the

[4] To be more exact, the rational choice is the one which *we have the best evidence to suppose* is most likely to succeed. Just as the bet which wins is not always recognizable, so the bet most likely to win is sometimes disguised from us by the circumstances, by limitations on our mathematical skill, etc. This added complication does not affect our behavior but only the definition. We still pick the bet most likely to succeed, as well as we can tell, and of course try to improve our judgment. Conversely, making a mistake (i.e., picking what happens not to be the best bet) is not necessarily irrational; that would be picking what we *know* isn't the best bet. Morons are not rational, but neither would we usually say they were irrational.

prudent, rational person may lose out to the hasty, impulsive person because the latter happens to be lucky. The best bet doesn't always win, but in the long run the prudent policy is much more likely to pay off. We do not say that an insurance policy was a bad investment just because we did not collect on it. The imprudent man who did not bother to insure himself may, by chance, escape financial disaster, but he is lucky and foolish, not clever. He could not know he was going to be lucky. If he really could be justifiably sure that he would not need insurance, he would no longer be simply lucky but the proud possessor of a capacity for seeing into the future. Indeed, it would become part of the rational approach to consult him. He would no longer be an example of the opposite approach. In general, there is no reliable alternative policy to being rational, because the rational approach operates on the invincible principle, "If you can't lick them, join them." Just as soon as a procedure can be identified as producing knowledge or whatever other end we are concerned with, it becomes part of the arsenal of the rational approach to that end.[5]

To sum up: until there is enough evidence of a procedure's reliability to justify using it, there is not enough evidence to entitle it to the claim of an alternative approach to the same ends; we do not talk of alternative routes to a place unless we are sure they both get there. And when there is enough evidence, the procedure is no longer an alternative. Reason is the only route to knowledge or to any other ends except the end of unreason, and that end conflicts with *all* other ends.

3. RATIONAL VERSUS RIGHT

Suppose the top scientist in the Army's ballistic missile division—let us call him Dr. Winter—comes to the conclusion, based on all the evidence, that an effective anti-intercontinental-missile missile is not practical. Various policies are changed in the light of his report, and a board of inquiry, looking into these changes, uncovers the fact that one of his subordinates, whom we shall call Dr. Spring, disagrees with him. For other reasons, largely political, they recommend that research be continued, and within three years an antimissile missile which can effectively intercept any rockets in existence is in fact developed.

It is clear that Winter was wrong and Spring was right. We often let our analysis of the situation stop at this point. To do so is extremely foolish, for the important issue in judging the relative merits of the two men is quite different. The basic question is whether Spring was right by good fortune or

[5] The master procedure for identifying reliable procedures uses evidence from their past success to draw conclusions about their future success. This involves a commitment to the idea that the future will resemble the past, which is discussed in section 6 below.

from good judgment. That a man inherits great wealth does not make him a good businessman, and a lucky guess does not make a good scientist. We must examine the evidence available to and used by Winter and Spring at the time of their disagreement in order to decide which of them, if either, made an error of judgment. It is not easy to do this objectively, since we now know who turned out to be right, but it is possible—and it is essential. We are quite likely to discover that the evidence supports Winter's judgment somewhat more than Spring's, and we may perhaps decide that it was the more optimistic spirit of the younger man that encouraged him in his view of the matter. In such a situation, we would have no grounds for losing faith in Winter's judgment nor any grounds for regarding Spring as irresponsible or naïve.

But our examination might show that Spring or Winter was *seriously* in error, in terms of the evidence available to them. All these possibilities are consistent with the fact that the prediction Spring made was right and Winter's wrong. Justice does not allot blame or praise where failure or success is due to the winds of chance.

We want to be right, about the future, about our beliefs, about our practical choices. The best way to be right is to be rational; i.e., the best procedure to adopt if one wants to be right is rationality. We know in advance that this will sometimes lead to failure on a particular occasion, but this is no reason to suppose it is not the best procedure available. Since we can only expect a man to do the best that is possible, we can never conclude that he *did* wrong just because he turns out to *be* wrong.

These considerations, simple though they are, will make it easy for us to give an analysis of responsibility in Chapter VI.

They should also make it clear why he can have the highest regard for the intelligence and achievements of the great scientists of the past without in any way believing that their conclusions are true. When someone asks whether Newton was right in believing in absolute velocities, he may be thinking of either of two entirely different questions. First, was this a well-justified, rational belief in terms of the evidence available to him (and recognizable as such)? Answer: Yes. Second, was this belief true? Answer: As things appear now, no. The first question is the important one in evaluating the individual, who lived *then;* the second, the important one in evaluating the view which he held, for us who live *now.*

4. RATIONAL VERSUS TRUE

What counts as *the most rational belief* obviously varies from time to time and from person to person, depending on what information is available. But *the truth* does not vary in this way. Now, our only guide to the truth is our reason, and that may point in different ways at different moments, as the evidence changes. We say, properly, that something is true if at the moment the best available evidence confirms it strongly. So what we *properly call* the truth will vary, but what is *actually* true does not.

Someone could twist this around and make it even more confusing by using the term "correct." (1) Aristotle had excellent reasons for thinking the Earth stands still and the stars move. (2) Therefore, it was correct for him to say that the claim "The earth is fixed, the stars move" is true. (3) Now, if it is correct to say that a claim is true, it must be true. (4) Yet this claim is not true, as we now know.

Such an argument often leads people to feel that truth is relative, but it is only our *best estimates of the truth* which are relative. The error in the argument is easily seen when we realize that "correct for him to say" is ambiguous. It either means "proper to say, in the circumstances," i.e., rationally justified, or it means "true." For the statements in the argument about Aristotle to be true, we must use the first of these meanings in statements 1 and 2 and the second in statement 3. If we write in these meanings instead of the ambiguous phrase "correct for him to say," we see immediately that the argument does not lead us into the contradiction between statements 3 and 4.

Other concepts in our language contain similar traps: for example, the concepts of knowledge and certainty. Before turning to them, we can sum up one important point in this section by saying that it may sometimes be rational to believe something and to say that it is true although it turns out (later) not to be true.

5. KNOWLEDGE AND CERTAINTY

What can we be certain about? It sometimes seems that all the things people have been most certain about in the past—the flatness of the Earth, the motion of the stars, the impossibility of a vacuum—have turned out to be incorrect. Surely we should learn our lesson from this and agree with the skeptic who says it is wrong to be certain of anything.

But our ancestors were by no means as far wrong as these favorite examples suggest. They were also certain, and they were right in being certain, that water could freeze solid and that it could put out fires, that wood could be burned and bent, that the process of tempering hardened iron but cracked flint, that bears eat some fish and some fish eat others, and so on. Their ventures into astronomy and physics were riskier than they had any way of knowing, but these claims were a very small part of what they believed.

Clearly, to say that something is certain is not just to say that one believes it is true. It is also to express great confidence in it: it is to say that it is *beyond rational dispute;* indeed, it is sometimes taken as equivalent to saying that it is *impossible that it be false.* Now, are we ever justified in saying this?

Take the claim that water eventually becomes a solid if its temperature is lowered. Could this really be mistaken—is it really possible that it is false? Well, water might suddenly lose its power of freezing. But we know of no substance which has ever done this in several thousand years of direct observation, and there is no sign of this having occurred in the several million years before that for which traces are open to study in the rocks and skies. Nevertheless, there is a sense in which it *could* happen, namely, that it is not a contradiction in terms to describe it. We shall never find a circle whose perimeter also happens to form a plus sign, because it is logically impossible that the properties of the two coexist; i.e., we cannot describe such a figure without contradiction. But water might conceivably retain enough of its other observable properties to be still correctly called water, although it no longer freezes.

This distinction has often led people to say that we cannot be certain of anything except matters of definition (which of course we *make* certain by so arranging the rules of our language). And indeed truths of definition are in a sense more secure than truths of experience, for while it is true we might someday find people referring to some drawing as "a circular plus sign," we can be quite clear that either the word "circular" or the term "plus sign" would no longer have its present meaning. "Plus signs are not circular" is a statement we make here and now, with, of course, the current English meanings for its terms. And it is only *that statement* of which we can be certain. The fact that the same signs may be used in Ethiopia today or in the United States in 1999 to mean "fish can't swim'" casts no doubts on the certainty of our present claim and its proper translation into the languages of other times and places. So these truths of definition are certain beyond any corrosion by time or whim.[6]

Other truths are certain too, however, even though they are not so certain. It is entirely proper to say, "It is certain that water freezes," although it is even more certain that water often has frozen and still more certain that plus signs are not circular. For to say that something is certain is not to say that nothing is more certain, i.e., that it is true by definition (that its contradictory is impossible by definition), but only to say that the evidence for it is so overwhelming that one could not rationally doubt it. We could put this by saying that its contradictory is so remote a possibility that it should be left out of rational consideration, that is, it is, in the usual sense, impossible. There are several different circumstances in which it is proper to talk of certainty about statements that are not simply definitional truths.

There is, to begin with, an important difference between the claims "I am certain" (or "I feel certain") and "It is certain." It is often proper for someone to say, "I am certain I locked the door before I left," because—after careful thought—he clearly recalls the action he mentions, a memory which he cannot

[6] See section 11 below.

rationally reconcile with the possibility of not having done it. And he knows his memory is usually very reliable. It does not, of course, follow that because *he is quite certain* he locked the door, *it is quite certain* he did. We may have photographic evidence that he did not. But we can move from the individual's frame of reference to the public one and consider whether we can meet the stiffer requirements that apply there, without denying the propriety of the individual's use of the term "certain." He did not claim objective certainty, only his own, and he met the conditions for his claim fully. What he believed was not true, but he was right to believe it.

In the public domain, we may do likewise; it is entirely proper for someone to claim "there *certainly* wasn't anyone in the office when we first arrived" if he has had a thorough look around and especially if he was accompanied by others who also looked around. This claim is not shown to be wrong by pointing out that it is not true by definition. It is true that someone *might,* in some sense, be possessed of the power of contraction and be hidden in a desk drawer, but that is not the sense of "might" that is meant to be excluded by the claim of certainty in this context.

Terms such as "certain" and "possible" are examples of *context-dependent terms;* i.e., their cash value in a particular case can be determined only by examining the context of the particular use. Good everyday examples are "very expensive" and "medium-sized." What counts as very expensive depends on the context, which might be a discussion of the price of frozen orange juice now or of peacock plumes in the seventeenth century. The use of the term will also depend to some extent on the financial status of the person making the evaluation. But this is not to say it is simply a subjective evaluation: for that, we reserve the phrase "It seems very expensive to me," to which someone may retreat when it has been demonstrated that "for what you get," dinner at the Tour d'Argent is "not really so expensive." No one can give a definition of "very expensive" as "so many dollars" or "so many dollars per pound," but this in no way proves that the expression lacks meaning. It is a term which refers to one end of a scale of comparative terms (including "inexpensive," "remarkable bargain," etc.) whose center is attached to items whose cost is about average for the class of items under discussion and not unreasonable by other standards, and it indicates a cost *very significantly greater* than this, sometimes also implying the lack of a corresponding increase in merit. It follows from this, of course, that someone who says that a pair of shoes at $75 isn't very expensive, on the ground that one pays much more than this for a good suit, has simply failed to understand how the term is used.

In the same way, objective certainty is at the high end of the justified-confidence scale. The points on this scale are attached to a degree of probability that depends on the topic under discussion and the gravity of the decisions which are to be made in the light of the assessment. It would be simply foolish to complain about the statement, made in the appropriate context, that we can now be certain of the feasibility of atomic power for ships, on the ground that it is not so certain as "$2 + 2 = 4$." Of course, such a statement could be attacked *appropriately* if, for example, we had specific reasons for thinking that the atomic piles used in marine power plants would explode at unpredictable and frequent intervals.

What we have said about certainty and truth applies equally to knowledge, for whatever can be said to be certain can be said to be known, and vice versa.[7] The context supplies the scale for the proper use of the terms, but, of course, the facts have the last word, and what we may have properly called certain at one time may turn out to be false. If it does, the claim of certainty must be now retracted, but making it at the earlier time will still have been proper. And, of course, very many of the claims of certainty made in the past have shown no signs of being misplaced. Indeed most of the statements that someone in the past would have produced if asked to give *carefully considered* examples of certainty have survived, e.g., that a man commonly referred to as Abe Lincoln was once President of the United States, that red tulips were often grown in Holland in the first half of the twentieth century, and so on. So we have the best of reasons for believing that certainty is attainable. Let us see if these exercises in exemplification and contrast have equipped us to deal with some of the old hands in the philosophical crew, for they often threaten a mutiny which would overthrow our relatively comfortable conclusions.

6. KNOWLEDGE OF THE FUTURE AND THE PAST, OF THINGS AND PEOPLE

Let us consider the following arguments:

1. We are always in the present and hence never in the past or future. Thus, we can never have direct knowledge of them: the future may be entirely unlike our present expectations of it (which are conditioned by the past), and the past entirely unlike our present memories of it (which may have been manipulated or have deteriorated in the present).

2. We have only our own experiences to consult directly, and these are not all the same as the supposed objects in the outside world which supposedly cause them. Hence, we can never have direct knowledge of the external world; it may not exist at all, and our experiences may be simply a very elaborate dream.

3. A given person can directly experience only his own pains and

---

[7] There are minor differences between the known and the certain. A man can be certain that something is the case, although in fact it is not, but he cannot know what is not the case. But we normally withdraw the claim that a claim was certain upon discovering that it was not true, just as we withdraw the claim that we knew it.

thoughts, never those of other people. He can thus never be certain that the other figures he sees actually have sensations and thoughts of their own: they may simply be acting *as if* they did, and he may be the only real person in the Universe.

The doubts raised by these arguments are not ones which normally disturb common sense, to which the contrary view appears obvious. But this is no better ground for dismissing the doubts than it was for dismissing doubts about the fixity and flatness of the Earth, which appeared obvious to common sense. It is relatively easy to convince people that the list of doubts we have just given constitutes a very serious threat to what we have always believed. Nevertheless, these doubts are based on a logical error, which is (roughly) the idea that we cannot be certain of anything except our immediate experiences. Following the lines of the previous section, it will be suggested that while immediate experience is usually *more* reliable than indirect evidence, it is perfectly possible for us to be justifiably certain of some inferred states of affairs of the kinds attacked by these three arguments.[8]

Each argument begins by stressing the nonimmediacy, the indirectness, of a certain kind of supposed knowledge. Taking this to demonstrate *weakness,* it then proposes a counterexplanation of the evidence on which we base this supposed knowledge. (This evidence comprises, of course, the experiences which we normally believe to bear on the nature of the remote entities, for example, our memories, which we think are a guide to past and future events.) Taking the *conceivability* of this counterexplanation to show that it is no

---

[8] They are, technically speaking, versions of the classical problems of induction, memory, other minds, and the external world, respectively. Three slightly technical comments, which can be skipped by the general reader, follow. (1) The general problem of induction applies not only to knowledge of the future but to knowledge of any state of affairs which we infer from what we see (or hear, etc.), e.g., to our knowledge that a skunk is in the vicinity, for the *confirmation* of such claims is always in the future and hence it and necessarily the claim are open to inductive doubts. (2) For this reason, induction is the most general problem of the set. Yet the other problems raise distinctively different further doubts, so that a solution of the problem of induction does not automatically solve them. For convenience, we concentrate on the future-doubting traditional form of the induction problem, although this cuts us off from an elegant alternative *reductio ad absurdum* refutation of the skeptic: (3) the skeptical doubts about induction are so sweeping that they are very nearly suicidal. The question, How can we know the future will be very like the past? almost admits the answer: by definition of the term "future" (David Shear, unpublished, 1956). The future must be distinguishable from the past for the question to make sense, and such a distinction would, it appears, only be possible if something in the future indicated a later time than the present. But time can only be indicated by recording cyclic processes of some kind (e.g., clocks, solar motions, decay processes); hence, for the question to make sense, there must be regularities continuing into the future, i.e., the question answers itself. The question concerns *all* regularities, however, not just the few that are necessary for chronology; so it can be rephrased to avoid this difficulty. Not everything we think of as a regularity does continue, of course, but more do than we need for recognizing the future.

weaker than the usual explanation, the conclusion is drawn that we have no grounds for picking this explanation. Let us consider a similar but simpler case and demonstrate a possible defense there.

Suppose someone said, "You can never know what is going on over the horizon, for you can never be there yourself to know it directly and if you use a messenger or a telephone or television, all that you really know from them is what you hear or see at your end; and, of course, this may be quite different from what is going on, for many reasons, such as the possibility of interference or deliberate tampering."

We would, commonsensically, probably reply that there are various ways of minimizing these possibilities by using guards along the way, armored cable, multiple independent channels, etc. Yet, how would we know that these precautions are working? Up to the horizon we can see and hence check them, but beyond that it seems we would be back to the old difficulty of relying on messages, this time about the precautionary devices, which might themselves be tampered with. Suddenly it seems as if our world has narrowed down to the span of the horizon, and looming up is the threat of similar arguments to constrict it further, until the sensations of the moment are all we know. And these we do not *know,* we simply *have;* so all knowledge has evaporated.

But the situation is not so desperate as it appears. Let us immediately concede the possibility, in the sense of conceivability, that our instruments may be misleading us. Remembering that the mere existence of such a possibility does not mean we must abandon claims of knowledge or certainty, we must now see whether we cannot make this possibility so remote as to be rationally insignificant. First, we employ a large number of independent telephones, television channels, chains of individual lines of sight, and other linkages between ourselves and the distant events, each concealed separately and protected in a different way. We thus make it immensely improbable that a deceiver (or random interference) could *simultaneously* pervert the messages with equal efficiency. Any *unsynchronized* interference will be obvious at our end, since the various instruments would give different accounts of the distant events. We also use guards whose honesty we have amply demonstrated and arrange for rewards which would exceed any feasible bribes. Finally we lay the most ingenious traps along the transmission lines and around the transmitters. Quite apart from these *precautions,* we have a very wide range of procedures and devices which will tell us *subsequently* whether any interference has actually occurred. For instance, we shall examine the cables to see whether they have been cut, the ground above them to see if it has been disturbed, and so on. We test the whole arrangement many times, subsequently checking both the account it provides of the distant event and the interference detectors. The arrangement always works. Now we can surely regard the possibility of error as insignificant and say, as we watch the screens and listen to the sounds, that we *know*—indeed that we can *see and hear*—what is happening at the UN or the Olympic games. And our actual historical experience closely parallels this imaginary experiment.

The skeptic has nothing left but the conceivability of error, and this he cannot inflate into a serious doubt. To do so he must produce a *serious* counterexplanation of the phenomena we perceive on our screens and the reports we receive from our guards and instruments. Every passing day that uncovers no evidence of archdeception despite the continuing use of telephone and television further weakens this possibility; and even on the first day it is too remote to make claims of certainty improper, as even a cautious and philosophically learned bookmaker would agree.

Let us turn now to the classical doubts about the future (or the past) and the world. We concede immediately that the future might suddenly be unpredictable chaos, beginning this very moment; that the world we think we see or remember might not be as it appears; and that the human beings in it might not be endowed with minds of their own. Let us ask rather for the *probability* of these counterhypotheses, the tangible support for them. It need not be great; indeed, the claim of certainty is easily undercut. But there is *none*, not a shred of evidence of any kind that errors on *this* kind of scale have ever been made. The doubt may be dismissed as not rationally significant, as based on rather elementary errors of reasoning.

But the skeptic answers bitterly. We ask for evidence improperly, he says, for his suggestion is that a *wholesale but successful deception* has been practiced on us, and just because it is wholesale and successful, there will be no evidence. Evidence would require that slips be made, i.e., that the deception not be successful. He is in the role, he suggests, of someone who has suddenly seen a way in which the death of the Princes in the Tower could have been accidental, though heretofore it had been supposed to be murder. It is a condition of such an account that it refers to *exactly* the same evidence as the current explanation; and it simply shows us that until some new evidence which distinguishes between the two stories is uncovered, we cannot be sure which is true. Now the special feature of the classical philosophical doubts is that *no* such distinguishing evidence is possible. Hence, we are eternally suspended between the two explanations.

This reply is based on a false though very persuasive analogy. The two accounts of a death may be in balance, but not simply because they are both *capable* of explaining all the known evidence. They are equiprobable because the various assertions that each makes about what actually happened are *about equally plausible*. Murder of royalty used to be quite commonplace, and accidents happen to everyone. When we turn to knowledge of events beyond the horizon, we see that the possibility of deception is not made a serious one by the mere fact it could account for what we directly observe. It would also have to be a serious candidate for explaining the apparently unbroken cables and the silent guards and the independent subsequent checks of what actually happened beyond the horizon. Similarly, the suggestion that other human beings are mindless not only must be able *in principle* to account for what we see but must be a serious possibility as an explanation of many other special features of the situation such as that, when asked, these human beings often say they are thinking, feeling, or intending, which activities surely imply they have minds. Now we are constantly asking questions of other human beings and are later able to see whether they are telling the truth or not, whether they used the terms used, whether they could have told the truth at the time when they told us an untruth, and whether they told us the untruth accidentally. We thus develop some skill in identifying liars, occasions when lies would have some point, lie-detecting instruments, and hence truthful informants. So we have good reasons for supposing that our informants are telling the truth when they say they, too, feel pain and reflect on the futility of anger. Again, the scale of the deception is such that some plausible motive for it, if planned, would have to be suggested; and the fact the deception is designed to mislead oneself rather than another also requires explanation. Even if the alternative is not dependence but simply a very peculiar kind of world, the egocentrism of the hypothesis is still a crippling handicap. In the face of these demands, the suggestion that there are no other minds is feeble. It can only be based on a failure to realize the force of indirect evidence for a conclusion, including the role of simplicity and symmetry as they are in this world.

Is the same kind of defense effective with respect to the other doubts? The independent existence of the outside world, other than as a figment of our mind, is supported by the colossal number of intellectual achievements produced within a short span by its entities, which could scarcely all be our own thinking and which can be subsequently checked, laboriously, by us. This is not, on this scale, a feature of dreams. And then, more important, there is the enormous difference between the limited span and degree of organization of dreams and what we normally regard as the real world. The elusiveness and variability of conditions in the dream world undercut any systematic attempts to establish that it is real. These differences need a specific explanation and are not bridged by the vague analogy with a dream. And the excitement, the shocking power, of the dream hypothesis is virtually eliminated if we start talking of wholesale, highly permanent dreams, since "waking up" could no longer be identified reliably. Systematic attempts to wake oneself up have no effect in the real world, although in the dream world they often result in waking up (a marked change in the flow of experiences), or it turns out to be impossible to make such attempts.

If these intrinsic differences between waking and dreaming states did not exist, we would probably be better justified in saying that the world had suddenly changed in a drastic way, instead of saying that we were "going to sleep," it still being a real world before and after the change. So to be a real threat, the dream hypothesis has to become so undreamlike that it is almost no longer a counterexplanation, just a different set of words for saying the same thing. This is not *quite* all there is to the superdream theory, for it is not just a trivial redescription of the facts, but the little more is just an idle hypothesis. Hypotheses which are so contrived as to produce exactly the same results as our normal interpretations are usually complex, and their components lack *independent* confirmation; thus they make, in conjunction, a very inferior alternative to the simpler account.

The most difficult challenge comes from the doubts about induction, simply because they are so general. (With a little ingenuity, however, one can make the doubts about memory or perception nearly as pervasive.) Let us suppose one tried to reply to the skeptic here by saying that (1) rather than casting doubts on a kind of knowledge, he is simply suggesting a particular hypothesis about the future, namely, that it will be extremely unlike the past; (2) we know very well what it would be like to have some evidence for such a possibility, namely, several past occasions on which there have been wholesale sudden changes in the course of events; and (3) there have been no such changes, as far as we know, and so his suggestion lacks serious support.

To this he can reply that we have assumed what we are supposed to prove, for we claim that the evidence is against his suggested possibility. But by this we mean only that there is no record of similar occurrences in the past. We have, he says, simply assumed that examining the past has some bearing on the future. It is exactly this assumption which he is questioning in the first place, and our reply has, he argues, simply taken it for granted.

Now, of course, the only *possible* kind of evidence about the future will be from the past and the present since they are all there are besides the future. So he is suggesting that, contrary to the ordinary belief, there really is *no such thing* as good evidence about future events, no such thing as a rationally calculated probability of a future event, and hence, of course, no certainty or knowledge about the future.

It is easy enough to show that if the future *is* like the past, our usual procedures for predictions are the best ones. And we know that until now the future *has* always turned out to be like the past. The problem is, How can we justify our great confidence that this will continue to be so? We cannot reply that our grounds are that it often has been that way, without assuming exactly what is to be proved, namely, that the past underwrites the future. And it is not enough simply to reply that the present use of the terms "evidence," "probability," etc., supports our usual practice; for they may have fallacious views built into their meaning, as into terms like "*lunatic*," which could hardly be called on to demonstrate that the moon really affects the insane. We would also have to show that the views built into these uses of the terms do not involve errors and that no less misleading alternative ways of using them are available.

Perhaps the best way to justify confidence in the future is to examine carefully what happens if we abandon it: to understand what we believe we must always examine the alternatives, the contrasts. Let us take the skeptic seriously: let us assume we agree with him that we really have no good reasons for supposing the future will resemble the past, indeed, none for supposing there will be a future at all. This surely has very definite consequences for our behavior. As a matter of fact, it is likely to prove fatal. For example, if we have no reason to think automobiles are lethal, why should we get out of their way? We have no reason to think they are not, either, but if we took every possible doubt seriously, we would not be able to move because of the risks of encountering lurking monsters, of the floor's collapsing; we could not eat because the food might be poisonous. Nor could we stay still, because the floor might collapse right there! And failing to eat of course might lead to starvation. If we were fortunate enough to survive a day of taking all such doubts seriously, we would have to concede that it is rationally preferable— since we wish to enjoy life—to act *as though* we expect the future to re- semble the past, for this is the way our bodies learn to react and fighting it is too hard to be feasible. Indeed, if we want to live, this is the *only* option we have and, hence, certainly the *best* means to the end of staying alive. For the skeptic's doubt does not give us any specific alternative suggestion as to how things will turn out; it simply removes all possibility of telling.

So we must act as if the doubts are foolish, but this is only to save our lives. In fact, says the skeptic, the doubts are well founded, and we should remember this. That is, although from habit and for good reasons *acting* to the contrary, we should really *believe* the future may suddenly evaporate. Now, if we are right to believe this, it should still affect our behavior to some degree. At least, it seems, we should take and not make long-term loans (since we are more likely not to be around for the pay-off), be a little less careful about breaking the law (since prison sentences are quite likely to be termi- nated by the end of the world or an unprecedented amnesty), and so on. Nor are these long-range considerations the only ones to be affected: the skeptic's doubts make chaos or the simple reversal of previous patterns quite possible within the next few minutes. Hence our bidding in bridge, our betting at the track, and our bluffing at poker should be substantially different. Indeed, the tone we use in bidding farewell to our wife in the morning should be different, for each day may well be the last, and likewise the enthusiasm with which we greet a friend, for we may never see him again. It is perfectly true that this attitude would soon wear off—one cannot say a thousand farewells as if each were the last—but this is simply a sign of slovenliness on our part.

We cannot sustain the attitudes that, according to the skeptic, are the only intellectually legitimate ones. Even our beliefs finally become corrupt in this way, but this in no way shows they *should* do so.

Yet there is a fatal error here, it appears. It is not the corrosion of the casual that cuts down our doubts; it is the carbolic of common sense. Why? Because to have the skeptic's doubts about the future implies that we have knowledge about the future and, hence, that our choice is simply between knowledge claims that are confirmed in the usual way and those that are not.

The skeptic thinks we are overrating the probabilities in our procedures because he believes there is no real way of inferring future states from present and past ones. We have already seen the hints that this has very strong consequences for prediction. *We* say that sunrise tomorrow will be at 6:08 A.M. and the next day at 6:11 A.M., using the standard formula. In *his* view, sunrise may not even occur tomorrow, or it may occur at any time in the twenty-four hours. Any time is a possible time, and no past experience can be relied on to support one of these possibilities rather than another. Consequently, he must view it as fantastically improbable that 6:08 will be the lucky hour: indeed, it is virtually certain sunrise will *not* be at this time. And he will be even more certain that it will not be at 6:08 A.M. tomorrow *and* at 6:11 A.M the next morning, as we predict. So he "knows" something about the future, and it is demonstrated that knowledge of the future is possible, since believing the opposite also leads to knowledge about the future. On this interpretation, his position is self-contradictory.

There is a better line of defense for the sophisticated skeptic. He should say that we have no reason to prefer one time for sunrise over another but deny that it follows all are equally likely. Then we cannot show that a particular time is immensely *unlikely*, i.e., that he is committed to saying he knows it won't occur at that time. Although this move is defensible in some very important cases (in which it avoids Laplacean paradoxes in probability theory), it is less plausible here. For here *we* are asserting probabilities of (effectively) 1; hence the skeptic must think the real value lower. That is, for his skepticism to have any practical impact, it must involve a commitment to a particular kind of alteration in the probability value; and from that kind of alteration it follows that he will bet differently and in extreme cases "know" something we deny, e.g., that in 10,000 bets he will be right more often than we are. The later arguments also apply to this version of the skeptic's position.

The story is not over, of course. If we both say we know what's going to happen and contradict each other, we shall want to find out which of us, if either, is justified. We wait two days, and it turns out that *our* predictions were correct and the skeptic's wrong. That shows that what we said was true and what he said was false. It does not of itself show we were justified (remember the Winter-Spring argument).

Indeed, although the months go by and the skeptic's predictions are always wrong and ours always right, he remains steadfast. He admits that human nature in this situation tends to take the easy way, to drift with the tide of events, but he maintains that this is mere laziness of thought and in no way indicates superior insight. For, he says again, we can give no good reason for supposing that a formula which has worked in the past will work in the future. *His* claims to knowledge—he prefers to say lack of knowledge— of the future are justified, he says, and ours are not. If his line of defense all along has been a resolute insistence that he has *no* idea what the probability is and that it may even be 1 (as we suggest), then he is not guilty of inconsistency; his lack of knowledge, if it is as complete as this, does not lead by a back door to negative knowledge. And his position of total ignorance, he says, is the only justifiable one.

We must attack this position directly. First we repeat our admission that the past is not an *infallible guide* to the future. Our claim is only that the past is a *good indicator* of the future, that it provides good, not perfect, grounds for prediction. Now any indicator of the future will have to be in the past (or the present, which immediately becomes the past) since if it were in the future, we should not be able to use it. And it can be only an indication, not an absolute guarantee, since we all agree the future is immensely complex normally and could conceivably be totally unlike the past. So it will be misguided to criticize a supposed indicator either on the ground that it is in the past or on the ground that it does not absolutely guarantee the future: one might as well criticize a screwdriver for not being a hammer.

The common-sense view is that the past does provide good indicators of the future. And it is true that we cannot give good reasons for this fundamental principle *in the same way* that we can give good reasons for a particular prediction to someone who accepts the principle. One can never give the same kind of reasons in support of a basic principle of reasoning that one gives based upon such a principle, for a basic principle, by definition, is one that sets different standards from other principles. Let us consider an example.

We can give reasons to show that $7 \times 3 > 4 \times 5$, namely, that the left side comes to 21, the right to 20, and $21 > 20$. But if someone now asks our reasons for supposing $21 > 20$, what can we do? We might simplify by subtracting 20 from each side and say, "Because $1 > 0$." But if this is also challenged, we cannot provide further proofs of the same kind; we can only say, "*This* is true by definition: 1 is a greater quantity than 0." And if doubts are raised as to the propriety of definitions from which this follows, we can only say, "They do the job they are supposed to do: they adequately embody the meaning of the terms they define; e.g., they make sense of the counting and adding of numbers." Notice that we have shifted gears here. We cannot go on giving mathematical proofs indefinitely; at some stage we must appeal to the obvious. This is not to fail to give a proof; it is simply to give a different kind of proof.

So if someone asks for evidence for the prediction about the sunrise, we can readily produce it from our records. But if he then asks what makes us think this *is* evidence, i.e., how *any* evidence from the past can support a prediction about the future still ahead, we can only reply that evidence is simply that material from the past which until now has turned out to be a reliable indicator of the future. And if doubts are raised as to the propriety of so using the term "evidence" (or "grounds," etc.), we can only say, "It does the job: it does connect the key elements in the concepts of grounds and evidence; it does identify indicators that lead from truths to further truths; such a use has led to true predictions, does not contradict other uses, and so on." We have had to shift gears; we cannot go on giving evidential support for the principle of evidential support, ad infinitum. At the end we can point to something much simpler and more conclusive, though to do this is to give a different kind of proof. We point to the fact that what we are calling evidence is living up to its billing.

After all, the choice is simply between the skeptic's predictions and guesses, which never work, and ours, which almost always do, and our success can hardly be due to luck. *It needs to be explained;* it is, from the skeptic's point of view, quite extraordinary. The explanation is simple; we have discovered that the future can be foretold from the past. No other explanation is plausible.

Belief in this claim produces our successes; doubt of it produces his failures. He says our belief is unfounded; but this either means that one cannot absolutely guarantee the future will be as predicted, which we concede anyway, or it means that we cannot support our belief by any other means than appeals to definitions or past successes. The appeals to definitions and past successes are circular, he says, since their propriety or relevance to the future is exactly what is in dispute. But he is simply calling attention to the fact that a principle of inference introduces a *new* kind of inference as legitimate and, hence, cannot be shown to be justified by the *old* principles of inference. The appeals to definitions and successes are always appropriate, always ultimate, and never intrinsically circular. For the only question that matters about the new kind of inference is, Do we on balance increase our stock of true conclusions by accepting it? (It is not, Can it be justified in terms of the old concept of a sound inference?)

Let us recall the series of extensions of the number system to include rational fractions and negative, imaginary, and transfinite numbers. *None* of these could be shown to be numbers by the old standards. Each was rejected at first for just this reason. Yet each can properly be argued to have its place within the system of numbers, whereas the non-Archimedean "numbers" and several other candidates cannot be so defended. The reason is that the added types of number have enough of the properties of the previously acceptable entities to make extension of the franchise *useful* for the purposes of mathematics. When we remember the contrast with the skeptic's unsuccessful alternative procedure or lack of procedure for predicting the future, it is clear that it is perfectly sensible to call our observations "evidence" for conditions about the future, even though it is not just the same as what is called evidence in other cases.

What we are saying then is this: As we notice the number of past successes grow, we see that the new principle does work, does what a good principle of inference should do. Consequently, we have good grounds for predicting that the future will continue to be like the past, since this is what the principle recommends. The skeptic tries to stick in his toes here by saying we only have good grounds for thinking the future has *thus far* turned out to be like the past. But we have an *absolute guarantee* of that; we are not talking about having an absolute guarantee, we are talking about having a basis for a highly reliable though not infallible inference, about the legitimacy of using the past as an *indicator* of what is to come. In making that move the skeptic is reverting to the assumption that the only good reasons are absolute guarantees. Now we have seen that the new procedure works; hence we have good grounds for admitting as good grounds the kind of evidence it recommends. Doing so, we are in a position to jump across the present moment into the future, for the new principle applies to all futures. And when the evidence is overwhelming, we may rightly claim *knowledge* of the future, as in the case of the time of sunrise.

Or we might say, very simply, that principles of inference are good if they work, bad if they do not, and we do not have to appeal to a further principle of inference to show this. For this is exactly what is meant by a good principle of inference.

7. KNOWLEDGE OF OUR OWN FEELINGS

There appears to be one area in which our knowledge is beyond dispute, and that is the area of our knowledge of ourselves. (Someone has put this rather skeptically as, "We know we think, we think.") At least we know when we are in pain: we would view suggestions that we might be mistaken about this as very odd. We may lie about it or misname our feelings, but, it seems, we surely cannot be *mistaken* in our knowledge of it. And we know when we feel happy. Even when we can be talked out of this state, we say, "I was feeling good until you reminded me that tax returns (or term papers) are due." But with more complicated states, we are less reliable as judges of our feelings. When someone announces, honestly enough, that he is in love, close observers may be in a position to challenge the claim with some success, suggesting perhaps that some affection, considerable dependence, and a desire to avoid other obligations are all that are involved. To some extent, these are persuasive attempts to correct the would-be lover's use of the term; but they may also be calling attention to facts the speaker has overlooked or under-valued or to the overall balance of the evidence, in the same way as one might correct the claim that a certain person is reliable, intelligent, or industrious. Similarly, the claim that one really likes Smith or has only feelings of gratitude toward Jones may be made honestly enough but be mistaken.

So we can sometimes be mistaken about our feelings but not about what we think they are nor, it seems, about our sensations of the moment. There are actually some grounds for suspecting the latter claim; those indeterminate sensations at the dentist which we can by an effort of will identify as merely pressure, noise, and heat, can easily appear as pains if we allow ourselves to become tense and nervous. We can sometimes be distracted by gaiety and talk which make us quite forget the pain in our side, so that we might give conflicting answers to inquiries about it, and so on. Yet there are certainly many clear cases in which we are perfectly entitled to claim that we know beyond any shadow of a doubt what we feel. And, by comparison with the cases in which we say, rightly, that we know when the sun will rise tomorrow or even that we know there are other people or shoes on our feet, such claims about feelings perhaps involve fewer hostages to fortune, take less of a chance that subsequent events and examinations will show them to be mistaken.

But the special confidence we have in our capacity to tell how we feel often tempts us into special pitfalls. People sometimes suppose that they can transfer this confidence to matters of external fact, just as long as they have a "feeling of certainty" about such matters. Someone at the office may say she suddenly feels certain, or that she "just knows," that something terrible has just happened at her house. Now telepathy is always a *possibility*, and her distress is certainly genuine; so of course we take the matter seriously in that we make, or encourage her to make, a check. But we do not suppose that her conviction is a legitimate basis for us to assume she is definitely right. And we do not blame a bank manager for refusing credit to someone who wants to back a horse he *knows* is going to win, even if he had a vivid dream of the race.

In short, the reliability of feeling-claims applies only to "inner states" (and not to all of these), unless it has been independently demonstrated by testing that a particular individual has feelings which are good indicators of the minds of others, the weather, or the stock market. And the reliability of our claims about inner states springs from the fact that *these* "inner states" are usually defined in terms of our feeling about them. So we can be pretty sure when we are happy because little more is packed into "happy" than our *feeling* that we are happy. It is impossible to be mistaken about one's *feeling* that a disaster has occurred, but this feeling may well be mistaken. The im-portance of this point is crucial to, and will be used in assessing, the argument for the existence of God based on religious experience (Chapter IV). And it is the key point in discussing any claims about alleged cases of intuition, insight, "sixth senses," etc.

One of the most perplexing puzzles in the theory of knowledge illustrates a related pitfall about private experiences. This is sometimes called the "traffic-lights problem," or the "reversed-spectrum puzzle." Our certainty about our sensations is sometimes (though rather misleadingly) said to stem from their immediacy and their privacy; but just because we alone have access to them, a special kind of *uncertainty* arises about them. How do I know that when *you* see the color green, you have the same sensation that *I* have when I see green? Might it not actually be the case that when you see *green,* you have the sensation that I have when I see *red?* It seems there is no way of ever finding out the truth about this, for all the tests we could perform would have the same results, whether it is true or not. For example, when we come to some traffic lights, both of us have learned to apply the term "green" to the same light, but the sensation it produces in us may be quite different. Tests for color blindness only test the intrapersonal capacity to *distinguish colors,* not interpersonal differences in sensation. Even marvelous developments in the study of the brain would only reveal similarities or differences between our brain states when looking at the same color, and these form only part of the mechanism associated with the sensations, not the sensations themselves. Your red sensation might be attached to the same kind of brain state as my green state.

The problem is fairly easily solved. It arises because of the persuasive suggestion, built into the way it is stated, that we can separate the color seen from the sensation associated with it. But one does not have a separately identifiable sensation from which one learns to infer that something green is in one's field of view. The situation is not like the case of the sinking feeling one has which "tells one" an elevator is descending. Whatever interesting things go on in the optic nerves and the brain, they do not produce a sensation which is then interpreted; they simply produce confidence that the subject is seeing something outside himself whose hue is conventionally called "green" in the English language. What he learns is that *objects* of that hue are called green, not that a certain internal sensation is an indication of external green. There is an internal state (of his brain) but not a sensation: he is not aware of the state of his brain but of the presence of a green object. The brain is the mechanism of knowledge, but the knowledge is not about the brain any more than knowledge of the time is knowledge about the mechanism of a clock.

Consequently, there is no possibility of your having a different sensation from mine when seeing the same color. Of course, you may have different *associated* sensations: blue may make you feel chilly and make me feel warm as we recall, respectively, the sea ice and the hot sky which provided our childhoods with their main examples of this color. But we do not use those sensations to infer that it is blue. We *see* that it is blue and have these sensations or associations as well.

And on a particular occasion, when I have learned the language, my claim that something is green is not the claim that you will feel or say the same thing about it; it is the claim that the something *is* the same color as those things which both of us were taught were green. You may be wrong, this time; or I may be.

Is this solution dependent on some special feature of vision, the fact that seeing does not necessarily involve having sensations? Could we not have a corresponding problem about the sensations which we get when riding in elevators or when being jabbed with a pin? We can certainly have a genuine problem in such cases, though in most cases not a serious one and in no case a deep, philosophical one, as the reversed-spectrum puzzle appeared to be.

You know how you feel when the elevator starts down. I know how I feel. Might our feelings be different? It is extremely likely that they are different. If, for example, I am the elevator operator or an experienced paratrooper, it is virtually certain that I shall not experience the sensation of one's heart popping into one's mouth that is common in those new to high-speed elevators. Similarly, you may well have an entirely different experience from that of a seasoned sailor when out on a rough sea, an experience known as feeling seasick.

Such differences are quite easily discovered by observation of the associated behavior or by comparison of descriptions. If it were seriously suggested that I might experience the feeling when the elevator drops that another does when it rises, one would immediately point out the obvious describable differences: the feeling of increased weight in the one case, of lightness in the other, and so on. But much lesser differences may become important, as when a lover frets over his beloved's coolness, despite her honest protestations of equal affection. At such moments, one may become very conscious of the limitations of our language or of our control of it in conveying nuances of feeling. But it is clear that the resources of poetry and music can be enlisted to pursue precise expression further; and in the end the difficulty is clearly not so much that a gross error may be involved as that slight differences in such cases are matters of great personal, rather than philosophical, importance. So the possibility of great hidden differences in our experiences, clouded over by the mask of words, is not a serious threat to our knowledge.

Another interesting puzzle related to the traffic-lights problem arises in studying the mechanism of vision. The light falling on the lens of the eye from external sources is projected onto the inner wall (the retina) as if onto the film of a camera or the screen of a cinema and in the process is reversed left to right and turned upside down. The image of a tree thus appears on the retina with its roots above its branches. The puzzle is, How can we possibly see things as being the right way up when the retinal image is upside down? An eminent contemporary psychologist has described this as one of the great unsolved problems in the psychology of vision. A short course in the philosophy of perception (or in the history of his own subject) would have revealed the antiquity of the solution, which is of course a purely logical one. The reader will no doubt see it quite quickly, since the problem itself involves a cruder form of the error behind the traffic-lights "problem."

Another version, sometimes encountered among neurophysiologists who lack training in logical analysis is this: Since the nerves transmit only electrical impulses, how can we possibly detect sweetness or softness or any of the many other qualities of experience, which are obviously *not* properties of an electric current? But one might as well ask how musical notation can possibly represent sounds, when it is entirely visual, or the Morse code tell us of high temperatures in Tucson. These puzzles are intriguing logical riddles, but as it turns out, they are based on misconceptions (in particular, on the idea that messages can transmit properties only by having them). This has led some people to call them pseudoproblems.[9] It has even been maintained that all philosophical problems are ultimately pseudoproblems in this sense. This is either a bad definition of "philosophical problems" or a false claim, but it is true that *part* of the puzzlement about *many* philosophical problems comes from incorrect logical analysis, a less exciting and less misleading way of putting the "pseudoproblem" claim.

8. INEXPRESSIBLE KNOWLEDGE

The precise nature of our feelings is hard to communicate, and for this reason we may not be able to say just what it is about them that we are certain of. But there is another reason which might make our experiences, feelings, and sensations incommunicable: they might be incommunicable to someone who has never had them. How can we really tell in words what it is like to be married for fifteen years to someone you hate? Words can scarcely carry the depth and complexity of such an experience, although a whole novel, play, or film might succeed. What is it like to be in weightless space? To die and be brought back to life? To change sex? To inherit wealth after a lifetime of starvation? To see for the first time as an adult? To be insane?

Of course, people who have had these experiences can tell us something about them—at any rate they can *say* a great deal about them. But with all the words, the quality of the experience is often not communicated. From reading, we might say that we have *some* understanding of the experience

[9] There is a genuine problem in the *neighborhood,* however, namely, how physical signals can produce mental effects, and perhaps it is partly this that puzzles the physiologist. It is discussed in the *Man* chapter.

rather than knowing exactly what it is like. When we talk about experiences and sensations, we use the language of analogy and examples and use it to strike a chord in each other's memories. If that memory contains no similar element, the analogy will not evoke a full response. A man born blind may understand *that* others "see"; he may know *how* they see, physically speaking; but he does not know *what it is to see.* And that knowledge, it seems, is inexpressible in words. But notice that for the very same reason it is not knowledge that a particular state of affairs is the case; it is simply the having of a particular and rather special experience. It has been called "knowledge by acquaintance" to contrast it with "knowledge by description," i.e., knowledge of the truth of some descriptive statement (Russell). The blind man misses an experience and lacks a convenience, but he does not have less information or fewer truths available to him. If it takes him a little longer to find out about truths involving colors, he can still discover them by using the testimony of instruments and witnesses. He knows that blood is red, orange between red and yellow, and blue the color of his daughter's eyes.

Remembering the traffic-light puzzle, which underlines the peculiarity of talking about there being visual sensations in normal cases of seeing colors, we can raise an interesting problem about knowledge by acquaintance. Suppose we improved one of the sensing devices invented to help blind people, so that it not only emitted clicks to indicate the distance to obstacles but also conveyed information about color and shape by using high-frequency tones of a specially modulated kind, instantly recognizable by the user. Let us assume we strap this detector onto the blind man's head, like a miner's lamp, or build it into an instrument that looks like a pair of goggles, so that as he turns his head it reports on what would be in his visual field, if he had one, via small earpieces, like those on hearing aids, which do not block out other sounds. With practice the user finds it no longer necessary to make inferences from the sound to what is within range of his "acoustical eyes"; he simply knows what is there, to a degree that makes him immediately as well informed as a moderately well-sighted person. He also hears ordinary voices much as we all do, but he has unconsciously acquired the ability to translate certain special sounds from his detector into information about color, etc. If he is a man who has recently lost his sight, we may suppose that after a while he finds that his memories attach themselves to the appropriate signal and that he is getting visual imagery which, though not as good as he once had, is just like that of someone with somewhat defective vision.[10] (Similarly, his hearing is

---

[10] There is some reason to think that the sound spectrum is extremely limited in information-carrying capacity compared with the visual spectrum, and so the "substitute vision" might be very much inferior. But the facts do not affect the logical point (remarks like this are one reason scientists find philosophers irritating).

slightly impaired, since we steal a small part of the sound spectrum to convey visual data.) Now the odd question arises, Is he seeing with his ears? In a sense, he is; he is seeing (and hearing) by sound. The channel through which the data come is not what marks the special quality of visual experience.

Suppose we tighten down the clamps on the example and see if we can squeeze out a more striking result. Let us assume we are dealing with someone who has never had vision and that after some months with the device he reports himself as having become oblivious to the fact that a sound is providing the visual data and instead conceptualizes them immediately in special terms. Objects which actually have different colors are conceived of by him as different in a quality to which he is (via his detector) immediately responsive and to which of course he gives the correct names of "green" and "red," which he has learned from us as being right for these. Is he having genuine visual experiences?

Why not? What do his experiences lack that ours have? It might be suggested that they must be different because they are coming from a different part of the brain, but the colors we see have no trademarks on them that identify their intracranial source. Besides, it is quite possible that the brain would do a little recircuiting and bring the usual visual areas or equivalent ones into play. It is at least possible that we would simply have a more complex case of the well-known effect of wearing inverting prisms in front of one's eyes: after a while, everything begins to look the "right way up" again, because we learn how to translate the new code automatically into the familiar language of vision.

Suppose we now succeeded in restoring normal optical vision to our "blind" subject. According to this interpretation, he would shortly succeed in amalgamating the signals from the new sense with those from his audiovision device and would find the special apparatus dispensable, but after readjustment he would not report any qualitatively new experiences.

If this were to occur, the special experience of vision is not as special as it seems: it is simply the capacity to discriminate the wavelength of radiation in a certain band of the electromagnetic spectrum with a certain degree of precision and allot the standard labels to it. This conclusion has interesting consequences for the question whether a robot could ever have feelings or whether the mind is simply one aspect of the functioning of the brain, which we discuss in the *Man* chapter.

Therefore, there *is* a point to the remark that you can't tell a blind man how blue the sky is or an eight-year-old what it is like to be in love, but the point is not that the words fail *you*; it is rather that your words would fail *them*. You do not have inexpressible knowledge, but you can do a trick they cannot do now. And you cannot teach such a trick by talking to someone who lacks the basic physiological abilities to do it.

9. KNOWING HOW

This leads us to discuss other cases of knowledge which, though in one sense expressible in principle, are still quite different from any expression of it. One may know how to wiggle one's ears, swim the eight-beat crawl, recognize Rembrandts, or act graciously, without being able to express the whole of one's knowledge in words. To put it more precisely, the proof one knows *how to do* something is *doing* it, not talking about it. The coach of one of Yale's greatest swimming teams did not know how to swim, but he obviously knew a great deal about swimming. (We sometimes put this by saying that such a person knows how to do something *in theory* but not *in practice*.) To know what blue looks like, what Rembrandts look like, or what it is like to swim the crawl is just another way of saying one can do something. It *is* a kind of knowledge, but it is a very different kind from that which can be produced as evidence or as a conclusion in a proof. In fact, we should distinguish (1) knowing how to do something, (2) knowing how to tell how one does something, and (3) knowing how to teach someone else to do something (which may be done by offering actual examples and nonverbal correction of the learner's attempts).

And all of these are again quite different from knowing a fact and knowing how one came to know it, in the sense of being able to explain the mechanism of vision or mental calculation. We may know something and have no idea how we know it or came to know it, just as we may eventually arrive at the Gare du Nord in Paris without having any idea how we got there. Uncertainty about the route does not affect one's certainty about arrival.

This fact is sometimes taken to mean that claims to direct special knowledge do not require powerful evidence behind them. But to say one does not have to be able to explain how one knows something is by no means to say it is not necessary for there to be good evidence for it, before it can be said *that* one knows it. One may not even have the evidence at hand, but it must exist. Knowledge claims are strong claims and require strong support, though the support need only be evidential, not explanatory, and the knower need not have either explanation or evidence in mind at the time of the claim.

10. UNEXPLAINED WAYS OF KNOWING

A brilliant clinical diagnostician will often be able to identify correctly an obscure condition in a patient (we check his accuracy by watching the patient's later development or by making special tests), although he cannot give us any precise rule by which to do the same. His students, under his guidance, acquire the skill by careful scrutiny of the patient's charts, history, and appearance, which are all the expert employs. They discover that just *this* sallow cast of complexion, together with *this* kind of slurred speech and an occupation in the metal trades, strongly suggests antimony poisoning. But they have to look and listen in order to get the cash value of this color and this slurring. This is a case in which someone knows how to do something, knows how to teach how to do it, but does not know how to state how he does it in a rule that a newcomer to the field could use to repeat the performance. In such cases, we can see hope for a scientist who wants to find out exactly how it is done. He might be able to pin down the clues objectively and give us an exact rule with terms in it for the precise color shades, etc.; and he might say that this rule tells us how to identify antimony poisoning and is the secret of the great clinician's skill.

But although it is the first, there is one sense in which it is not the second: the clinician is not using this rule to make inferences, and he has not been keeping it hidden from us; he has simply acquired a reliable response to cases of antimony poisoning from many hundreds of exposures and attempted diagnoses. He is like the man who can identify green but knows nothing about the physiology of vision. The clinician may be confident that the skin color has something to do with it, but he does not know exactly what it has to do with it. He is simply an instrument, for detecting this and other conditions, which has been calibrated by experience and which can be used by himself as well as others. We discover in a very simple way *that* pigs can detect truffles and pigeons know how to get home, but we do not thereby discover *how* they do it. Clocks tell the time but they cannot tell how they tell or what it is they tell. It is really we who tell the time from clocks, but it is still not true we all know how to explain escapements, drive trains, and balance wheels. For some time intervals *we* are quite good clocks, but we do not know how we do that either. A knower needs no blueprints.

There are even simpler examples that demonstrate how we may know something without knowing how to say how we know it. When one has worked in a timber mill for a few weeks, one acquires the capacity to identify a piece of lumber on the other side of the yard as a 14-ft. 6-in. length of 2½ in. × 3½ in., a skill entirely mysterious to the new arrival. How does one do it? Just by looking, but now one can see something that others cannot when they look at the same thing; one can see what its dimensions are.

This, like the clinical example, is a case of possession of a certain kind of skill or know-how, and the particular performance involved is that of recognizing or perceiving a certain state of affairs (instead of swimming or baton twirling). In such a case "knowing how" produces knowledge of a fact. The lumber judge simply has a perceptual skill that most of us lack, like absolute pitch. Similar "knowledge skills" are illustrated by the possessor of a "photographic memory," or by a "lightning calculator," or by a water diviner, clairvoyant, telepath, hexer, and so on, if these exist. The difference between the lumberman's skill and the rest of these skills is that most of us could acquire his skill if we tried, whereas the other talents are relatively uncommon or entirely mythical. In all these cases, we notice that the knowledge produced by the special skill is not completely unavailable to others; it is simply not so *readily* available, either not available so quickly or not from the same position, etc. This is no accident; this is an essential feature of knowledge skills, unlike performance skills.

Even if someone is absolutely confident of skill in mind reading, fortune-telling, or communication with the spirits of the dead, we do not suppose that this confidence guarantees that he is right. It is impossible that he be mistaken about his feeling of confidence, but he may certainly be mistaken in the claim he is confident about. Putting it another way, we probably do not doubt, for example, that he *feels he can* read minds; what we doubt is whether he *actually can* read them. In all these cases, there is no insuperable difficulty in testing the claims made: some extremely ingenious experiments have been devised by parapsychologists to test the claims of communication with absent people, alive or dead.

What we test is the claim to knowledge of a special kind, and to reject it we can show either that the claimed "knowledge" is false or that it is impossible to tell whether it is true or false and hence impossible to justify the claim that it is true. In testing the claim of communication with the dead, we first try to demonstrate that the "medium" has obtained information from some other, more ordinary source: private inquiry, lip reading, skilled guesses based on the inquirer's dress and talk, or even telepathy. As long as these *could* provide the information which is being offered as a communication from the dead, we say that it cannot be known to be such a communication and hence that we cannot know that anyone survives death as a disembodied spirit (since this is the most important evidence for that conclusion). Sometimes, however, the evidence is extremely difficult to dismiss in this way. Arrangements have now been made by contemporary researchers to communicate information when they die—should it be possible for them to do so—which will be virtually inexplicable by any other hypothesis.

The crucial point of these considerations is that a knowledge claim, "I know that X is the case," may be shown to be false without anyone knowing whether X is true or false. We simply have to show that the speaker cannot justify any certainty about X's being true. Remember that mere confidence only justifies a subjective-certainty claim ("I *feel* certain X is the case"); a knowledge claim requires objective certainty ("It *is* certain X is the case"). We may criticize someone for feeling certain when the evidence is inconclusive, we may feel that rationally he *should not* feel certain, but we cannot deny that he *does* feel certain. We *can* deny that he knows or that X is certain. Of course, he does not have to produce evidence from which we can infer X directly; he need only produce evidence that he is a good instrument for detecting that X is the case, and this requires no explanation of how he does it.

The usual method of testing knowledge claims is simpler. It consists in arranging for an *independent check* of the alleged knowledge. We check the lightning calculator's claim by working the same sum through slowly, that of the man with the photographic memory by keeping a real photographic record, and so on. If we have no independent check, then we have only the confidence of the claimant to go on, and, without in the least questioning his honesty, we cannot ignore the possibility that he is mistaken. After all, it constantly happens that someone *honestly* claims she is *certain* she saw Mrs. Spring at the market this morning, when in fact Mrs. Spring is at a conference in Geneva with her husband.

If eyesight (which we know can work) is fallible, then "second sight" is doubly dubious. Moreover, we know very well that many people would very much *like* to have special powers and that it is a common occurrence for our wishes to master our judgment. So there are two competing explanations of the feeling of certainty about knowledge that could only be telepathic; it may be well based (in which case it is knowledge) or it may be a product of wish fulfillment and some lucky coincidences or shrewd guesses. Before we accept knowledge claims that are very firmly held, we *always* need to ask whether an alternative explanation of the conviction is better supported.

It is sometimes thought that our ignorance as to *how* a clinician, lumberman, or telepath operates should throw doubt on his conclusions. Perhaps, it is suggested, such people (and ourselves) should not be permitted to say they *know* something by using their special skill unless we know how they know. That this view is mistaken is obvious since (1) it would dismiss all memory-based claims from the realms of knowledge (e.g., "I know I drove to work this morning") because we do not know how the memory operates; (2) it would make all vision-based claims to knowledge unsound up to the time when eye structure and function were worked out (and surely people both before and after that day were *equally* entitled to say they could see the sun shining); and (3) it implies that only people with training in physics should believe what they hear on the telephone, since only they know how it works.

Let us now attempt to give a general analysis of statable knowledge. We are *entitled to say* (or *justified in saying*) that we know something (or that it is certain) when we believe it on very good grounds, and we will be *right in saying it* if what we believe is true. If it turns out to be false, we retrospectively retract our claims of knowledge or certainty; instead of *saying that we knew* (or *it* was certain) Mrs. Spring was here but she wasn't, we say we *thought* (or *we* were certain) she was here but she wasn't. It will still be perfectly possible to say that we were *at the time* justified in saying we knew she was here, but it is no longer justified to say this. (Similar analyses apply to other knowledge-incorporating terms like "seeing" and "hearing.") The subjective claim does not have to be withdrawn, because it correctly described our feelings. The objective one must be withdrawn, because it involves a claim as to what was actually the case, as well as a claim about our feelings, and the first part of this turns out to be wrong. So we have to replace it with the subjective claim.

If we have really thought about the matter carefully, there is often an objective but guarded claim we could have made that would not have to be withdrawn. We can say that in terms of the evidence available it was highly probable she was there, i.e., it was rational to attach considerable weight to that belief. Even if it turns out she was not there, looking back we can still say that it *was* highly probable (if, in fact, the evidence was very good) but—as it happens—not true. But of course the probability claim is much weaker than the knowledge claim and is often too weak for the situation. We can be safer if we use it, but we cannot be as useful: we shall not be conveying what we are often perfectly entitled to convey by the knowledge claim.

We could sum up this analysis by saying that claims to knowledge of this kind are simply claims that certain statements are true and as such they need good evidence to justify them. We can get good evidence if we use a thoroughly reliable instrument, such as a good thermometer, our eyes, or a proved diagnostician. Reliability is tested by making comparisons between readings and the facts as they turn out to be, and it requires no knowledge at all of the principles on which the instrument is constructed. "The facts as they turn out to be" are usually inferred from *extremely* good evidence at a later date, and of course even these inferences may conceivably be wrong. Knowledge is an immensely complex structure like others in this world, not unchanged by time but not a mere fantasy for that. That each of its tiny elements has a remote though sometimes significant chance of failure does not make the chance of simultaneous failure of the whole structure in the least significant.

11. LOGIC, THE FRAMEWORK OF KNOWLEDGE

The system of scientific and common-sense knowledge can only be communicated or expressed by using a language. For a language to serve as a means of communication between two persons it must have some common meaning. The meaning of some terms in language is partly given by "attaching" them to objects in the world; in this way, for example, we are taught the names of individuals and colors. Thus a common language, if it includes such terms, is possible only if we have common experiences. A test of understanding such terms is seeing whether they are applied to the "correct," i.e., conventionally associated, objects. It is not possible for someone to understand what "green" means and deny that it applies to most trees in midsummer, the way trees are now. But, of course, it is not an indispensable part of the meaning of "green" that it be the color of summer trees in every future summer, for trees may change and then we'd use other standard examples.

Now there are other rules governing the meaning of terms which do not involve connecting them with the external world. These are internal rules of the language. We do not have to look to see that something that is dark green all over is not bright red all over at the same time. When we talk about something as being a certain (single) color without qualification, we are talking of a property that describes its whole surface and has its meaning simply because it excludes the other possible colors. The color scale, like the length scale, works by dividing and labeling the range of possibilities and would lose its meaning if the possibilities were not separate. If red were not distinguishable from green, it would not be red; if 6 in. were not distinct from 1 in., it would not be 6 in., and if pawns were not different from queens in chess, they would not be pawns.

These general truths which express principles of the grammar of our language are often described as *logical* or *definitional* truths, by contrast with *factual* or *empirical* truths, which might conceivably be false. Now, of course, we might conceivably change our use of the terms in our language so that *green* means "shiny," and then something could correctly be said to be green and bright red all over at the same time. But that can happen *only* if we change the meaning of the terms, and it does not nullify the original truth. For in that new language the old logical truth will still be around—if the language is adequate for ordinary purposes—as it is in French or German, wearing a slightly different linguistic guise. If the new word for dark green is "dreen," then the old truth will now be expressible as "Nothing can be both dreen and bright red all over at the same time." Logical truths do not cease to be truths when the language changes: they simply have to be expressed in different words. But an empirical truth may just turn out to be wrong, without any change in the language.

Some of the logical truths involve words like "not," "and," "or," etc., which are not the names of anything. "If two claims are not both true, at least one of them must be false," is an example. It is a definitionally true statement; that is, it expresses part of the meaning of "true" and "false" and "are," etc. It expresses a rule of our language. There is nothing mysterious about the source of such truths: a language must have some rules if it is to be used communally, and these rules are not factual remarks about the world but merely conventions in a language which is used to describe the world (among other tasks). These are not "laws of thought" or "assumptions about the structure of reality."

People have sometimes argued that these are truths about the language and hence there is a sense in which they are about the "world" (in an extended view of the world). But even if we take this position, they are about a very special part of the world, namely, the part we use to describe the other parts, so that we can still distinguish logical from factual truths. The rules of the game of describing are the rules of a language which we created, and they are true because we *choose* to use that language; their truth does not depend on the way the *rest* of the world is.

This immunity to falsification (by discoveries about the nonlinguistic part of the world) is the special feature of logical truths that makes it important to distinguish them from empirical or factual truths. Now even when the linguistic conventions change, the logical truths are not falsified but simply require reexpression. This makes it very misleading to say that logical truths are truths *about a* language (since such truths would indeed be falsified by changes in a language). It is much better to say they *express* or *exhibit* the rules of a language than to say they *describe* the language. "Pawns that reach the opposing back line become queens" describes what happens to chess pawns; it expresses a rule of chess: it does not describe chess except in a very roundabout sense. Similarly, "If a proposition is not true, it is false" expresses a rule about propositions.

There are some interesting borderline claims that are partly rules of the language and partly truths about the world, as you would expect in a language which is constantly changing. These can be called quasi-definitional truths or quasi-logical truths. "Ripe lemons are yellow" is a good example; over a period of many decades lemons might gradually change so that when ripe they are the red of pomegranates and do not pass through a yellow phase en route. Would that show they really should not be called lemons any more? Well, let us suppose they are still just the same inside, taste the same, and grow on trees which appear exactly the same; would it not be more appropriate to say that lemons had evolved, just as we say the horse has evolved through the ages? The concept of a lemon seems to have that much flexibility in it. If we followed this line of argument, we should say that "Ripe lemons are yellow" is not a definitional truth, which inclines us to say that it is a factual truth.

But against this we must observe that exactly the same possibility appears to exist with regard to every property of lemons. They might change in *taste* but not in any other respect, as the result of atomic fallout, and that is the way we should describe it; we would not say, "There aren't any more lemons." We could put this by saying that the concept of lemon is an abstraction from a certain cluster of properties, no one of which is essential to the concept but a number of which must be present for it to be correct to call something a lemon. The extreme case in one direction, in which the properties *have* to be present, is a purely logical truth ("Bachelors are single male adults"). In the other direction, in which some properties have absolutely no effect on the meaning, the claim that such a property applies is a purely factual truth ("Lemons made up 11.5 per cent by value of the interstate commerce of Florida in 1939"). We hesitate to call this a property of lemons because it is not characteristic of them; but a property does not have to apply to every single lemon to be characteristic.

So there are some claims that are neither purely logical nor purely factual, and in the evolution of a language these may change their status in the course of the years. This is one reason why reading the history of philosophy, even in English, often requires considerable sensitivity to linguistic nuances, since the same words constantly shift their meaning in such a way as to convert eighteenth-century facts into twentieth-century definitions.

There should also be clear recognition of the *complexities* involved in expressing the rules and developing their consequences in a perfectly precise language. The work of Euclid was not a matter of offhand recitation of the rules of the language of geometry, any more than the work of Whitehead and Russell and their successors in modern symbolic logic is a casual formulation of the language of logic. There is often a possibility of human error in the formulation of the more complex logical mathematical truths, even if there is no possibility that a particular claim will be falsified by events in the physical world. One might say that when it can be established, the certainty of logical claims is wholly impregnable, whereas that of factual claims is not, but that establishing logical certainty can be just as hard and fraught with risk as establishing any factual truth. The proofs of many famous theorems, like the Herbrand theorem, have stood unchallenged for many years and then turned out to be faulty. Even a perfectly sound mathematical proof, when it can be identified, only establishes its conclusion if its premises are sound, and the history of mathematics is strewn with the wreckage of discarded axioms. An axiom may seem entirely obvious until some of its more complex consequences are uncovered, so that the truth of axioms is constantly subject to retest by independent examination of the truth of their consequences. The situation is very like that in testing physical hypotheses. Of course, merely to discover that an axiom is not as indisputable as we had supposed (Euclid's parallel postulate) does not imply its error; we may still take it to define one particular subbranch of the subject (Euclidean geometry), a maneuver which has no exact counterpart in physics.

Given all these qualifications, however, $3 + 1 = 4$ and its relatives are in no danger whatsoever. Nor, of course, is the claim that the Sun currently has more than four planets. But the latter claim is not true by definition; it represented an important discovery in the history of science, and it is informative about the world precisely *because* it goes beyond the definition of its terms. For that reason, it is more open to disproof, though it may still be certain. Complex logical truths or mathematical theorems are informative *without* going beyond the definition of their terms by revealing what was packed into those definitions. But complex factual claims are not elaborations of the rules of a language; they are elaborate descriptions of the particular way this world happens to be, out of the infinity of ways it might have been.

So our knowledge does not "depend" in some dubious way upon assumptions about the truth of a particular system of logic.[11] If we wish to express our knowledge in English, we obviously must adhere to the rules of English grammar, but we can express it in Swahili or Urdu and use their grammars. We assume a grammar, in a sense of *assume* that just means "use," but this kind of assumption does not make our knowledge vulnerable to hidden errors, because it simply means we adopt a certain convention in order to utter. There are alternative logics in the sense of alternative grammars for alternative languages, but that does not show that a particular logic (the grammar of a particular language or group of languages) is dubious or suspect. It is inviolable, since we make it true—the only question is whether it is rich enough to express the distinctions we are interested in. If it is not, the distinctions do not become false, only inexpressible. So logic, which is the development of the common and important features of the grammar of the words involved in reasoning, is not an Achilles' heel in the system of knowledge; it is just a book of rules for the language without which we could not say that Achilles had a heel or distinguish having one from being one.

Logic is the great instrument of philosophy, and to discover and test the more subtle principles of logic requires considerable attention to and skill in analyzing the subtleties of language. This does not mean that philosophy is about language any more than physics is about mathematics. It is just that you cannot do good work in the one if you cannot use the other. Many of the most interesting concepts in both physics and philosophy are best explained by using sentences which are neither purely factual nor purely logical but quasi-logical. In this sense, these concepts and claims about them express truths about the world as well as truths about language. The difference between philosophy and physics is that you cannot make logical analyses of physical concepts unless you know all about them, i.e., know physics; but the philosophical concepts of the primary problems are the great concepts of our intellectual language, and we already know how to talk about them. The relevant facts about them are largely built into that language, just as the relevant facts about the clusters of properties that we call lemons are built into the many quasi-logical claims about lemons whose truth we know. Sometimes other facts are relevant, too, and for these we must turn to the appropriate science. There is thus a most important and very strong sense in which philosophy is about the world and not just about language, although it does not exclude the simultaneous truth of the claim that philosophical analysis requires a great deal of linguistic analysis and very little factual investigation of the nonlinguistic world.

[11] The part of logic discussed here as the grammar of terms like "proposition," "true," etc., is usually called deductive logic, and some of its principles have their own names: the law of the excluded middle, etc. Inductive logic is the study of the other principles used in ordinary scientific reasoning.

12. THE LIMITS OF REASON: ENDS VERSUS MEANS

We have been extolling the advantages of rationality and the security of its foundations. It is time to stress certain limits on reason. Although reason extends far beyond the sciences into the fields of law, history, mathematics, philosophy, and literary criticism, its scope is not universal. At the level of primitive tastes it serves merely on a stand-by basis. That you prefer one flavor of ice cream and I another is not, today, a sign that one of us must be right and the other wrong. These are reports of likings or feelings, and the feelings evoked by external sources are frequently very different for different individuals. We do not insist that everyone on the boat has to be seasick before we can believe one man who says he's feeling seasick. In Chapter III we shall see whether the assessment of beauty is like the assessment of logical or factual truths or more like the assessment of strawberry sundaes and seasickness.

The recognition of the comparative immunity of taste from rational criticism has led some people to suppose that reason can only criticize means and not ends. We have already seen the difficulties with this supposition, and we shall now summarize them. The suggestion is generally true but extremely dull in the context of a particular task of rational evaluation. If we are going to evaluate dishwashers in order to decide which one is the most rational for us to buy, we begin by putting down a list of the properties that are important to us; the amount of hot water used per cycle may be an important factor for us though not for others, etc. Only when we have listed these properties and have an idea of their *relative* importance to us, can we begin the evaluation process, which requires comparing the performance of the available candidates with regard to each of these factors. In this sense, reason only comes into play when the ends have been determined.

But this remark is rather trivial, since the ends themselves are subject to rational criticism. We may, for example, be much better off to buy a new, larger-capacity water heater and pick the best dishwasher regardless of the water consumption. This will be true if the economical dishwashers are enormously inferior to the others and the cost of a new water heater is not very important to us. Or it may be that strong independent reasons exist, in terms of baths for guests, using the dishwasher on laundry day, etc., which make the new water heater a rational choice.

Still, the ends-defender says, discussions of these kinds are going on far down the scale of our values, and they all depend on our higher ends, our goals in life, etc. In some sense, indeed, this is true: if we do not want clean dishes, then none of this talk about dishwashers matters; and if we do not want to live, we shall not care about clean dishes. But exactly what are the ultimate ends with regard to which it is being suggested that reason has no jurisdiction?

Is it that we value *life itself?* Clearly this goal falls under rational scrutiny, too, as the patriot contemplates suicide to avoid revealing revolutionary plans, the martyr considers his own sacrifice, the drug researcher decides to use himself as a patient, and the hero volunteers for hazardous duty. Moreover, valuing life is itself far too general a goal to yield the rather specific preferences we need for our dishwasher evaluation.

It is clear that the more specific goals arise from differences of taste in choosing a particular kind of life, but the trouble is that reason is by no means irrelevant here, either, in the stand-by sense. If commercial strawberry flavor turns out to be cancer-inducing, it is no longer rational to choose strawberry-flavored ice cream. In fact, continuing to have a passion for that flavor smacks of irrationality and *is* irrational if it is possible to give up such tastes and one does not do so. Any end, at any level, is potentially subject to rational assessment insofar as it is a matter of choice whether we have it or not and insofar as we have any other independent goals at all. Now almost all ends, certainly those of life, food, drink, and happiness, are to some extent controllable by strenuous conditioning and self-discipline, as the Japanese suicide-bomber pilots, the self-burning Buddhist monks, and the hunger strikers make clear. And there is no one who has only one aim, by which all his decisions are determined; the abstract aims are too general, and the specific ones not general enough, to provide a basis for the whole range of decisions he must make. Hence, all ends are subject to rational scrutiny.

The system of a man's values is a net and not a knotted string. It is a web that stretches across our lives and actions and connects them with the threads of reason. It may be true that a net only ties holes together, but it still has to have some points of attachment. The rational tension in the cords often makes it necessary to adjust these points of attachment, as we add new connections or the old holding points move around, but this internal tension is not self-supporting. There must be points of attachment, and they should be secure ones. No point of attachment is immune to these adjustments; so there are no ultimate values, in the sense of unquestionable or indefensible ones. But certainly some values are more important than others; that is, more numerous threads run from them. A child begins with certain wants, and these get modified by his environment; he learns to think, he acquires new tastes, and these changes lead to self-modification. Eventually, all his values are either new or have a new importance. But they sprang from the interaction of rationality (or irrationality) with his original values and his environmental constraints. If human beings were very different in their infant needs or very different in the constraints which are brought to bear on them, they could well have wholly different later values. Reason bears on and changes values but does not create them *ex nihilo.* If this is a basis for saying there are limitations to its powers, then we can say that. But the picture of ultimate values, from which all others hang like onions on a string, is completely wrong.

There is another point which might also lead one to conclude that reason has limits. Obviously, our knowledge and our reasoning power are limited. Our reason leads to less-than-ideal choices and beliefs insofar as it depends on incomplete knowledge, or is itself deficient. So it is only productive of relatively good choices and beliefs, not always the best ones. And that is, in a way, a limitation, though it is a limitation in about the same way that it is a limitation of a perfect pocket knife that it is not a felling ax.

Now we shall turn to an area where the extent of the limitations on rationality comes into focus and where the solution to the primary problems consists in exhibiting these limitations clearly.

ART

0. THE PROBLEMS

Is it possible to evaluate works of art objectively, or are such judgments essentially matters of taste? Is anyone's opinion better than that of anyone else in judging the merit of works of art, or natural objects such as sunsets and sunflowers, or hybrid objects such as gardens and girls? There are more numerous problems about judging art than about judging nature, but the fundamental problem in both cases is that of judging aesthetic merits, and it is common to gallery-going and girl-watching. Are very good copies of extremely beautiful natural objects very good works of art? (Is photography an art?) Is intelligibility to the contemporary audience, or social or psychological significance, or great technical skill a crucial requirement for great art? Are there greater and lesser arts?

1. OBJECTIVITY AND MATTERS OF TASTE

Matters of taste are not always *mere* matters of taste. There is a story about the composer Darius Milhaud and a young lady who came to speak with him after he had given a talk on the appreciation of modern music, in which he had extolled its virtues by comparison with the older traditions. She disagreed with him completely but could make no impression on him; finally she asked, "But Mr. Milhaud, isn't it all ultimately a matter of taste?" to which he replied, "Yes, indeed it is, ma'am—good taste and bad taste."

Our main problem is to decide *which* kinds of "matters of taste" are involved in evaluating art. To the extent that judgments about art are in any sense matters of taste, they are often not *mere* matters of taste in the extreme sense that liking a particular flavor of ice cream is a mere matter of taste. For artistic taste may certainly be informed rather than uninformed, and it is often said to be sophisticated rather than naïve, or highly trained rather than instinctive, although these latter distinctions need explanation and justification. But even if these distinctions are allowed, the puzzle about objectivity is still meaningful: it is a request for a decision whether the dissenter, informed or not, is *wrong* or simply *different,* whether he is making a *mistake* or simply showing that he was not born, or trained, exactly like other people.

This chapter is devoted almost entirely to a discussion of the objectivity problem and should be seen as a development of the discussion of the role and limitations of reason in Chapter II. We there gave an outline of rational-evaluation procedures in pragmatic contexts and criticized the idea that reason can assess means and not ends. In later chapters we shall examine other areas in which reason is sometimes said to be irrelevant: the provinces of theology and ethics. Can we stretch the process which works so well with evaluating consumer goods and other practical issues, and even with life ideals, into the realms of art, religion, and ethics? Very different answers must be given to these problems.

2. AESTHETICS

The field of philosophy concerned with works of art and natural beauty and the status of judgments about them is called aesthetics; it involves the discussion of many interesting problems which do not qualify as primary problems, e.g., the analysis of the concepts of drama, metaphor, balance, realism, irony, aesthetic object, aesthetic experience, and art. We may call such discussion *elucidatory aesthetics.* We may think of this discussion as concerned with understanding the aesthetic language in much the same way as we might concern ourselves with understanding the language of a certain tribe or the technical language of some group in our own society. In the case we are discussing, the group is that of the artist (when talking *about* his work) and the art (music, literature, etc.) critic, the art historian, and the connoisseurs, who, in turn, are talking about and trying to understand the artist's work.[1] But an art critic not only attempts to understand and explain an artist's work (*elucidatory criticism*); he is frequently concerned with evaluating it: hence, presumably, his title as "critic." And, in the same way, the philosophy of art is concerned not only with the analysis of the concepts and categories used by the critic but with the justification of whether the critic's assessment of a work of art is good or bad, better or best, in this and that respect (*evaluative criticism*). We may call the theory of evaluative criticism *evaluative aesthetics*.[2]

In terms of our analogy between understanding the language of a tribe and elucidatory aesthetics, we may think of evaluative aesthetics as the attempt to decide whether the tribe's beliefs about the Universe around them, once understood, are well supported. In terms of the analogy with the technical language of a subgroup of our own society, the comparison is with the assessment of the merits of the claims made in the technical language of quantum mechanics, theology, or astrology.[3]

It is clear enough that evaluative aesthetics presupposes some elucidatory aesthetics, since we can hardly assess claims if we do not understand them. In

[1] Even though much of what is said in this chapter applies equally to judgments about natural beauty, cumbersome phrasing would be required to make the remarks apply as they stand; so we shall chiefly use the language for discussing art. Our conclusions may be transposed in most but not quite all cases to the general field of the evaluation of beautiful objects. For one thing, "beauty" is a word which is much more important in the vocabulary when we are assessing works of nature than works of art; a great drama such as *Hamlet* is not normally something which we call beautiful, and the same is true of some orchestral works, paintings, novels, and performances. There are other important differences between works of art and works of nature, for example, the extent to which the problem of unity does not exist for works of nature, except in a very different sense, and the absence of the tendency to confuse the merit of the artist and the merit of the work of art when appreciating sunsets, starry skies, and sweet sirens (although some theists persist in the confusion).

[2] There are certain kinds of aesthetic judgment which may be properly called evaluative but which are not directly concerned with the question whether a work of art is good or bad; for example, the assessment of a particular work as in the style or school of Ingres, or as earlier rather than later baroque, or as a parody of or a satire on Salinger may be said to be an evaluation of it (meaning, roughly, a technical classification of it). It is usual, however, for evaluations to be directly or indirectly connected with the grading of works in terms of their merit, and it is with this kind of evaluation that we shall be primarily concerned.

[3] The *philosophical* task in each of these examples is really to decide whether there is any way to establish these claims rather than to decide them; but to do this one must look at representative examples of the evidence and see how it actually bears on the claims made. The philosophy of art criticism or of science cannot be wholly separated from the practice of the art critic or the scientist.

fact, the two divisions of aesthetics are even more closely bound, because what we *can* mean by aesthetic terms is restricted by the extent to which they can be substantiated objectively. What is meant by "The sun is rising" depends in part upon what the astronomers can establish, and the phrase has consequently changed enormously in meaning since it was first employed. Correspondingly, what is meant by calling a work "trite" or "banal" depends a good deal upon the extent to which the evaluations of merit implicit in these terms can be substantiated. There are more complicated as well as simpler cases than these, and we shall begin with the simplest.

Since all of us are familiar with a very wide range of nontechnical aesthetic judgments ("It's a great, good, clever, dull, or lousy novel, film, painting, play, photograph, or view") and these appear to be typical of the judgments about which skeptical doubts are usually expressed, we can attack the primary problem without any need for detailed examination of the technical or semitechnical language of the critic. The discussion will in fact involve some reference to the development of the technical vocabulary, partly to see whether it really does have the same logical character, and our conclusions are intended to apply in general to technical as well as nontechnical descriptions.

3. TYPES OF AESTHETIC CLAIM

Claims made about a work of art may be entirely nonevaluative or entirely evaluative, just as they may be nontechnical or highly technical; and any mixture is possible. Nonevaluative claims may of course be among the grounds for evaluative conclusions, but one should be careful not to add unconsciously the further assumptions needed to complete this kind of argument when classifying the basic claims themselves. For example, the fact that the dialogue in a novel is inappropriate to the social stratum of the characters may be a simple and obvious fact. It is not evaluative, but if you assume or can show that this novel should be realistic in this respect, an evaluative conclusion follows.

Some of the semitechnical language of criticism packs the value judgment into the terms used; if dialogue is "banal" or "trite," it is to that extent lacking in merit (exceptions are still possible, e.g., for a work that is deliberately trying to exhibit the banality of life). But using evaluative semitechnical language like this of course requires that we be able to establish deficiency of merit in the dialogue in order to justify applying the terms. The value conclusion comes out of such claims more easily, but it is correspondingly harder to justify the claims. If it is *just* as much harder, then giving reasons cannot help us to reach evaluative conclusions in aesthetics. Reasons only help us to establish conclusions insofar as they are easier to establish than the conclusions themselves, just as definitions or explanations only help us to understand a word or puzzle insofar as they are simpler than the word or puzzle they define or explain. It is this primitive logical fact which poses the most savage threat to the whole structure of aesthetic evaluation.

Here are examples of two categories of aesthetic claim not so far discussed:

Nontechnical, nonevaluative:

> The novel is set in Barsetshire; its chief character may reasonably be supposed to be a Tory; the talk is quite unlike that of the landed families of the time; it contains no serious discussion of social problems; it is unusually long.

Technical, nonevaluative:

> There is an undercurrent of concern with the problem of the social responsibility of the rich; the plot is developed without appeal to fate; the style is reminiscent of Thackeray; the novel is basically satirical, although the tragic element is occasionally predominant; the villain is a grotesque and haunted figure; the baroque flavor is curiously muted by the simplicity of the theme.

Examples of nontechnical evaluative ("boring") and semitechnical or technical evaluative ("banal," "better brogue than Burns") claims are obvious enough. It is most important to see that arguments, indeed bitter, irresoluble arguments, may perfectly well arise over claims in any of these categories; the fact that they are somewhat more likely to arise over valuational claims is simply because the stakes are greater there. A man's status is at stake with his taste, and his taste is revealed in his evaluations. But, of course, one's prestige is also involved in being right, and this is at issue whenever one makes even a nontechnical, nonvaluational claim about a work of art.

Aesthetic claims, like any others, may be put in the form of very mild, highly qualified assertions ("It seems to me . . .," "I think . . .") or of blunt, definite, unqualified assertions ("It is the case . . .," "There can be absolutely no doubt . . ."), but however qualified in this sense, the aesthetic claims are still present and open to attack or support depending on the particular claim and on the views held about aesthetic claims in general. Hence the distinction between strong and weak claims in this dimension, of qualification, is not the same as the distinction between matters of personal preference and matters of objective fact. Of course, the unqualified language is rather inappropriate if art is just a matter of taste, and someone who thought it was only that probably would not use such forms of words. If he did and the matter were *not* one in which an objective decision was possible, we could either say that he was claiming more than he was entitled to and was wrong or that he was "really" only expressing a taste, though he used a form of words normally reserved for stating a fact. The second alternative is like saying that if we cannot really show there is a God, then claims like "God exists" should just be thought of as an expression of attitude, even if the speaker thinks they express a fact. In the field of ethics, the corresponding view is that categorical moral claims like "Adultery is absolutely wrong" are only expressions of enthusiasm for a purely parochial attitude and not references to a set of absolute moral standards. When there are no objective standards to support the literal interpretation, then, according to this view, the meaning of the claim should be reinterpreted. When you cannot literally mean "The Sun is rising," then your statement must be taken to mean that it looks *as if* it is rising or that its location relative to the horizon is rising. But in a field of knowledge in which the true situation is not apparent, it is somewhat gratuitous to make such a reinterpretation. There are probably still some people who think the sun does move up from beneath the sea, and they are just wrong. If there are no gods or no absolute standards in art or ethics, then a great many people will be wrong when they make certain claims, though there may be others who use the same words to express more moderate claims which may be true.

In conclusion, it is important to notice that many evaluative claims are (explicitly or implicitly) comparative, and the more restricted the range of comparison, the weaker the claim is, and thus the easier it is to establish. To claim that one mystery novel is better than another is generally to make a weaker claim than to claim that it is a very good mystery novel (though not, of course, if the second novel is itself one of the best), and the claim that it is a very good *mystery novel* is in turn a weaker claim than the claim that it is a great *novel,* which is in turn weaker than the claim that it is a great *work of art.* The advantage of reducing the field of comparison in this way is that it may prove possible to reduce it to a point at which fairly strict standards can be agreed on as defining the genre (the type of artistic work in question). In terms of these narrow standards it may be quite easy to apply objective procedures for supporting an evaluation of merit: good mystery novels simply cannot have great loopholes in the plot, for example. But to succeed in this task of relative evaluation, or comparison, is typically only to postpone the day for a certain kind of reckoning: the reckoning on the merits, significance, etc., of the particular genre. Nevertheless, we can achieve an important kind of objectivity in aesthetic judgments of merit by restricting the range of our claims in this way.

Our main concern in this chapter is, however, with the more difficult problem whether one can objectively support absolute, not comparative, judgments of merit about art. That is the problem to which most people have an answer, an answer which they express when they say, "Modern art is junk," or "The true stature of Mondrian is only now emerging," or "I know everything about art, but I don't know what to like."

4. OBJECTIVE REASONS

At this stage it is essential to set out some of the requirements for a system of reasons that is to have objective status ("carry weight," "justify a claim," "constitute good reasons," "prove anything," etc.) in any field, practical, normative, or scientific. First, in their usual linguistic form reasons have certain grammatical characteristics; they are assertions (possibly only implicit in what is actually said) which bear on some other hypothesis or assertion that is said to "follow from them," or be "the conclusion which they support," or be "the conclusion to which they point," and so on. Second, to be good reasons for believing the conclusion, the assertions have to be true. Reasons must, in short, be *facts*. Third, it also has to be true that such facts do make the conclusion probable (or certain). This is the requirement of relevance, of a sound *connection* between the reason and the conclusion. The connection may be definitional or factual; especially in the latter case it is often given as one of the reasons for the conclusion. The connection, like any reason, must exist and be recognized, but it does not have to be quotable (remember the diagnostician and the lumberman examples in Chapter II).

If a reason or a connection is not quotable, it may still be possible to show that the conclusion which it is supposed to support should be accepted by others besides the one who recognizes the connection, but the others will not be in possession of "reasons for coming to the conclusion," only of "reasons for believing it." Think of a good tracker who may see a change in the stride pattern of a hunted animal that indicates increased fatigue to his experienced eye. He cannot give you an exact rule that makes his conclusion (rather than a mere slowing of gait) probable, but *he* has a good reason for the conclusion, namely, what he sees; and *you* have a good reason for believing the conclusion, namely, his known merit. But his reason for believing the conclusion is not your reason, and it cannot be presented to you as a ground from which you too can infer the conclusion. Although our main concern here is with reasons which *can be communicated,* i.e., with reasons in their linguistic form, we must also consider cases in which reasons can be recognized or even exhibited although they are not stated. Suitable training in tracking would make it possible for you to recognize the force of his reasons, as he points to certain features of the animal's tracks, even if you do not have a common language in which to express them. Perhaps the same sort of thing can be done in aesthetic training. In any case, whether or not the connection between the reasons and the conclusion is statable, it must exist.

By contrast with the requirement of connection, there is the fourth requirement for a system of reasons, *independence,* and about this and the following requirements we shall say rather more than about the first three because they are the critical ones for the objectivity of aesthetic evaluation. The independence requirement demands that we be able to know the reason or reasons for a conclusion without first having to know the conclusion; otherwise we can never use the reasons as a means of getting to the conclusion. This is an easy requirement to misinterpret. It is not enough that the reason say something *different* from the conclusion, for it may make a more specific claim than the conclusion and still be such that it cannot be known without knowing the latter. (But *sometimes* we can know a more specific claim without knowing the more general one.) Nor does this requirement rule out reasons which definitionally (deductively) imply their conclusions. One may know the axioms of geometry and not know Pappus's theorem, which follows from them, and yet they might be said to be excellent grounds for supposing Pappus's claim to hold. (Normally, however, grounds are facts whose connection with the conclusion is *easily* seen or shown.)

The important notions of definition, explanation, argument, and proof all involve an independence criterion (in its more general form it can be called the requirement of enlightenment or informativeness) because they are all part of the business of knowledge conveying and knowledge enlarging and you cannot convey knowledge to someone who already has it or enlarge knowledge by a process that requires the enlargement before it can proceed. The requirement is sometimes expressed in terms of a ban on what are called circular definitions or question-begging arguments. Speaking of circularity in definitions is a loose way of referring to the independence criterion. It is useless to define *strong* as "the opposite of weak" unless there is a way of identifying weak things that does not involve deciding whether they are strong. Definitions are not merely equivalences: they are also attempts to express the meaning of a term in language which is *easier* to understand and certainly *capable* of being understood without understanding the defined term, i.e., independent.

It is indeed usual to impose a somewhat stronger requirement than independence on reasons. Reasons are normally required to be not only independent (i.e., such that we *can* know them without knowing the conclusion) but, as a fifth requirement, more easily known or proved. Otherwise there would be little point in proposing them as grounds for the conclusion, since we could as readily establish the conclusion. We shall call this fifth requirement the *simplicity* requirement; it clearly applies equally to definitions and explanations and to reasons and proofs.

Now one cannot usually tell from a single definition or a single reason whether it violates these requirements. The merits of the definition of *strong* given above depend on how *weak* is defined (and *opposite*, of course). Similarly, a proof usually cannot be classified as unsound, with regard to this criterion, until we know how the terms in it are to be tested and applied. Of course, a headline like "Shriver Says [Peace] Corps Succeeds because of Its Effectiveness"[4] tends to be self-incriminating, but when people talk in circles, the circles usually have more than a single-sentence circumference.

The sixth and last criterion that must be met by a set of reasons is that of having *indisputable* (or *demonstrable*) *starting points*. In the course of giving an argument, we must eventually be able to appeal to reasons which are not only true but can be seen or easily shown to be true. Otherwise we have not established the conclusion but merely linked it to other claims. These indisputable claims might be matters of definition or readily observable facts. *Indisputable* does not mean "undisputed," nor does it mean "impossible to dispute": it means "*rationally* impossible to dispute." So the mere fact that people have agreed the earth is flat or Gauguin good, or that they have not so agreed, does not show the indisputability criterion to be satisfied. For what is indisputably true in these cases is not the conclusion we are interested in but some premises from which it is in fact very difficult (though some have thought it easy) to get the conclusion. We *can* see that the horizon is level from a boat or a camel, just as it would be if the earth were flat; and we *can* see that nearly everyone likes Gauguin, that his painting has certain qualities, such as bright colors and Tahitian themes. The problem here is to establish the remaining axioms.

The secret of proof is to build a bridge out to the island conclusion from the shore of established truth. It may be helpful to elaborate some of our requirements on objective reasons in terms of this analogy. The requirement of relevance or connection is the requirement that the bridge actually get us to the island we are trying to reach. The requirement of independence ensures that the bridge begin somewhere other than on the island, the requirement of simplicity ensures that the somewhere else be easier to get to than the island, and the requirement of indisputability makes sure that the starting point is in fact the mainland of known truth. The requirement of truth insists that each of the piles of the bridge go down to bedrock. The grammatical requirements are not essential but amount to a request that we use such construction materials that people will recognize the result as a road on a bridge.

The independence, simplicity, and indisputability criteria apply to a group of reasons, like a proof, not to each individual reason. It is these requirements that are the most difficult for systems of aesthetic evaluation to meet. We may show that certain considerations in the language of critics are treated linguistically as if they were reasons (grammatical criterion), we may find there is complete agreement that they apply in a particular case (which is sometimes a fair indication of meeting the criterion of truth) and that whenever they do apply there are excellent reasons for believing the work of art to be good (connection criterion), but they may still be wholly lacking in "proof power."

---

[4] *Wisconsin Daily Cardinal*, Nov. 17, 1964.

For the decision that the considerations do apply in a particular case may require that we have already decided that the work is good, so that they cannot possibly serve as a stepladder to this conclusion.

It would be too severe a complaint to say that in these cases the critic's considerations are incomprehensible or uninformative, as is sometimes suggested. Other critics and connoisseurs may understand that the production of these considerations indicates attention to certain kinds of features rather than others: they have a *focusing function*. To say that a work's merit (or defect) lies in its perfect composition (or lack of it) is certainly to say something comprehensible, and indeed it may be to give the actual reason for one's judgment. But the question whether it is a *good* reason is a different question, which involves several tests. And these include deciding whether one can objectively establish the presence of perfect composition without first having to decide whether the painting is good. A man who can run off ten shots inside a ½-in. circle at 100 yds. is an excellent shot, but we need not know that in order to count the holes in the target and measure the range; so these facts provide us with good reasons for concluding that he is a fine shot.

When investigating the question whether the reasons are independent of the conclusion in the required sense, it often becomes clear that the opposite error is equally hard to avoid: the error of making them so independent that the connection is broken; i.e., they become irrelevant. A rather striking variation of this error occurs when a critic cites a particular quality, perhaps passion, as beneficial on one occasion and detrimental on another, i.e., when he is apparently guilty of *inconsistency*. If there is no extenuating circumstance, such as the presence of other relevant circumstances, then it is clear that even within the critic's system of appraisal there is no reliable link between passion and merit, and hence it is illegitimate for him to appeal to passion as a ground for his conclusion about merit.

Sometimes this kind of inconsistency is disguised by using one word for a quality like passion when it is going to be regarded as a merit and another when it is to be a demerit. A nice example of this, from the field of music criticism, occurs in the following quotation: ". . . This performance reminds us of what Tebaldi sounded like shortly after she first came to international attention; the voice was lighter and a bit freer than it is now, quite round and lacking in that quality which can be regarded as a virtue (when it's known as 'bite') or as a defect (when it's known as 'edginess')." [5] Distinctions like this are perfectly legitimate as long as there really is some difference between the two kinds of passion—perhaps one is more crude than the other. But if no such difference exists, use of two different terms is just a disguise for inconsistency. If inconsistency does occur, it will still be true to say that one of the *critic's* reasons for praising the first work was the passion it con-

[5] *Records in Review,* Wyeth Press, 1964, p. 398.

tained and *his* reason for condemning the second work was the same, for "his reason" means roughly the factor (of the kind in which we are interested —here, proved properties of the work of art) which caused him to come to this conclusion. And of course, the same factor may produce different effects (conclusions) at different times, depending on the critic's relationship to his wife, mistress, or digestion.

Of course, we could *say* his reasons were different if all we mean by this is that they had different effects. That is, we could say that his reason in the first case was the passion$_1$ he saw in the object, and in the second the passion$_2$, where passion$_1$ is passion that happens to have led him to a favorable conclusion, and so on. Obviously at this stage, where there is no *intrinsic* difference between passion$_1$ and passion$_2$, although one leads him to a judgment of merit and the other to the opposite conclusion, we have lost the *connection* between what can be objectively identified in the object and its merit, for it is only passion that can be so identified, and this, as such, is not connected with merit or defect but sometimes with one and sometimes with the other. But we cannot avoid this difficulty by using the more restricted terms, for they violate the criterion of independence, since even the critic cannot identify passion$_1$ as distinct from passion$_2$ without having already decided on the merits of the work of art. Hence, the requirements of consistency, independence, and connection must be juggled with great care, for concentration on one of them very often leads to a fatal oversight of another.

Some aspects of the preceding points have been expressed by other writers in terms of a requirement of generality. Good reasons, it is said, must be *general* reasons; what is good about one work of art must, if it occurs elsewhere, also be good there. This formulation, which is a kind of extra-strong requirement of connection, is incomplete because it is satisfied by passion$_1$, which is, of course, an entirely general merit, but of no value for objective evaluation. Our requirements of independence, etc., provide the necessary tightening of the requirement of connection without having to refer to generalization. The idea that logic requires us to derive our reasons from precise generalizations is especially misleading in art, where such generalizations are very hard to find and even harder to pin down to a particular case. It is often true that we feel more confident of the merit rating of a particular work of art than of any precise generalization. Yet it is not the absence of such generalizations that makes objective evaluation of art difficult; it is the more fundamental deficiences of connection, independence, consistency, simplicity, or demonstrability.

The insistence on general reasons may have definitely harmful effects. It is clear that, without any inconsistency, one may hold that the same evidence of passion is a merit in one play and a drawback in another just because the first play is a tragedy and the second a comedy of manners. Reasons certainly do not have to be general in a stronger sense than this. Could one not say that the real reason for merit in such cases is the combination of passion and tragic atmosphere? *This* would be generalizable, but it is not a reason. There is a crucial distinction in the language we are trying to analyze, the distinction between reasons and genres.

Reasons are the factors which sway us, good reasons those that should sway us, and both appear on the scene only after certain categorizations have been made, only when we have located the object to be appraised in the appropriate region of logical space. It is clear enough that different reasons apply to the appraisal of cars, by contrast with clothes dryers, but our reasons for condemning a clothes dryer do not include the fact that it is a clothes dryer. They *presuppose* such a classification: they do not undertake to make it. Similarly, if being a poor likeness is offered as a criticism of a painting, it has already been classified as a representational portrait, with regard to which such a complaint is appropriate. This distinction, between reasons and categories, is often overlooked because reasons can also be given for the classification, so that part of the process of defending an evaluation often involves giving such reasons. But reasons at the second level of defense are not made into reasons at the first level just because they are reasons which may arise in the same argument. So there is a perfectly good sense in which one can give the same reason for believing one painting good and another bad, without inconsistency. But one can also be inconsistent in doing this if no distinction of categories can be defended.

This point may be expanded by the realization that it is not only general classifications that determine the relevance of a particular consideration or the direction in which it bears but also considerations of mood, period, style, technique, materials, and so on. Hence the idea that the appraisal of each individual work of art may call for its own standards of criticism, which at once charms and frightens us, is not entirely absurd. There can still be standards even when the combination appropriate to a particular work is unique. Nor is this idea incompatible with the only sense in which the generalization requirement is legitimate, i.e., the sense in which it demands that a system of reasons be consistent, connected, and yet independent. For as long as there might be considerations of type, etc., which differentiate two paintings, there can be at least one critical generalization which will apply to one of them and not the other.

It is too strong a requirement to insist that the critic always be able to *formulate* this distinguishing generalization, just as it is too strong a requirement to demand that a man who has found the cause of an automobile's refusing to start be able to formulate the general conditions under which this cause will have that effect. A good critic can often persuade us of the cogency of a particular reason for condemning a particular work of art without going into the very general question of the range of applicability of that reason to other works of art. But of course it is helpful and desirable if the generalization can be formulated, and it provides a very good defense against the claim of caprice or inconsistency. In sum, reasons do not have to be generalizable, except in the sense that they must be applied consistently, and they are inconsistently applied only when they are used to draw different conclusions between two works of art which cannot be said to differ in any respects that are relevant to critical categorization.

With these general logical considerations we have set the stage for the major task of this chapter: an assessment of the extent to which aesthetic evaluation really is or can be objective and rational.

5. THE JUSTIFICATION OF AESTHETIC CLAIMS

We shall consider five views about the justification of aesthetic evaluations. (1) The skeptic thinks they are just decorated opinions, lacking any objective foundation. The others hold that such evaluations are essentially similar to (2) scientific claims or the claims of (3) a sensitive, (4) a specially skilled person, or (5) a salesman.

We have already examined the process of rational evaluation in the preceding chapter, using the "performance and profile" method.[6] The key question is whether we can apply this rational procedure for substantiating evaluations, which is sometimes rather loosely called the scientific approach, to the field of aesthetics.

If we were only concerned with substantiating a claim of personal preference, the procedure seems entirely redundant. How can you be called on to *prove* to yourself or to anybody else that you really like something? Not by means of this kind of analysis, surely. Rational evaluation appears to be useful only when combining preferences with objective-performance measures is complex enough so that we are not very reliable at doing it in our heads. But this comment underestimates the procedure. We are often committed to many preferences, at many different levels of appreciation, and the rational-evaluation procedure can take us back to the more fundamental levels and show us that we really *should* like something that we had not immediately appreciated, i.e., that we stand committed to it because of some very pervasive preferences whose application here we had overlooked. The rational process cannot provide reasons for all our preferences, at all the times we have

[6] The process of comparing the objective qualities of the objects (their "performance") with the ideal set of qualities desired (the consumer's "utility profile") and weighing the deficiencies in terms of the relative importance of the ideal qualities. Exactly the same kind of procedure can be employed in applying complex nonevaluative terms, such as the names of species or psychoses or aesthetic types like the novel, although we shall not elaborate on this procedure here, since it bears on the problems of elucidatory rather than evaluative aesthetics. This technique by-passes or resolves the classical difficulties of defining abstract terms and ideals.

them, but it bears on almost all, at almost every stage of our development. Its aim, however, is not so much to show someone that he *does* like something but that he *should,* and it can often do this with respect to his own preferences. As one moves away from matters for which objective performance is readily established, it becomes easier for the immediate impression to override the projection from other commitments. "You really *should* prefer Oxford to Cambridge, with *your* interests, even though you don't like the atmosphere as much so far" sounds possible, but substitute a passage of Ovid for Oxford, of Catullus for Cambridge, and the probability of persuasiveness diminishes. But it does not vanish. Personal preferences are not always *immediate, subjective preferences.* Usually it is relevant to assess them in the light of a person's long-term overall preferences, and often we can bring some *external standards* to bear on personal preferences. One is open to certain kinds of criticism if one's preference is for heavy smoking, or snobbish schools, or sentimental stories. Of course, aesthetic evaluations are typically intended to be more than statements of personal preferences; even if highly qualified, they aim higher. "I think Kazan is a better director than Huston" is modest but open to destruction if we can show Huston is the better of the two; the speaker would have been *wrong* to think the reverse. And there is always one particular way in which even expressions of personal preference are open to criticism. "I *like* Huston better than Kazan" would be a sign of *poor taste* or poor judgment if it were demonstrable that Kazan is better than Huston, and no one likes to concede that he has bad taste.

In general, then, the issue is not simply whether it is true that you think Kazan is better than Huston or that you like Kazan more than Huston; we are also interested in whether you should think or like in that way, i.e., whether you are right or wrong to do so, conceding that you do. It is clear that this distinction is important in the practical sphere; we may concede that you like the Corvette better than the Cobra as a competition car, or Investors Diversified better than the Dreyfus Fund as a conservative investment, and we may still prove that you are quite wrong to do so. Perhaps we can show that you have overlooked certain obviously relevant factors, used unreliable figures about other factors, made an error in combining the results, etc. Insofar as you are rational, this will lead you to alter your preferences. Can we pull off this kind of trick in the aesthetic field?

In the simplest possible view, the sensitivity view, we need not go this far with the detailed analysis, since artistic appreciation is something you simply have or do not have. The gifted ones in this world appreciate the finer things; the clods dig pops. This is simply one of the intuition family of philosophical positions. It suffers from the usual difficulties,[7] which are particularly aggravated in the aesthetic field, where there are such wide

[7] Discussed briefly in the *Knowledge* chapter, and with reference to faith, religious experience, and the conscience in the *God* and *Morality* chapters.

variations in people's "intuitions": in short, we have no way of telling the clods from the clevers if the court of last appeal is people's feelings. The usual move here, often implicit in the simple sensitivity position, is to start talking about sophisticated versus unsophisticated taste. But this is just adding another swearword unless we can both give some *independent* way of identifying sophisticated taste and show that it is *superior*. The most common response to this challenge is to appeal to *experience, exposure, training,* etc., in short, to attempt a comparison with a skill. And this suggestion deserves careful examination.

6. SOPHISTICATION VERSUS SATIATION

There certainly are some genuine skills in the field of aesthetic judgment and analysis, for example, the skill involved in identifying a piece of pottery as an Attic red-figured neck amphora, or in recognizing a piece of chamber music by Buxtehude, or in tracing the historical development of perspective. These are skills because we can often establish the claims involved in some independent but definite way. Nevertheless, we run into difficulties even in the nonvaluational field. Learning how to use "baroque" acceptably in various fields is a skill and not a mere routine application of a definition, because the term is not precisely definable. The term is *so* vague, however, that it is believed by many critics to be useless. It is still meaningful, and the ability to apply it is still a genuine skill, in the sense that it is universally agreed it does apply to some periods and styles and does not apply to certain others, and you can learn to label these correctly. But it is not sufficiently precise to be of much value to the critic, for there is a *very wide and important range* of cases in which (1) there is no way of deciding who is right and who is wrong and (2) one writer applies the term and another denies its applicability. The same difficulty applies to the concept of the Renaissance in history.

The situation in using these technical but nongrading terms is closely matched when we turn to the grading field (i.e., to terms with a commitment to intrinsic value), for we find the experts still disagreeing violently, not just over who is good but over what is trite, sentimental, overlong, balanced, inspired, sensitive, and so on. Just as agreement does not establish truth, disagreement does not prove there is no truth. But lack of agreement combined with the absence of a reliable, even if difficult, test does hurt the suggestion that evaluation is a precise, teachable skill. In short, there is no ultimate demonstrability.

One can agree that a trainee astrologer, phrenologist, or psychoanalyst has acquired the skills of his trade when he can cast a horoscope, read the conformation of a skull, or conduct an analysis in a way recognized by the other experts as professionally competent. This still leaves considerable room for him to disagree with them on the particular details of a particular case. In the same way, one can argue that exposure to, thought about, and the capacity to fit most of the well-known works of art in a particular field into one's own system of evaluation in such a way as to give a *substantial overlap* with the evaluations (and classifications) of many other recognized critics are the basic requirements for an art critic to be regarded as competent. We might also include the need to understand much of the technical terminology involved in other art critics' approaches and considerable understanding of the technical terminology employed by the artist (this being particularly important in certain fields). Knowledge and performance of this kind constitute the trade-union membership card; they entitle one to disagree without being called ignorant and incompetent, except by people who possess no better credentials than one has oneself.

But while these credentials may be adequate for admission to a trade, they do not suffice for a noble profession. The trade is the trade of talking art critics' lingo with a skill indistinguishable from that of an art critic. The noble profession for which we are looking would entitle a man to be called a savant, a man with deeper insight into true artistic value, a more profound knowledge of the way things really are in the world of values. Astrologers not only cast horoscopes according to procedures which they more or less agree are the appropriate ones; they claim to be able to tell from these horoscopes how a man's future fortune will fare. It is only that high aspiration which makes the jargon worth learning. A psychoanalyst not only believes himself to have learned how to talk in a certain jargon about people who exhibit symptoms of a certain kind; he also believes that he is able to identify the causes of these symptoms. The art critic not only thinks that he has learned how to chat about surrealism, cubism, and so on; he also thinks that he has learned how to tell what is good from what is bad, in the way that a nutrition expert can tell you whether a particular diet is healthy and a painting expert can tell you whether a particular painting is a Cranach. But how can a critic believe that he can really do this when succeeding decades, indeed, different continents in the same year, even different critics on the same Sunday in the same city, give incompatible evaluations of the Pre-Raphaelites, abstract expressionism, *l'art moderne,* Schoenberg, Wagner, Arabic music, Thackeray, Eliot, Calder, Victorian Gothic?

It just will not do to say that the experts agree, on any reasonable definition of "expert" and to a significant degree of agreement. What is worse, to the extent they do agree, their agreement may simply be a sign of the domination of one school of thought or fashion. There is no stopping point in the constantly changing cycle of attitudes and approvals of art; the situation is deplorably similar to that in the field of women's fashions, where the eye is conditioned to approve of this and disapprove of that in a way which changes with the succeeding years and finally comes full circle, so that what has been thought the worst may quite soon be thought the best.

Of course, there is much agreement among the critics' group at a particular time concerning a number of historic figures and some contemporary ones: the Rembrandts, Monets, and de Koonings. Such agreements are of little significance; they can be seen as the group's tacit compromises without which, its members recognize, no posture of objective judgment could possibly be maintained. As the agreements tend to evaporate and recondense on other nuclei with passing years, this interpretation is confirmed. To the student of the pseudosciences, this kind of hollow accord is a common phenomenon: the ingroup of practitioners creates the illusion of esoteric knowledge with empty arguments, a complex jargon, and the practice of obscure debate. What marks a real science is very simple: it is the ultimate demonstrability, the pay-off that can be seen with the naked eye, the predictions of eclipses or sunrise, of death or recovery, of dishonesty or crime, of explosions or precipitations. It is the elimination of the possibility of contagious bias, the jump from agreement to truth. If the only check on the experts' expertise is the experts' agreement, we do not have experts. Agreement over Beethoven today does not mean a thing; it is the *stability* over time of such agreements, the extent to which agreement is reached on *highly novel artists* without knowing their background, and, above all, the extent to which consequences of the evaluations can be checked *independently*. What the experts identify in the new year's designs as good cars had better last longer, corner faster, run smoother—do something we can check on—or they are not experts, just gossips. And that is where the art critic's situation is peculiarly difficult. What *can* he produce to meet this challenge? Is his problem a sign that his field is more difficult or that it lacks all objective standards for evaluation?

Even though there is no general consensus among experts as to the merits of different movements and schools in art (especially if we include the non-Western tradition) and even though this would not be very significant if it did exist, since it is readily explicable as contamination rather than insight, it is perfectly true that the student of art, as he undergoes greater experience of the subject, does alter his taste; and there are indeed certain overall tendencies in this alteration, depending upon the field of art he is studying and the teachers to whom he is exposed. Perhaps this tendency can be construed as the approach to true perception of worth. But this conclusion cannot be drawn, for to discover that experience produces changes does not tell us whether it is proper to think of these changes as progress toward a greater skill in evaluation, comparable to the changes that occur as someone becomes increasingly expert in the identification of the works of a particular painter, or whether they are to be thought of simply as a sign of satiation with the simple pleasures, a sad consequence of exhaustion of the individual's reservoir of primary sensitivity. But surely there cannot be absolute parity between the taste of the tourist entranced by Keane's bug-eyed urchins and the gallery goer who has gradually come to see the subtleties of the *settecento* schools? Is this not a *refinement* of discrimination?

That we learn to differentiate between—as we describe it—the value of art objects which we previously found indistinguishable or to reverse earlier orderings of merit is not enough to show that our present evaluation is more accurate. To justify that description would require that we demonstrate in some *independent* way the truth of our present judgment. If there really were a remarkable consensus among people from quite different backgrounds with respect to the works which they come to judge admirable after much study, then we would be able to make something of a case for talking about "coming to see the lasting virtues as opposed to the flashy or superficially appealing attractions." Here, the virtues and merits would be the pleasure-giving qualities. But if the same objects give pleasure to some experienced viewers and displeasure to others, they can hardly be called virtues in this sense, and no other sense presents itself. Now there are some areas in the arts in which this kind of virtue ascribing (or denying) is rather easily justified. One thinks, for example, of the performing arts, in which certain skills are quite definitely required even to achieve a performance, let alone a smooth or effortless-seeming performance. Here indeed is an area in which a very considerable measure of agreement exists and the language of merit can be employed insofar as that agreement does exist. But when it comes to the examples of the arts that decorate our homes or fill our galleries, appear on our plates or emerge from loudspeakers, then the consensus vanishes, and we are talking the language of expertise in a domain in which there are no experts. Of course, there may be a secondary kind of expert, the one whose skill consists in the capacity to foresee how taste will go, a skill that may arise from a more acute sensitivity to what informed critics will come to like than they themselves possess. But this kind of insight by the avant-garde cannot justifiably be described as insight into the *real* value of the works unless we can show that those of equal learning and different estimates of the works' merits are wrong.[8]

[8] "Even in science or on the stock exchange or in ordinary life we sometimes hesitate to condemn a belief or a hunch merely because those who believe it cannot offer the sort of reasons we had hoped for. And now suppose Miss Gertrude Stein finds excellent the work of a new artist while we see nothing in it. We nervously recall, perhaps, how pictures by Picasso, which Miss Stein admired and others rejected, later came to be admired by many who gave attention to them, and we wonder whether the case is now a new instance of her perspicacity and our blindness. But if, upon giving all our attention to the work in question, we still do not respond to it, and we notice that the subject matter of the new pictures is perhaps birds in wild places and learn that Miss Stein is a bird-watcher, then we begin to trouble ourselves less about her admiration" (John Wisdom, "Gods," reprinted in *Philosophy and Psychoanalysis*, Blackwell, 1953, p. 163).

7. *THE ARTIST'S MERIT AND THE ART'S MERIT*

Just as in the interesting cases of aesthetic evaluation of works of art we cannot produce an independent test to demonstrate the security of some starting points from which a chain of reasons might be built to support an evaluation, so it is with the identification of great merit in the artist himself. It is not a gross blunder on the part of the layman to look back at the early paintings of Pablo Picasso and say to himself, "Ah, so he really *has* great talent, for once he could paint in a way that very few can; so there must be something to what he's doing now, even though I don't see it at first." For to be able to do something that is very difficult for most people *is* a merit of a kind; and if we know that someone has achieved this goal and does himself consider his next stage of development a natural extension and no less difficult, then we are not unreasonable to entertain the same hypothesis.

But the inference to the merit of the work from its difficulty is by no means unassailable. It was partly the influence of primitive art that led to Picasso's change; men who have acquired great skills may find the continued practice of these skills boring, their effects no longer original, and so return to explore the realm of children's painting or discordant sound. How *they* feel about what they do is a product of many factors and not simply a matter of their recognition of the greater artistic merit of their latest output; it may be immensely more satisfying to them, but their need for satisfaction may include demands that are important from the artist's point of view but not from the spectator's. The need to meet new challenges may lead a sculptor to feel that his work in carving carbide is the pinnacle of his output, but to a very experienced critic it may seem far cruder and less talented than his other work. There are no reasons for supposing either man to be right at the expense of the other. That there is a connection between technical skill and merit is revealed in the fact that one is very loath to praise a work highly if one knows it can easily be produced by anyone with no special training at all. But that connection tells us very little. The product of a modern artist, even if it cannot be shown that it would be difficult for him or an amateur to do, is *different* from what any given amateur would produce. And the difference might reflect a difference of talent, for some talents are "natural." Conversely, the mastery of some technique that is manifestly difficult or impossible for most of us may simply show that its master is a hard-working or statistically unusual man, not that he is a great artist rather than a skilled artisan. So the Skeptic's doubts cannot be shown to be ephemeral, nor the Sensitive's claims to be absurd. Yet this is no impasse, for in a tied game *of this kind* the decision must always go to the Skeptic. The positive claim is being made by his opponent, and as long as there are no grounds for believing that there are objective standards in a field, it is simply irrational to suppose they exist. Is it not equally irrational to doubt they exist if you cannot show they do not? Indeed not, for standards can only be said to exist if they can be demonstrated; "standards" which cannot pass the tests for standards are not standards at all.

In general, there is a different vocabulary for the appraisal of skills and their product from that used in appraising artists and theirs. When we look at the extraordinary filigree work of some of the early Indian silversmiths or the minute ivory carving involved in the "nested-ball" curiosities of the Far East, the term that comes to mind is "remarkable." It is not an automatic guarantee of approval of the subject as beautiful or as great art: it is a commendation of the performance as one that exhibits great ability or industry.

But the appraisal of ability is not unlike the appraisal of an art work within an extremely narrow genre, without commitment as to the value of the genre, as when we refer to one of Agatha Christie's detective stories as "extraordinarily ingenious" or "a fascinating puzzle." We might call them extremely good *detective stories;* but we make no commitment whatsoever as to the absolute artistic merit of the category of detective stories, i.e., no commitment as to the absolute merit of the author's work in the realm of fiction, let alone in art as a whole. Some merit is implied, but only the merit of a technical master.

The same applies to performers who tackle extremely difficult music. We may regard them as enormously talented, without in any way suggesting that the work they are performing is of any merit. Indeed the expert in some literary or painting genres is very like the performer.

There is, of course, a connection between talent in the artist and merit in the work of art: a great work of art must be a sign of talent in the artist. This does not entitle us to infer from talent in the artist greatness in all his works of art, but at least the former makes the latter possible: hence the impact of the early Picasso on the layman. The layman can infer the greatness of the artist from the early work, and from that greatness the merit of the later work, a merit he cannot see directly. Were it not for this, he would find himself quite unable to dispel the threatening hypothesis that the late-period work is all a kind of joke on the consumer. Nevertheless, his inference is a very shaky one; it is only slightly better than nothing at all.

And so we still find ourselves lacking any kind of a sound basis for many of the most important judgments of aesthetic merit.

8. THE APPEAL TO A COMMON LANGUAGE

It is not that there is no agreement about what is *beautiful.* There must be some agreement; otherwise there could hardly be such an adjective in the language. When we are children, we are introduced to the word "beautiful" by reference to examples, usually of natural objects and scenes that arouse in us all a somewhat similar response, as we can tell from the roughly similar way in which we generalize from the examples which are used to introduce the word to us. But, of course, this degree of agreement is not enough to settle the kind of disputes in which we are interested as adults. We also acquire the meaning of "beautiful" from the learned linguistic opposition to "ugly" and the identification of certain objects as ugly; and similarly for "pretty," "lovely," "plain," "dull," etc. That is, the agreement as to applications need not come in immediately, but it must come in somewhere if a common language is to be learned. Agreement does *not* have to be complete for the language to be communal, just close enough to separate the use of this word from that of other words.

Let us compare the concept of beauty with the concept of justice. Not all adults agree that every particular court decision is a just one, and yet it is clear that the nature of their disagreement and the extent of their agreement are such as to make the notion of justice a very great deal more objective than the notion of beauty. What disagreements there are, other than those based upon different estimates of the real facts of the case, are often due to subtle disagreements about the moral role of the concept of justice. This matter may be argued rationally, and in the *Morality* chapter an attempt is made to do this. But the attempt to give a theoretical analysis of the beautiful, despite the millenniums during which the search has continued, has led to disagreements just as profound as the disagreements today about which specific art objects we should call beautiful. Put crudely, the inescapable fact is that the primary role of the concept of beauty is to identify objects that are pleasing to us, in a way that is different from, though not sharply different from, the way in which an object which is a remarkable bargain, or is of remarkable historic importance, or is the product of a remarkable business achievement may be pleasing to us. Even the exact nature of these distinctions is not well analyzed, but it is indisputable that the main function of the adjective "beautiful" is immediately connected with what is pleasing to us in a particular way. It is not so with the concept of justice, nor with the concept of truth, nor with the simple concepts of red, or loud, or round, or rough. And what pleases us varies very much as between people and as between the stages in the development of one person. Therein lies *one* source of the difficulty for objective aesthetics.

It would, however, be quite wrong to suppose that aesthetic evaluation is the mere identification of personally pleasing objects. Those who use the vocabulary of evaluation recognize that it has a commitment to objectivity quite unlike that of phrases such as "is pleasing to me" or "is beautiful," in which objectivity simply amounts to a projection of consensus about pleasingness. Judgments of aesthetic merit must be analyzed as claiming more than mere expressions of pleasure, typically as implying the achievement of certain standards within a particular category. The question is whether that more can be shown to be justifiable—whether there *are* standards within genres which all observers must acknowledge. The situation is reminiscent of a certain kind of experiment in the psychology of perception. A series of letters are projected onto a screen which is viewed by the subject through a fixed pair of eyepieces. He is asked to write down what he sees; then the lighting level is lowered, and he is told that the letters have been changed and he is to write down what he now sees; the process is continued, and at the limit we find subjects continuing to write down letters that they believe firmly they see, although in fact no letters are being projected at all. We begin by learning the word "beautiful" and more merit-laden words in circumstances in which there is no doubt about their proper use; as we proceed to study the more complicated and refined developments in art, it becomes increasingly difficult to establish that any of us are seeing something that is really there for all of us, until at the limit we have simply to choose between various seers, each of whom claims to see clearly what is there, when there is in the background always the haunting suspicion that all are deceived.

9. OBJECTIVITY PROBLEMS IN ELUCIDATORY AESTHETICS

Some of these skeptical doubts about evaluatory aesthetics carry over into the field of elucidatory aesthetics. Let us think back to our analogy between the art critic and the psychoanalyst. Each has a conception of his activities that involves both a claim to objective truth and a component of communal agreement. Each believes that he has learned not merely a language with which he can talk about certain phenomena to a certain group of people but a language which expresses *truths,* both evaluative and elucidatory, about those phenomena. In particular, the analyst feels qualified to make evaluative judgments about the psychological well-being of individuals and evaluative judgments about various ways of treating them. The objective component in these judgments is connected—not in a very straightforward way, but inescapably—with the objective question of changes in the health, happiness, and behavior of the individual under discussion, as judged by persons *other* than psychoanalysts (including the patient). If none of the treatments judged to be good by analysts led to more improvement than occurred in those not undergoing psychoanalysis, as judged by a nonanalyst, and none of the treatments judged to be bad by analysts led to differential deterioration detectable to the outsider, we would be strongly inclined to suppose that psychoanalytic therapy was a complicated delusional scheme. There would certainly be serious question whether its practitioners were entitled to pose as therapists or to charge people for their services.

Now the objective facts about the efficacy of psychoanalytic therapy are not very encouraging. It is not possible to point to studies which establish its efficacy to the degree that we consider minimal in the case of an allegedly therapeutic drug. (The enthusiasm of some ex-patients does not, of course, give us grounds for supposing that they have improved *as a result* of this particular treatment to a degree that would not have occurred anyway.) In the face of this difficulty or perhaps for other reasons, some psychoanalysts have produced an appraisal of their activities which has an interesting analogy in the field of aesthetics. They have argued that their claim is not one of therapeutic efficacy but solely one of improved understanding; they are offering insight and not improvement. They may add that they have some reasons to suppose that insight does lead to improvement, but this is not something that they are disposed to guarantee. One might liken this move to the shift away from evaluative claims to elucidatory claims ("I can't tell you whether electronic music is great music, but I can explain it to you"). The objective commitment is, however, still present even in the weaker type of claim and often exceedingly hard to establish.

We may readily concede that in the elucidatory field there is a wide range of analytical remarks, some of which can be construed simply as claims of the form, "It is *possible* to see this as being so and so (this music as cheerful and bucolic)." And these remarks are surely rather easy to support. But others are of the form, "So and so really *is* a representation of so and so," and it is these that provide the difficulty for us. When the analyst says that a certain dream figure represents the patient's father or that a certain childhood experience is the origin of the present marital infelicity, he is not merely saying that this is one way in which one might see it. He is saying that this is a *correct* way to describe the situation, and when the art critic says that the circular format of the "Madonna della Sedia" dominates the internal structure of the painting or when he says that the work clearly reflects the influence of Raphael's teacher, he is making a claim that goes beyond any analysis in terms of how things look to him or even to a group of observers. To the scientifically trained student of psychoanalysis or aesthetics, it is impossible not to be overawed by the difficulties involved in any attempt to support such claims. As possibilities, they are interesting and illuminating: they encourage us to see things in a new light, to contemplate them from a new point of view, and in so doing to enlarge our perspective of the object of contemplation. But as claims on whose truth someone may stand, they are in the far reaches of that swampland which science is ever attempting to reclaim, where reclamation is possible only by prodigious labor for enormous periods and where the risk is always great that one will find only quicksand, for which not reclamation but replacement is the only feasible remedy. Explanation as well as evaluation has objective standards, and true explanations are not the same as possible explanations, except in fields in which truth is no different from a dream. And the criteria of truth for explanations must be built up, from indubitable starting points, in just about the same way as the criteria of truth for evaluations.

In sum, we must concede to the skeptic the impact of much of his criticism. The claims of evaluatory aesthetics and much of elucidatory aesthetics, in the disputed areas, must be viewed with great reservations. They are like the stimulating assertions of a man long exposed to human nature but committed to a system of thinking about it, such as reincarnation, which is fundamentally superstitious in the sense of going far beyond any rational foundation.

So the possibility still remains that a great deal of sophistication is the bastard offspring of satiation and indoctrination. To the extent that this is true, a sophisticated person's taste is *in no way* superior to that of the naïve person; indeed, the case is better for the opposite view, for the child's enjoyment of sunshine or a flower is perhaps a finer and certainly a more universal experience than the jaded aesthete's cultivated appreciation of a chipped but costly fragment of pre-Columbian pottery. One can see the aesthete's situation as sad rather than superior, a sign of the decline of taste rather than its refinement. One can see it either way, and so it cannot be seen as simply the development of *better* taste.

10. PROVABLE DIFFERENCES IN SENSITIVITY

Not all differences of taste are due to differences of training or exposure. There seems to be no doubt that hereditary sensitivities (to the *natural* properties of objects), likings, and discriminatory capacities vary considerably from one person to another in the auditory, visual, and other sensory dimensions, and there seems no reason for doubting that this variation affects our taste very much. One's tendency is to argue that the greater the powers of sensory discrimination, the more "sensitive" a man is and hence the more highly his taste should be respected. A logical extension of this tendency might be to recommend that the individuals with lower discriminatory capacity examine paintings by means of sensitive colorimeters, whose sensitivity exceeds that of any human eye. Would their judgment, based upon this kind of examination, be in an even more privileged position than that of the individual with good natural visual sensitivity? Not their judgment of the *merit* of the work of art, surely. Such devices assist them in making certain factual judgments about the differences in hue in the painting or certain regions of the painting, just as the use of an oscilloscope might enable one to give considerably more sensitive analyses of the music wave form produced by various instrumental combinations than the human ear can manage. For someone to argue that he can prove that the music is better than the music of another composer by appealing to a complex feature of the wave form, however, is surely absurd. How could he justify the claim that this feature of the wave form constituted a merit in the work, if it is a feature not noticeable by any listener? It seems reasonable to suppose that a man's task in evaluating a work of art is to judge it in terms of what he sees in it or can be brought to see in it, or perhaps in terms of what others can be brought to see in it, without the use of instruments. The use of instruments may enable him to see what amounts to a different or a new object, or aspect of the object, and that may in turn be evaluated. But its evaluation will not be that of the original object.

Here again, however, we are tempted by the analogy with those other kinds of perceptual tasks for which increased discriminatory power is reliably correlated with increased skill. As the veterinarian develops his diagnostic skills or the timber cruiser becomes more adept at identifying the species and condition of trees from their winter appearance, he is relying upon and improving a capacity to discriminate visual cues that the beginner cannot discriminate at all. The advantages of this refinement of perception are immediately demonstrable by independent checks, and the development of diagnostic instruments is entirely appropriate. But in the field of taste, the increase of discriminatory power does not automatically lead to any ability other than the ability to discriminate; it does not lead to the ability to identify a condition which is a reliable indication of merit. In aesthetic evaluation the end of the road is evaluation, not differentiation. And most evaluations are not confirmed (or weakened) by the discovery that others can come to the same conclusions, or that many of them do, with or without special training or instruments. So discriminatory abilities do not appear to help us in the quest for objective standards. It appears that the distinction between "I find this very pleasing" and "This is very good" is, in a *large and important area* of aesthetic evaluation, a distinction which does not mark a difference. Or one can say it marks a difference of intention but not of real cash value; it is like a very big check drawn on a very small account.

There are other difficulties about the supposition that increased discriminatory skills serve to support their fortunate possessor's aesthetic evaluations. For the extent to which a man can systematize and verbalize what he perceives is in many cases a far more important component in his taste than the capacity for minute discrimination, important though the latter may be for a bloodhound or a camera light meter. The capacity for seeing things as a whole, seeing the relationship of their parts to their total organization, is in many forms of art far more important than being able to observe a slightly larger number of distinct elements or variations in the object itself. It is virtually certain on statistical grounds, as well as because of a lack of awareness of such limitations by those who suffer from them, that some of the great art critics have been significantly color-blind. Similarly, it is a consequence of a well-known fact of psychoacoustics that *most* of the great music critics have a hearing range one-third smaller than that of one-third of the audiences who hear the music they review. These facts about the discriminatory limitations of critics are not wholly irrelevant, but they are not of very great importance because so much of the complexity of a work of art, from texture to tempi, is still available to the critics, and it is in appraisal of the organization of this complexity that they perform their most valued task. Yet there can surely be little doubt that these perceptual differences have a significant effect on many of their judgments and at least some of their evaluations. Once again we must conclude that the defensible approach to their remarks is to look for suggestions as to what one may see or hear oneself. We must take their evaluations as clues to their overall reaction, which may be interesting enough to induce us to reappraise the work for ourselves. But we must also be prepared to go beyond their judgments (or perhaps not so far), realizing that what they see or hear is probably importantly different from what we see or hear, in a simple physiological sense to which praise or blame is irrelevant.

As an extreme case, it is salutary to consider the extent to which the evaluations of a wholly color-blind man are immune to criticism by the rainbow-sighted group. He sees the world as a projection of black, white, and shades of gray, and we see it in color, but who has ever shown that color motion pictures are aesthetically better than black-and-white ones or that water colors, just because they are in color, are better than pen-and-ink drawings? We may like them better, and it might happen to be the case that they are done by better artists, but who could show this? It is not even clear that it is harder for the artist to do great work in the more complex domains: opinions on this question vary from field to field. What the color-blind man can see *is* limited: he does not notice differences we notice; he cannot feel some of the clashes we feel, some of the harmonies to which we respond. But everything at which we look presents itself to him, too, for appreciation in his terms, and what possible defense can one give for the claim that his appraisal is *inferior* to ours? Appealing to the original perceptions and discriminations made by the *artist* is of singularly little significance, since many artists have been or have become seriously color-blind or deaf and since aesthetic appreciation extends to natural objects for which there was no artist at all. We are (probably, but not always) right to say that the properties of the object of which the color-blind man takes account in his appreciation constitute a more limited range than those to which we respond. We are wrong to suppose that the judgment based on the wider range is better: it is simply appreciation of something a little different and more complicated. Our judgments are no more to be thought of as better than his than are those of a critic watching a color film to be thought of as better than those of another critic watching the same film shown in black and white.

There is not even a natural terminal point in the process of developing increased refinements of taste, at least not in one's own lifetime. After twenty years of decorating one's houses with modern furniture, one may gradually come to feel that its simple lines are not enough and turn to antiques. But exactly the reverse process may occur. Indeed, both swings of the pendulum can occur for the same person. So evaluative claims in aesthetics should not be regarded as claims about the consensus of others or about one's own eventual beliefs, nor do they concern anything else that can be independently identified. A more sophisticated taste is different from a simpler one, but there is no interesting sense in which it is better, except the sense from which the art dealer benefits, for it is certainly true that sophisticated tastes are more expensive.

11. IN DEFENSE OF EDUCATING TASTE

It does not follow from this that it is pointless or mistaken to undertake the serious study of art forms in the usual way, by reading books and taking courses or perhaps by essaying some minor practical undertaking in the field. For this may lead not only to a better appreciation or understanding in the domains where objective sense can be made of this concept but also to an enhanced pleasure in the viewing of art; moreover, it may well be pleasurable in itself, and it may stabilize one's taste. In this respect it is no different from the fact that knowing something about trees and birds makes living in the country more interesting and enjoyable. All that follows from the criticisms of the skeptic is that such training grants no license to regard all one's present evaluations as more *accurate*. One's evaluations may be better sometimes and, somewhat more frequently, one's elucidatory remarks will be better; but neither all nor even a majority of one's most important evaluations will be superior, in any useful sense. After all, they will be contradicted by the evaluations of others with just as long and thorough training; yet even if this were not true, there is nothing to distinguish mere conformity from universal recognition of truth in this area. So the skeptic says, and what can we say against him as long as our appeal is to innate or trained sensitivity and skills?

12. INSIGHTS FROM ART

But has not the history of art been a history of *discovery*, of research into reality? Do we not *learn* from art and from education about art, learn more about the world around us and the artifacts in it? Is this not a way of saying that art and art education form part of knowledge? Now of course it is true that we can learn many facts about art and its history and techniques. Classifications can be learned (who's who in Impressionism), and the meanings of many terms. But that is not the debatable part of this view of art. What were the artists *discovering*, what did they really *learn* about the world and themselves, and what kind of knowledge is artistic insight? These are the hard questions.

The exploration of our potential responses to art is a delicate and dangerous task, but it is one the original artist must undertake.[9] He introduces or abandons or distorts perspective; he uses blues where reds appear to the eye, the grains of pointillism in place of the apparently smooth natural shades, a shirt attached to a canvas to play the role of an art work. Each move is a trial rocket, springing up from his imagination and perhaps catching ours up with it. If it does, we come to see his work and that of others in a different way, and so we enlarge our experience and enrich our senses. We may legitimately talk thus; we may say to the novice, "Don't look for recognizable subject matter cleverly represented in two dimensions; look instead at the care lavished on the texture of the paint, the exploitation of the interaction between three colors as a pure phenomenon." And he may come to respond; but if he does not, he only shows that art for him is not what it is for you. You cannot say what the Pollock is telling us, only what it suggests to you; you cannot say it is as good or better than the Turners he does admire or even than the odd drawings he finds on the covers of some science-fiction magazines. You are equals before the bench of a nonexistent court of higher appeal. The artist learns what the lover learns, the taste of a new slice of experience, and we may learn this from him. Painting, particularly, is today a succession of New Taste Thrills, a situation admirably analyzed by Rosenberg in his essay "The New as Value." [10] But what the painter learns is not the kind of learning that can be written down and added to our libraries, and the title "truth" ill becomes its independent ways, though truths may follow after. It is the wayward stuff of experience, ragged and bold, lawless; words do not fit it well, and only through the way they fail to clothe it do we sometimes learn a little of it from another. The artist is not saying something, and the critic cannot tell us what it is, in any way that makes them right where others might be wrong. And so they teach us only by teaching us how we *can* see things; we learn of possibilities, not of facts, except the

[9] Among the many differences between the arts which we do not explore in detail in this chapter is one we should mention here. In the field of music, for example, we distinguish performers from composers; each is an artist, but for the first, techniques (in the sense of physical skills) provide a more substantial part of the requirements for merit. In painting we lack this distinction between performer and composer, but it is helpful to think of it as an analogy to the distinction between the skilled but routine portraitist and the innovator. The first may be great as a performer is great but not as a composer is great. It is easier to evaluate performers than composers, because (partly through their connection with difficulty) the techniques can be judged much more objectively. We here discuss the harder task, that of evaluating the great originators.

[10] Harold Rosenberg, *The Anxious Object*, Horizon Press, 1964.

fact that these are possible. We learn that we can come to see a single line as the back of a nude in a Matisse figure drawing, that we can see a swarm of Seurat's spots as a riverbank, that we can see a shirt as an as-if-it-were-a shirt. How far can illusion take us; what are the limits of our projective power? Can we really come to see the Emperor's nudity as *haute couture?* It is not clear; but the skeptic stands ready to remind us that we surely should not be charged *very* much for a bathing suit that is bottomless as well as topless, for a shirt on canvas that is just a shirt on canvas. We may say it's not *just* this, it's art: it's not just adolescent lyrics, a bad voice, and four chords on a guitar; it's folk music. We are right; yet he isn't quite wrong. Self-deception is as close to sophistication as solipsism is to sanity.

13. THE SCIENTIFIC APPROACH

Is there not a more systematic alternative than this? In these fields where disagreement is rife, is it not appropriate, indeed imperative, to search for *hidden* standards to which implicit appeal is being made by the critics, in the hope that a systematic procedure for combining them may be constructed which will lead to more general agreement? Might not aesthetics be in a prescientific stage?

This hope has inspired aestheticians for 2,000 years and with some interesting results, though without success in the intended direction. The difficulty can be very simply described. If the criteria which we are proposing as criteria of merit are described in a way which is straightforward enough to make it possible to tell when they are present in a particular work of art, it turns out to be impossible to get any agreement that they are, in fact, really criteria of merit; and the criteria that experts agree on as general criteria of merit, they cannot agree on applying to specific cases. In short, we cannot satisfy the requirements of demonstrability and connection simultaneously.

An excellent analogy is available from the field of morality. Ask the question, What is morally wrong? You get two kinds of replies: rules for identifying moral evil that are easy to apply, like "Lying (or drinking, or killing) is wrong," although moralists cannot agree on the exceptionless truth of these, or rules like "Sin (or unjustified killing, or excessive drinking) is wrong," although moralists cannot agree on the cases to which these rules apply. Now in morality there is a way to handle the difficulty via an analysis of its essential functions. But what are the essential functions of criticism in the aesthetic fields? To increase our understanding of works of art—certainly, elucidatory criticism has an important function. But even there, objective understanding is hard to identify; it seems rather that several equally "good" interpretations are often possible. And whereas the moral evaluation of specific acts has, in morality, the enormously important role of identifying the action which in fact we should take (for taking it can be supported by a whole chain of reasons), in aesthetics evaluative judgments cannot be shown to carry corresponding weight. It is certainly true that we should admire what is great art, condemn what is ugly, and so on, just as we should be in favor of what is morally good and against sin. But as to the questions whether we should be in favor of art that is representational, or that portrays the struggle of the worker, or that transcends the bounds of realism, or that takes account of the Greek laws of proportion, we cannot find answers from a more detailed consideration of the role of such criteria in the general function of art. And when we get down to the level of specific works of art, there is still less certainty. Many people, it is evident, can formulate in an internally consistent way sets of practical rules governing evaluation which systematically condemn the very works that others find to be exemplars of *their* highest standards.

A recent writer,[11] drawing with great scholarship upon previous attempts and adding his own considerable insights, has proposed a set of General Canons for aesthetic evaluation. These identify criteria which are said to be desirable but are not upheld as strictly exceptionless necessary or sufficient conditions. In this respect his attempt is surely more realistic than those of many of his predecessors. For even the canons of evaluation in a field of applied science are no more than tendency statements; an example would be a canon such as "The V-8 engine is the best choice of power plant in the design of all but the smallest automobiles, by comparison with any other configuration or number of cylinders." This is a sound and useful principle but not an exceptionless one.

Thus far the analogy with the canons of merit in the practical fields is sound enough, and we have avoided the error of overgeneralization. But when we turn to the actual content of the General Canons we run into the other horn of the dilemma. Each of Professor Beardsley's three Canons identifies a particular quality as a desirable one, and the three qualities are *unity, complexity,* and *intensity.*[12] Let us consider the first of these as an example.

It is certainly true that unity is a desirable quality in certain realms of aesthetic assessment. Gombrich recalls ". . . when I read the proofs of my *Story of Art* how I discovered to my mortification that I had said of nearly every work of art I particularly admired that it formed a 'harmonious whole.' " [13] But surely there are other realms of aesthetic assessment in which it has no relevance at all, for example, in the judgment of beauty in a mountain landscape. There are certain other areas where it still seems in-

[11] Prof. Monroe Beardsley, *Aesthetics,* Harcourt, Brace, 1958.
[12] Of "human regional qualities," for which these are given as examples: vitality, vividness, beauty, tragedy, grace, irony.
[13] Gombrich, *Raphael's Madonna della Sedia,* Oxford, 1956, p. 13.

appropriate; one thinks of those schools in painting and in photography which have revolted against the constraints of composition: the action painters at times and some of the coarse-grain specialists in the photography of the 1950s. It would be hard to deny that unity is a value when it refers to elements which are difficult to unify and worth unifying and which the tradition of the art form in question requires to be unified. But now the Canon has become trivial. Moreover, it is clear that even when present unity is not necessarily of any merit. Think of a painting consisting of concentric circles tinted in the successive colors of the rainbow framed in a circular frame concentric with the circles, or with any colors, including monochrome, which we believe would be unifying. This is surely not presumptively good art because of its unity; it is almost certainly trivial, and so its unity does not in any way guarantee its value. We must argue (and Professor Beardsley suggests something like this) that unity is only a merit in conjunction with certain other properties and that it is a very *small* advantage for a work to be unified in the absence of these other properties.

Our problem can now be quite simply stated: when can we identify something which needs unity and has it to a degree or in a way that does constitute an advantage? It seems all too clear that the degree of agreement about when unity is needed and present to the needed or desirable extent does not exceed the degree of our initial agreement about the merit of the work of art. Of course, on many occasions critics would agree that a novel by a new author lacks unity or exhibits an unusually well-integrated plot-subplot counterpoint. There are women whose beauty almost no one would deny. The argument of this chapter concentrates attention on the error of concluding from this kind of agreement that there is a correct answer in all or even most cases. It is hard to resist putting whole subjects under the heading of subjective or objective, but the fact is that the most important and interesting subjects, theoretical physics and literary criticism, for example, are a mixture. When we come to look at the critics' reactions to the alleged scandal of French painting in the 1960s, or Henry Miller's novels, or the work of a young contemporary American poet, is the criterion of unity objectively applicable without begging the question? Insofar as the criterion is brought up at all, it is as much disputed as the merits of the picture. Even when its presence is not disputed, it is not clear that unity is a merit rather than merely a characteristic of the work, like its realism. It does not seem at all plausible to argue that appeal to this criterion provides us with a system of objective reasons in the sense we need. Until the contrary can be clearly shown, we can only conclude that nothing is gained by the appeal to unity: it does not even fulfill the criterion of independence, certainly not that of simplicity.

It seems clear enough that similar difficulties will apply to Professor Beardsley's other Canons. Nevertheless, although such canons cannot provide us with a firm foundation cn which to build aesthetic evaluations, a particular set of them does provide us with the ground plan of a particular structure of aesthetic analysis. Professor Beardsley's set gives us the grammar of one possible language of elucidation and appraisal, not a language with any objective claim to validity but a convenient and common one. Once we have been trained in a certain way, we come to see faults and virtues as falling into certain categories; and this breaking down of the total aesthetic object into components or aspects, each with a valuational plus or minus attached to it, is part of the process of teaching a system of elucidatory or evaluatory aesthetics, part of the persuasive propaganda for *an* elucidatory schema that leads us to evaluations. It is ideological salesmanship. But of course this function of the Canons is essentially different from that of canons of practical evaluation in the applied sciences. There, there is little dispute about the identification of the advantageous qualities (strength of structural materials, durability of finishes, economy in manufacturing costs, etc.), and it is easy to prove that these qualities, in the degree to which they are present, *are* advantageous. In short, the "scientific model" of justification cannot be applied to aesthetic evaluation, and it appears to be the only one which can give any objective foundation for that activity.

The career of the scientific model of aesthetic judgment has many parallels in philosophy. One of the more interesting is the attempt to provide practical criteria for *meaningfulness.* The history of the so-called verification principle closely parallels the career of any given formulation of canons for aesthetic merit. At first it was cast in a form in which it was easily applied, a sharp-edged instrument for the separation of the meaningful from the meaningless, the meritorious from the undeserving. But then it was observed that the sharp edge was not cutting along quite the right line: some extremely important and clearly meaningful items (in the usually accepted and apparently sensible sense of "meaningful") were being discarded by its application. We attempt to refine the formulation of the principle, and in so doing we gradually blunt the edge of our instrument until eventually we are left with the merest truism, with the suggestion that propositions cannot be meaningful unless they have some consequences that make them in some way really distinguishable from their denials. And even about this we occasionally have doubts, although we can still find occasions on which it is clearly the appropriate principle for condemning pretentious nonsense. The fatal feature of the dialogue in such cases is that we appeal to the cases in which we are sure of the conclusion in order to decide whether our principles are correct and that we never get to the point at which we might appeal to the principles in order to decide which cases are meritorious. The reasons are not independent of the conclusions. When this is true, we have failed to establish a useful criterion; and it *is* true with regard to meaningfulness and aesthetic merit.

14. THE ROLE OF REASON IN CRITICISM

Despite the emphasis that has been placed in the preceding pages upon the power of the skeptic's position, it certainly does not follow that reason has *no* place in art and literary criticism. The rational-objective part of these activities is not enough to decide the issue in all cases or even in many of the most important elucidatory and evaluative disputes. But when it comes to discussing the merits of a particular short story, play, film, painting, or novel, some very closely reasoned analysis is often possible and properly persuasive. Once an artist or an observer has set his foot upon a certain path, has placed himself and the particular work under consideration in a certain category, then we often can and do bring to bear the full apparatus of subtle rational analysis to demonstrate the extent of success and failure. The strength of our argument in such a case is not extinguished by the ever-present possibility of errors, by the recognition that despite its demerits, viewed in the most appropriate category in which we can now locate it, the work of art *may* indeed set some new fashion, create a new category for itself, and thereby show our critical complaints to be misplaced. This is no more disturbing than the recognition of police investigators that building a prima-facie case against a particular suspect may in the end prove to have been an endeavor whose results are entirely swept away by the discovery of new evidence that proves him innocent. Such discoveries are not so common as to make the case building pointless: it is often good enough to convict a man.

Now it is often quite easy to identify a novel as a detective story or a spy story and a painting as a commissioned portrait of some notable public figure, to be used as a memorial to him. And, just as detective stories must have plots which contain no inconsistencies or absurdities, so portraits of this kind must exhibit some readily recognizable resemblance to the sitter or not be regarded as good portraits in this context, though they may, of course, have other claims to merit. Marches must have a certain meter, fugues a theme, parodies similarities to their subject, and satire a target. When we achieve agreement about the categorization of a work of art, then it is often possible to bring to bear some fairly specific criteria. And the nearer we get to the performing arts and the so-called minor arts or the crafts, the more nearly similar the situation becomes to that of appraising processes and techniques in the applied sciences. A similar kind of focusing occurs as the consumer's interests are more precisely clarified: we approach a decision as to what can be said to be good "for someone with his interests."

15. THE PECULIARITIES OF PAINTING AND PHOTOGRAPHY

Painting today is in many ways a very special case among the arts. For one thing, it is all composers and no performers. In music it is considered a worthy goal to become a great performer, a great interpreter, contributing *something of one's own,* together with exceptional technique, to the reproduction of a style of music that may be several centuries old. But in painting the aim of becoming a preeminent Pre-Raphaelite or a topical Turner obviously lacks appeal in the academic ateliers, and yet talent and even originality can as easily be demonstrated in that way as in the days when the Guardis and Canaletto put Venice on canvas. Overemphasis on the search for novelty inevitably leads to absurdity, to the worship of the trivial, because it is at least novel to *worship* the trivial. To condemn the present condition of painting as involving such overemphasis and its consequences is only to voice one possible view; what is objectively clear is that in a field in which serious artists are constrained to be composers, not performers, it is much harder to make judgments of merit in terms of some set of generally acceptable standards. The current conception of originality is far too crude, and it produces expectably crude noveltymongers.

The situation of photography is very like that of classical landscape painting done today; it is, typically, an exercise in the representational tradition, a "performing art," requiring very considerable technical skill, especially if the more advanced techniques are involved, and an artist's eye for composition, form, and texture. It is quite wrong to conclude that because quite good representation is obtained fairly easily with a camera, the first-rate photographer is not an artist. The difference between the work of the untrained shutter snapper and the professional is as clear as in any art. And of course there is now a highly skilled group of nonrepresentational photographers whose use of color, particularly, is truly original and most striking. It is true that the skill required to obtain a fair likeness in a portrait in oils is much less easily come by than the ability to take a candid snapshot. But the goal of art, even portrait art, requires much more than those minimal skills, and clearly the recognized portrait photographers have developed a technique sufficiently different from that of the amateur to lead even people uninterested in the status value of their names and unmoved by most painting to pay willingly for their talent. This difference does not make Karsh and the others objectively great except insofar as it is identified with their technical mastery and success in achieving the goal sitters have in mind. On that definition, of course, your old Aunt Flossie's snapshot of the family around the Christmas tree may also qualify. It is often supposed that, in the photographic field, we can discover a general tendency for the trained student to tend toward identifying the same workers as outstanding. In fact,

Karsh or Stieglitz has his bitter denunciators among professionals. Yet none of them would pick Aunt Flossie's work as being as good as Karsh's. To that extent the field may be one degree more objectively structured than painting, in which Auntie Flo and the chimpanzee next door win prizes and thereby suggest that merit is an easy virtue there.

It is often salutary to refer discussions in aesthetics to examples from arts that have been less often worked over by philosophers, for example, architecture or industrial design. No matter what its visual charms, a house which requires that food from the kitchen pass through the bedrooms in order to reach the dining room has a design defect in that respect, and if in addition it lacks the appropriate roof overhang for the latitude, appropriately thick batts in the roof insulation system for its microclimate, acoustic barriers between children's playrooms and the study, and adequate grading to prevent the runoff from the parking lot from flooding the garage, it is inconceivable that it be regarded as an example of good architecture. It might still have attractions worth pointing out, perhaps enough to make it a valuable or desirable house, although a badly flawed one. Similar considerations apply to body styling in the automobile industry and to the design of furniture and flatware. Reason can play a decisive role in the elimination of candidates even though election of a winner, if several qualify, may involve imponderable reactions to appearance and style as well as to structure and function.

Sometimes the classification of the arts into greater and lesser ones is done in the reverse order of the extent to which practical considerations dominate evaluation, but such an arrangement would be better described as identifying *pure* arts by contrast with *applied* arts. It is not persuasive to claim that pure mathematics or pure theoretical physics or pure art is any greater than applied: the inclination of many is to say the opposite, and there seems to be no ground for supporting one view as against the other. One can only use the term "great art" conventionally, to refer to painting, music, architecture, and literature, as opposed to the lesser arts and the performing arts. And then the fact remains that the "greatness" of some of the great arts and the great artists in them is not only indefinable; it is, in the important sense, indefensible.

16. THE ART CRITIC AND THE AUTOMOBILE SALESMAN

There is a certain domain of our own everyday activities in which the role of reason is in many ways similar to its role in evaluatory aesthetics and, to some extent, in elucidatory aesthetics. It is the domain of legitimate persuasive discourse, that respectable working relative of prostitute propaganda and proper logic. Let us take as an example a knowledgeable and enthusiastic but honest automobile salesman, perhaps somewhat easier to imagine than to observe. Exactly what can he legitimately undertake to do in his dialogue with a prospective purchaser? He can discover the customer's needs, interests, and knowledge and the extent to which these are modifiable, inconsistent, and inexperienced. If lucky, he may be able to demonstrate the superiority of one of his offerings by direct proof from facts about performance, convenience, comfort, and so on. He can do more: he can work with his own enthusiasm and knowledge on the customer's tastes insofar as they are modifiable and as a case can be made for modifying them, and he can then produce the evidence that a particular model best meets this revised set of needs and tastes. He may exhibit new dimensions of appraisal, the criteria for their application, and the pleasures of their exploration. In so doing he shows how the object may be seen and appreciated in other, different, and still—or perhaps more—rewarding ways.

This point has some interesting consequences. It suggests the illegitimacy of wholesale condemnation of "content aesthetics" (e.g., in biographical program notes), or "the intentional fallacy" (reference in evaluative discourse to what the artist was trying to do), or emphasis on transonic performance specifications of high-fidelity components. For these are part of the complex of an art work as a human endeavor and an object of human appreciation, and it is entirely legitimate to incorporate them into that which one evaluates and to regard the totality as an art work in context. One cannot show the insight obtained from biography to be less valuable than that gained from the study of other art; it is valuable insofar as it *makes* a thing of value, and it does that for many people with more success than "pure contemplation." To judge an artist or one of his works on the basis of that work alone is unsound, for we may learn from other works more about his language of expression. And that we may also learn from stories of his life or his age. We must come back to the work, but we have only ourselves to please and nothing to prove; so we should develop our interests in whatever dimensions of appreciation we find interesting.

When the salesman is talking about a car which, for a customer with the appropriate interests, would fill the bill better than any of the alternatives and fill it very well indeed, the only way he can legitimately refer to it in the presence of a quite different kind of customer is by saying such things as "It's a magnificent car, for somebody who can get by with only two seats," or "Nothing finer has ever been made, if you don't take account of the price," or "Where luggage capacity and not a compact turning circle is the primary consideration, this is unequaled." These are evaluations, and they are reasonable enough; but they have no impact on the present customer, in the sense that they should lead him to purchase the car. Such cars are simply not ideal from his point of view. He can see how they might be highly satisfactory for someone with a different set of interests, and in this sense the salesman has performed an elucidatory task for him. But they do not have any direct appeal because he lacks the appropriate interests. If those *were* his interests, the evaluation would follow. In the same way you may come to see the merits, perhaps even the genius, of Klee and Miró for someone who does not think the representational element important; but you are not thereby moved to suppose that it is appropriate to regard them highly yourself, if you *do* value representation. Genius may be perverted, or it may be a genius for the trivial. It is not merely that you do not *like* Klee and Miró; it is also that there is no reason for you to evaluate them as of the first rank. Nor can you propose your own favorites for that exalted position. You can view with attention but with reservation the suggestion that you should so adjust your interests as to find them ideal. There can be a case for this adjustment, as we have seen; but it is never a universal case, only an optional one.

It is important that the good salesman can not only lead the customer to see hidden virtues in the merchandise, without changing his taste, and to see the *overall* advantages of one alternative in a very complicated choice. He can also lead the customer to see that his tastes, if they are further cultivated in their present or in some even more satisfying form and if their consequences are thoroughly examined, will inevitably commit him to the recognition of the merits of something which at first sight he did not see as being meritorious. The role of knowledge and of reason in bringing about a correct judgment of merit is here considerable, and so it is with art. Nevertheless, it is more nearly true than false to say that judgments of greatness in art are usually best construed as largely expressions of personal preference for the particular work or for a particular way of rating art and artists.

GOD

0. THE PROBLEM AND ITS STATUS

What kind of God, if any, exists? This is the primary problem about God, and it is simply stated. Nothing else about the issue is simple. And the problem's complexity is matched by its profundity. No other problem has such important consequences for our lives and our thinking about other issues, and to no other problem does the answer at first seem so obvious. There *must* be a God, for how else could the Universe have come to exist, or life and morality have any point? So one feels. The informal versions of the arguments for the existence of God are probably the oldest and the most widely known of all philosophical arguments. But the centuries have not been entirely kind to them, and many contemporary theologians have wholly abandoned the attempt to prove that God exists, the original task of natural theology.[1]

Even if the arguments do not provide conclusive proof of God's existence, it is often thought that the situation allows a free personal choice. After all, it is said, the failure of positive proofs is not the same as finding a disproof. We shall find, however, that the failure of positive proofs *here* would *not* leave a personal choice open; it would necessitate atheism.[2] Consequently the validity of the arguments is of absolutely crucial importance. An effort has been made here to present the arguments in maximum strength of numbers and individual force, and a stronger method of combining them than has previously been made explicit is provided.

1. OUTLINE

In a preliminary section we shall discuss the following: (2.1) the concept of God, (2.2) the relation of a belief in God to religion, and (2.3) current views about proving there is such a God. Then we shall examine (3.1) the competence of reason in this debate and (3.2) the possibility of faith as an alternative to reason here. In section 4, we shall discuss the consequences if the arguments are *not* conclusive, and in section 5 we shall look at the reasons for considering them separately and at ways of combining them. Section 6 contains the arguments themselves and commentary on them.

2. GOD AND RELIGION

2.1 The concept of God   Gods are more numerous than religions, and to do justice to all their natures is a task for comparative religion, not primary philosophy. Our task is to decide whether any of the usual ones exist, and it is simplified by the fact that they share some common properties. God is

[1] *Natural theology* is to be distinguished from *revealed theology;* the first consists of conclusions about God that can be inferred from the natural world, while the latter elaborates on further truths obtained by divine revelation.

[2] Definitions: A *theist* believes there is at least one God, an *atheist* believes there is not, and an *agnostic* does not know (negative agnostic) or thinks neither conclusion is well supported (positive agnostic). (The atheist may believe there is no God because he thinks the concept is essentially self-contradictory, or meaningless, or because he thinks it is wholly superfluous, or because he thinks it is factually false. It will be shown below that superfluity is an adequate ground for atheism rather than agnosticism.) The *monotheist* believes there is only one God; the *polytheist,* that there are several. Theism is one kind of *supernaturalism,* while atheism is usually associated with the universal possibility of *naturalistic* explanations, which involve only entities of the kind used in ordinary scientific and logical theories. The *humanist* is an agnostic or an atheist with a moral commitment to the value of human life and dignity. The *theologian* is a specialist in the philosophy of theism.

normally conceived of as an extremely powerful Being (certainly more so than any man), and as extremely wise and good (certainly more so than any man). (Something will be said later about wicked gods.) These properties of God are normally taken to guarantee—or else must be supplemented by—(1) a capacity to act and to have acted at almost any place at almost any time (which does not imply the capacity to perform many or all of this large number of possible actions) and (2) a very extensive knowledge of past, present, and future events on the Earth. These specific powers make God *capable* of simultaneous, informed intervention on at least many of the occasions when a moral agent would be obliged to act.[3] Power, wisdom, and goodness, thus interpreted, are the properties of what we may call Basic God, and the question with which we are chiefly concerned is whether any Being with these or greater powers exists. If there is an *infinitely good, omnipotent, omnipresent, and omniscient* God, then there is a More-than-Basic God, which of course is a stronger claim. If there is no Being with as much power as Basic God, of course there cannot be a More-than-Basic God. And a Being lacking any of the properties of Basic God would not normally be thought of as supernatural, as divine, as deserving prayer, reverence, or worship. A highly moral being on another planet, even assuming he commands technological powers considerably superior to our own, still falls short with respect to the special combination of knowledge, powers, and interests that makes God capable of listening to and acting on the prayers of His children here on Earth. And this shortcoming would surely disqualify him from the relevance and the reverence due a Deity.

Of course, an Air Force pilot in a well-armed vertical–take-off plane could no doubt inspire worship in many a primitive tribe, and his counterpart from another planet could do likewise in a large number of Westerners. Zeus and the lesser gods in Eastern polytheistic religions have only this Sub-Basic status. But the existence of such "gods" is not what the intelligent theist is maintaining today; he would certainly require *at least* Basic God. Indeed, many would cavil at this splendid supervisor and require in addition that His achievements include Creation, Redemption, and some infinite powers or perhaps *necessary* existence. Worship of a merely Basic God would be thought of as idolatrous. It is a crucial step in the argument of this chapter to show that an important part of the discussion can by-pass the disputes over these additional powers. For if it is possible to show that there is no entity as powerful (good, etc.) as Basic God, it follows that no *more* powerful entity can exist.

But the most unsatisfactory feature of these and other recently popular approaches is that they make it unfashionable to consider seriously the traditional arguments which are still the main motivation for theistic belief in

[3] This is operational omnipresence.

most theists. Hence the commitment to the new theology in most of its students simply lacks any foundation; they have no real idea of the reasons for that approach. In such a person the view is just as superficial as that of the doctrinaire theist who has never heard and cannot handle the standard arguments against his position. The "new theology" is thus far too often an intellectual fad in the worst sense and can never be more except for the few who do the work required to understand the difficulties with the alternatives.

Attempts have occasionally been made to define God in a very different way: as the infinite Universe, the essence of beauty, truth, or love, the course of history, the Ground of Being, whatever a person believes in most deeply, and so on. These are misleading and intellectually trivial suggestions, for the existence of these things is not what theists have been asserting and atheists denying for two or three millennia. Neither their existence nor their importance is open to much dispute, but since they are simply natural phenomena or idealizations from them, they are grossly miscast as the central entity of a theistic religion. They are not Supreme Beings; their power, if any, is not at the disposition of their intelligence, if any, nor governed by their morality, if any. It may be true that God is love, that God is the Universe, but it cannot be true that God is *only* these things. They have their own names and properties, and to graft the concept of God onto those stems is a cheap attempt to establish His existence at the expense of destroying His character. The most charitable way to regard these recent moves in theology is as wholesale revisions of the content of theism to make it intellectually acceptable without cutting it off completely from the traditional literature. But they are not new analyses of old religions, they are new religions, albeit acquiring most of their supporters as hand-me-downs from sterner creeds. The more honest position is to concede the truth of atheism and argue only for the merits of a demythologized Christianity (for example), a Christianity with an inspiring but human Christ. This position is close to the "God is dead" school; but the real question is whether God was ever alive. For the rest of the discussion is about the rather personal question of which sage one finds to be inspiring.

A particular merit of the Basic God definition is that it appears not to be self-contradictory or incomprehensible. More elaborate definitions run into problems about conflicting infinite properties (Can an omnipotent Being create an immovable object? Can an omnipresent Being act at one place?) which make them susceptible to logical attacks such as the ones which prove the impossibility of a greatest prime number or a construction for squaring the circle. The extreme version of the temptation to expand God's powers results in a definition whose terms are beyond human mental power to grasp (a definition defended on the grounds that God *is* beyond our comprehension); as we shall see, that temptation is a trap that destroys theism.

2.2 *The relation of theism to religion*   Almost but not quite all religions that commonly bear the name are theistic—perhaps polytheistic, perhaps monotheistic, but committed to the existence of supernatural beings. Certain forms of Eastern religions, however, particularly Buddhism and particularly those versions of it that try to recover the original views of the Buddha, are naturalistic. Buddha on his deathbed is said to have told his disciples who were proposing to sanctify him and worship him in effigy that this would be a betrayal of all his teaching. Such Buddhists are usually thought to believe in the transmigration of the soul, i.e., its reincarnation in another body after the death of an earlier body; so their views might be held on this basis to be supernaturalistic. But the case is not very persuasive and surely not the chief reason for regarding Buddhism as a religion. The feature of Buddhism, Confucianism, and Taoism which distinguishes them from the work of a lone philosopher is the production, acceptance, and practice by disciples of a systematized morality or "philosophy of life," or both, involving reference to "spiritual" as opposed to "merely material" values or attitudes. The great social and economic structure of the usual religions results from this and only indirectly from any supernaturalistic content. In the case of Buddhism the novelty was the suggestion that the motive behind the action and not the mere form of the action is the key moral issue, contrary to the views of the then-prevalent Hinduism. It was not long after the death of Buddha himself, however, before the religion became divided, and over the centuries it declined in its country of origin as its followers reverted to polytheism with its easier answers.

So it seems that the only common element in what are normally called religions is that they all produce a distinctive, codified morality. Now this is not an adequate identifying feature of religion, since many groups that are obviously not religious in nature have a morality, too. For example, the Chicago mobs had (and may still have) a fairly definite "moral code," which bore remarkably little resemblance to the Christian ethic but involved the prohibition of certain kinds of intragroup behavior, and a set of values which was quite articulate if not legal.

If someone is anxious to have a simple view of the world and to give the appearance of having made a profound philosophical discovery, he may propose that we call any commitment to an organized set of values a religion. This has the charming result of making mobsters religious, an achievement which probably outweighs the contribution of St. Paul in all his missionary endeavors. But it is only a verbal trick or, to put it more accurately, a mistaken use of the term. There are important social and psychological similar-

ities between Communism and the major religions, despite protestations to
the contrary by some Communists and anti-Communists, but we do not have
to elevate the Bolsheviks to an undeserved and unwanted sanctity by insisting that there are no important differences. The most obvious of these,
of course, are the Communists' absolute denial of any supernatural entities
and of existence for ourselves in a life beyond the grave, their deterministic
view of man, and their view of morality as lacking intrinsic validity, as
being a mere instrument in the class struggle. Few religions would agree
on the first three points, especially in the West, and none on the fourth.
This is surely adequate ground for saying that while a state of mind very
like religious *fervor* and perhaps even a worshiping *attitude* to some entities
are to be found outside religion, this is not enough to show that the place
they are found should be thought of as essentially indistinguishable from
a church. We are all grown-ups now and should be able to accept the fact
that in this world differences between importantly different things are often
not sharp in *all* respects: the Mafia and the Inquisition and the Mau-Mau
do not have to be irreligious in order to be bad.

The classical Western religions of yesterday and today are readily distinguishable from humanism, fascism, or atheism because of their commitment
to theism and hence are more directly affected by our discussion here. Indeed
it is typically the case that these religions attempt to justify their distinctive
moralities in terms of God's wishes or commands, i.e., by appeal to their
theism (for example, in arguing that suicide is wrong because it destroys
something given to us in trust by God). It is, therefore, extremely important
in evaluating such religions to be clear about the evidential basis for their
belief in the existence of that God. The contribution of those religions which
lack a theistic basis for their morality can be assessed in terms of the criteria
presented in the *Morality* chapter. Of course, the social institutions of a
theistic religion may continue to exist even when most of its theologians and
many of its officers are no longer theists in any significant sense. This may be
thought to support the conclusion that *theism* is not an essential part of such
religions, but it only follows that *the claim that theism is readily demonstrable* is not crucial. For it seems most likely that theism is still the basis
for most religions, at least in the West, in the sense that few people would
become religious if they were brought up to believe that theism was *false*.
Yet theism is not all there is or can be to a religion; in particular, its truth has
very little bearing on the question whether religion is or has been a great
force for good.

2.3 Current views of the arguments   It is perhaps worth reporting that
belief in the conclusiveness of the arguments for theism, among trained
theologians, is now quite unusual. The official position of the established
churches, where they have one, is generally against their validity, and the

position of the most popular theologians of the time is even more widely skeptical. The most notable exceptions to this situation are theologians of the fundamentalist Protestant churches, who think the argument from Scripture is sound, and many Dominicans and Jesuits, who think the proofs given by St. Thomas Aquinas are sound. In this respect they go beyond any clear commitment of the Roman Catholic Church to which they belong. The official position of the Holy See is not *demonstrably* stronger than the claim that the arguments, while suggestive of a path to and the nature of God, are not binding on the reason. That is to say, a man may be honest and intelligent and yet find them wanting.[4] If he does so, it is a sign that God has not given him a certain further capacity or disposition called faith, insight, or grace, which is necessary to make the arguments appeal compellingly. This lack is not his fault—is not a punishment—and hence in this view it is not a sin to be an honest atheist. Presumably the atheist serves part of the Divine Plan, perhaps as an instrument to test men's faith. (This position is not universally accepted; St. Thomas's view was that atheists should all be killed.) This situation is of comfort to the open-minded, since it means that intelligence, study, and an honest heart—and not fear of the consequences—can provide a complete basis for the proper decision. Nor can one "play safe" by believing in God without reason, for this kind of dishonest theism is simply a betrayal of the reason God gives man and hence is more sinful than honest atheism.

Of course it has long been felt, by most of those who are outside the established churches but who have professional training in the study of such arguments, that they are not sound. But this does not tell us whether these persons are of this view because of their disavowal of religion or outside religion because of their judgment about the arguments. Besides, there are exceptions to this generalization and in recent years a most interesting development in contemporary logical discussions has concerned the suggestion by notable philosophers that the most powerful argument of all is one that almost no recent theistic theologians have taken seriously: the so-called ontological argument.

So one can only conclude that the status of the arguments is not a matter of general agreement even among theists. This is the case not only because the arguments themselves are by no means easy to assess but because there are a number of controversies about the relevance or significance of the whole approach through the arguments. It is to these general issues that we must now turn: the question whether reason rules here or whether faith should be conceded dominion over this territory; the questions whether the arguments are stronger jointly than separately and whether atheism is ever justified even if the arguments should fail.

---

[4] A stronger interpretation is often put forward, but the available documents do not establish it beyond dispute, even among Roman Catholic theologians.

3. GOD AND REASON

3.1 *The relevance of reason* Does it matter whether the arguments are sound? Indeed, should we be trying to reason about God at all? It is often said that such an attempt is hopelessly inappropriate, and indeed it is sometimes said to be sacrilegious. By His very nature God transcends merely human categories of thought, and to attempt to imprison Him in them is a simple fallacy. The attempt, in fact, demonstrates that some other, limited being is under discussion, not God Himself. Our enterprise and, indeed, our very definition of "God" in terms of human concepts are thus doomed from the start.

But a mountain that is infinitely tall does not thereby cease to be a mountain; those who lived in its shadow would not lack good reason for saying that there was a mountain near them just because none could determine where the end of the shadow was to be found. A God that exists everywhere is nonetheless present here and now. A God that is perfectly loving is at least as loving as a human being who loves with all his human heart. An omnipotent God is at least as powerful as you and I; indeed He is certainly more powerful than any human being. So we *can* legitimately begin by looking into the question whether there is any reason for thinking that this world is inhabited (or permeated) by a Being who is superhuman in respect of His knowledge, power, and love to the extent set out in our definition.

If such a Being exists, then we might or might not be able to go on to argue that It is *infinitely* powerful, etc., or the grounds we uncover may immediately lead to that conclusion. Despite a common belief to the contrary, this task is obviously possible in principle. We have already learned, from the fossils and footprints of the dinosaurs, that there were once beings on the Earth's surface with greater physical power than human beings. There is nothing in the least self-contradictory about a human being reasoning to the conclusion that there are beings with *more-than-human* power, just as the big-game hunter frequently reasons to the presence of elephants. One might as well argue that it is impossible to reason about the existence of beings with *less*-than-human power—after all, they are just as different from us. Indeed we can go further; the whole of modern particle physics involves reasoning about the existence of beings with properties that are so fundamentally different from the ones with which we are familiar that comprehension in the sense of simple analogy with the familiar is almost completely lacking, but the success of applied physics shows that such inferences are not only possible but very effective. And mathematics readily demonstrates the possibility of reasoning to the existence of infinite entities and properties.

So there is a clear possibility of direct proof of the existence of a Being with wholly unfamiliar powers, and there is nothing inappropriate about approaching that possibility via the simpler stratagem of discussing the finite and more comprehensible Basic God, however different this may be in itself from the mighty God of our fathers. It is different but not irrelevant. After all, if someone can show there is nothing on the Earth's surface stronger than a man, then there are no elephants; and if his first claim is true, he need not go into detail about the other properties of elephants. This is likely to seem very irreverent to elephant lovers, but it is an exceptionally powerful procedure, because it also shows there are no gorillas, dinosaurs, or tigers around. And on the theist's side, the Basic God step has advantages, too. Some of the worst difficulties with the claim that there is a God around arise over the particular properties that are ascribed to the particular version of God favored by, for example, Christianity. Although we shall later discuss some of these, the first part of the argument will not require us to look into any details about such questions as whether God is a Trinity or a Unity. So an approach via the existence of Basic God makes it possible to show there is a God that many would consider worthy of awe, reverence, and prayer even if the difficulties about the more complicated entities of certain religions are insuperable.

But surely there could be arguments which would show that a Being with truly immense powers exists, even though they would not in any way show that a lesser Being existed; and by showing that no such lesser Being exists (if indeed that can be done) would one not in fact only be showing something which many theists would grant anyway? The mightiest arguments of the theologians are aimed higher, it might be said, and for better or for worse they bear on a different question. God is not just *more* of everything or even the *most*. He is different in kind from other things: He is the *Creator* and not just a jumbo-sized friendly handyman, and so on with the other properties.

These points are good but irrelevant. Direct proofs of a More-than-Basic God will certainly be considered; but theism does not depend on their success, since a Basic God might be all there is. So their role is limited. Conversely, grounds for believing that there is nothing *as or more powerful* than Basic God eliminate both kinds of God. There can be a God even if He is not Basic, but there cannot be a God that is not at least Basic.

In a somewhat desperate move, some theologians have argued that the words we use to describe God do not have their ordinary use at all. All religious language is symbolic and not to be taken literally, they say. This move throws out the baby of belief with the bath water of mythology; it is too sophisticated for its own good. In the first place, almost all believers and potential believers, past and present, take the usual claims about God's nature to be something like the truth, even if not quite literally true; and it is to them we are addressing these discussions. The points made will not be vulnerable to the possibility that analogical or symbolic reference is the best we can do (in any comprehensible sense of "analogical" or "symbolic"). In the second place, if we try to take the sophisticated position seriously and ask what it is about religious belief, interpreted in this way, that distinguishes it from the beliefs of a pagan or an avowed atheist, we find that either there is no agreement on the answer or the answer is that no such distinction exists. The latter comment has been taken to be the profound discovery that everyone is "really" religious or even theistic (for example, because everyone has some "ultimate concern" about something or believes in the existence of substance). But, of course, it equally well proves that everyone is "really" irreligious or atheistic; if there is no difference between chalk and cheese, you can just as well call the stuff on the supermarket's cold shelves chalk as call the stuff on the blackboard cheese. There is a real difference between almost everyone who believes in the existence of God and everyone who does not; the difference is that the two groups disagree about what a thorough census of all existing entities would show and only one of them thinks it would include an intelligent Being with supernatural powers, concerned with our welfare. Attempts to eliminate this residual content in theism, common in recent "liberal" Protestant theology, are the survival attempts of a system of belief that sees its only salvation in camouflage but fails to see that what is indistinguishable cannot be indispensable.

Someone who wanted to adopt a really disproof-proof position here (many have been tempted, and at least one Indian philosopher has succumbed) could *define* God as the Unknowable; or he could say that whatever else God is, He is certainly unknowable. The only trouble with this position is that you really cannot eat your cake and worship it too; there cannot be any reason for worshiping, or respecting, or loving, or praying to, or believing in such a God. The Unknowable may be evil, stupid, inanimate, or nonexistent; a religion dedicated to such a pig in a poke would be for the feebleminded. If religious belief means anything at all, it means belief in something whose properties may not be entirely clear but which are at least worthy of respect (most have said, humble adoration). Such a Being is not wholly unknowable, since we know some very important things about Him, such as His goodness. We may certainly say that He is not fully knowable, and the ensuing discussion does not assume that God is fully knowable. The theist's claim is that there is a good supernatural force, perhaps with many mysterious properties. And the atheist's claim is simply that the God of the great religions has quite enough properties to make him, on the one hand, worthy of respect and, on the other, nonexistent.

The extreme form of the defense against the relevance of reason is therefore itself indefensible. There are no obvious mistakes in the attempt to reason about God. One can all too easily get carried away by catchy little slogans like "The finite cannot comprehend the infinite," "Man cannot presume to judge God," "God takes up where Reason gives out," and so on. Their merits, if any, lie in their potential use as tricky titles for sermons in fashionable suburban churches. They have no force as a defense against skepticism or as a support for belief. We can be quite sure there *is* an infinite sequence of digits after 1, 2, and 3, and we can be quite sure there *is not* an infinitely long ribbon in our typewriter or an infinitely heavy nuthatch sitting on the bird feeder; so the preacher just has to get down from the pulpit and do some hard, logical work to show that there is some special reason why an infinite God cannot be reasoned about in the same way. Why should the human mind be incapable of dealing with the infinite in theology but not in mathematics or cosmology, where it is a commonplace and well-defined part of the subject?

Yet, a more profound point is involved behind the scenes here. There is a nagging nervousness about talking as if there were no limitations on the power of the human reason. After all, there *must* be a certain parochialism about our present views and a certain poverty about our capacity for analyzing the evidence. We have only been thinking systematically for a few millenniums (some would say, centuries), and in that short span we have constantly found ourselves abandoning the absolute convictions of previous generations. How then can one have any degree of certainty about the existence or nonexistence of a Being so different from the beings of our immediate experience and so vastly superior to ourselves in thought?

The point is very weighty, but it is not decisive here. In the first place, the very nature of the Being we are now undertaking to discuss makes Him approachable by reason. For God, Who is often said to be ever present, is at the very least *able* to be present almost anywhere at almost any time—He is ever accessible. If He lacked this power, He would be of little concern to us. We cannot be certain about the existence of beings on other planets just because they are on other planets and not here, and thus far we have not been close enough to see if they do, in fact, exist. But a Being that is here, indeed often said to have been here since Creation—such a Being, with the opportunity and the power and the interest in doing something that would prevent or improve an imperfect work, would surely have to leave some traces in *this* world. Indeed, whether He created the world or merely had the chance to change it, the world itself must to some extent be a reflection of His character. If we can show that the world is best explicable in terms of a Divine Plan, we have the best reasons for theism. If the world is simply a natural phenomenon, whose natural properties are grossly imperfect for our needs and not improved by any unseen force, it seems at first sight as if we would have some kind of reason for thinking Him less than good, powerful, and wise. So reason can in principle both prove and disprove the existence of God.

Second, even if it were in His nature to be anonymous, the nature of our basic question still makes an answer possible. For we are not discussing the question whether the existence of God is possible but the question whether it is likely. And, as we shall see, the absence of all evidence for God's existence would make it most unlikely that He exists.

We are ignorant of many things that exist in the Universe, of course, and we always shall be; but the whole reason for concern about God is His immense importance for our affairs here and now, and we are not blind about the here and now.

3.2 Faith and reason   We must now contend with the suggestion that reason is irrelevant to the commitment to theism because this territory is the domain of another faculty: the faculty of faith. It is sometimes even hinted that it is morally wrong and certainly foolish to suggest we should be reasoning about God. For this is the domain of faith or of the "venture of faith," of the "knowledge that passeth understanding," of religious experience and mystic insight.

Now the normal meaning of *faith* is simply "confidence"; we say that we have great faith in someone or in some claim or product, meaning that we believe and act as if they were very reliable. Of such faith we can properly say that it is well founded or not, depending on the evidence for whatever it is in which we have faith.[5] So there is no incompatibility between this kind of faith and reason; the two are from different families and can make a very good marriage. Indeed if they do not join forces, then the resulting ill-based or inadequate confidence will probably lead to disaster. So faith, in this sense, means only a high degree of belief and may be reasonable or unreasonable.

But the term is sometimes used to mean an *alternative to reason* instead of something that should be founded on reason. Unfortunately, the mere use of the term in this way does not demonstrate that faith is a possible route to truth. It is like using the term "winning" as a synonym for "playing" instead of one possible outcome of playing. This is quaint, but it could hardly be called a satisfactory way of proving that we are winning; any time we "win" by changing the meaning of winning, the victory is merely illusory. And so it proves in this case. To use "faith" *as if* it were an alternative way to the truth cannot by-pass the crucial question whether such results really have any likelihood of being true. A rose by any other name will smell the same, and the inescapable facts about "faith" in the new sense are that it is still *applied to* a belief and is still supposed to imply *confidence in* that belief: the belief in the existence and goodness of God. So we can still ask the

[5] For faith to be well founded, especially faith in a person, it is not required that the evidence available at a particular moment justify exactly the degree of confidence one exhibits. There may be overriding reasons for retaining trust beyond the first point of rationally defensible doubt (see the discussion of attitude inertia in the *Morality* chapter). But this minor divergence does not seriously affect the discussion here.

same old question about that belief: Is the confidence justified or misplaced? To say we "take it on faith" does not get it off parole.

Suppose someone replies that theism is a kind of belief that does not need justification by evidence. This means either that no one cares whether it is correct or not or that there is some other way of checking that it is correct besides looking at the evidence for it, i.e., giving reasons for believing it. But the first alternative is false since very many people care whether there is a God or not; and the second alternative is false because any method of showing that belief is likely to be true is, by definition, a justification of that belief, i.e., an appeal to reason. You certainly cannot show that a belief in God is likely to be true just by having confidence in it and by saying this is a case of knowledge "based on" faith, any more than you can win a game just by playing it and by calling that winning.

It is psychologically possible to have faith in something without any basis in fact, and once in a while you will turn out to be lucky and to have backed the right belief. This does not show you "really knew all along"; it only shows you cannot be unlucky all the time (see *Knowledge* chapter). But, in general, beliefs without foundations lead to an early grave or to an accumulation of superstitions, which are usually troublesome and always false beliefs. It is hardly possible to defend this approach just by *saying* that you have decided that in this area confidence is its own justification.

Of course, you might try to *prove* that a feeling of great confidence about certain types of propositions is a reliable indication of their truth. If you succeeded, you would indeed have shown that the belief was justified; you would have done this by justifying it. To do this you would have to show what the real facts were and show that when someone had the kind of faith we are now talking about, it usually turned out that the facts were as he believed, just as we might justify the claims of a telepath. The catch in all this is simply that you have got to show what the real facts are in some way *other* than by appealing to faith, since that would simply be assuming what you are trying to prove. And if you can show what the facts are in this other way, you do not need faith in any new sense at all; you are already perfectly entitled to confidence in any belief that you have shown to be well supported.

How are you going to show what the real facts are? You show this by any method of investigation that has itself been tested, the testing being done by still another tested method, etc., through a series of tested connections that eventually terminates in our ordinary everyday reasoning and testing procedures of logic and observation.

Is it not prejudiced to require that the validation of beliefs always involve ultimate reference to our ordinary logic and everyday-plus-scientific knowledge? May not faith (religious experience, mystic insight) give us access to some new domain of truth? It is certainly possible that it does this. But, of course, it is also possible that it lies. One can hardly accept the reports of those with faith or, indeed, the apparent revelations of one's own religious experiences on the ground that they *might* be right. So *might* be a fervent materialist who saw his interpretation as a revelation. Possibility is not veracity. Is it not of the very greatest importance that we should try to find out whether we really can justify the use of the term "truth" or "knowledge" in describing the content of faith? If it is, then we must find something in that content that is known to be true in some other way, because to get off the ground we must first push off against the ground—we cannot lift ourselves by our shoelaces. If the new realm of knowledge is to be a realm of knowledge and not mythology, then it must tell us something which relates it to the kind of case that gives meaning to the term "truth." If you want to use the old word for the new events, you must show that it is applicable.

Could not the validating experience, which religious experience must have if it is to be called true, be the experience of others who also have or have had religious experiences? The religious community could, surely, provide a basis of agreement analogous to that which ultimately underlies scientific truth. Unfortunately, agreement is not the only requirement for avoiding error, for all may be in error. The difficulty for the religious community is to show that its agreement is not simply agreement about a shared mistake. If agreement were the only criterion of truth, there could never be a shared mistake; but clearly either the atheist group or the theist group shares a mistake. To decide which is wrong must involve appeal to something other than mere agreement. And, of course, it is clear that particular religious beliefs are mistaken, since religious groups do not all agree and they cannot all be right.

Might not some or all scientific beliefs be wrong, too? This is conceivable, but there are crucial differences between the two kinds of belief. In the first place, any commonly agreed religious beliefs concern only one or a few entities and their properties and histories. What for convenience we are here calling "scientific belief" is actually the sum total of all conventionally founded human knowledge, much of it not part of any science, and it embraces billions upon billions of facts, each of them perpetually or frequently subject to checking by independent means, each connected with a million others. The success of *this* system of knowledge shows up every day in everything that we do: we eat, and the food is not poison; we read, and the pages do not turn to dust; we slip, and gravity does not fail to pull us down. We are not just relying on the existence of agreement about the interpretation of a certain experience among a small part of the population. We are relying directly on our extremely reliable, nearly universal, and independently tested senses, and each of us is constantly obtaining independent confirmation for claims based on these, many of these confirmations being obtained for many claims, independently of each other. It is the wildest flight of fancy to suppose that there is a body of common religious beliefs which can be set out to exhibit this degree of repeated checking by religious experiences. In fact, there is not only gross disagreement on even the most fundamental claims in the creeds of different churches, each of which is supported by appeal to religious experience or faith, but where there is agreement by many people, it is all too easily open to the criticism that it arises from the common cultural exposure of the child or the adult convert and hence is not independent in the required way.

This claim that the agreement between judges is spurious in a particular case because it only reflects previous common indoctrination of those in agreement is a serious one. It must always be met by direct disproof whenever agreement is appealed to in science, and it is. The claim that the food is not poison cannot be explained away as a myth of some subculture, for anyone, even if told nothing about the eaters in advance, will judge that the people who ate it are still well. The whole methodology of testing is committed to the doctrine that any judges who could have learned what they are expected to say about the matter they are judging are completely valueless.[6] Now anyone exposed to religious teaching, whether a believer or not, has long known the standard for such experiences, the usual symbols, the appropriate circumstances, and so on. These suggestions are usually very deeply implanted, so that they cannot be avoided by good intentions, and consequently members of our culture are rendered entirely incapable of being independent observers. Whenever observers are not free from previous contamination in this manner, the only way to support their claims is to examine independently testable *consequences* of the novel claims, such as predictions about the future. In the absence of these, the religious-experience gambit, whether involving literal or analogical claims, is wholly abortive.

A still more fundamental point counts against the idea that agreement among the religious can help support the idea of faith as an alternative path to truth. It is that every sane theist also believes in the claims of ordinary experience, while the reverse is not the case. Hence, the burden of proof is on the theist to show that the *further step* he wishes to take will not take him beyond the realm of truth. The two positions, of science and religion, are not symmetrical; the adherent of one of them suggests that we extend the range of allowable beliefs and yet is unable to produce the same degree of acceptance or "proving out" in the ordinary field of human activities that he

[6] More precisely, a judge is said to be "contaminated" if he could know which way his judgment will count insofar as the issue at stake is concerned. The famous double-blind experimental design, keystone of drug research, achieves reliability by making it impossible for either patient or nurse to know when the real drug, rather than the dummy drug or placebo, is being judged.

insists on before believing in a new instrument or source of information. The atheist obviously cannot be shown his error in the way someone who thinks that there are no electrons can be shown his, *unless some of the arguments for the existence of God are sound.* Once again, we come back to these. If some of them work, the position of religious knowledge is secure; if they do not, nothing else will make it secure.

In sum, the idea of separating religious from scientific knowledge and making each an independent realm with its own basis in experience of quite different kinds is a counsel of despair and not a product of true sophistication, for one cannot break the connection between everyday experience and religious claims, for purposes of defending the latter, without eliminating the consequences of religion for everyday life. There is no way out of this inexorable contract: if you want to support your beliefs, you must produce some experience which can be shown to be a reliable indicator of truth, and that can be done only by showing a connection between the experience and what we know to be true in a previously established way.

So, if the criteria of religious truth are not connected with the criteria of everyday truth, then they are not criteria of truth at all and the beliefs they "establish" have no essential bearing on our lives, constitute no explanation of what we see around us, and provide no guidance for our course through time.

4. THE CONSEQUENCES IF THE ARGUMENTS FAIL

The arguments are the only way to establish theism, and they must be judged by the usual standards of evidence—this we have argued. It will now be shown that if they fail, there is no alternative to atheism.

Against this it has commonly been held that the absence of arguments *for* the existence of something is not the same as the presence of arguments *against* its existence; so agnosticism or an option remains when the arguments fail. But insofar as this is true, it is irrelevant. It is true only if we restrict "arguments for the existence of something" to highly specific demonstrations which attempt to establish their conclusion as beyond all reasonable doubt. The absence of these is indeed compatible with the conclusion's being quite likely, which would make denial of its existence unjustified. But if we take arguments for the existence of something to include all the evidence which supports the existence claim to any significant degree, i.e., makes it at all probable, then the absence of such evidence means there is *no* likelihood of the existence of the entity. And this, of course, is a complete justification for the claim that the entity does not exist, provided that the entity is not one which might leave no traces (a God who is impotent or who does not care for us), and provided that we have comprehensively examined the area where such evidence would appear if there were any.[7] Now justifying the claim that something does not exist is not quite the same as proving or having arguments that it doesn't, but it is what we are talking about. That is, we need not have a proof that God does not exist in order to justify atheism. Atheism is obligatory in the absence of any evidence for God's existence.

Why do adults not believe in Santa Claus? Simply because they can now explain the phenomena for which Santa Claus's existence is invoked without any need for introducing a novel entity. When we were very young and naïvely believed our parents' stories, it was hard to see how the presents could get there on Christmas morning since the doors were locked and our parents were asleep in bed. Someone *must* have brought them down the chimney. And how could that person get to the roof without a ladder and with all those presents? Surely only by flying. And then there is that great traditional literature of stories and songs which immortalize the entity and his (horned) attendants; surely these cannot all be just products of imagination? Where there is smoke, there must be fire.

Santa Claus is not a bad hypothesis at all for six-year-olds. As we grow up, no one comes forward to *prove* that such an entity does not exist. We just come to see that there is not the least reason to think he *does* exist. And so it would be entirely foolish to assert that he does, or believe that he does, or even think it likely that he does. Santa Claus is in just the same position as fairy godmothers, wicked witches, the devil, and the ether. Each of these entities has some supernatural powers, i.e., powers which contravene or go far beyond the powers that we know exist, whether it be the power to levitate a sled and reindeer or the power to cast a spell. Now even belief in something for which there is *no* evidence, i.e., a belief which goes *beyond* the evidence, although a lesser sin than belief in something which is *contrary* to well-established laws, is plainly irrational in that it simply amounts to attaching belief where it is not justified. So the proper alternative, when there is no evidence, is not mere suspension of belief, e.g., about Santa Claus; it is *disbelief*. It most certainly is not faith.

The situation is slightly different with the Abominable Snowman, sea serpents, or even the Loch Ness monster. No "supernatural" (by which, in this context, we only mean wholly unprecedented) kinds of powers are involved. Previous discoveries have been made of creatures which had long seemed extinct, and from these we can immediately derive some likelihood

---

[7] This last proviso is really superfluous since it is built into the phrase "the absence of such evidence," which is not the same as "ignorance of such evidence"; but it is included for the sake of clarity. When we are investigating the existence of God, we naturally attempt to discuss all the evidence, conclusive or not; so if this comes to naught, we would be left with no alternative to atheism. Fence sitting with the agnostic is not only uncomfortable; it is even indefensible.

of further discoveries.[8] Footprints or disturbances for which no fully satis-factory alternative explanation has yet been discovered (although such an explanation is by no means impossible) have been seen in the Himalayan snow and the Scottish lochs. It would be credulous for the layman to believe firmly in the existence of these entities. Yet it would be equally inappropriate to say it is certain they do not exist. Here is a domain for agnosticism (though perhaps an agnosticism inclined toward skepticism). For the agnostic does not believe that a commitment either way is justified, and he is surely right about strange creatures which, while of a new *appearance,* have powers that are mere extensions, proportional to size, of those with which we are already familiar on this Earth. There is some suggestive, if by no means conclusive, evidence for such entities; and the balance of general considerations is not heavily against them.

But when the assertion is made that something exists with powers that strikingly transcend the well-established generalizations we have formulated about animal capacities or reasonable extrapolations from them, then we naturally expect correspondingly better evidence before we concede that there is a serious likelihood of having to abandon those generalizations. It is en-tirely appropriate to demand much stronger support for claims of telepathy or levitation or miraculous cures than for new sports records or feats of memory in which previous levels of performance are merely bettered to some degree, in a way that is almost predictable. On the other hand, it is entirely prejudiced to reject all such evidence on the ground that it *must* be deceptive because it contravenes previously established generalizations. This is simply to deify the present state of science; it is the precise opposite of the experimental attitude. It is right to demand a stronger case to overthrow a strong case and to demand very strong evidence to demonstrate unprecedented powers. It is irrational to require that the evidence of these powers be just as commonplace and compelling as for the previously known powers of man or beast: one cannot legislate the exceptional into the commonplace.

We can now use a set of distinctions that would previously have seemed very abstract. First, let us distinguish a belief which is wholly without general or particular evidential support from one which can be directly disproved. The claim that a race of men lives on the moons of Jupiter or that a certain cola causes cancer of the colon is entirely unfounded but not totally impos-sible. The view that the ratio of a circle's circumference to its diameter can

---

[8] We would not normally say this general consideration is *"evidence* for the existence of the Loch Ness monster"; evidence, like proof, must be rather specifically tied to a claim. But these general background considerations set the stage for proofs, and they directly determine the legitimacy of total skepticism or complete confidence. We re-gard them as relevant considerations, and the present claim is that without even these no option but atheism is possible.

be expressed as a fraction is demonstrably untenable, as is the view that some living men are infinitely strong, or that any man is or has been unbeatable at chess, or that the FBI has wiped out the Mafia. We normally say that a claim is *well founded* if there is evidence which is best explained by this claim. We may say it is *provable* if the evidence is indubitable and the claim is very clearly required. If there is no evidence which points to this particular claim, although some general background considerations make it not too unlikely that something like this should be true (Loch Ness monster, mile record broken twice in 1980), we would say there is *some general support* for the claim. We shall say it is *wholly unfounded* (or *wholly unsupported*) if there is no evidence for it in particular and no general considerations in its favor, and *disprovable* if it implies that something would be the case that definitely is not the case.

Of course it is foolish to believe a claim that is disproved, but it is also foolish to believe a wholly unsupported claim, and it is still foolish even to treat such a claim as if it were worth serious consideration. A claim for which there is some general or some particular support cannot be dismissed, but neither can it be treated as established. The connection between evidential support and the appropriate degree of belief can be demonstrated as shown in the diagram on the next page, which is quite unlike the oversimplified idea that the arrangement should be:

Provable	Theism
Disprovable	Atheism
Neither	Agnosticism

The crucial difference is that both "unfounded" and "disprovable" correlate with atheism, just as the two corresponding types of provability correlate with theism; hence the agnostic's territory is smaller than he often supposes.

Recalling that to get even a little evidential support for the existence of a Being with supernatural powers will require that the little be of very high quality (*little* does not mean "dubious"), we see that the failure of all the arguments, i.e., of all the evidence, will make even agnosticism in the wide sense an indefensible exaggeration of the evidential support.[9] And agnosticism in the narrow sense will be an exaggeration unless the arguments are strong enough to establish about a 50 per cent probability for the claim of theism. Apart from the wide and narrow senses of agnosticism there is also a distinction between a positive agnostic and a negative agnostic.

[9] Technical note: Attempts to formulate the general principle of evidence involved have usually run into difficulties related to those made familiar in the discussions of the paradoxes of confirmation. For example, negative existential hypotheses in natural language can be supported by the failure of proofs of their contradictories, but positive existential hypotheses are not made plausible by the failure of disproofs of their denials.

EVIDENTIAL SITUATION	APPROPRIATE ATTITUDE	NAME FOR APPROPRIATE ATTITUDE IN THEISM CASE
1. Strictly disprovable, i.e., demonstrably incompatible with the evidence. 2. Wholly unfounded, i.e., wholly lacking in general or particular support.	Rejection	Atheism
3. Possessing some general or particular support; still improbable.	Skepticism but recognition as a real *possibility*; not to be wholly disregarded in comprehensive planning but to be bet *against*.	Skepticism
4. Possessing substantial support but with substantial alternatives still open; a balance of evidence for and against; about 50 per cent probable.	Suspension of judgment. Make no commitment either way; treat each alternative as approximately equally serious.	Agnosticism (narrow sense)
5. Possessing powerful evidential support; some difficulties of inadequacies or significant alternatives remaining; probable.	Treat as probably true; bet *on*.	Pragmatic theism
6. Possessing overwhelming particular support and no basis for alternative views; beyond reasonable doubt; provable in the usual sense. 7. Strictly provable, i.e., as a demonstrably necessary result of indubitable facts.	Acceptance	Theism

Agnosticism (wide sense) [brace spanning rows 3–5]

A *positive agnostic* maintains that the evidence is such as to make his position the correct one and those of the theist and atheist incorrect. *Negative agnosticism* is simply the position of not accepting either theism or atheism; it does not suggest that they are both wrong—it may be just an expression of felt indecision or ignorance. The difference between negative and positive agnosticism is like the difference between a *neutral* who says, "I don't know who's right—maybe one of the disputants, or maybe neither," and a *third force* who says, "Neither is right, and I have a third alternative which *is* right." Obviously, the negative agnostic has not progressed as far in his thinking as the positive agnostic, in one sense, because he has not been able to decide which of the three possible positions is correct. The view of the negative agnostic cannot be right, but his position may be the right position for someone who has not thought the matter through or who lacks the capacity to do so.

In practice, an agnostic's position is often the product of an untidy mixture of factors. He may never have happened to come across an argument for either theism or atheism which struck him as compelling; a rough head counting has revealed intelligent people on either side; his nose for social stigmas indicates a slight odor of intellectual deficiency attached to theism by contemporary intellectuals and a suggestion of unnecessary boat rocking or perhaps rabid subversion attached to atheism. This makes the agnostic fence look pretty attractive; so up he climbs, to sit on top. But now we put the challenge to him. Is he incapable of thinking out an answer for himself? If so, he is intellectually inferior to those below; if not, he must descend and demonstrate the failings of the contestants before he is entitled to his perch. Agnosticism as a position is interesting and debatable; agnosticism as the absence of a position is simply a sign of the absence of intellectual activity or capacity.

5. COMBINING AND SEPARATING ARGUMENTS AND EVIDENCE

There used to be a standing joke in the Rationalist Club at Melbourne University about the theologian who said: "None of the arguments is any good by itself, but taken together they constitute an overwhelming proof." Alas for the simple approach; the instinct of the theologian was better than the formal training of the rationalists, although the error is not easily stated. There used to be a small book on the market which contained 200 "proofs" that $-1 = +1$; entertaining though these are, they do not make it one bit more likely that -1 really does equal $+1$, for they are all invalid. If you knew nothing about mathematics, even about elementary arithmetic, and the only way you could find out whether $+1$ equaled -1 was by counting the number of alleged proofs in each direction, you might reasonably conclude that it did. But if you were seriously concerned with the truth of the matter, you would want to investigate the validity of the proofs for yourself; and you would find that they were all unsound. So there is no advantage in numbers, *as far as mathematical proofs go.* They either do the whole trick or nothing at all.[10]

The situation is different with scientific proofs, whereby we hope to do no more than show that one conclusion is so probable as to be beyond reasonable doubt. Let us suppose you are investigating a murder case. There are three clues. The first one points most strongly at North as the suspect; the second, at East; the third, at West. Obviously, you could not argue that South had been shown to be the culprit from a consideration of any one of these clues by itself. Yet there are circumstances in which you can put them all together and conclude that South was, *without any doubt,* the murderer. Here we have a number of "proofs" (items of evidence) which separately do nothing to establish a particular conclusion but which add up to a good proof of that conclusion. How is this possible? The point about probability proofs is that they do not make the alternative explanations completely impossible and may indicate a second-best hypothesis. So, although the first clue is North's handkerchief at the scene of the crime, you also know that South is North's roommate and may have borrowed his handkerchief, while no one else could have done so without considerable difficulty. And although the second clue is that East very frequently had violent arguments with the victim and had been heard to threaten him with injury, it was also true that South stood to gain by the victim's death since he inherited his job in a public relations firm. And West's professional skill at judo, which ties in well with the victim's curiously broken neck, is not such as to make South's army training in the basic karate blows an irrelevant consideration. So South is by a long way the most likely murderer. In the same way, with respect to those arguments for the existence of God which are of the probability-increasing kind, we shall have to consider not only whether they make God's existence likely on their own but whether some of them make it a sufficiently good alternative explanation so that when we take all the arguments together it is the best overall explanation.

Obviously this can happen only if the *same hypothesis* receives support as an alternative in each case, for example, the hypothesis that South is the murderer. It would not work at all if the first clue made a secondary suspect of one man called South and the next of a cousin of the first suspect, also

---

[10] On the frontiers, this is not quite true. There is a large realm of metamathematical inference which is very like ordinary scientific inference, especially in prime-number theory and in foundational work. Reasoning from examination of samples, from analogy, and from the preponderance of expert opinion is here not without weight; but these are not the procedures of mathematical proof.

called South. After looking at all the arguments in this kind of situation, we would not have any one candidate who was better qualified than any other; we could not even say that it was probably someone from the family of South, for as a matter of fact this is less likely than that it was one of the other three, North, East, and West.

It could be argued that the greatest confidence trick in the history of philosophy is the attempt to make the various arguments for the existence of God support each other by using the same term for the entity whose existence each is supposed to establish. In fact, almost all of them bear on entities of apparently quite different kinds, ranging from a Creator to a moral Lawgiver. The proofs must, therefore, be supplemented with a further proof or set of proofs that shows these apparently different entities to be the same if the combination trick is to work. Otherwise the arguments must be taken separately, in which case they either establish or fail to establish the existence of a number of remarkable but unrelated entities.

It can sometimes be argued that considerations of simplicity require one to adopt the hypothesis that only a single entity is involved, when the alternative is to introduce several special entities. But the circumstances in which this is legitimate are quite limited; we do not, for example, argue that simplicity requires us to assume that the murderer South is also the unknown person who stole some bonds from a bank the day before the murder. We would have to show some connection through means, opportunity, motive, or *modus operandi,* before the identification could be made at all plausible. Simplicity is a fine guide to the best hypothesis if one can only decide which hypothesis is the simpler. Although there is a greater simplicity in terms of the number of entities involved if we say, for example, that the Creator is the moral Lawgiver, there is a greater complexity in terms of the number of explanations required, since now we must explain why and how one entity could perform these two functions. In short, we have really got to give a plausible specific reason before we can identify the two criminals or the two theological entities, since simplicity is now clearly gained by either alternative, and until we do so, any commitment to such an identification is wholly unfounded.

If only a very weak case can be made for the claim that the same entity is involved in the different arguments, the "linkage proof," it will mean that the separate arguments must be much stronger (though they need not be individually adequate) for the conclusion that God exists.[11]

Instead of attempting to establish monotheism, one can, of course, frankly accept the arguments as separate proofs of the existence of separate beings.

---

[11] A formal statement of the probability inequality is surprisingly complex, but easily developed.

Roughly speaking, such a polytheist loses one god for each argument that fails and in this sense has a more vulnerable position. But the monotheist may still lose one property or power of his God for each argument that fails and thus fail altogether to establish the existence of the Being he has defined as God, Who has *all* these properties.

It is possible that monotheism owes some of its current support to the feeling that few if any of the separate arguments are without defect and hence *must* be combined for strength. But if this is so, it is surprising that more attention has not been paid to the linkage arguments, which then become crucial.

Another factor acting in favor of monotheism is the feeling that it is less difficult, in the face of the increasing success of naturalistic science, to postulate one supernatural being than several. (But it may be that only the *combination* of properties is supernatural.) To this extent there is a kind of negative justification for the widespread and curious claim that Christianity was in some sense the precursor of modern science with its allegedly unifying theories, but the causal relation is reversed. Christian theology may have been fleeing into monotheism from the shadow cast ahead of the development of Babylonian and Greek science.

6. THE ARGUMENTS ARRANGED AND ASSESSED

6.0 Outlines The following brief outline will serve as a guide to this section. The numbers of arguments given are approximate, since what is to count as a separate argument is partly arbitrary. Previous writers have usually not made so many distinctions as are made here, though the reverse is occasionally true.[12] The arrangement here reflects a compromise between logic, tradition, and the desire to avoid boredom.

BRIEF OUTLINE
6.1 The arguments for the existence of God
    6.1-1 As the best explanation of certain facts, taken individually (about thirteen arguments)
    6.1-2 As the best explanation of certain alleged facts (about three arguments)
    6.1-3 As the result of a certain definition of God (one argument)
    6.1-4 As the best belief (about two arguments)

---

[12] For example, there is no discussion of H. W. Wright's argument that God's existence is required to achieve the final unification in man's system of knowledge, and demonstrates its validity by performing this function. It is no worse but less popular than several arguments that are discussed and may provide the reader with a moment's exercise.

6.1-5 As the best explanation of all the facts, taken together
6.2 The arguments against the existence of God
    6.2-1 As a myth
    6.2-2 As an impossibility on some definition
    6.2-3 As an impossibility on any acceptable definition
6.3 Explanations of the belief in the existence of God

DETAILED OUTLINE

6.1 The arguments for the existence of God
    6.1-1 God's existence as the best explanation of certain facts, taken individually
        6.1-1A The cosmological (or first-cause) argument
            FACT: Something exists
                  Version 1. Causal sequence
                  Version 2. Contingency sequence
        6.1-1B The Prime Mover argument (argument from motion)
            FACT: Something moves
        6.1-1C The teleological argument (argument from design)
            FACT: Some things and processes in nature are coordinated with others in goal-directed activity
        6.1-1D The argument from the efficacy of reason
            FACT: Logic, mathematics, and physics work
        6.1-1E The argument from justice
            FACT: Some apparent injustices are never corrected in this life
        6.1-1F The argument from morality (naïve form)
            FACT: Some people have a sense of right and wrong
        6.1-1G The argument from morality (sophisticated version)
            FACT: Moral language is not self-contradictory
        6.1-1H The arguments from truth, beauty, reality, perfection (the general form of the argument from values)
            FACT: Some people have a sense of truth, beauty, reality, perfection
        6.1-1I The argument from comparative value
            FACT: Some things are commonly said to be less true, beautiful, real, perfect than other things
        6.1-1J The argument from diversity (the henological argument)
            FACT: There are many different things that are commonly said to be good, true, and real
        6.1-1K The argument from Scripture
            FACT: The sacred writings report supernatural events and claims

6.1-1L The argument from religious experience
FACT: Some people report having religious or mystical experiences
6.1-1M The argument from hope
FACT: Some people hope for God's existence
6.1-2 God's existence as the best explanation of certain alleged facts
6.1-2A The argument from agreement (*e consensu gentium*)
ALLEGED FACT: The peoples of the world have always agreed that there is a God
6.1-2B The argument from miracles
ALLEGED FACT: Miracles occur or have occurred
6.1-2C The argument from revelation
ALLEGED FACT: Some individuals have had the existence of God revealed to them
6.1-2D The argument from the greater happiness of the converted (reward version)
ALLEGED FACT: Theists are happier than agnostics or atheists
6.1-3 God's existence as a result of a certain definition of God
6.1-3A The ontological argument
DEFINITION: God is the most perfect Being (or that Being than which no greater can be conceived, etc.)
6.1-4 God's existence as the best belief
6.1-4A The argument from the greater happiness of the converted (intrinsic-merit version)
6.1-4B Pascal's wager
6.1-5 God's existence as the best explanation of all the facts, taken together
6.2 The arguments against the existence of God
6.2-1 God's existence as a myth
6.2-1A The Santa Claus argument
6.2-2 God's existence as an impossibility on some definition
DEFINITION: God is omnipotent
6.2-3 God's existence as an impossibility on any acceptable definition
6.2-3A The argument from the existence of pain and evil
DEFINITION: God is good, potent, and present
6.3 Explanations of the belief in the existence of God

6.1 The arguments for the existence of God

6.1-1 God's existence as the best explanation of certain facts, taken individually

6.1-1A The cosmological (or first-cause) argument

Statement of the argument.   The Causal Version: Everything we know came from (was caused by) something else; so we must conclude that the Universe as a whole came from something else, and the something from which it came is the Creator, God.

The Contingency Version: Everything that exists either exists because of the existence of something else (we call this *contingent existence*) or it exists of itself, being in no way dependent upon the existence of anything else (this is *necessary existence*). It is impossible that there be nothing but contingent beings, for the existence of these things is not self-sufficient. So there must be a necessary Being, and this we call God.

Assessment of the argument.   Let us begin by working with the causal version,[13] which is an attempt to answer the question, Where did the Universe come from? (The other version will come in later.) We shall treat it from the scientific as well as the logical or philosophical point of view. This will make the answer much longer but more watertight—and also perhaps more interesting in itself because of the various scientific possibilities that arise. Philosophically speaking, this kind of approach recurs throughout the book and reflects the belief that our views and concepts must be hard-hammered on the world's anvil before we can trust them to keep a useful shape by themselves.

Where did the Universe *as we see it today* come from? Astronomers can tell us with more or less reliability: the answer lies within science. But where did the Universe *originally,* or *ultimately,* come from? It seems that no scientific answer will do for this question, for any such answer can only be about matter or energy or other scientific entities, existing somewhere, sometime. About these we shall still want to know, Where did *they* come from? It appears that we shall have to look to something outside science for a real answer, and that something will be more fundamental than science, since it is only because of it that any scientific entities exist at all, and *it* will not depend for its existence on scientific entities.

But there is something odd about the original question. Suppose someone says to you, "Have you or have you not given up your unpleasant habit of unnecessary lying?" This question is intended to make you answer either Yes or No. But if you answer Yes, you are conceding that you once had the habit; and if you answer No, you are saying that you not only once had it but that you still have it. In both cases, you are giving the impression that you used to lie. Suppose you never had that "unpleasant habit." Both the answers Yes and No will give the wrong impression. It is easy to see that in such a case one should refuse to give either of these answers and

---

[13] In Thomistic theology, both versions are said to be causal; the first is said to be about "causes *in fieri*," and the second about "causes *in esse*." Whereas the first is obviously causal in a common sense, the second is not; and we shall not here make the very powerful assumption that it is, in order to avoid falling into the web of causal language which may embody the crucial error.

instead say something like, "I have never had the habit; so the question does not arise." In a court of law we might say this is an *improper question*: it rests on an unjustified assumption. Is it possible that our question about the Universe is equally misleading, that it looks like a question which should have a straightforward answer, whereas it is really an improper question? Instead of giving an answer of the kind it suggests, can we instead point out some unjustified assumption that underlies it?

Now, some questions about the Universe are certainly improper. *The Universe* is usually taken to mean "everything there is," and there are many questions about whole collections that do not make sense, even when the same question asked about any single thing in the collection would make good sense. For example, one can ask of any given Canadian (or any group of Canadians) whether he or she (or they) is taller than all other Canadians. But one cannot ask of the Canadian population as a whole whether it is taller than the rest of the Canadian population. There isn't any "rest of the Canadian population" in this case; so the question does not make sense. It assumes there is, and this assumption is unjustified; the question is thus improper. It is senseless to spend years searching for the answer to an improper question: it does not have an answer (of the suggested kind), not because it is a difficult question but because it is not a sensible one.

Consider the question, Where is the Universe? We can ask of any object within the Universe where *it* is; indeed, we can ask this of any group of objects, like the Sun and the planets. The answer is always given by reference to *other* objects within the Universe. The Sun is in the Milky Way, we say, naming the galaxy of which our solar system is part. But when we ask where *everything that exists* is located, what can we mention in our reply? There isn't anything left to refer to. We cannot give a location without referring to something that has a known location. It is like trying to explain the way to Piccadilly to a man in Trafalgar Square without mentioning any places or directions.

We might say, "Piccadilly is located on a map," but this would not be giving directions to it; it would be a trivial remark about Piccadilly in the sense that it would tell the questioner nothing he did not already know. Similarly, we might say, "The Universe is located in space," but this would be evading the issue. The question is, *Where* in space? To sum up, the Universe does *not* have a location, because things can have locations only relative to other things and, by definition, there are no other things besides the Universe. So the question, Where is the Universe? is an improper question.

Similarly, there is no answer to the question, How fast is the Universe moving? The velocity of something is always relative to something else, and there isn't something else besides the Universe. It is quite difficult to find out how fast the Sun is moving relative to a star like Sirius. It is not difficult to find out how fast the Universe is moving; it is not something which a great astronomer may one day calculate: it is an absurd task because the Universe cannot have velocity.

Of course, we might one day decide to give a meaning to the phrase "the velocity of the Universe," but as it is used at present, it has no more meaning than "the sex of the Universe." It *looks* as if it has more meaning because the Universe can be split into components, each of which has a velocity. Put them all together, and it seems odd to suggest they can *lose* this property. But every Canadian has a height relative to other Canadians; put them all together, and the nation does *not* have a height relative to other Canadians.

What about our original question? Let us take it in stages. First we ask *whether* the Universe came from somewhere or something else. It appears that everything now within the Universe comes from something else: must not the Universe itself have come from somewhere or something else? Indeed not, and indeed it could not; any answer will be inappropriate because the question is improper. We can only answer by mentioning some *place* or some *thing*, natural or supernatural. But the things we mention exist themselves and hence are part of the Universe itself, and the locations we mention exist only in relation to existing things, i.e., in relation to parts of the Universe. So, whatever we are referring to will itself be part of the Universe and hence something whose origin is part of the problem at hand. The only remaining possibility appears to be that the Universe comes from within itself, is self-originating; if this does not prove to be a satisfactory answer, we must say that the original question is improper and that the Universe is not the kind of thing that comes from anywhere or anything.

Of course, if we mean by "the Universe" just the material things which make it up (on some specific definition of "material"), then it is conceivable that these things all come from some nonmaterial entity such as a God or a magnetohydrodynamic vortex. But, in the first place, the argument gives us absolutely no reason to believe this. In the second place, this conception would simply postpone by one stage the fundamental question, Where did the whole Universe ultimately come from? because in the new terminology this will simply amount to, Wherever did the God (or vortex) come from? The persuasiveness of the cosmological argument comes from the way it tricks us into thinking that the *whole* Universe *must* have come from a supernatural Being. But we can only say that the *material* Universe *may* have come from a supernatural Being. The whole Universe cannot have come from *any* (other) Being.

The only conclusion to which we are forced by this argument is that *either* the Universe provided its own origin, *or* it did not have an origin, *or* it is not the kind of thing that can possibly have an origin, just as it cannot have a location or velocity and just as the Canadian nation cannot have a height relative to the rest of the nation.

Now, does it make sense to say that the Universe "came from itself"? It is like saying that someone "owes a debt to himself"; the meaning can only be metaphorical, not literal. We might say that someone owed a debt to himself if he had promised himself a holiday after a period of hard work and had then been forced by circumstances to postpone it. "Promising to oneself" might still be said to be metaphorical, but it is a metaphor which now has a very well-understood use. Similarly we might say the Universe comes from itself if we find evidence that space regularly "condenses" into matter as steam condenses into water. This would still be explaining one metaphor with another, but it is not hard to think of evidence that would lead us to say that large volumes of space regularly produce a neutron or an electron.[14]

Now, certainly, the Universe could then be said to be *self-perpetuating,* but would this be the same as *self-originating?* Where did the *first* particle come from? From empty space? Whether or not we say it came from empty space, it seems very odd to suggest that the first particle (or even God) came from itself, since there would be nothing from which it could come until it had already come. All that would be left of the meaning of "came from itself" would be "did not come from anything else." Now if that is the only meaning we can give to self-origination, the loophole in the cosmological argument lets everything out. For we quickly saw that all the argument showed was that the Universe either came from itself or was not the kind of thing that comes from anything. And the interpretation we have now suggested of the first alternative reduces it to the second. So scrutiny of the problem of the Universe's origin quite rapidly reveals that it can have none (which is of course a much stronger conclusion than the claim that we cannot discover its origin).

Some further examination of the scientific and logical alternatives helps to clarify the inevitability and internal consistency of this answer.

The picture which dominates one's thinking about the origin of the Universe is the picture of some substance springing into existence in empty space. If that picture is realistic, then the need for an explanation of the

---

[14] As in the steady-state cosmological theory of Bondi and Gold, which led to the somewhat inappropriate name "continuous creation" for the process (more correctly, "continual creation"). The name is inappropriate because mere regular appearance is not creation. We can call it "spatial condensation" or "the mitosis of mass," terms which are rather less inappropriate. Each suggests a different kind of phenomenon, and we shall concern ourselves primarily with spatial condensation. Space-matter transformation, because it is rather less mysterious, is scientifically as digestible as mass-energy transformation or action at a distance, both once banned as absurd in the sense in which they are now accepted.

event it depicts seems inevitable. We shall see that the picture is wholly inappropriate, in some cases obviously so and in other cases for more subtle reasons.

In the first place, there is something very puzzling about the idea of space before the Universe's existence because it seems that space is space *between* and *around* things, so that "space without things" is a contradiction in terms. Now one might decide that one can give some meaning to the concept of wholly empty space,[15] or one might deny this. If one can give this concept some meaning, then it would be possible for the Universe to have come from this empty space in just the way in which particles might currently be appearing from what empty space we now have. If it is of the nature of empty space to fill itself, that would just be a law of nature like the law of gravitation and the answer to the question, Where did the Universe come from? would be, "From empty space, as matter always does." And now, at last, we can reach an end to the questions. For there is surely no need to explain where empty space came from. So here is one naturalistic possibility; space has the inherent disposition to coagulate into matter, and it is this process which has fired and fueled the Universe.

But we may not—indeed, it will be argued that we cannot—make sense of the idea of wholly empty space; or, on the other hand, we may have no reason to believe in the condensation of space into matter. The question, Where did the *first* particle come from? which seems to be the heart of our original question, would then have to be approached in a different way.

In either case, the time has come to notice that this is another example of a question with a built-in presupposition. It assumes that there had to be a first particle or particles. But there are two possible kinds of Universe where there is no first particle at all. Let us suppose that we were able to go back in the history of the Universe, making a note of the moment at which each new particle came into existence, from whatever source (space, other particles, etc.). These times will form a numerical sequence, which might look something like this:

Most recently appearing particle	5	millimicroseconds ago
Next most recently appearing particle	7	millimicroseconds ago
Third most recently appearing particle	13.6	millimicroseconds ago

Now it may simply be the case that we keep on finding earlier and earlier particles, indefinitely. The sequence will go on and on: 5, 7, 13.6, 14.01, 16, 23.4, . . . Although it is not quite so regular, this sequence is something like the sequence of even numbers: 2, 4, 6, 8, . . . That sequence has no end at all. It is surely possible that there is no end to the sequence of times when particles appeared in the Universe. In that case, the Universe

[15] *Empty space* usually means the space between or around things: *wholly empty space* would then be empty space without spatial boundaries.

had no first particle for just the reason the series of even numbers has no last member: there is always another one beyond any candidate that is put up as the last one. The Universe would, if this is the case, be infinitely old. And in this case the answer to our question, Where did the first particles in the Universe come from? would be, "The question is improper; there *were* no first particles." So, in this case, the idea that the Universe came from empty space and in that sense needs explanation is quite mistaken. The Universe, at any given stage, came from the Universe at an earlier stage, and so on. It did not have a beginning; so its beginning needs no explanation, and each of its infinitely many states has an explanation.

It is hard to grasp the idea of an infinitely old Universe. It is all very well to allow infinity in mathematics, but can there really be a physically existing infinity? One way to persuade oneself of the legitimacy of the idea is to ask oneself whether one thinks the Universe must *suddenly* come to an end. There seems to be no absolute necessity about this, and hence, turning our gaze backward in time instead of forward, there is surely no necessity for the Universe to have begun at any time. Hence it may be infinitely old.

There is a second possibility. The Universe may be only a few billion years old, and it might *still* be the case that there were no first particles.[16] This is much harder on the imagination, but it can be demonstrated easily enough. Suppose the sequence of times when the particles were formed begins to slow down after a while, instead of continuing at a more or less regular pace. It might behave like the following sequence: . . . 70, 80, 90, 95, 97.5, 98.75, 99.375, . . . This sequence, after reaching 90, proceeds in the following way; each term jumps half the gap between the last term and 100. Since 90 is 10 units from 100, half of this is 5 and the next term is 95. Similarly, 95 is 5 units from 100, and half of this is 2.5; so the next term is 97.5, and so on. It is obvious that no term will ever reach 100 (because it will always be half of the last gap away from 100). It is also obvious that there is no last term (since, given any term which was alleged to be last, we could immediately construct the next term by subtracting it from 100 and adding half of the result to it). So there would be an infinity of previous particle births—we could never exhaust the history of events in the Universe—but all this would have happened within a definite, limited time, less than 100 units of age.[17] There would have been no first particles; so we could not sensibly ask where they came from. Nevertheless, in this

[16] We talk about particles as an example; the same argument can be applied to anything, including events, fields, plasma, and gods, although not to all possible entities of these kinds.

[17] There is an interesting analogy between this case and the situation in low-temperature physics, in which we can never attain absolute zero but may find an inexhaustible range of phenomena as we get nearer and nearer.

case, it does not seem quite absurd to ask where the Universe came from, even though it consists of nothing but particles and we can explain where each of them came from. For the picture still haunts us; there is all that time before the Universe existed when there was nothing but empty space. But the two possibilities we have just been discussing are exactly alike in having no first state in their history at all and hence no stage which could be said to have come from empty space, even if one can make some sense of such an occurrence. So in neither case is a legitimate question about the origin of anything left unanswered. And this suggests that there is something peculiar about our picture, for it applies about as well to the Universe with an infinite history but a finite age as to the entirely finite Universe; in each case, there is the blank black screen and then, suddenly, *things!* And in one of these cases the picture is just misleading, for nothing that needs to be explained is unexplained. Or is that quite fair? We must now consider the picture in greater detail.

Of course, even if it is true that in [18] an entirely finite Universe some existing thing or things must in some sense have come from nothing, it is hardly plausible to call such things supernatural. There are no grounds for supposing they are supernatural in any normal sense and, in particular, no reason for thinking "they" are a single entity, as monotheism suggests. They may simply be the original neutrinos or fields which are no different from any other neutrinos except that they were the first. Since we already have the best scientific reasons for supposing that things like neutrinos and the fields exist, the most plausible view would be that some of *these* simply came into existence without cause. We only add a further mystery, not eliminate one, by introducing an entirely new kind of (supernatural) entity to create all other entities. No study of contemporary matter has shown it incapable of spontaneous generation or even no longer involved in such a process, as the steady-state model suggests.

The primitive appeal of bringing in a Creator is probably that we feel we can understand the origin of the Universe better if we say someone or something created it than if we say part of it just existed. That is, we bring in a type of explanation which is very helpful in ordinary contexts where the artist, for example, creates a work of art where none was before. But that is not creation of *matter* from nothing; it is the creation of an *arrangement* but only a transformation of materials. A creation "explanation" of the Universe is hopeless since such a creation has to be more than

[18] When we talk of God as being one of the things "in" the Universe, there is no suggestion that He would just be one of the objects of which the Universe is composed, as a wall is composed of bricks. *The Universe,* as it is here used, just means "everything that exists"; it is a label for the group of existents. If God exists, He is in that group, whether as ground for the existence of all the other members (whatever that means) or in any other role.

a rearrangement of previously existing materials by a previously existing entity. We have to pay the excessive price for this explanation of introducing a Being whose own origin is exactly as unexplained as that of the first material objects and whose nature and creative procedures are additional unfathomables. In short, the act or process of divine creation, rather than being an explanation, not only is itself unobservable and incomprehensible, with no observable effects that distinguish its product from a naturally but spontaneously originated Universe. It is also supposed to be performed by an entity whose own origin simply reintroduces the mystery which it was His function to eliminate.

A second reason for the appeal of theistic creation is perhaps that it is all right for a *mysterious* Being to have a mysterious origin, whereas this is not plausible for ordinary material things. So, instead of seeing that the introduction of a God simply substitutes two mysteries for one (the mystery of His own origin and of the way He creates matter, for the mystery of the origin of matter), we think it actually explains where the Universe came from. It is about as explanatory as telling a child who asks where the rainbow comes from that the light elves weave it. We cannot avoid the questions: "*How* do they do this?" "Where do *they* come from?"

Perhaps there is a third kind of reason that pushes us toward the theistic "answer." An inanimate first stage does not "have within itself," in any obvious way, the intelligence, beauty, and morality that later appear on the Earth. We instinctively feel that a Creator could produce *these* out of Himself. But not only does this raise the question of how He acquired the capacity to produce these properties; it is simply a logical error to suppose that what is in the effect must be in the cause in any similar form. Intelligence can evolve from unintelligent matter in a fully comprehensible way. It is a triviality that the initial state of the Universe contained the *potentiality* to "produce" intelligence; false, that it was actually intelligent.

The idea of "coming from nothing" or "just appearing" is now due for further examination. It seems to mean "came from empty space" or "from nothingness." We shall see that all that these phrases mean is "did not come from anything" or "just exists." In that case, the full answer to our original question, Where did the Universe come from? will be, "It does not come from anywhere, any more than it has a velocity or a location: it just exists."

We have already seen that the infinitely old Universe could not have anywhere to come from, even nothingness, since it occupies all past time. Yet it is here, and hence *it* must be said simply to exist. So this kind of answer is sometimes correct.

The Universe which has an infinite history but a finite age or one with a finite history and a finite age is a little trickier to handle. After all, a certain number of billion years ago it did not exist at all; then, a little later, it existed. Surely we could plausibly say it came from nothingness, from empty space? But what is the "it"? There is no first stage in the infinite-history universe; so to say the Universe just appeared is not to say that any particular state just appeared: each state came from a preceding one; none lacks a perfectly ordinary kind of explanation. All that can be meant by "just appeared" is that after a certain point in time there was a Universe; before that, none. There was no state of affairs that just appeared, and hence it is false to say that this Universe just appeared, for it is only its states and their relations that appeared. Now let us consider the fully finite Universe.

In the first place, how can one make sense of the claim that there was, at an earlier time, wholly empty space *in which* there appeared the primitive form of the Universe? Surely if something appeared, it must have appeared *somewhere*, but in wholly empty space there is no sense to the idea of a location. It is for this very reason that the concept of wholly empty space is essentially meaningless, for space that is incapable of allowing location is surely not space at all. Notice that the one scientifically acceptable use of the idea of appearing from nothing—the continual-creation cosmology—refers to events that do have a location since the hydrogen atoms appear among the other things in this Universe.

Now the picture that grips us has a temporal as well as a spatial dimension. It is not just that the first things appear in the middle of that illicit screen (illicit because it smuggles in location, via a field of view, when location is inconceivable). It is that time passes while the screen is blank and then, in that time stream, there appears the first entity. But there are also grave difficulties about the idea of there *being* any time "when" there was just empty space. Certainly we can give sense to the idea of the Universe's having a limited age: it means that every time something has happened, it has been during a limited historical period. It is tempting to suppose this is equivalent to saying that before this first event there was a time when nothing happened, "empty time," so to speak. Yet the concept of "time passing while absolutely nothing happens" is like that of space without content, or counting without units, or squares without lines: it is a self-contradiction, an empty phrase. It is not merely that there would be grave practical difficulties in telling how much time passed in the absence of any existing things; it is that there *could not* be time passing any more than there could be a view passing a train window if there was nothing outside the train. One is easily led to think there is sense to the idea of periods of time before the world began because it is easy to think of periods of time when nothing happens *in an empty container.* But it is what happens *outside the container* that makes sense of the passage of time. If there is nothing outside, there can be no sense to it. The Universe has no container, it only has contents, and if it has none of these, there is certainly nothing outside it.

It is easy to construct a *number* which is larger than the number of years in the age of the Universe and just call it "an historical date from the pre-Universe period." The interval between any two of these dates is then a period in prehistory, and so we "prove" there were times when there was nothing. But constructing a number which we call a date does not guarantee that there is a real time to which this date refers. We measure height in numbers plus the units of feet and inches, but constructing the description "—6 ft. 6 in." does not guarantee that this is a height. The meaningful numbers for height begin at zero, for temperature at —273.6°C, and for time at the time the Universe began, if it did.

Thus even the Universe of limited age does not come from nothingness, since there was no previous time and no empty space from which it could have come. It simply exists without having come from anywhere. And this will be true whether or not it has an inexhaustible history. So the answer to our original question is that the Universe is a kind of entity that exists without coming from anywhere, just as the Canadian nation is a kind of entity which exists without having a father, although both are composed entirely of things with these properties.

Of course, this kind of answer seems mentally indigestible or evasive to many people when first they hear it. Sometimes they express their difficulty by saying, "But look; the fact is that the Universe *does* exist, and there *must* be some explanation of this fact—it can't be just an *accident* that it exists." Or they may ask what *sustains* the existence of the Universe, whether finite or infinite in age,[19] or why the Universe is just the particular age that it is.

These questions raise some different points, although much of what has been said is relevant. They are really of the form, *Why* does the Universe exist? (or, Why has it existed for just *so* long?), rather than of the form, *Where* does the Universe come from? We must, of course, begin by asking ourselves whether the questions are proper questions at all. The question, Why does the Universe exist? looks like the question, Why does the Princeton Institute for Advanced Study exist? That is, it asks for the purpose or function of a complex entity. Now it is perfectly clear that the purpose or function of the Universe cannot come from its role in some external agent's plans, since there can be no such agent. Does it make sense to talk of a purpose or function conferred on the Universe by some part of it, perhaps an intelligent spiritual part of it?

Some believers in gods do see the Universe as part of the gods' plan.

---

[19] The contingency version of the argument is absolutely independent of and hence in no way refuted by the possibility of an infinitely old Universe, a fact which many critics persistently ignore, although St. Thomas Aquinas clearly saw this point and for that reason put the argument in contingency form, stating that this would apply to a Universe of finite *or* infinite age.

But our previous discussion points up the inadequacies of this kind of suggestion since it merely raises the corresponding problem about the gods: Why do the gods exist? We can hardly explain their existence by reference to supergods, since that will clearly only push the question back one further stage. So the introduction of the divine is just as useless here as before. We should see at once that there is no hope of an "ultimate" answer to the question, Why does the Universe exist? in terms of the plans of any entity. We may be part of the plans of a god or a biological experiment by aliens from another planet, but interesting though this would be if true, the gods and the aliens obviously have to answer the same question about themselves that we are raising about ourselves (or, by failing to do so, demonstrate themselves to be less intelligent than their progeny). Of course, there might be an infinite regress of planners, each one part of a higher being's plans, but for someone who begins with the idea that he wants an ultimate explanation, this step-by-step answering will not be satisfying. He must eventually recognize that his request is self-contradictory, since his insistence on an *ultimate* answer rules out every *legitimate* answer and any introduction of a "self-planning" (or "unplanned but planning") Being is simply a concession that there are things for which no external planner is necessary, i.e., a denial of his original position. And if he is prepared eventually to concede this, he must do so at the beginning and just say, "Parts of the Universe exist because of planning by other parts, but parts of it may simply exist without being part of any plan."

Now the Universe certainly functions in certain ways that are well known to scientists. For example, it expands and probably derives the energy for its expansion from certain thermonuclear processes. One might perhaps say that the Universe exists in order to fulfill these functions. But this is only a misleading way of saying that it obeys certain laws—misleading because the phrase "in order to fulfill" suggests purpose again.

Does this mean that the Universe exists by accident, by chance? Not at all: that is a false dilemma. We have argued the Universe cannot be part of a plan, but it does not follow that its existence is a chance affair. For processes *within* the Universe, these might be said to be the only alternatives,[20] but the Universe itself is not a process within the Universe. It is not the kind of entity which is created or appears, and hence the possible ways in which this might happen are not covered by the alternatives of "deliberately planned" and "accidentally occurring." Neither alternative can be given any meaning for the Universe as a whole.

But what *sustains* the existence of the Universe? After all, it exists rather than not exists, whether or however it came into existence. At any

---

[20] Even this suggestion is not very plausible. See the discussion of the teleological argument below.

specific level of inquiry, we can give specific answers to this question. At the physical level, for example, we can explain that material substances maintain their existence because of molecular bonding forces, and then we can explain these in terms of nuclear bonds, and so on. At any given stage of science, such a quest will eventually come to the frontiers of knowledge. We normally expect to find these shifting with time, but they need not shift—there may be an ultimate law or theory. Whether our explanations go on developing forever or reach some ultimate laws is irrelevant: the same conclusion applies. We know that either the sum of all the explanations or the final theory cannot itself require explanation.

It is easier to feel comfortable with this situation in the infinite-series case than when there is an ultimate law, because it is easier to see that there is something improper about the question, How do you explain *all* these explanations? than about the question, How do you explain *this* (fundamental) law? After all, why should collections of explanations themselves require explanation? But to assert of a particular law, fact, or explanation that it is immune from explanation, unlike all its predecessors in the sequence, appears inconsistent with normal scientific procedure.

This may partly explain why many scientists view with great distaste any talk about having reached the last frontiers, the ultimate laws, of physics. No doubt they also dislike this kind of talk because it subconsciously encourages apathy about further investigation. But *if* we ever knew we had one of the fundamental laws, *this* is what it means to call them fundamental. The chances are against our ever being entirely sure we have one; but in quantum theory, chances and all, we seem to have reached the insubstantial bedrock of one great structure in physical knowledge. And in the relation between the distribution of mass and the curvature of space we may have another. Even though it is easier to accept an infinite sequence of explanatory laws than a finite sequence, the logical situation does not justify any distinction; there will always be *something* about the Universe which does not require explanation of the kind we are talking about here, whether it is a whole infinite sequence or the last law of a finite one. To put this conclusion back into the language of the last paragraph, there must always be certain features of the structure of the Universe which do not depend for their existence on any other features. This is a simple consequence of the logic of explanations and is no more surprising, when understood, than the fact that when we count we have to begin with some number. When we set out to explain the Universe, we have to begin somewhere unless it so happens that the Universe is infinitely complex, in which case we never find or need an ultimate starting point. There is no point in asking *why* the chain of explanations does not have a beginning, if it does not; or why it has *this* beginning rather than another, if it has this beginning;

or why it is only as old as it is, if it is only that old, for we have passed into the realm where explanations are no longer indigenous. Suppose someone asks *exactly* how many times 0 goes into 1. There is no answer, because even an infinity of zeros will not make up 1 and certainly no finite number will. For any finite divisor of 1, like ½, ¼, or ⅛, no matter how small it is (that is, no matter how close to 0 it is), there is an exact answer; but for 0 itself there is no answer at all. Some questions just do not make sense in the limit, and so it is with the present question, Why does the Universe exist? If it is pushed to the limit and answers about the function and relation of the parts of the Universe are rejected, it simply becomes an improper question.

One cannot expect someone who encounters these suggestions for the first time to find them so clear and convincing that he will never again have the feeling that there really is something about the existence of the Universe that needs explaining even when all the scientific accounts have been given or their inexhaustibility has been recognized. One cannot alter the mental habits of many years overnight. The situation is very like that in the early days of relativity theory and non-Euclidean geometry. The ideas of an absolute space and time and of Euclidean geometry were so deeply ingrained in the mind of those best qualified to study the new theories that they often refused to regard the new ideas as sensible. The idea that space may be finite in volume but without boundaries, to take one example, is extremely indigestible at first. It must be explored, discussed, examined, and compared with other ideas; it must be worked with until its potentialities have been thoroughly understood and can then be evaluated. Eventually it comes to be seen as a new conceptual tool, a liberating break-through in our patterns of thought. It may be hoped that mature reflection on the simpler suggestions discussed here will convert their alien inevitability into a natural grace.

To sum up the difficulties with the cosmological argument, (1) there is no necessity for there to be any uncaused state in the history of the Universe, since there may be an infinity of caused states; (2) there would be an uncaused first state of a Universe with a finite history, but this does not constitute an incompleteness in our understanding, since the idea that a causal account is possible or needed for that first state is indefensible (and the same can be said of the infinite totality of states in case 1); and (3) in particular, there is no apparent reason to suppose that the uncaused state (or the infinity of states) has any of the moral, intellectual, or supernatural properties of God.[21]

[21] There can be a Universe with an infinite history, a finite age, and a first state (if we add the lower bound to the states in an infinite bounded sequence). This does not merit separate discussion.

6.1-1B *The Prime Mover argument* (*argument from motion*)

Statement of the argument. Things move; generally they derive their motion from the motion of other things, but it is impossible that everything should have derived its motion in this way, for else there would be no motion at all. So there must be an entity whose motion is not derived from the motions of other entities; this is the Prime Mover, God.

Assessment of the argument. This argument, which is closely analogous to the cosmological,[22] perhaps more clearly trespasses across the boundary from logic into science. There is no logical reason why spontaneous slow or sudden decay of matter could not lead to its collapse and hence to motion. Moreover, there is no reason why the original state of the Universe could not be one involving relative motion of its parts. And there is no reason why there could not be an infinite sequence of stages in the history of the Universe, each passing on its motion to the next. Finally, there is no reason why the situation in which there does happen to be a first state containing unmoved movers should be regarded as having the remotest religious significance.

6.1-1C *The teleological argument* (*argument from design*)

Statement of the argument. The properties and behavior of many things in the Universe, whether they are different parts of the same thing or different things, are highly coordinated with each other in their attempt or tendency to attain certain goals. The mind and limbs of a hunter, the stages in the evolution of the eye, the colors of a camouflaged butterfly and that of the bark on which it normally rests to avoid its enemies, and the curious property of water that prevents natural bodies of water from freezing solid in the winter and killing the fish therein are commonly offered examples. It seems that these coordinations could not be accidental but must be a part of a master plan for the well-ordering of life and objects on the Earth, and there has to be a planner for a plan. This Planner is God.

Assessment of the argument. The first weakness in this argument is the assumption that highly organized results, even those occurring in a pattern involving a goal state, must be due to a plan. They may in fact be due to the operation of either natural laws or chance, or both. The extraordinary coincidence between the positioning of stalactites and stalagmites in the great limestone caverns, such that there is always one directly below the other, is not due to chance nor to a plan; it is due to the fact that the lower one is formed by the water dripping off the upper one. The remarkable distribution of numbers in the results from an unbiased roulette wheel, such that there is a closer and closer approximation to the same

---

[22] As are several other arguments not discussed here precisely because they raise no new points.

proportion of each possibility the longer this random machine operates, is purely due to chance; indeed it is the very evidence that only chance is operating. The interlocking patterns in the world of living creatures are simply the result of the laws of natural selection operating on the random mutations of genes; chance produces the initial variation, and natural selection, i.e., their suitability to their environment, determines whether they stay around long enough to reproduce or reproduce more effectively than the other forms then present. Consequently, the forms that do survive exhibit considerable suitability for their environment. The argument from "design" is simply a fallacious argument from *functional order* to a *designer;* it is fallacious because there is a much better explanation of the order, namely, the operation of evolution. This is a much better explanation because it involves only claims that can easily be supported by evidence and follows immediately from these claims. We can even demonstrate the evolutionary process in a laboratory, controlling its rate and modifying the direction it takes by manipulating the conditions (energy supply, population density, mutation rate, etc.). At this stage in the history of science it seems entirely clear that this *is* the explanation. Hence, introducing any new and hitherto-unknown entities such as a supernatural planner is entirely indefensible.

The steps in the evolution of inorganic chemicals into organisms are now as unmysterious as the steps in the evolution of man from simple organisms, and we may refer to the combination of both processes as the evolution of man from nonlife. The first of these steps is perhaps the most important for the teleological argument since it bridges the gap from the clearly nonpurposive to the clearly purposive. For those unfamiliar with the research, the basic process is the shuffling around of inorganic ions in water, with the action of wind, evaporation, and lightning discharges, which eventually results in their linking up end to end into long-chain organic molecules; these then act as templates to which similar ions attach themselves laterally until a second chain forms alongside the first, from which it is separated by physical or electrical shock, giving the beginning of the reproductive process. And now the competition for survival of various organic compounds formed in this way begins, in terms of their relative stability, speed of formation in the "soup," etc.; eventually some of these systems build up some internal articulation, component coordination, and transformational feeding—and life is on its way.

The supporter of the teleological argument does not usually give up at this point. He will say that we have merely pushed the difficulty one stage farther back. The question now becomes, Why are the *laws of nature* and the *properties of matter* such as to produce the remarkable patterning that we observe? The argument does not assert that the Planner intervenes at the last step in the process of planning, only that the order in the final product requires that there be a planner somewhere. Behind the superficially random operation of the roulette wheel, there is actually the operation of other laws of whose nature and application we are not aware at the time we spin the wheel. Our ignorance leads us to call the result random, but fundamentally this process, too, is one exhibiting design. If we achieved an historically complete account of contemporary order, carrying it back to an originally existing mass of plasma (or whatever it was, if it was), the question becomes, Where did *that* material get *its* special properties, such that the intelligent activity and coordinated properties of contemporary things were able to evolve from them? And if the Universe had no beginning, the question still arises about the particular laws that it obeys.

This move is not simply an extension of the original point but a shift to quite a different and wholly dubious arena for the argument. For at first we asked for an explanation of certain effects in the world of nature which are clearly present. And such explanations are commonly given—as they can be in this case—by appealing to the nature of the entities involved and the laws governing their behavior. We can even explain some of these laws and properties in terms of other laws and properties. But the request to explain the ultimate laws and properties, or *all* the laws and properties *together,* is just like the misguided request to explain the existence of the first material state or of an infinite totality of states (which we discussed in connection with the cosmological argument). If this still seems arbitrary, let us examine what happens if we are more permissive.

Suppose there is a Designer. It appears that He will Himself be an existing (or once-existing) entity of considerable complexity, containing within Himself the potentiality of producing all the complex properties that emerge in the order that we eventually see. Where did He get that complex order or potentiality of His own? Either it came from somewhere else, and so on to infinity, or we admit that there is at least one complex (or complexity-generating) intelligent entity whose nature does not require explanation. Both possibilities ruin the original argument.

If it is acceptable to think of the search for the explanation of functional order producing an infinite series of answers, then there is no need to bring in a designer at all. And if we are to say that all order comes from a designer but that his own properties do not come from any other source at all, then we might as well admit from the beginning that there can be entities whose design does not require any further explanation; and if that is so, then the most obvious candidate for this exceptional status is the primordial matter of the Universe's earliest state, if there was one (or its ageless governing laws, if not). From these properties we can, in principle, give a scientific account of the development of all stages in the Universe's history, including that of its living denizens. And fundamental properties are not themselves subject to explanation, simply because there is nothing else in terms of which it could make sense to explain them.[23] (At this point we achieve an identity between one form of the teleological and one form of the cosmological arguments.) To introduce a designer is simply to postpone the problem one stage *and* to saddle oneself with a surplus entity—the old story.

But, the theist is sometimes heard to say, surely it cannot be absurd to be asking why the world was initially just the right way to bring about the present state of affairs rather than some other state—surely *that* isn't an accident: it is a clear case of one alternative's occurring, when others might have, which is just the kind of phenomenon that we seek to explain scientifically.

This version of the question involves another assumption and a very familiar one at that; it is the assumption that the world was arranged to bring *us* about. But if the world exists at all, it has to have *some properties*. These might have been such as to lead to no sensate beings, indeed to no coagulations of matter at all; it so happens that that is not the way things were, for otherwise there would be no one to discuss the teleological argument. But there did not have to be anyone to discuss teleology; so there does not have to be a reason why there is or why there are sensate beings at all, in the sense of an overriding plan. What happened is just one of the possibilities. If we decide to throw a die ten times, it is then guaranteed that a particular one of the 6^{10} possible combinations of ten throws is going to occur. Each of them is equally likely; each of them is entirely distinct from each other possibility. And each of them, if we study it closely, has interesting properties. Now it would be pretty silly for the combination that happens to come up, to sit and look at itself and suggest that there had to be a designer who deliberately manipulated the fall of the die in order to bring about the particular combination that did occur. The request for an explanation in terms of planning in such cases is appropriate only when what occurs is *contrary* to the laws of chance. It is not contrary to the laws of chance that there should be intelligence in the Universe any more than it is puzzling that an unbiased die should throw the series 1, 2, 3, 4, 5, 6, 1, 2, 3, 4. It would be very puzzling if this happened many times in a row, but there are not several universes in a row: there is only one. That one happens to have some order as well as some disorder. Why does it have some order? Because it has to have some properties to exist, and it happens to have these.

[23] In fact, explanations are not simply one-way affairs, and the picture of a stopping point is unrealistic. There is no terminus because the system of explanations is a net and not a chain. (Similarly, in the cosmological argument, there are loopholes we have not explored—the possibility of closed rather than linear times, for example, which makes a first cause impossible.) But let us make it as hard for ourselves as possible; even then, the argument does not work.

Still, this leaves one with the impression that we are accepting a cosmic accident without questioning. But it is misleading to talk of this as a matter of accident rather than as a matter of design, since the possibility of design is absolutely meaningless with respect to the Universe. To call the Universe an accident suggests that it *might* have been planned but was not. This does sound odd; the truth is simpler—the Universe isn't the kind of thing that occurs, or is the way it is, either by design or by accident. It just is.

Could there have been a designer? Indeed there could have been one; our brief career may be the laboratory project of some Ph.D. student in the exobiology department of a university on a distant planet in a distant galaxy, or it may be remedial play for some retarded third grader. But such a designer is not the designer of the *Universe*. He would in his turn require a designer if the argument from design were sound. Could there have been a (capitalized) Designer? Indeed there could, if by this we mean a Being which gave form to all the Universe and which derived its own form from nothing outside itself. But there is absolutely no reason to think that there ever was such a Being, and the argument from design in no way supports the idea that there was. For the argument's own assumptions would require us to demand an answer to the question of the origin of the Designer. And the very conception of such a Being is fraught with conceptual problems; it is just another mythical entity, which appears to help but turns out neither to be required to explain the order we can see nor to be capable of explaining it without introducing more puzzles than it solves and so not to be in any way likely to have existed.

And even if it had at one time existed, there would be no reason why it should exist any longer, no reason to think that it must be good, or powerful enough to intervene in the workings of its design once it has been set going, or able to foresee the outcome of its designing activities. In short, a Designer is not the same as God, and the teleological argument lends no support at all to the claim that there was a Designer.

6.1-1D *The argument from the efficacy of reason*

Statement of the argument. One of the more striking arguments attempts to show that the very act of criticizing the arguments is self-refuting and God-supporting. How do we criticize the arguments? By using our reason. Why should we trust our reason? From long experience we have discovered that it gives us reliable indications of how reality will turn out. How can the operation of the human reason (or of the brain on which it depends) be a reliable guide to the operations of the rest of the world? Surely not by chance alone. It could not be mere chance that there is a close relationship between the outcome of the mental processes leading to a prediction and the events predicted; it must instead be due to prior arrangement by some master planner—indeed the very Planner whose existence the skeptic so arrogantly attempts to disprove!

Assessment of the argument. Of course this argument blatantly ignores the alternative that every biologist today would think of: the fact that organisms are constantly modified by their environment in the processes called learning and evolution. It is indeed *not* chance that the brain's predictions work; it is the result of 1 million years of development, which produces the ability, and years of learning that convert it into a working skill. Brains that did not work during that million years did not consistently survive, and the ones that do not learn now survive with difficulty, if at all. Brains that did work efficiently, i.e., in harmony with reality, not only survived but reproduced themselves through the mechanism of heredity, and thus there evolved the present modest achievement of human reason. Improvement for 1 million years is not mere chance, and it is not a miracle; it is the pedestrian operation of natural forces. And it completely explains the efficacy of reason, such as it is.

6.1-1E *The argument from justice*

Statement of the argument. It is clear that in this world the just do not always get their due reward and the wicked often go unpunished. The balance must therefore be redressed in the hereafter by the Great Judge, which is God.

Assessment of the argument. This argument probably packs more punch in a pint-sized package than any three of the others. It not only attempts to prove the existence of God in two sentences, but on the way it establishes the existence of life after death and makes three assumptions of such enormous magnitude as completely to undercut its conclusions.

The first assumption is that operating in the Universe is a Principle of Conservation of Justice such that deficiences in one part of the Universe must be made up by surpluses elsewhere. This is so confidently maintained that the argument unhesitatingly insists upon the existence of another phase of the Universe, the "next world," to provide room for the compensating process, since it evidently does not occur in the section we can see. Unfortunately, before we can use a principle like this to do such important work we have to check its references. What is the independent evidence for this principle? It will not do any good to say that it is needed to ensure that justice is done, since that is exactly what we are wondering about. Maybe the Universe is just one of those places where things do not always go right, with respect to justice as well as horse races. Maybe injustice can only be corrected on the Earth, and there is no hereafter where it will be fixed up. This is not such a comforting arrangement; but it may be a more grown-up way of thinking about the world, and it is certainly more likely on the available evidence.

The second assumption is that redressing such a balance of injustice would require a divine personality. There is no reason to think that such an arrangement might not be part of the way the Universe naturally and impersonally works. Even if we were to be persuaded that the Universe operates on a principle of moral conservation, that is no guarantee that someone has to be running it.

The third assumption is that a Redresser of wrongs and Rewarder of Righteousness has any power over this world, that is, is God. Such tidying up may occur *only* in the hereafter. So the argument is not tied to a key element in the concept of God, His presence, and is thus not only wildly invalid but partly irrelevant.

6.1-1F *The argument from morality* (*naïve form*)

Statement of the argument. Many people have an acute moral sense, which could not be explained in the way that we can explain the ordinary senses of sight and touch, for the moral sense is not responding to physical stimulation in that kind of way. It must have been implanted for our guidance by some higher Being, concerned with our welfare and anxious that we should have guidance in our behavior.

Assessment of the argument. Some of the arguments simply compete with alternative explanations of the same facts, and when the alternative is a simple and satisfactory one in terms of some well-known mechanisms of a material or psychological kind, the argument is of no value at all. So it is here; the "instinctive" response to moral situations is too easily explicable in terms of the training of the individual throughout his childhood and is so like many other "instinctive" responses, such as those to artistic creations, to cooking of various flavors and substance, and to skin color or facial bone structure, that it is now hard to believe that anyone should have thought it so puzzling as to require a supernatural explanation.

The best attempts to strengthen the argument involve a move of the following kind: A moral rule is more than a prudential rule, and only behavior that obeys the latter kind can be explained naturalistically, for only such behavior is adaptive (i.e., survival-oriented). But the assumption in this move is simply without foundation; human beings can be conditioned to or may inherit wholly irrational patterns of behavior, as well as moral behavior which is not wholly irrational and not even maladaptive in evolutionary terms, since it is oriented to the survival of the race.

It is not even important to settle the question whether we are justified in calling the moral response instinctive in a precise sense; if it really is inborn, which is almost certainly true only to a limited degree, if at all, this would still present no serious difficulty. There are many examples in nature of inborn responses to complex situations which, since Darwin, it would be absurd to regard as divinely originated, such as the nest-building behavior of birds or the predator-recognition responses of ducklings. We need look no further than evolutionary theory for an explanation of such patterns of behavior. As a matter of fact, there is enough diversity of moral response between different human beings, at some levels, to found an argument for the existence of a Moral Confuser rather than a Moral Guide. For completeness' sake, one must point out again that any entity whose existence was established by this argument would lack much of being the God of our fathers (He could be impotent, dead, and so on) and would have to be shown to be Him by some further argument which no one has yet succeeded in formulating.

6.1-1G *The argument from morality (sophisticated version)*

Statement of the argument. It is a logically necessary presupposition, for moral language to make sense, that there should be an objective reality which is the source and enforcer of morality. Since no such source is evident and moral language does make sense, there must be a next world or a higher reality containing the Source of all good and a Judge who arranges true justice.

Assessment of the argument. Surely moral language could be objective and concern ideals that are not in fact realized anywhere, although we strive toward them (or at least some of us think we see good reasons for striving toward them). For comparison, we might think of the language of geometry. No one can draw perfect circles, but we know what properties they have and we can evaluate actual circles as more or less perfect. So perfect circles do not exist, but the conception provides us with an objective standard nonetheless. Moral evaluation is likewise possible without the existence of a morally perfect Being. And the deficiencies of the argument for justice apply to the suggestion that there must be a Supreme Judge who balances the moral ledger.

There is another version of the defense here which has particularly appealed to philosophically trained theists. The suggestion has been that moral rules are essentialy *imperatives*: they hold whether or not we are thinking of them, and the only possible basis for imperatives is an entity whose imperatives they are.

While it is true that moral rules are not in some *simple* way equivalent to factual statements, it does not follow that they cannot be adequately founded on factual statements in a *complicated* way (as is attempted later in this book). Whether they can or cannot be so founded, the analogy with imperatives is only an analogy. "Killing for pleasure is wrong" is not the same as, though it may imply and it may be useful to think of it as very like, "Do not kill for pleasure." The analogy with nonmoral evaluative statements like "Soldering stainless steel with ordinary rosin-core solder is wrong" is much better. In particular, the analogy with imperatives is not nearly close enough to justify the conclusion that an Imperator is required; it is not even clear that one is required for imperatives.

6.1-1H *The arguments from truth, beauty, reality, perfection (the general form of the argument from values)*

Statement of the arguments.   Some people have a sense of truth, beauty, reality, and perfection, and this cannot be explained unless there is some external source of the standards to which they are responding.

Assessment of the arguments.   The learned responses to claims, art objects, etc., which we label by the words "true," "beautiful," etc., are not simple reactions to the presence of a simple property but a complex reaction to many features of the object of assessment. But there is not the least difficulty in accommodating this kind of learning in a psychological theory, and there are no grounds whatsoever for arguing that it bespeaks external injection. Even if it did, there would be in this (as in the preceding and subsequent arguments) further steps in the proof for which it is extremely difficult to give any support, for the Originator of the aesthetic sense is not at all obviously either good, powerful, or present.

6.1-1I, 6.1-1J *The argument from comparative value and the argument from diversity (the henological argument)*

Statement of the arguments.   Some things are commonly said to be *less* true, perfect, etc., than other things; and *many* things are said to have these properties in some degree. For there to be scales of comparative merit there must be an entity that has all these properties in perfect form; and for there to be multiple instances of a property, there must be an entity in which it is unified. The perfect exemplification and unity which is thus called for is God.

Assessment of the arguments.   The implausible logic on which these arguments rest has so little appeal that they have been out of style since logic began its modern development. They are included only for completeness' sake and as an exercise for the reader.

6.1-1K *The argument from Scripture*

Statement of the argument.   The Holy Writ, whether it be the Old or the New Testament, the Koran, or that of some other religion, tells of events of a supernatural kind and reports many claims by its holy figures to represent supernatural forces. We may conclude from the reliability of these sources that these claims are to be accepted.

Assessment of the argument.   Suppose we are about to reexamine the records of an incident in the Second World War in which a group of men were alleged to have displayed cowardice during a night patrol. They claim to have been attacked by and to have been running from extraterrestrial beings in a flying saucer. It is an incident which has since been much publicized; the men concerned have been tried for their part in it and much was published and spoken in their defense. No records survive other than their own recollections, recorded only when the case came up many years later; they were all aware of earlier similar claims of extraterrestrial contact, many turning out to be false alarms. What kind of confidence can we have in their account? None. We are not in a position to deny it flatly, but it would be absurd to accept it as if it were good evidence for what they say happened. They embody almost every property of the unreliable witness, and they are speaking many years after the event. As a basis for changing views that we have on all other occasions found to be true about the world it is entirely insignificant. Of course, it is a hint that there may be or may have been something on Earth that we have not yet fully understood, the kind of hint that is always a stimulus to the open and probing mind. The investigation of such claims and their contemporary equivalents is indeed an interesting quest and is chiefly the concern of parapsychology.

When we turn to the Christian analogue, it would be surprising if there were not an historical teacher called Jesus and almost as surprising if he were not an unusually gifted psychic (i.e., psychosomatic) healer. Beyond that, the probabilities begin to count against the claims of the New Testament. Some of the miracles are easier to reconstruct than others, but none of them is any more impressive than the accounts of mighty works to be found in a hundred other places, referring to later and less distant lands and leaders. Just as the Christian disregards these, so the neutral observer must disregard them all, for they have such poor support evidentially, and their interpretation is so close to the emotional springs of the observers, that one familiar with the effect of emotion on perception would think ten times the number of reported miracles no indication of their actual occurrence. Similarly, the suggestion that the Bible is self-validating because the predictions of the Old Testament prophets are fulfilled by the New Testament events is based on inadequate exposure to the predictions of astrologers and others whose apparent success is impressive but whose only insight is into the normal frequencies of various events in human behavior and the value of ambiguity. *In the long run* they are almost certain to appear to do very well. But so would (and in practice so does) anyone who deliberately attempts such a performance; and, of course, both are helped by the psychological tendency of the audience to notice the successes to a greater degree than the failures. In sum, the assessment of Scriptural evidence is an exceedingly technical task; and the expertise required is not simply Biblical scholarship but familiarity with the psychology of belief, the sources of perceptual and recall error, and the relative frequency of such reports and confirmation of them in both religious and secular contexts.

Apart from the question of the happenings reported in the Bible, which are like in kind to those discussed under the heading of the argument from miracles below, there are the remarks by Jesus about his own relation to the Almighty. These are perfectly natural explanations for a man to suggest who discovers himself to have remarkable powers and believes that there is a God with even more remarkable powers; he modestly sees himself as a chosen instrument, as merely the transmitter of powers that come from beyond himself. It is, after all, exactly what the leader of almost every sect from the dawn of time has said, and honestly enough. Yet honesty and modesty are not enough to generate truth, and we have to ask whether there is not a better explanation of the performances that actually occurred; but of course we have no way of being even reasonably sure what these were. It would be wildly premature to invoke God, even if the Biblical descriptions were literally true, which is fantastically improbable. As things stand, the Biblical record provides no kind of foundation for supernaturalism, though there is a great deal that encourages morality and possibly research into the limits of human powers, for quite certainly we have not yet learned to heal where we could heal or to master the strength which some of us exhibit in rare moments of stress.

6.1-1L *The argument from religious experience*

Statement of the argument.   We have already discussed this argument implicitly in Chapter I and again in the introductory part of this chapter, for it is the claim to direct, rather than inferential, knowledge of the existence of God. The argument may be stated defensively or aggressively, either as the claim to a private experience from which no conclusions are supposed to follow for anyone else or as the claim that there are certain gifted people in this field, as in music or the other arts, who should be believed because of their conviction, the agreement between them, or the reliability with which they are able to tell us about some aspect of life.

Assessment of the argument.   Supporters of the argument often think that doubting it is like doubting the word of an otherwise honest person; after all, if someone you trust tells you that he has seen an ivory-billed woodpecker during a trip deep into the swamps of Florida, who are you to be sure he was mistaken, even though the species is known to be very rare? But there is no similarity between the cases. What one sees in the swamps is seen with one's eyes, and the reliability of one's eyes is constantly being checked. We would certainly not believe a person's report if he were known to be half blind. Furthermore, the specific skill of recognizing birds would need and can be given definite, positive support. Is it absolutely certain that your friend would not take a pileated for an ivory-billed woodpecker, which, after all, he had never seen previously? We would expect him to be highly reliable in identifying unmarked photographs of the two species, for example. Much of this implicit testing we forget because much of it is so well entrenched in the ordinary procedure of survival in our daily life that we do not think of it as a part of a testing program. But it is an essential part of the grounds for accepting visual reports of unusual experiences.

When it comes to accepting reports that involve some alleged *new* sense that has never been tested in the routine of daily life, special tests must be passed before *anyone* has any grounds for thinking the reports reliable. It is easy for someone to imagine that he saw something he did not see; it is even easier for him to "sense that some presence is nigh," to use a common description of the religious experience, for the sense that gives him this report is not one with the built-in training of our usual senses and is all the easier for the emotions to use as a projection screen.

That the millions who are brought up in a nervous and stress-provoking world and taught the tradition of religious experience and symbolism should produce thousands who claim to have had religious experiences is not surprising but entirely to be expected. Such experiences do not confirm each other in the way that the reports of independent judges do, for each of the people involved has a background containing the same elements which are projected into the emotional religious experience just as into the dreams, art, and literature of that culture. In the old days, the days of the Old Testament, those who saw God brought back a prophecy, and the children of Israel knew they spoke truly, for their prophecies were fulfilled, according to Scripture. But the God of those tales, if ever He was here, is not dispensing prophecies now; so the success of His prophets no longer provides any reason to think He is here. Therefore, we cannot suppose that those who think they have experienced His presence are any more reliable guides than those who have seen the great vision of the Universe as a mighty engine at last delivering itself of man, who turns to drive it faster still, a noble and natural conception.

6.1-1M *The argument from hope*

Statement of the argument. It is inconceivable that the millions who hope that God is nigh should be disappointed.

Assessment of the argument. This is another curiosity from the old war chests of the evangelists, still to be found often enough in the lay context. It is an elevation of wish fulfillment to the status of an axiom. "I wish; therefore I am right." Alas, no. "I wish; therefore there is an explanation of why I wish." Very probably true, and very unexciting. There is a close connection with the next argument.

6.1-2 *God's existence as the best explanation of certain alleged facts*

6.1-2A *The argument from agreement* (*e consensu gentium*)

Statement of the argument. The peoples of the world have always believed in gods, and such a remarkable degree of agreement *must* be more than chance: it can be plausibly explained only as a sign of the actual presence of a God.

Assessment of the argument.   One possible explanation of wide agreement on a claim is that the claim is really true and that its truth is readily recognized. This is why people agree that our arms are attached to our shoulders. Another explanation of agreement is that those who agree have been told the claim is true by men who should know and would not lie. This was the situation with the old belief that the sea off the African coast was boiling. Another explanation is that there seems to be good evidence for the belief, although in fact the reasons are not good. To this category belonged the beliefs that the Earth is stationary and flat.

If grave objections arise to apparently plausible arguments that have, up to a certain moment, been widely accepted as establishing a conclusion, then they can hardly be met by appealing to the popularity of the belief. That popularity is easily explained, whether the belief is true or not, by the fact that it *seems* well supported. What we have to decide is whether it *is* well supported, and that means reexamining the usual reasons.

So the agreement on theism, which is actually so far from universal as probably to be a minority belief today, tells us nothing about its truth, since this is not a matter in which the simple perception or reasoning for which the untrained person is highly reliable is adequate.

Suppose that today, when education is more widespread than ever before, theism is a minority belief in the world. We could reverse the argument and use it to "prove" the *nonexistence* of God. ("As education becomes better and more general, theism becomes less widespread. . . .") But a Western Christian would immediately object that the atheism of the Socialist states is not spontaneous, being rather the result of propaganda and restrictions from a central government. Then he has admitted the irrelevance of agreement when an alternative explanation of the agreement can be given, and, of course, we can give several alternative explanations of the moderate agreement on theism of Westerners. Counting heads is not a good guide to the truth, as the *early* Christians were proud to acknowledge.

6.1-2B *The argument from miracles*

Statement of the argument.   Miracles have occurred and can be reasonably explained only as acts of a God.

Assessment of the argument.   There are three types of definition of *miracle*. A miracle may be defined as an unexplained event, an inexplicable event, or an act of supernatural intervention into the natural order of events. The first definition makes every unsolved crime an act of God, which seems a shade sacrilegious. The second guarantees a god in any gambling world,[24] which seems a shade optimistic. The third definition is the important one. But the evidence for the occurrence of miracles in *this* sense is in an unhappy state. We have discussed the deficiencies of the Scriptural record as a proof of miracles at that time. The records of recent miracles are slightly more thorough but no more encouraging to the critical investigator. Let us consider "miraculous cures" as a typical class of supposed miracles.

First, it must be stressed that faith healing is a commonplace and exciting phenomenon, both within the churches (especially in the Christian Science church) and outside, a phenomenon about which far too little is known. The medical profession objects to it or denies its existence under the title of faith healing but acknowledges its potency as "the bedside manner," "the placebo effect," or "suggestibility phenomena." Its success depends, not on the *truth* of the sacred or profane convictions of the patient, but merely on their existence. "Only believe and ye shall be saved" is a very profound truth, naturalistically interpreted. So, even if faith healing were inexplicable, it is not a support for supernaturalism but a commonplace of secular medicine.

Second, if we adopt a stricter notion of miracles than this, we cannot fail to note the minute number of serious candidates that have occurred in recent times, which increases the probability that they are mistakenly diagnosed as such, since there is always a small chance of error (hallucination, lying, etc.).

Third, when we examine such records as are available, we discover an astonishingly *trivial* collection of cures. Of the half-million or so visitors to Lourdes in a given year, only a tiny handful are identified as benefiting from miraculous cures by the two committees (medical and theological) that the Roman Catholic Church has appointed for this purpose. Among these, the evidence available for the common arthritic crippling cases often involves "before-and-after" X rays showing the same bone structure, so that the reported long-term lockage of the joints can be thought of as psychosomatic even if not psychogenic. Where the closing of a fistula or the cessation of hemorrhage or discharge is an element of the miracle, we are again dealing with physiological activities that are already known to be on the borderline of nervous control, and we may regard the cures as demonstrations of

[24] A gambling world is one in which the laws of nature are ultimately statistical rather than deterministic. On the best current interpretation of quantum theory we live in a gambling world. This has the consequence that certain individual events in the world of fundamental particles cannot be predicted and perhaps in certain respects cannot be explained to the degree of precision that we can measure. But this in no way supports the view that there is a supernatural agency whose actions account for the inexplicable residue of physical behavior; indeed, it makes it almost impossible.

great promise for the future of psychosomatic medicine. But the suggestion that we could build a case for divine suspension of otherwise exceptionless physiological laws, rather than for some extension of the psychosomatic domain, can be based only on hope.

When we turn to the carnival side-show kind of miracle that gets on the news wire every few years, the bleeding statues, the Virgins-in-the-sky and unfading-crowns-of-roses performances, we come up against a truly profound absence of any evidence that is based on careful examination by those with extensive knowledge of similar cases and the usual down-to-earth explanations. But we are also struck by a feature of many "miracles" which has led some theologians to dismiss them and even warn of possible heresy in thus naming them. While it may be thought a shade melodramatic for the Good Shepherd to be speaking from the whirlwind, writing on the rocks with letters of fire, or turning back the waters of the seas to save His children, it is inconceivably insulting to suppose that He is now reduced to the present minor meddling in medical marginalia. As a sign of His presence, these performances are indecipherable; as a reward, unjust; and as a contribution to the reduction of suffering, derisory. Far from being explicable only in terms of God's intervention, the contemporary "miracles" are wholly inexplicable in those terms.

6.1-2C *The argument from revelation*

Statement of the argument. Some people have been fortunate enough to have had the existence of God revealed to them; hence for them (and, to the extent they are trustworthy, for us also) His existence is incontrovertible.

Assessment of the argument. This is simply the question-begging form of the argument for religious experience. Instead of accepting the fact of religious experience and asking whether the theistic hypothesis is the best explanation of it, the critic here simply asks for the evidence that people have really had the existence of God revealed to them. No account of their experience by itself can contribute to the argument in any way; there must be some independent evidence of its veracity or their expertise. And this is notably absent.

6.1-2D *The argument from the greater happiness of the converted* (*reward version*)

Statement of the argument. The greater happiness of the converted can be most plausibly interpreted as a reward from God to the believer, or as evidence that His way is best and hence that He must exist.

Assessment of the argument. To this argument we may reply as follows: First, there is no evidence that the premise is sound, since the world contains and has always contained vast numbers of men who do not accept any given faith or any theistic faith at all and in these vast numbers there does not appear to be a greater proportion of unhappy men than in the multitudes of believers. Second, even if there was any evidence that belief in God brings happiness, this would hardly show that there was a God, unless one makes the assumption that the believers' happiness could be explained *only* as a divine reward for their belief. In fact, it is easy to see that there is another and more natural explanation for this supposed effect, namely, that the mere belief makes them happier, just as the belief of members of a football team that their team is the best in the country may make them feel and play better even if it does not make the team the best, i.e., even though it is not true.

Moreover, it is difficult to work out what the function of this supposed reward could be. It can hardly be intended as a beacon to attract others, for it is so doubtful whether it exists that the only instrument for detecting its presence that God has given man, that is, his reason, does not give a clear indication that it is there. So what is God rewarding the believer *for?* Unless some of the arguments for theism are correct, the reward is essentially for ignorant luck or bad reasoning. If some of the arguments do work, it is so difficult to see that they do that the uneducated will have to be rewarded for luck or penalized for their misfortune or incapacity.

So the happiness is not a reward; but neither can it be evidence of God's existence for any other reason, since the counterexplanation (in terms of the mere belief's being the cause of the happiness) cannot be ruled out.

So this argument is rather strikingly lacking in merit, beginning as it does from an unsubstantiated claim and proceeding by an invalid inference to a conclusion which appears to imply that God is running a gaming room.

6.1-3 *An argument for the existence of God as the result of a certain definition of God*

6.1-3A *The ontological argument*

Introduction and statement of the argument. Perhaps the most fascinating argument of all, this claims to establish God's existence from a mere definition. Such establishment would be a spectacular achievement if the definition were acceptable and the proof watertight, since there could be no possibility of factual discoveries' undermining its conclusions. The cosmological argument's first premise, that something exists, is impregnable, but the foundation of the ontological argument would be even stronger. The argument has had a checkered career. Although proposed by St. Anselm, it is currently not accepted by Roman Catholic theologians. Curiously enough, some contemporary analytical philosophers have come to esteem certain forms of it more than any other argument or even to accept it as sound, and the usual summaries in histories of philosophy of Kant's "definitive criticisms" are certainly inadequate to refute every sophisticated version of it.

One form of the argument is this:

1. God is, by definition, the most perfect possible entity (i.e., the entirely or fully perfect entity).
2. An entity would be less than perfect if it did not exist.
Therefore, God exists.

Premise 1 is a reasonably plausible definition of God, although we would have to be shown how to get His usual properties out of it. Premise 2 clearly requires some defense.

A version of great historical importance, which incorporates a partial defense of the second premise, is this:

1. God is that Being than which no greater can be conceived.
2. If God did not exist, we could conceive an entity with all His properties which also existed, and such a Being would then be a greater Being than God, which is impossible.
Therefore, God must exist.

The most important feature of the argument, logically speaking, is the fact that it attempts to proceed from a mere definition to a conclusion about what really exists; this will be discussed first, before questioning the second premise. The discussion will be aimed at showing that there is a shift of meaning in the argument; the sense of the conclusion in which the argument is valid is not a sense in which the conclusion establishes the existence of a supernatural Being. The recent reformulations of the argument which have found some support turn out, on close examination, to be different from these only in adding additional dubious premises and in concluding that God's existence is not only provable but provably necessary. The treatment that follows is powerful enough to handle the stronger forms, even if the added premises were acceptable.

Assessment of the argument. Suppose we define God as the most perfect existing thing. Then, in an obvious sense, it follows from this definition that He exists, just as it follows from the definition of a square as an equilateral quadrilateral that it has four sides. In this sense, when we say that a certain property "follows from the definition" of a certain term, we simply mean that this property is part of the definition; i.e., the term cannot be properly applied to anything unless it has this property. So if we had defined God in this way, we could not properly apply the term to something that did not exist. A definition does not normally provide any guarantee that there is in fact something to which it applies; we can define geometrical figures which could not possibly exist, like the trisex, which is a six-sided triangle, or the squound, which is a round square.

If we define God as the most perfect existing thing, then if nothing at all existed, there would certainly not be a *most perfect* existing thing and so no God. If there were only one existing thing, perhaps a lump of rock, that would be God. If there were just two lumps of rock, absolutely identical in every respect, there would not be a God, because there would not be any most perfect thing. Looking back, we notice immediately that the ontological argument simply assumes there is *one* fully perfect Being (or Being than which no greater can be conceived). This is an unwarranted assumption but not a crucial defect for theism, only for monotheism.

If we have defined the term *squound* to mean "a geometrical figure which is perfectly square and perfectly round," then it follows from the definition (we might say, *it is true by definition*) that a squound is square, and similarly it follows that it is round. Does that show that there is *in fact* something that is both round and square? Not at all; it just shows that anything that could properly be called a squound would have to be both round and square; it does not tell us whether there is any such thing.

Now suppose someone is doing a crossword puzzle and the clue says "something that is both round and square." He says, "What on earth can that be—is there any such thing?" You might say, "Oh yes, that's what a squound is." When you say, "Oh yes, that's what a squound is," you do not mean that this thing can be found in the real world or even in the ideal world of geometry, you just mean that there is such a term or such a concept—you simply mean that there is a name for such a thing, though you know we shall never come across something to which we can apply this name. The context makes it perfectly clear that this is all that you have in mind. Thus the remark "There is something which is both round and square" can be perfectly correct in one context (in which all you mean is "in the dictionary") and plain wrong in another (in which you are suggesting that such things really exist). Remembering this, one can make sense of the remark that there are some things that are *necessarily*, i.e., that have to be, both round and square, although there are no things that are *really* round and square. It would just mean that squounds are by definition both round and square but they do not exist in reality. If we include, as we often do, anything that has ever been defined as a thing, then some things are round and square. If we use *things,* as we often do in other contexts, to mean actual entities rather than mythological or imagined or merely defined entities, then we are right to say *nothing* is both round and square, just as we might say, "There are no such things as ghosts."

In the same way, if God is defined as an absolutely perfect existing Being, it would be possible to say that God necessarily exists but that we didn't know if he *really* or *actually* existed. We could perhaps put this point less misleadingly by saying that He exists *definitionally,* but it has not been shown that the definition applies to anything; i.e., we do not know if He really exists.

Now let us try another turn of the logical screw. Suppose we define a *supersquound* as a squound that *really* exists. It looks as if we have at last squeezed some real existence out of a definition. But all we have is the same situation in a slightly messier form; a supersquound now has *real* existence *definitionally,* but that does not tell us whether it *really* has real existence, i.e., whether it really does exist. In fact, elementary geometry makes it plain that it does not. True, it is a contradiction to say that supersquounds do not exist—a definitional contradiction, like saying that a squound is not square. But that does not mean that supersquounds really do exist any more than squounds do; it just means that it is a contradiction to call something a supersquound and say it does not exist, whereas that is not true about squounds. We have got the existence, all right, but only in the definition.

Now suppose that we define God as being *absolutely perfect* and as having *real existence.* Just as with supersquounds, we can say that while it is definitionally required that such an entity have real existence, there may not be any such entity. If, on the other hand, God was just defined as *anything* that has real existence, then we already know that in fact there are such things, and so we can tell that there is a God; actually, we should know that everything is a God. But if we give Him a second property by definition, such as being entirely perfect, it obviously will require further investigation or another proof to find out if there really is such a Being, that is, to see if anything (in the real world) combines the two properties now in the definition. There are many levels of existence, and there are different ways of checking on their population: one just cannot jump from conceptual existence to geometrical existence or actual existence. For example, there are obviously rough triangles in the real world, since we can draw them; it is not obvious there are rough six-sided triangles, and thinking up a name for such an entity certainly does not settle the question affirmatively. Similarly, there are perfect circles in the geometrical world, (i.e., the concept is full of properties and free from contradiction), but that does not show there are perfect squounds. Moreover, our factual or geometrical knowledge that certain things do really exist does not guarantee that something entirely perfect really exists, at *whatever* level of existence, beyond the merely definitional, that is appropriate for God. And we cannot get that further proof that there is such a thing just by adding the property of real existence to the definition, because all that does is tell us that we cannot apply the term "God" until we find something entirely perfect that really exists. Indeed it follows from this definition that even a demonstration that something entirely perfect exists in the imagination is not enough to justify calling it God; we shall require a demonstration that something entirely perfect really exists.

Finally, let us suppose that someone could prove that any being that was entirely perfect [25] would automatically have to have real existence. If this is true, then even if we define God only as the entirely perfect Being (without explicitly adding the further property of real existence), we shall still be able to say that He definitionally has real existence (since this has been proved to follow necessarily from the one property in the definition). To say this, let us remember, simply means that we cannot correctly call an entity God unless it has real existence. Such a proof would just show that real existence is built into perfection; it would show that it is part of the concept just as inescapably as if it were added explicitly. So if such a proof *could* be given, it would be a contradiction to say that God (defined as the entirely perfect Being) does not really exist, in just the same way that it was a contradiction to say that a supersquound does not exist. But these are only definitional contradictions, and the one about God no more guarantees that God really exists than the other guarantees that supersquounds really exist. And that is the weakness in the ontological argument.

When we put existence into the definition (explicitly or implicitly), we make it part of the concept, and this makes it very tricky to express the distinction that we normally make between the existence of a concept and the existence of the thing to which the concept refers (we have the concept of Martians but, thus far, no Martians). But the distinction is there, however tricky it is to express.

What Anselm thought he had done was to show that as soon as you have the idea of God you have to concede His real existence, because the conception involves the notion of real existence. But even if the idea does involve real existence (and that part of the proof also fails), you simply realize that it cannot be applied correctly to an imaginary entity. You can put this, if you like, by saying, "He exists definitionally" or "He exists necessarily"; but then you must remember that supersquounds exist definitionally, too, and it does not do them a bit of good in the race for reality. The difference between the existence of a God and that of a supersquound is that a simple proof exists to show there is no such thing as a supersquound because the concept is a contradiction in terms, while the concept of God as perfect cannot be simply shown to be contradictory.

A persuasive variation on St. Anselm's approach is sometimes put by an enthusiast as follows; Look, he may say, you have tentatively accepted my proof that total perfection guarantees real existence. Now, it could

[25] For brevity, we use "entirely perfect" as the defining property rather than "such that no greater can be conceived." The argument applies equally here. Later, we shall discuss distinctions.

hardly be denied that the *concept* of a fully perfect Being exists, since we are now talking about it coherently and I have given a proof that this concept implies another property, namely, real existence. Since the concept of the fully perfect Being exists and since we have proved that such a Being cannot have merely conceptual existence but must have *real existence*, it follows that God does really exist. Here is the proof that cannot be given in the case of the squound, whose existence is impossible by its very nature, or in the case of the centaur and the unicorn, whose existence is factually lacking. Unlike them, God cannot be a mere creature of the imagination: it is *of His very nature to exist*; He, unlike them, exists necessarily, could not be nonexistent.

But there is a logical slip in the argument. "The concept of the fully perfect Being exists." Correct. ". . . such a Being cannot have merely conceptual existence but must have real existence." Correct—meaning that the concept definitionally involves the notion of real existence and so cannot correctly be applied to anything that has only conceptual existence. But what follows is only that we *cannot* say the perfect Being exists as long as all we know is that the concept exists, since conceptual existence is *not* enough for a perfect Being. Remember the supersquound; in one sense it is a contradiction to say that such things do not really exist, because it is part of their definition that they do, and we can put that by saying they necessarily exist. But this in no way affects the brutal and provable fact that you will never find any real thing which you can properly call a supersquound in a book or in a geometrical system, which can be perfectly well expressed by saying that they are necessarily nonexistent. Thus necessary existence (in one sense) is even compatible with necessary nonexistence (in any more-than-definitional sense of existence)!

When you are defining a new kind of entity, you can be said to be "giving" it various properties. But you are only giving them to the concept. When you analyze a concept, you can be said to be "finding" that it has certain properties. What you give or find are the conditions for applying the term. The more numerous properties you give or find, the harder it will be, in general, to discover anything that meets all these conditions. In particular, by giving (or finding) the property of real existence in a concept, you make it that much harder to apply it to anything; and if it also has the requirement of total perfection built into it, it is really going to be tough to find anything to apply it to. So a concept's chances of application to anything go down with the discovery (or addition) of "real existence" in its definition, as with the discovery of any further property; far from being a guarantee of employment, that property is likely to be a real handicap.

In a nutshell, the logical point is this: the sense in which it is true that God "necessarily exists" is not a sense from which one can conclude that there has to be a God. The first claim is translatable as "Nothing can be properly called God that does not really exist"; the second claim is "God really does exist," and you cannot get either one from the other.

There is a further problem in the ontological argument, arising from the premise which claims that perfection guarantees (or requires) real existence, a premise which we have thus far accepted. The discussion of this is not, however, nearly so crucial to the argument as the preceding points.

Perhaps the best case for the unblemished (i.e., absolute) perfection of anything can be made for abstract geometrical figures or special numbers like 0 or 1. It is hard to see any respects in which these could be said to be *imperfect*. Does this not suggest that substantial existence is actually detrimental to perfection? It is obvious that no circle we ever find in reality is a perfect circle. It is indeed obvious that a geometrically perfect circle could not exist in reality. To do so, it would have to have a circumference of some definite thickness in order to exist at all, and if it has this, it is not perfectly circular, because a sufficiently high magnification would show the jagged edges of the line of molecules that made up the circumferential line. The suggestion is that perfection guarantees nonexistence, at least with repect to geometrical figures and with respect to physical existence of the kind that is necessary for portrayal.

In general, are there not physical limitations of some kind on any actual entity? Either it is not perfectly strong, or it is not perfectly formed, or it it not perfectly uniform, or it is not perfectly good. It seems that the exact opposite of the ontological argument's conclusion is the right one. *Conceptions* can be perfect; but that is just because they only exist in the mind or, to put it another way, it is just because they need meet only the requirements of a definition and not those of reality that they can be perfect. For the *totally perfect Being*, all the practical difficulties would be compounded, and it would seem to be even less possible that it should exist than that a being perfect in only one respect should exist.

How do we decide if existence is one of the qualities that can be said to contribute to perfection? Is roundness one of the qualities that contributes to perfection? Clearly it does in the case of circles. But, if so, then the same argument would surely show that squareness is also one of the perfect-making properties, since it is an essential part of the properties of a perfect square. But if *both* roundness and squareness are properties that the fully perfect Being must have, then the fully perfect Being is a contradiction in terms, and that presumably shows it does not exist. It seems clear that what is to count as a fully perfect entity of a certain kind will depend in a very crucial way on the kind. If we start talking about an entity of no specified kind and try to make it fully perfect in every respect, we shall either have to give it all the properties that make entities of any kind perfect, which contradict each other, or we shall have to pick some of these in an arbitrary way, a move which will hardly produce a convincing argument. For instance, if we include *existence* as one of the properties that is sometimes necessary for perfection, then the example of the geometrical figures will show that its opposite should also be included, so that an argument can equally well be given to show the *nonexistence* of the perfect Being. Certainly we shall have difficulty showing that existence, rather than nonexistence, is a necessary property of perfection.

Could we save the perfection version of the argument by demonstrating that God must be one of the kind of entity whose perfection requires existence and not one of the kind that appears to require nonexistence, like geometrical figures? Perhaps we might define God as the most perfect *power*. Now nonexistent power is surely less perfect than existent power; so it appears that God would have to exist in order to meet this definition. The "greater-than" version of the argument really incorporates and perhaps improves on this point and so must be preferred. Even so, it seems clear that Hercules was more powerful than any mortal even though he never actually existed and odd to say that he would have been more powerful still if he had existed. It is really best to say bluntly that an imaginary God is less effective than a real one, so that the description should be "a God than which no greater can be conceived." In this form, the argument suffers only from the basic flaw discussed earlier.

6.1-4 *God's existence as the best belief*

6.1-4A *The argument from the greater happiness of the converted (intrinsic-merit version)*

Statement of the argument. Even if the arguments for the existence of God are not good, there may still be a kind of reason behind the theist's position. It is sometimes reasonable to have a belief for which there are no reasonable grounds. If you live in Nazi Germany, talk in your sleep, do not trust your wife not to turn you in, and do not think Hitler is a good man, then you should leave your wife or Germany, or try to get Hitler to leave Germany, or, failing these, try to believe that Hitler is a nice man, settling with your conscience in some suitable way. The belief is not reasonable in itself, but adopting it is reasonable for you, given that life is more important to you than believing a lie about this. Of course, we cannot control our beliefs directly by an act of will. Learning is partly an automatic process; otherwise, we would learn very little when we are young and hence never be in a position to learn a great deal when we have learned how to learn, e.g., by learning how to read. Moreover, it is not thought to be proper to control one's beliefs to suit one's pocket: truth is generally thought to be a value in itself and not just a means to the end of one's convenience. But most of us have slyly realized that what cannot be done openly can be left to the efficient and rather unscrupulous unconscious mind with considerable confidence, and thus we come to adopt many beliefs for convenience. This often has short-term survival value for the individual, in that it makes it easier to get along with people in his immediate environment where they are likely to be upset by disagreement with beliefs that they hold to be very important. And, in a more positive way, theism may for some be the key to a happy life. Thus, for many men belief in God may be reasonable even if theism is not logically supportable.

Assessment of the argument. The individual's practice of adopting beliefs for short-term advantages has no long-term survival value for the society that condones it on any scale; it simply corrupts that society's view of reality, and the day has always come when the arrogance or ignorance of such a corrupted view has lead to foolish wars or laws and the decline of the society. This observation has given us a celebrated argument for truth-seeking as an autonomous value and hence, in the practical sphere, for freedom of speech, freedom of the press, and academic freedom. This sequence of freedoms protects those who vote, those who inform those who vote of current news, and those specialist informants who commit themselves to the study, discussion, and teaching of controversial topics. Only with these fences can we prevent the society from drifting into the marshes of mental sloth in which the economically successful culture tends to bog down. When an educational system finally succeeds in retaining enough independence to convey this argument to each succeeding generation, the day may have come when the pathetic cycle of cultural degeneration from the founding fathers or the frontiersmen to the fat friars of the fourteenth or the fortieth generation can be halted without losing a war. No country which virtually prevents, by law or by practice, those who share the viewpoint of its ideological competitors from expounding that viewpoint in its schools and universities can hope to deal realistically with those competitors, for it has abandoned the serious study of their viewpoint. To imagine that serious study is possible without any exposure to the reality of an enthusiast for the view studied is wholly naïve. This might not be applicable if the alien viewpoint were so unsound as to be incapable of support by a man truly knowledgeable in the field, but this qualification clearly applies to neither capitalism nor socialism, theism nor humanism, pacifism nor militarism, bohemianism nor puritanism.

For these reasons, cutting oneself off from exposure to discussions about the nature and origin of the world involves a tremendous personal risk. An irreversible commitment to a religion with theistic and other beliefs on the ground of the supposedly beneficial effect of this belief is a form of self-betrayal that has potential moral and practical disadvantages of an overwhelming kind. That is not to say there are never *any* advantages for *anyone* in such a belief. There are indeed times when it is of great comfort to believe that there is Someone up there who likes you, Someone who will remedy injustice or recompense undeserved misfortune; otherwise, the present may be just too much to bear. Almost the whole structure of a religion has the function, anthropologically speaking, of increasing psychological support to its members, through the ritual, the music and other arts, the dogmas, and the paternalism. But these gains should no longer be necessary for the moderately educated person in a modern society. The dangers for the society and the individual in adopting theism and the usual associated beliefs on these grounds are that they promise that human errors on this Earth are remediable and that they tend to make their supporters think they may count on support from supernatural sources in civil or military battles against those with different views about this world and the next. Perhaps most seriously, especially when institutionalized in a religion, such beliefs tend to provide ready-made answers to the primary problems of philosophy and morality, which everyone should think out for himself, insofar as he can. Ready-made answers let one down when one is subjected to pressure, for then we realize that we do not really see exactly why they are true and hence how seriously should one take the answer one has hitherto accepted? The claim that for a particular individual it is more beneficial to believe in God than in man and nature alone is generally quite without foundation. It is usually based on a naïve feeling rather than on comparative data and is generally based on ignorance of the risks. To adopt such a belief simply because it *might* do you more good than harm is really to abandon any concern with the truth.

It must be clear that *none* of these considerations bears on the question whether there is a God; they bear only on the question whether it is a good idea to believe there is. The mighty results of Émile Coué, whose patients used to repeat many times a day, "Every day in every way I am getting better and better," and found themselves much improved by this exercise, are an example of one kind of statement that can make itself come true by being believed; and the football coach or political candidate who says, "We're going to win," in a determined voice, is another. But theism cannot be saved in this way; God cannot be created by belief in Him. A man must be very sick if he can find no better therapy than to adopt theism after having seen the state of the case for it and the irrelevance of its therapeutic efficacy, if any, to its truth. Still, if that therapeutic efficacy far outweighed the grave social consequences of theistic commitment, someone would have to struggle hard with his conscience before he could publicly attack theism. But if the case is rather the other way, a man will need strong proofs before he can get up and pronounce his support for belief in God, for he may corrupt those for whom theism is no benefit. Which way *is* the evidence? Is theism today an advantageous belief, on balance, or not? The answer to this psychological question is not clear, though probably there is no answer "on balance" in this highly individual issue. In this kind of situation, one must therefore speak what one takes to be the truth and give reasons for what one says, in the hope that by wide and full discussion we may come closer to the truth. For truth has at least enough merit to merit consideration in an otherwise evenly balanced case.

6.1-4B *Pascal's wager*

Statement of the argument. Assuming that it is possible to exercise some control, conscious or unconscious, over one's beliefs, one might argue for belief in theism in terms of its consequences in the hereafter rather than in the present life. The argument now associated with Pascal is as follows: If you believe and there is a God, He will reward you hereafter. If you disbelieve and there is a God, He will punish you. If there is no God, neither attitude will lead to reward or punishment. So the only possible gain is obtained by believing, and the only possible loss by not believing; therefore, it is rational to adopt a theistic belief.

Assessment of the argument. The argument has the formal charm of Pascal's great mathematical proofs but unfortunately lacks their validity. There are two insuperable objections to it. God is no fool, and if your reasons for belief are the expected gains this argument leads you to expect, He will undoubtedly see you as a hypocrite whose devotion to Him is in no way virtuous but indeed is aimed to extract a reward from Him for something which had inadequate intrinsic meaning for you. So He will punish you. On the other hand, if the skeptic's doubts are honest doubts, attended to regardless of their unpopularity and not the result of failure to think hard about the matter, God will, of course, understand this, and, being a just God, He may well regard this as more worthy of reward than the self-seeking of the gambling theist. So the argument really leads only to the conclusion that we should make up our minds with the greatest care of which we are capable, which naturally includes study of the atheist position.

The argument rests on another assumption that invalidates it formally. It assumes that there is only one possible version of theism, when in fact there are many possible gods in whom one might believe, either singly or separately. If it is true of some of these that "the Lord thy God is a jealous God" and says "Thou shalt have no other Gods but me," then the gambling theist may find that he has backed the wrong horse, even if it comes from the right stable, and thus may be punished even though he is a theist. Let us suppose, conservatively, that there are 100 possible jealous gods from which he has to choose. Suddenly the force of the argument is deflated; there is no percentage in favor of belief at all, since there is overwhelming likelihood of being punished in any case. The first criticism now becomes more important still and makes honesty look as if it is probably the best policy, even in gambling terms. It certainly is on theological, naturalistic, and moral grounds.

6.1-5 *God's existence as the best explanation of all the facts, taken together.*

Statement of the argument.   So the arguments are insufficient to establish the existence of God, if we take them one by one. As we have already pointed out, however, this is not the end of the matter. It might well be that a stew made of the leftovers would be enough to sustain God's existence, even if each course was insufficiently nutritious by itself. Remember the detective example, in which one suspect was the best although not at all likely insofar as any individual clue was concerned. It is an essential requirement for the combining move that the parts of the arguments we combine refer to the same entity. The God to which most of the preceding arguments explicitly refer is obviously different in almost every case. Even if the arguments were sound as stated, we would have to go on to examine the attempts to show that the entities involved are really the same. Since the arguments are not good in themselves, i.e., there is a better explanation than the theistic one in each case, we need to ask whether any *set* of them lends residual support to the theistic hypothesis. One way in which this might occur is that they might lend *some* support to the entities they explicitly try and fail to establish and *these* entities might be identical. But even if this procedure does not work, there is still the possibility that the arguments jointly support the existence of some *other* entity besides the one it was their explicit purpose to support; for example, the cosmological and the teleological arguments might give some support to the existence of a supernatural *moral* agent, even though failing in their primary purposes. Another way of seeing the point at issue here is to see that it is too easy to cut the arguments down if we treat each of them as if it had to bear the whole load of establishing theism. It must be unfair to regard *that* requirement as the sole criterion of their contribution, and that is all we have thus far considered explicitly.

Assessment of the argument.   In the first place, do the arguments lend any support at all to the conclusions they explicitly espouse? Given that the teleological argument does not itself prove the existence of a Designer, does not the evidence of order in the Universe make it at least probable? This is not an easy question, and its consequences for natural theology appear never to have been thoroughly discussed. In what follows we ignore, for simplicity, the further difficulty for the theist of the possibility of a Designer's having *once* existed but by *now* being dead.

If there were a Designer, then indeed it would be *more likely* that there would be some traces of his handiwork (i.e., some order) than if there were no Designer. It is perhaps not *certain* that there would be such traces, since He might wish to keep His activities secret. There would, however, be little sense in calling Him a Designer if the Universe were chaotic.

If it could be proved that a Designer would necessarily be an undetectable Designer, then we could not even claim that the existence of such an entity makes order *more* likely than its nonexistence. But such a proof appears impossible, indeed, absurd; so we can make this modest claim.

It may even be plausible to claim that if there were a Designer, then it is quite probable that there would be some order. Many logicians have held that this means we should take signs of order to be evidence for design. This is a mistake or at least an abuse of the term "evidence." For something to be evidence for an explanation, it is essential not only that the explanation explain the evidence but that there not be an entirely satisfactory alternative explanation. The fact that North was in Dallas at the time Lee Harvey Oswald was shot is not evidence, even weak evidence, that he did it, since it is perfectly clear that Jack Ruby did it. We might be able to prove directly that North did not do it, perhaps by showing that he was in another part of town. But even if we cannot do this, we could not say that there was some residual likelihood of North's being the culprit, if at the same time we agreed that Ruby really did do it. In the same way, if the order in the Universe really is explained by evolution (insofar as it calls for any explanation), there is no possibility of arguing that it also supports the hypothesis of a Designer.

On the other hand, if the explanation in terms of evolution is weak, then there is some residual strength in the hypothesis of the Designer, which is certainly a *possible* explanation. It is clear that we are to ask not merely whether there is a *better* case for evolution than for Design but whether there is a *wholly satisfactory* case for evolution, as there is for the guilt of Ruby. If the answer is that the case is not wholly complete, so that there is a residue for a Designer, then we must go on to see if there is supporting evidence of this kind, for the same entity, to be found in the residue of some other argument or arguments. If there was, then there would be a case for the existence of God (or at least a Designer) of a perfectly respectable kind, despite the individual failure of the arguments.

But when we attempt to follow up this lead to a new "combination argument" for the existence of God, we find ourselves faced by insurmountable barriers at the very beginning. For there is not the least inadequacy about the evolutionary explanation, except for minor technical details that need filling in, none of which gives any promise of permanent irritation. It is as if we have found the murderer—eyewitnesses, motives, weapon, and all—but have yet to find where he learned to shoot. This fact is not needed to complete a satisfactory case against him but only to fill out a case of which we are already and correctly confident. If some serious breakdown were to appear later in the part of evolutionary theory that we currently find well supported, then we would turn with interest to the alternatives. They are there, waiting to be called into service. In the same way, the observation that our friend South happens to own a gun of the kind that we know was used in the murder of Oswald does not make it true to say, "There is some evidence that South committed the crime." If the currently well-identified suspect turns out not to have done it, then we may well turn to an examination of anyone else to whom the clues, as they then appear, point. But the clues have no surplus force left in them at the moment. Like tiny compass needles, they can exhibit allegiance to only the most powerful agency nearby. Before the development of evolutionary theory theism presented a conceivable though, even then, an ultimately unsatisfactory alternative. Today there is no such alternative.

Is there some evidential force left in the order of the Universe for the existence of some other kind of entity, not a Designer, that might be made into God with the help of corresponding evidence from other residual arguments? (After all, that South has a gun can certainly be evidence for *other* conclusions about him even if not for his homicidal achievements when the only available homicide has been preempted.) But what could such an entity be? The suggestion that the order in the Universe indicates the presence of some entity with nondesigning but supernatural powers is badly in need of specific support, for no such possibility is apparent. How could evidence of order bear on some property unconnected with arranging order, i.e., designing?

So, in the case of design argument, this possible and relevant move in the logic of the subject turns out to make no gain. May it not be more successful with some other argument? In principle, yes; but as we work down the list (and this the reader should do for himself), we do not find any single case in which the residual strength is significant for the main conclusion or for any other theistically relevant conclusion. In some cases, such as the cosmological argument, there is *nothing* left over for the theistic hypothesis because, once understood, it can be seen to be entirely nonexplanatory when taken by itself, rather than simply inferior to another, better account. In other cases, such as the arguments from Scripture and religious experience, the situation parallels that of the weak form of the teleological argument. And, of course, with many of the arguments, there isn't even any evidence that needs to be accounted for in the first place, since they are based on an unwarranted factual claim, as in the case of the argument from agreement.

Nevertheless, when all the facts and alleged facts are taken together, there is a collection of material that would undoubtedly be *unified* by the discovery that there was a God. Could we not, therefore, appeal to the principle of simplicity to support theism as an overall explanation? It seems doubtful that one could justify dismissing this attempt to support theism as wholly mistaken. But to agree to this is like agreeing that it would be unifying to suppose that almost all crime in New York City is due to a small organized group: it is neither entirely inconceivable nor is it without explanatory charm, but there is not enough evidence to put it into the realm of serious consideration. So the verdict on theism, despite this move, must be "unfounded" rather than "disproved," and not just unfounded in the sense of lacking enough foundation to make it a good bet but unfounded in the sense of lacking enough foundation to make it sensible to take it into account at all in any practical considerations. In other words, it is beyond reasonable doubt that it is false, and yet it is not so absurd as to be excluded from the possibilities to which we would turn if there were some radical change in the evidence or in the status of the alternative explanations that currently displace this theory at every point of its application to puzzling facts.

There is a special difficulty about theism, however, which makes the unifying maneuver rather less interesting as a way of giving it support—quite apart from the possibility of direct disproof, to which we turn in the next section. We might put the point like this: The evidence for theism is either good now, or else it never will be good. For let us suppose that tomorrow it turned out that indisputable miracles were occurring all over the place and that religious mystics began to agree on many novel and testable claims. This might well be construed as grounds for theism, but the God involved would surely be a Johnny-come-lately and hence not the entity that we have been talking about. The best explanation of the evidence we have just described would be that a god had *arrived;* there would be absolutely no reason to think that he had the access to all times and places that is part of the nature of the God to whom theists pray now.

The situation would be rather different if we were to discover evidence that evolutionary theory was fundamentally mistaken. G. G. Simpson has suggested that this would be the case if we found a human skeleton in a coal seam. Such a disastrous counterexample to the evolutionary time scale would threaten the only factor that makes the slow processes of evolutionary selection capable of handling the enormous changes that have taken place in the form of life on Earth. Of course, we would first think of alternative hypotheses and check these out: for example, the chance that the discovery was fraudulent, that the seam was a later, man-made deposit, the possibility that this was actually the skeleton of an extraterrestrial being of a humanoid species, and so on. Even if these attempts at salvation failed, the evidence for evolution is so strong and immediate that all we could say would be that it appeared not to be the explanation of *every* item in the historical and contemporary catalogue of life. And, of course, this does not lend direct support to a *supernatural* theory; the unexplained is not supernatural. The position of theists before Darwin and Wallace was not well founded; it was simply less hopeless than it was by the end of the nineteenth century.

So there is little hope in the possibility of changes in the evidence, since they fail to give adequate support to the hypothesis we are now talking about, namely, that there *is* (now) a God. It is perhaps even more important to see that no matter what changes take place in the evidence, they cannot bear on the question we are discussing, which is whether it is *now* appropriate to be a theist. If the evidence changes with regard to the belief that the Sun is going to keep burning for a great many more years, it still will not show that the lunatics who now claim it is about to go out were not lunatics. The view that they held happened to turn out to be right, but this in no way shows that they were right to have held it. So it is with the theist; even if the evidence did change and some basis for theism did appear (at least for a theism of the then and there), this would not in any way show that the theists' claim in the here and now is defensible.

6.2 The arguments against the existence of God

6.2-1 God's existence as a myth

6.2-1A The Santa Claus argument

The most exhaustive study of all the proofs, indeed, of all the evidence for the existence of God, has thus far failed to reveal any grounds for rational belief in theism. Having understood this and having seen the weakness in the attempts to show that there are advantages in holding the belief even if there is no evidence for it, we must conclude that there is no more sense in believing in God than there is in believing in Santa Claus. The qualifications are very important, because the case for theism is initially much more plausible and cannot be overthrown without a good deal of work and thought and because there is at first sight much more hope for psychological advantage from theism than from Santa Clausism. But, in the end, the situation is the same except for those rare individuals or societies whose social or psychological needs are so desperate that they cannot face the truth.

The ancient myths chiefly concern creatures of whose existence no *disproof* could be given, but that lack scarcely affects our view that there is not now, nor was there ever, a centaur, a unicorn, a Zeus, a Circe, though indeed it would be sad if we could find no interest or pleasure in the stories of their lives. Since earliest times the myths have been not only an embodiment of primitive explanatory hypotheses but also more and less than this. For example, they frequently contain obvious inconsistencies, even within the one culture, as Radcliffe-Brown recognized long ago in his study of the Andaman Islanders. And so they must be seen as serving emotional needs as well as intellectual ones, as providing the background and reinforcement for the rituals and a greater sense of ease with—or even control over—the mysterious and threatening, than can be attained by mere verbal description.

They are the fabric of tradition, a source and repository of inspiration; they are more than fairy tales and yet not just bad science. All this is true, and in its light must be seen the hypothesis that God is a myth; but it is none the less true that a myth is not a good explanation, and widespread encouragement of this particular myth undercuts a correct understanding of the Universe's and man's origin, nature, and destiny.

6.2-2 *God's existence as an impossibility on some definition*

Statement of the argument.   God is omnipotent; so if He exists, He can create anything and He can move anything. In particular, He can create an immovable object, and He can move it, which is a contradiction. It follows that He does not exist.

Assessment of the argument.   The argument is not sound even against the existence of an omnipotent God, because it merely shows that the laws of logic are not the kind of constraint that can be fractured by a strong right arm, even an *infinitely* strong right arm. And, even if the argument worked, it would require only a minute qualification to God's potency to accommodate it. (In this respect it is an inherently weaker disproof than the attempt based on the problem of evil, discussed in the next section.)

It is no limitation on the powers of an omnipotent God that He cannot make square circles or divide 5 into 7 without leaving a remainder. It is not a sign of power to break laws of logic, because it is only a sign of contradicting oneself. So if an immovable object is immovable *by definition,* then it is no reflection on God's omnipotence that He cannot move it. Of course, He can destroy it, envelop it, make it permeable, etc.; so this hardly inconveniences Him.

Could He create something which was not only immovable but indestructible, impermeable, infinitely extended, etc.? This is the question whether infinite power includes the power to limit that power, and the answer is as much a decision about how to use the term "omnipotence" or "infinite power" as a discovery. Since it is often argued that God's nature is necessarily the way it is, then it would be necessary that He be omnipotent and hence a logical impossibility that there be limitations on His power. So, again, this is no limitation on His power if the argument that He necessarily possesses omnipotence is sound. If it is merely a fact that God is omnipotent, then we may or may not decide that such a claim includes the power to give up some of that power. If the decision is affirmative, then an omnipotent God *can* create an immovable object (and thereby lose some omnipotence), and if the decision is negative, He *cannot* (by definition). In neither case is the existence of an omnipotent God made impossible, since in the first case there is no necessity for Him to create the object and in the second no possibility that He will do so.

6.2-3 *God as an impossibility on any acceptable definition*

6.2-3A *The argument from the existence of pain and evil*

We have thus far considered only the argument for atheism based on the failure of the arguments for theism. But it happens to be the case that the claim of God's existence can be disproved and not merely undermined completely. The disproof is not particularly easy and is quite independent of the preceding argument, so that understanding or accepting it is not necessary in order to see a conclusive case for atheism. But the disproof is, of course, a very strong basis for atheism in its own right. It is not an absolute *contradiction* to assert that God exists and that there is inexplicable pain and evil. It is just that unless there are really impregnable proofs that God exists, the existence of inexplicable evil *virtually* precludes it, in the same sort of way that a life of virtuous acts disproves the allegation of wickedness.

Suppose that God was defined as an invisible, intangible, intelligent, good Being with no material power at all: a Benevolent Wraith. We have absolutely no grounds for belief in the existence of this entity, of a specific or a general kind, and so it is mandatory to be completely skeptical, i.e., to be an atheist about its existence. In fact, we have a kind of general ground for believing there are no such entities, namely, the lack of any related entities that look as if they have such relatives. But we can hardly offer a *proof* such a Being does not exist; we can hardly exhibit facts which appear to *contradict* the existence claim. Now suppose that it is a definitional property of Santa Claus that he is visible and that he lives in a large cavern exactly at the North Pole, except on Christmas Eve. Then there would be a way to prove that he did not exist: we could go to the North Pole and cut down through the ice to bedrock and show that no one was there. Some beings are such that their nature involves their detectability-in-principle; [26] some are not. *Both scientific and theological entities, unlike those of the myths, have to be of the first kind.* The philosopher who defined God as the Unknowable might appear to provide an exception, but his form of theism contradicts every accepted creed, for these tell us that God is loving, is the Ground of Being, etc., that is, express supposed knowledge about God. If God does not leave tracks, only a fool would try to follow Him. A scientist who qualifies the properties of the ether to a point at which he has made it totally undetectable has made it irrelevant to our thinking—has eliminated it as a scientific entity, though his work might still be part of the history of science. We shall now

---

[26] Detectability refers to investigations in this world, not the next. Theism would be *meaningful* even if its only consequences referred to a hypothetical life hereafter; but that would be a theism that was necessarily wholly irrational here and now (and also unrecognizable as theism).

try to show exactly why even the minimum properties of a Basic God require that He be detectable in our common experiemce and how we can be sure that the traces He would have to leave if He existed are not present. If we think God is omniscient, omnipotent, or the Creator, the argument against His existence becomes very much simpler and stronger.

First, if God exists and is able and good, He would have to inform us what is good if we were not able to work it out for ourselves, for otherwise we would be doing evil through ignorance, when He could prevent it (at least to a substantial extent) by an act well within His power. This would be a gross, repeated sin of omission, and He is presumably incapable of such a sin. It is not surprising, therefore, that the theistic religions all have moral codes which are supposed to have divine sanction, having come either direct from God speaking to man or through a prophet. Even though these codes, as interpreted now, differ on very important issues, they do share some common ground. For example, it is almost universally held that the infliction of pain on children for the sake of the pleasure it gives the sadist is immoral, that the taking of life for the sake of increasing one's wealth is wrong, and so on. Moreover, it is clearly held to be wrong to permit the commission of such an act when it is possible for one to prevent it without serious harm to oneself or more harmful results to the others involved. A theist cannot believe we are mistaken to think these actions immoral when all our systems absolutely commit us to this view; otherwise God would be grossly immoral not to correct us, especially when we teach these rules to our children, till then innocent. There is no point to giving a man free will, i.e., the responsibility for his actions, if it does not matter what he does; and if it does matter, then he still cannot be held responsible if he neither knows instinctively nor can find out what he should do. Contrary to a common suggestion, this difficulty cannot be resolved by supposing that God is good in some other sense than the one human beings use, since that amounts to saying he is *not* good in our sense, which means he is not God in the sense we are discussing.[27]

Now there are many occasions when it is difficult for us to be certain whether a particular action is or was the right one, because the long-run consequences are too hard to assess. There are others when even the facts of the immediate case are disputable, as when we sentence a man to prison or death after a long trial in which he pleaded not guilty and the jury deliberated for many hours. Nevertheless, there are still innumerable cases in which we are not in any doubt at all as to whether an action was right, for example, if a judge dismisses a case because he has been bribed to do so. The possibility that in *all* or even in *most* such cases we are wrong because of some

[27] An extreme form of the idea that what looks bad is not has been attributed to Boethius: "God is benevolent, so He cannot do evil; He is omnipotent so what He cannot do is nothing; hence evil is nothing."

invisible and never-discovered long-run consequences is simply the possibility that our moral codes are almost wholly useless and misleading.

Nor is it possible to argue that no pain or evil has really occurred to innocent sufferers on the ground that it will all be made up to the victims in the life hereafter; there is no good reason to believe in a life hereafter and also no good reason to think one can make up for undeserved agonies, i.e., expunge the wickedness of allowing them to occur. What would we think of the suggestion that rich men should be allowed to indulge their sadistic pleasures on unwilling victims just as long as they "adequately recompense" the victims with a large sum of money or other reward? There are no grounds for assuming that there is any such thing as adequate recompense for suffering certain agonies of the spirit and the flesh.

It follows that we can often be certain that something which is really and not just apparently evil has happened, such as the sadistic murder of a child, and it is equally obvious that we can often be certain that it could have been prevented if there had been someone there who had some modest physical power, an understanding of the situation, and some interest in preventing evil or pain. God, by His nature, must know about and is capable of an interest in preventing the occurrence of a great deal of such evil and pain to those who have not deserved it. It follows that He would, if He existed, prevent such things from occurring, and since they do occur, He does not exist; the existence of this kind of evil is the evidence which *disproves* the existence of God. A corresponding argument applies to much hideous pain not caused by human actions.

The millions of words that have been spent in attempting to show that this is not a disproof have been a comfort to many, but they have not produced any serious difficulties with the argument and can be briefly summarized. They consist in attempting to show either that the evil we think we see is not really evil or that its presence does not indicate a serious deficiency in God's power or goodness. We have already seen that for us to be mistaken about most of the extreme cases we see as evil would itself imply a deficiency in God. We need only handle the other move.

The usual version of this move is that man has been given free will by God and that it is as a result of man's own responsible actions that evil comes about. But this suggestion succumbs to the same criticism as the other alternative, for it involves the gross moral error of supposing that a bystander who could but does not prevent evil can excuse his inaction by saying that the evil was not done by him. The falsity of this is as certain a moral rule as any we have, and a God could not let us believe it to be true if it were false. Thus, if there is a God, this cannot be an excuse; it follows that a good God could not stand by and allow preventable evil to occur except perhaps as merited punishment. And it can hardly be maintained that little children are being justifiably punished when they are kicked or beaten to death by drunken parents. So there is no God.

Moreover, as the Thomists have long recognized, the problem is how to account not only for evil actions but for the terrible results of natural disasters and the accidental results of human actions which they call "natural evil." A good Being cannot stand by and allow the pain and deprivation that follows on earthquakes, floods, and mechanical disasters if He can prevent or mitigate it or the event. If there were a God, He would have to prevent these events or their effects, up to the limit of His powers. Obviously, there are many such events that even a man could have prevented, had one been present, for example, by warning of an avalanche or a flood. So God's power or interest in any given place is less than a man's, which means He is not God. We are wholly without evidence that on even one occasion supernatural intervention has prevented or mitigated evil acts or natural disasters.

The basic fact is that we tend to use a double standard in judging the negligent causation or toleration of pain and suffering, the standard being much stricter when judging human behavior than when judging divine behavior, an absurdity we can hardly tolerate just to salvage the claim of theism. To the suggestion that it is our ignorance of the facts which makes it appear that evil is being tolerated, we must reply that if that kind of ignorance is that serious a possibility, then ethical behavior is *not* a serious possibility, for we could never be sure of the right thing to do. We know quite enough about the connections between events to know that many hideous deaths serve no useful end, indeed, are often unknown to other human beings.

The situation is a desperate one for the thinking theist; for this is a straightforward proof of the nonexistence of God, even though it is constantly glossed over as though there *must* be something wrong with it, like the claim that the Emperor is wearing no clothes. Three popular countermoves remain: the suggestions that evil is necessary for moral training, that it has already been reduced to the minimum by God's constant work, and that it is necessary in order for us to understand what we are choosing when we choose to do good (or evil).

Might it not be best for man to have to face natural disasters and the evil of his fellow men by himself, without outside assistance? Would he not become dependent on that aid, if he knew it was going to come about, and thus become weaker in his endeavors to counteract sin and suffering, like a spoiled child? The suggestion is enticing but only because we think of the way in which it is best to train our own children. There is a fatal difference between ourselves and God, fatal for this apologia as well as for us. *We* do not have the power to eliminate most of the evil in the world before our children mature, and for a child who is to grow up in such an imperfect world it is certainly better that he develop the fortitude and the independence that are the best equipment for fighting fate. But this has *nothing to do* with the question whether it is any justification for a Being Who could make the world a better place to refrain from doing so on the ground that it would spoil people. We never accept this excuse from a man who thereby attempts to defend his lack of interest in humanitarian projects, and it is only one more example of the double standard that we should consider this to be a permissible defense of divine *laissez faire*.

How do we know that God is not in fact preventing things from being much worse than they are? The answer is simple: there are so few unexplained occurrences of the sort that lead to an improvement of the worst conditions in the world that one moderately energetic philanthropist could account for them in his spare time; indeed, they are probably just due to modest human beings. As supernatural performances, these are simply not in the right league. If this is God working at His maximum capacity for good, then it is either futile or immoral to pray for His help, since it can be given, if at all, only at the expense of others, presumably more needy. Moreover, by concealing His actions He does less good (and it sometimes must take more of His limited energies) than if He were to leave some signs of miraculous intervention on behalf of good causes, for that would both give heart to the good and discourage the evil intender. Even if God is not omnipotent, He is surely intelligent enough to do His little bit in the most effective way. Since He does not, He is not.

So, given the world the way it is, it is certainly better that we should not be spoiled while we are being trained by having all unpleasant experiences kept from us; but that scarcely shows that every unpleasant experience is beneficial—a husband who used this excuse for not trying to stop a truck from running over his wife would rightly be condemned. The "who-knows-what's-really-for-the-best" line is as absurd in defending God as in defending a murderer who pleads that his crime might, for all we know, have been for the best. The world is indeed a cruel place, and we should not disguise the fact from our children; nor should we deny that one reason for the cruelty is the absence of a God to prevent even a few of the more senseless or selfish results of natural disaster and human ignorance or viciousness.

The conception of God as your friendly neighborhood Divinity, i.e., Basic God, is not majestic enough for many religions or religious people. Nevertheless, their God always has, by definition, all these homely virtues and powers and more; so if no being with even these powers exists, no Almighty exists.

Turning now to another suggestion, we find that evil's existence cannot be defended on the ground that unless it occurred we could not know what it was; a man who does not make mistakes in arithmetic knows very well what a mistake is, as a saint knows of sin and decides to abjure it. We could choose between good and evil from the knowledge that evil is the avoidable absence or opposite of good. Hence, by knowing good directly, we can under-stand evil. But this move is in any case a puny one, since it could never be argued that we need *all* the evil there is in order to recognize it.[28]

Just suppose for a moment that God was around and able to intervene at least some of the time; would His doing so without disguise undercut our moral fiber entirely? The situation would then be what many primitive people thought was (and still think is) the case, namely, that when we are especially favored or particularly deserving we will occasionally "get a break" and the crocodile will be turned away, the rains will come, and the fever will go. This gives them ground for hope even when natural succor seems impos-sible; it would be a better world if it were true. But it has turned out that there are no cases in which there are good grounds for expecting or, later, diagnosing supernatural intervention, so that not even a weak God is around. A ten-year-old but suitably well-informed child whose only action was to inform others of the plots of very evil men could abolish organized crime in a year, working part time, but this task is beyond or beneath whatever gods there are. The suggestion that such acts would not be in our long-run best interest is as feeble as the suggestion that our police should not be improved, for the two suggestions are morally equivalent. We do not need to answer the question whether God should prevent all misery, which may be beyond His power or His inclination, for it is clear that if He were merely to prevent some and show us that He had, He would not only provide an incentive for the moral life, which is surely itself desirable, but also strengthen our wills against adversity. Of course, it is possible that there is a God who has and uses power to do good but is incapable of using it in any circum-stances in which His intervention would be detectable. This "Gagged God" has less than the powers of a human in a crucial respect, and hence is sub-Basic. That He should have to give us evidence of His existence, and not do so, is impossible because of His other properties, for the reasons discussed in this section.

Now God made or can influence not only the world but also the people in it, which gives rise to the final awkward question about human evil: Why does He not make or affect those who turn out to be evildoers in such a way as to make them better people? This again is within human powers, since clearly some parents do a better job of bringing up their children than others do, though most of us are not very good at it; it is surely within even the most modest divine powers. Surely some human beings would not have been so evil if they had begun with or at some stage acquired a slightly better *disposition* toward their fellows or slightly more interest in less immoral objectives, and for this deficiency God is to blame. The saints were human; we do not lose free will or virtue by receiving inspiration to do better. People

---

[28] A very fancy defense against the problem of evil is due to S. M. Thompson: ". . . . just as it is *true* that there is *falsehood*, so it is *good* that there is *evil*."

in general could easily have been made or inspired to be better. And similarly, with regard to pain and misfortune; Paradise is not immoral! Certainly the world could have been a less cruel place without disaster. And if God's energies are already being expended on *secretly* making it less cruel than it would otherwise be, He is laboring most inefficiently, which implies less-than-human power or intelligence, i.e., that He is not God.

The idea that some improvement would ruin the world as a testing ground is untenable. In the first place, God could scarcely be testing in the sense of finding out what we will do, since He presumably knows the answers already, or could discover them by means of a less savage examination. And if He is testing us as a way to *teach* us something, on the face of it the lesson appears to be that any evil is more than He can handle. Teaching is best done by giving plain examples, e.g., of the existence of a powerful force for God. It is inescapable that a world in which God made or influenced some people to be like the saints would not be one in which man was devoid of virtue, even though God had arranged it; and it is equally inescapable that it would be a less evil world and one within God's powers to arrange. That there are no grounds for supposing He has done this shows that He does not exist. The intellectual infection of the theistic myth is so pervasive that even today few of us can read such a remark without inwardly recoiling and instinctively raising sad cries about man's ignorance, his incapacity to judge God, as if these slogans will ward off the baleful light of the truth, the truth that we are alone. Truths are often most unpalatable, especially truths about ourselves, and the history of the resistance to this truth is a history of sad truths about ourselves. We are still an extremely primitive tribe.

6.3 *Explanations of the belief in the existence of God*   Why do people believe in the existence of God? There are three possible kinds of answer. It might be because God (or the devil) leads them to this belief. It might be because there seem to be good reasons for believing in the existence of God. And it might be because the belief fulfills some psychological need or needs that drive them to it regardless of the evidence. There is a common tendency among agnostics and atheists to start with the fact that theism obviously does offer some powerful emotional support to the believer and then to imagine that this entirely explains belief and thus shows that there isn't any God. Such a suggestion is clearly fallacious and about on a level with the suggestion that atheism is simply a rebellious or adolescent phase in the development of the mature individual.

It has been a central commitment of this chapter that the belief in the existence of God should be taken on its merits, as a claim about an entity whose existence explains certain features of the world, until it turns out not to qualify in this category. Even when a belief can be shown to be without rational foundation in the sense of logically adequate proofs of or evidentially weighty arguments for its truth, it is still inappropriate and insulting to start hawking around explanations of the persistence of the belief in terms of the psychological needs it fulfills. For as long as the arguments for the belief are plausible—that is, *look* good—to people with the training of those who accept them, the belief may still be said to be a rational one for those people, in a perfectly respectable sense—almost the same sense in which we would say that belief in Newton's laws of motion and gravitation was perfectly rational until the advent of relativity. The explanation of people's holding such a belief is simply that they consider it the best explanation of some puzzling features of their world. The father-surrogate theory is gratuitous insofar as this analogy holds.

But there is today some difference between the example from the history of science and the one from the history of theology, and there is in consequence some room here, as well as in one or two other exceptional cases, for the appeal to psychological explanations. The difference from the example drawn from the history of science is that enough counterarguments and evidence to make theism a very poor bet have been around for a long time, available and comprehensible to most educated people, and hence it *is* appropriate to ask why it has taken so long for them to achieve the currency in the educational system that has been accorded the counterevidence that has outmoded even quite recent scientific positions.

It should not be forgotten that getting changes in knowledge into the scientific curriculum is a very slow process, but there is still a difference of many orders of magnitude between the speeds of the two changes. In some countries the power of the established churches has been the main factor in maintaining the conspiracy of disregard for intellectual (as opposed to lazy) atheism. After all, since the churches are still able to prevent the teaching of many straightforward scientific truths in many states on the ground of an alleged incompatibility with their doctrine, it should hardly be surprising that on the basic issue of a challenge to their central claim they can exert considerable pressure. And it is also important not to underestimate the unconscious or simple-minded appeal of the argument that because the major opposing world powers are atheistic we must stand against them on that ground as well as on whatever moral grounds we think relevant.

Is there any need to look further for an explanation of the deficiency in the educational system that results in university graduates never having heard any serious criticism of the cosmological or teleological arguments and being unable to conceive that a secular morality is possible? It is not clear that other explanations are necessary. But the fancier psychological hypotheses *may* be a factor here, and they certainly are present in the personal histories of some highly intelligent men, fully familiar with the theological situation, who become adult converts to religion. For such men often make no pretense of having been persuaded on rational grounds, and it then becomes scientifically appropriate to look further for an explanation. The many theories for these and more general commitments are well known: "mankind's greatest obsessional neurosis," "the opiate of the masses," "the source of true security," "the projection of the father figure," and so on. The only comment on the application of these theories, in the limited realm of their proper domain, that seems appropriate here and now is that it is obvious that no one of them gives a universal explanation. In different people different factors or different combinations of factors operate, just as in the case of explaining why people marry.

When people say that it is inappropriate to treat religion or theism as if it were basically a matter for rational discussion, they often support this by saying that man really isn't rational anyway. What they have in mind is that he is much less than fully rational. But this is unimportant; he is also much more than fully irrational, and you do not withhold food from children on the ground that they are not in a starvation coma. It seems more than likely that theism and theistic religions rest on a foundation that is, in fact, *crucially* rational in the sense that when the arguments have been fully exposed and the alternatives to theism fully explored, most people will abandon any serious commitment thereto, even though they may have some natural psychological predisposition toward theism. It is entirely true that reading or hearing a thorough discussion once, even with understanding, does not often produce a deconversion. But it is very common that a reasonable man, having once heard such a discussion, cannot avoid recurring to it in his thoughts again and again, and at last the slow caustic of reason cuts away the clay on which the mountain of his faith was founded.

We cannot conclude the chapter without recurring to the theme of the opening section. No other issue in the field of human thought has such widespread consequences for our lives as this one, and few others have as much intrinsic interest; yet it is hard to think of any topic on which there has been so little change in the level of its treatment in educational institutions in two thousand years.

Perhaps the most constructive way to end is to describe the supportable beliefs that most nearly approximate theism as it has been defined here. The idea of two or more conflicting deities, including one with evil intentions, is much easier to reconcile with the evidence of pain and evil. But though we cannot be said to have strong evidence against it, we have none for it either, and hence atheism would still be obligatory for the reasons discussed first.

In the East today, as in Europe earlier, there are religions whose holy figures, sometimes called or treated as gods, are not so much superhuman as supreme among humans. The commitment to belief in these religions sometimes is so mild a reinterpretation of historical facts as to make them rationally defensible, though usually other beliefs which are harder to defend are involved in the same religions. Some versions of Christianity involve a similar approach to the Christ figure: the story of Christ is said to "demonstrate the possibility of a certain way of life," a *moral* way of life, whether or not He actually had the supernatural powers usually ascribed to Him. And theism is not added to the Christ story: it is an optional supplement. This is an unacceptable, indeed heretical, view in the eyes of many churches, but it is defensible, inspirational to many, and perhaps the only legitimate heir to the title of Christianity.

For the less Christian traditions, there is the possibility of identifying God with the great abstract ideals of truth, love, justice, wisdom, being, etc. We do indeed, and rightly, pay homage to these; they do indeed inspire us to action, good actions and the search for understanding; and they do indeed exist. The idea of their coalescing into one entity is a trifle more convenient than correct; possibly this gesture to monotheism can be salvaged by judicious use of the "metaphorical metamorphosis move" ("The use of a proper name here does not literally mean that only a single entity is involved; it must be seen as an essentially metaphorical use of language . . ."). Perhaps a return to this somewhat Platonic view will be the eventual destiny of theism. Religions have long incorporated such views, even in the West. Indeed, even belief in such a God would probably be regarded as gross superstition by a great many Unitarians and Quakers today.

MAN

Is man more than a very complex machine? Is he more than a very talented animal? Is the mind a different kind of entity from the body? Does man have a soul? Does the soul, or the mind, or any other part of us exist before or continue to exist after our body has ceased to function? Does the mind control the body, or the body control the mind, or both? What is the value of man? Why is he here?

1. INTRODUCTION

The primary problem about God is His existence. The existence of man is not in dispute, and the primary problem about him is his nature.

Discussions of the nature of an entity of a very complex kind are often best conducted in terms of a succession of contrasts. If we wish to understand the nature of science, it is valuable for us to examine the contrasts between science and technology, science and myth, science and the humanities, science and art, and so on. These distinctions are not in the same dimension, like the distinction between a tall man and a short man. Each distinction pins down a different dimension, and only a composite of them all gives us a picture in full perspective. This chapter will be organized around a series of such distinctions, some of which are themselves of a very complicated kind. We shall begin with distinctions of a very broad kind, like the distinction between living and nonliving things, and use them partly as exercises in the making of this kind of distinction and partly as preliminaries to the analysis of man's nature. The location of this chapter in the sequence of the book simplifies our task in some respects. Many of the answers to questions we raise in this chapter are normally given in terms of the relation of man to God. For example, man's purpose in life is said to be to do God's will or, in more primitive theology, to attain Paradise; or man's nature is said to be divine or to incorporate original sin. Since we have argued that the hypothesis of God's existence cannot be supported, it is only necessary to examine the nature of man in much more local terms. There still remain many puzzles.

2. LIVING VERSUS INANIMATE

Once upon a time most biologists believed that all living things incorporated a special substance which all inanimate things lacked: protoplasm. Some distinctions in science can be made this way—at one time, for example, one could identify acids quite effectively as substances that contain a free hydrogen radical. Other distinctions, however, do not depend on the presence of a particular kind of part or constituent but on a particular arrangement or function of the parts. Examples are the distinction between a voltmeter and an ammeter, or a cube and a pyramid made of the same set of blocks, or a left-handed and a right-handed spiral molecule. It has turned out that the search for protoplasm in the above-mentioned sense is rather like the search for the particular part that is in every voltmeter and absent from every ammeter, in every cube and absent from every pyramid. There is no substance or part the presence of which marks exactly the group of living things. Life is simply the name we use for those naturally evolved semisolid entities which can convert some of their external or internal environment (1) for use as their own constituents, in the process of repair and growth, and (2) into energy which they employ for further interactions with the environment and each other, typically including the search for and processing of food, the defense of their physical integrity, and the production of further entities of the same kind. Such a definition is chiefly in terms of functional rather than constitutive properties, and it would be a happy accident if all and only those things that fit it had a common constitution. (It does happen that all living things on this planet are based on carbon-hydrogen-oxygen compounds, but of course these compounds are inanimate themselves.) Even this definition is not a strict translation for any possible context but merely describes the term's present use. We can certainly imagine intelligent flames, clouds, and energy concentrations which would be said to be living, although not solid or not naturally evolved. Their possession of intelligence would more than counterbalance their lack of articulation: functional characteristics are more important than developmental or structural ones.

The spectrum of actual entities that spreads out along the dimension from the clearly inanimate to the clearly animate begins with such objects as rocks and furniture; proceeds through crystals, flames, hurricanes, and viruses to the algae and the microscopic animals; and culminates in what are regarded, on this planet and from our rather biased point of view, as the "higher" animals, including Homo sapiens. When it was discovered that some viruses could be crystallized out of solution and remain in the chemical form of a crystal for indefinite periods, subsequently manifesting all their lifelike properties when dissolved into a solution again, it became something of a problem to decide whether they should be called living organisms or not. If the decision was affirmative, it certainly meant the abandonment of the protoplasm criterion, since there seemed to be no substance present in viruses that is common to all other life. And yet the viruses behaved in every way like primitive forms of life. At the time it seemed to be more important to come to a definite conclusion than it does today. The viruses threatened the clarity and simplicity of a venerable distinction, and it is always scientifically appropriate to attempt to preserve simple theories and simple classifications by looking for mistakes in any observations which suggest the existence of intermediate or aberrant cases. We eventually concede defeat, however, when the world is too complex for our categories. We now face with relative equanimity the fact that any precise definition of the living organism, such as one finds in the beginning of biology textbooks, must cut the continuous spectrum from the inanimate to the animate at some relatively arbitrary point. One can even retain the protoplasm definition of living organism if one restricts one's attention to biological entities considerably more complicated than the virus and the bacteriophage. Protoplasm is then identified with the protein jelly in cells, in which metabolic change occurs. For it is true that most living organisms are made up of cells, in most of which this kind of substrate is identifiable. This is an important empirical fact about the world, but it no longer packs the big punch implied in the concept of protoplasm as the essence of anything we could reasonably call alive. A biologist who discovered strange plants and animals on another planet, whose ecological role corresponded closely to that of plants and animals on this planet, would not hesitate to refer to them as plants and animals, even if they were not made up of cells and hence contained no protoplasm. So the concept of living organism, to a biologist, really involves something other than the mere possession of protoplasm, since it would be unhesitatingly applied in cases in which protoplasm is absent. And even on our planet many biologists feel that it is entirely appropriate to describe the larger viruses as living organisms, despite their lack of cell structure and hence of protoplasm.

This discussion has illustrated two important points about the logic of definition, points which we shall need on several occasions in this chapter. First, when we are trying to express the meaning of a major concept of a science or of our prescientific language, a concept like alive or man or machine, we cannot expect to find a definition that exactly *translates* the concept into a simple conjunction of other concepts, each of them essential. Typically we shall find it possible only to give a roughly equivalent *description*, most of whose components look irrelevant because their absence in a particular case does not prove that the term should not be applied. But this irrelevance is illusory, for although no individual component may be essential, (1) the presence of several such properties is often a completely adequate proof that the term should be applied, (2) no properties other than those given are relevant, and (3) the absence of any one may count to some degree against the term's applicability. Thus, an entity which was intelligently defending its planet from alien invaders would surely be called alive even if not substantial like our typical life-forms. But in arguing that a flame should not be considered, literally, as a living entity, it is not inappropriate to appeal to its lack of solidity, for that is one of the (lesser) elements in the cluster of concepts for which the term "life" stands, as the term is understood today. This more complicated picture of definition is considerably more realistic than the "translation" ideal and helps us to solve several puzzles in this chapter.

The second point to be noted now concerns the relation between ordinary concepts and their scientific counterparts, e.g., between "living thing" and "living organism," or between "acid to the taste" and "acid in chemistry," or, perhaps, between "memory" and "data-storage banks in brain." Why do we have our ordinary concepts? Because they meet a need in the commerce of ordinary language; because in some family of contexts there is utility in having a single label for a particular cluster of properties. Of the clusters that are important enough to deserve a label, some raise questions that we cannot answer from the resources of ordinary observation or previous scientific knowledge, questions which lead us to create a new or expand an old science: What *is* life? How does *the memory* work? In the new framework of concepts that we then develop as part of the theory language of the new science, there are new pressures and new relationships and, eventually, new elements in addition to the ones with which we begin. In fact, the original concepts themselves begin to develop a separate identity when used in the scientific context. They get pushed around until they achieve the most useful relationship to their scientific neighbors. Eventually they may even cease to be the best embodiment in that company of the original notion, which is now better matched by a rather complex combination of scientific properties. (The term "acid" is a good example.) In such cases, it is simply wrong to say that the "real meaning" of the ordinary concept is that of the current version of the scientific one. It is true that shades of red are "really" certain wavelengths in the electromagnetic spectrum, meaning that in the perfectly real world of the physicist that is all that they are. It does not follow that this is the real meaning of the term "shades of red" when ordinarily used. Similarly, a psychologist investigating the emotional significance of shades of red might come up with a correlated concept or set of concepts in the psychological theory language. And so might a neurophysiologist concerned with the brain activities that go on during the perception of shades of red. Each can justify a remark of the form "Shades of red are merely (only, actually, simply, really) just XYZ's," as long as we understand this as having an implicit clause which adds "in terms of the psychological (or neurophysiological) conceptual scheme." *And* as long as we understand that a few other qualifications may be necessary to compensate for the drift in meaning due to local pressures, i.e., because of the need to provide the most useful concept within that science's system even at the expense of weakening the link with the original ordinary-language concept. "Red is really XYZ" often means "The most efficient vocabulary for a theory about the (physical or . . .) aspects of what we normally call red objects has XYZ as the nearest equivalent to 'red.' "

Thus, our functional definition of "life" comes reasonably close to representing the concept's normal *meaning*, whereas the protoplasm definition does not, even though the latter comes close to picking out the same class of objects. (Men are the only featherless, tailless bipeds, but that is not what "man" means; if a strain of tailless kangaroos or featherless chickens developed, we would not call them men.) The additional leeway available when defining "life" in biology, in the interest of improving the conceptual system of the science, is still not usually thought quite to justify the protoplasm definition. But some biologists have preferred to sacrifice the simplicity of the connection between the scientific and the everyday ideas of life in the interest of simplifying the basic concept of the scientific field. Others, with an engineering rather than an evolutionary approach to biology, have devised definitions in terms of goal-seeking behavior, homeostasis maintenance, or the consumption of negative entropy. None is notably superior; each illuminates an important feature of the living entities we know. Unlike those previously discussed, all these include some entities which we would normally say were not living, such as an antiaircraft gun plus its controlling computer, or a thermostat-controlled heating system, or a self-charging battery-operated yacht lighting system. This fact in itself does not destroy them as good scientific definitions, but it warns us to be cautious about accepting them as a sound basis for philosophical arguments, which are usually about the non-technical concept. It is of course sometimes the case that an ordinary concept is basically confused and needs to be replaced with one more carefully thought out, and it is sometimes the case that *certain* problems about an ordinary concept are best answered by switching to a particular scientific framework and its associated version of this concept. But it is also sometimes the case that a genuine problem is avoided rather than solved by such a switch in the name of scientific clarification—and in the philosophical problems about man this danger is especially prevalent.

Man is one among the living organisms. We have argued that this fact about him reflects no essential difference of constitution from the nonliving but merely a difference in the degree of complexity of internal and external functioning. The rest of this chapter follows through the same theme of attacking oversimplified distinctions which spring from our anthropocentric bias in the study of ourselves.

3. LIVING VERSUS DEAD

Whereas inanimate things have never been alive nor ever will be, dead things were once alive. The contrast between dead and alive is a contrast between things of a kind that had the same potential, only one of which is manifesting it at the moment. The contrast between living and inanimate is a contrast of potential. It would seem natural to say that the death of an organism is the cessation of those processes which are necessary for the continued life of *the organism as a whole*. Of course, many *parts* of the organism may remain alive for some time (human hair continues to grow on the corpse) or indefinitely (some of the microorganisms of the intestine). Although some parts of an organism have some life of their own, associated entities with full migratory potential (some parasites, such as fleas) may—just because of their relative independence—be regarded as not being part of the original organism. In the case of some symbiotic relationships or of inseparable Siamese twins, even when neither entity can survive the death of the other, we still think of there being two entities, rather than one with two parts, a decision which stresses the importance of independent control of body movements, reproduction, etc., in the concept of an individual entity. So the death of a whole does not necessarily mean the death of its parts, and parts cannot be distinguished from partners by their incapacity for independent survival.

Another borderline area concerns the state of suspended animation. A frog can be frozen and still revive when thawed out years later. We have mentioned that a virus can exist in an inert crystalline form; until it has been redissolved, it is simply a complex chemical. If it is crushed while in this form and hence rendered incapable of further life, has it been killed? Did it die at that moment? We are tempted to say Yes, because it has lost the capacity for life; and to say No, because it was not (in one clear sense) alive at the time of the destruction and perhaps also because, unlike a chrysalis, it would not *automatically* develop into a future living form. Or is it better to deny the appropriateness of a Yes or No answer here and to say instead that a state of suspended animation has been terminated?

In conceptual problems like this, as with many essentially moral problems, the illuminating power of analogy is the main instrument of argument, and a key analogy here is with sleep. From the point of view of the organism (if a virus or a frog can aspire to a point of view), there is no difference betweeen a dreamless sleep and suspended animation, and to kill something in its sleep is surely to kill it. Even the differentiating fact that it will *naturally* awaken from sleeep to enjoy its birthright to life hardly swings the verdict, since there are (1) natural circumstances in which this is false and (2) others in which the same is true of the crystallized virus. The act of destroying the suspended entity is thus surely equivalent to killing it. So we must conclude that suspended animation is closer to life than to death because the capacity for life, for this entity, has not been terminated.

It must not be concluded that suspended animation is just a living state. For this conclusion leads to unacceptable conclusions about the "medical-miracle" cases in which people who are said to have been "dead for several minutes" are revived. If we say that some people are alive as long as it is possible to bring them back to full life, we would have to say these people were not dead. But there are good reasons for saying they are dead, namely, that the autonomous bodily processes necessary to life have stopped. There is a brief period when artificial stimulation or an organ transplant can get them going again, but it is misleading to say that during this period they are alive. This situation is essentially similar to the suspended-animation case, and we might describe the organism in both kinds of case as being in limbo. Thus we have three states of animate things: life, death, and limbo.[1]

[1] The concept of limbo originated in Christian theology. It was the place to which the souls both of those born before Christ and of unbaptized infants went. These could hardly be sent to heaven, since they were not Christians, nor to hell, since it was not their fault they were not Christians. In short, limbo was a category created to handle awkward cases. There being no souls of the kind for which limbo was designed, it seems kind to replace them with some bodies which are a little awkward to fit into a simple biological classification. As medicine progresses, the time span after death in which we are in limbo will, in general, increase. With the improvement of electronic freezing devices, it may be possible to throw human beings who are dying of an incurable disease into frozen limbo to await the day when a cure is discovered for that

Borderline cases do not destroy a distinction, only its simplicity. The distinction between living and dead has had its share of attacks. It is certainly true that the death of a human being does not mean the end of the existence of many nonliving components of the human being, such as the constitutent atoms of the brain or some of the highly stable macromolecules in the skeleton, which can survive 1 million years or more. But this in no way shows that the human being has not died, any more than the presence of all the component pieces on the floor shows you have not broken the window.

A more interesting way of supporting the idea that death is an illusion is the usual religious claim that we achieve personal immortality through the survival of a spirit or soul conceived as the essence of personality. It is clear that this belief serves important functions in the psychic economy of many people, whether alone or in conjunction with other beliefs, making death seem less frightful, morality more meaningful, life more significant. But if we are concerned simply with the truth of the claim, it must be confessed that very little can be said for it. Divorce it from the indefensible belief in a divine man-centered creation and redemption, and it amounts to a piece of special pleading for one of the primates, one smarter but less agile than the gibbon, wittier but no funnier than the chimpanzee, weaker and meaner than the gorilla. Or else it becomes the general claim that all animals (and why not plants?) survive death, a claim which is simply fantasy. There is not only no shred of evidence to support such a claim, but it is clearly contrary to the evidence that greets our eyes and instruments if we care to watch the entity we have known dissolve into its component parts in the process of decay. Against this apparently obvious conclusion arguments of two kinds have been brought. The first are general arguments based on the nature of the person, and the second are specific arguments based on what is supposed to be direct evidence for "survival" (after death).

We have already dealt with one argument of the first kind at the beginning of the last paragraph. This was the funny little argument that a person is no more than the electrons (or energy, etc.) of which he is made and that since these survive his apparent death, he does not really die. Of course, this is just a verbal trick. The reason for its failure is repeated in the other arguments of the same kind: all depend on an incorrect analysis of the concept of a person. A person is one particular combination of his components, with a certain gradually varying character, memories, skills, form, and actual history. When that combination no longer exists, the per-

---

disease. In either case, the temptation still exists to suppose that limbo is a place people go to and to ask them what it is like. Treating the reports of those who return to life from limbo as reports on one zone of the hereafter is as inappropriate as treating the reports of the astronauts as descriptions of heaven. Rip van Winkle may have had dreams, but he didn't go anywhere.

son does not exist either. Indeed, exactly the opposite premise provides a better argument for immortality. For it *is* true that a person's personality is not a material entity like his nose or his liver, and hence, it is argued, the decay of his physical body does not mean the end of his personality. Unfortunately, the important logical distinction between the physical body and the personality (which is a property *of* an entity *with* that physical body) does not in any way support the factual possibility of the latter's surviving the former's decease. A man's shadow has no weight, no thickness, no texture; indeed, it can hardly be called a material object at all, and it certainly cannot be identified with a man's body. But it does not survive that body's departure any more than it survives the Sun's departure. In short, complex physical objects can have complex properties or associated entities, not all of them physical, but the important logical differences between some of the properties and the object itself do not in the least support any claims for an independent existence of the properties or entities.

Sometimes the smashing blow of death is softened by stressing the sense in which a man can be said to live on in the memories of him that friends retain or in the monuments his hands have wrought. But to suppose that this shows man to be immortal overestimates both the memories of friends and the power of a metaphor. For it is only metaphorically true, when true at all, that one "lives on" in others' memories. Their memories are memories of a man who is dead, and the existence of those memories is not his existence.

The more specific arguments for human immortality presuppose a weakened version of this type of argument. At least, it is said, since the human personality is something quite different from the body, it *could* survive the death of the body (granted that the fact that it could does not make it in the least likely that it does). Now, the argument proceeds, there have been a number of manifestations of the continued existence of the spirits of the departed, including séance phenomena, ghosts, successful prayers to the dead, promises contained in ancient documents, and so on. These constitute the positive evidence for the possibility demonstrated by the logical argument.

Some impressive counterarguments to this proposal, ranging from very high-powered attempts to prove that the notion of disembodied existence is really meaningless to criticisms of specific items of evidence, have been advanced. While it is true that there are deep difficulties about giving a fully systematic account of the ghostly life, it does not seem possible to rule out as inconsistent all the ways in which this can be constructed. One may, for example, construe the spirit as possessing a body visible and tangible (only) to other spirits but registering its presence on no material meters (except perhaps in the peculiarly charged atmosphere of haunted houses). The real trouble seems to be the deficiency of substantial evidence for survival in the light of the very thorough search for it that has been continued for millennia. The results of the ghost-hunting game in the last quarter century, when investigative techniques have been reasonably sophisticated, are vastly depressing to anyone who hopes for interesting results. The scientific investigation of the effects of prayer to the departed has been no more fruitful, and the same must be said of the scriptural evidence.

By contrast, the lodes of mediumistic phenomena, on which the quasi-religion of spiritualism is founded, exhibit some occasional flashes of golden ore. There are a number of remarkable, indeed, classic cases, including some puzzling cross correspondences between several independent sittings intended to communicate with the same dead subjects, which are not easily explained without recourse to the hypothesis of the presence of the dead men's discarnate intelligence. Unfortunately, an hypothesis with this degree of generality and so contrary to a number of general considerations and observations cannot be given a secure foundation by a few scattered puzzling reports. These reports do make it impossible to dismiss further research as absurd; they convert a mere logical possibility into a proposition with a small but nonzero probability. They do not, however, make survival an option on which it would be reasonable to bet, even given modest odds. They are not even in the same position of strength as the sightings which were held to support the existence of Martian canals with all that would have implied. For the spirit hypothesis involves more complex chains of inference before it can exclude the possibility of the medium's obtaining the evidence in any natural though dishonest way or through the use of some abnormal sense, such as telepathy or clairvoyance, whose existence in no way supports the survival hypothesis.

Fascinating though the literature of survival research is, then, it does not provide us with anything more than a thorough education about the experimental investigation of allegedly supernatural phenomena. And there is no other source of evidence to support belief in our survival of bodily death. We die, and then we rot; and that is the only reward or retribution for our life as a whole that we shall ever receive. The meaning of man's existence lies within his life and not beyond the grave.

4. MAN VERSUS ANIMAL

Various distinctions between man and the other animals have been put forward as the key difference that led to, or now proves, man's superiority. The number of real distinctions to have survived careful analysis is very small. Something can be made of the opposed thumb but not very much of its necessity for tool using or toolmaking, and besides the cretinous potto's hand has more nearly perfect opposition than ours. Something can be made of the brain-weight–body-weight ratio but not enough to put us significantly ahead of the dolphins, and so on with the sense of humor and the use of a language. The idea that we are the only rational animal either means that we alone are intelligent, in which interpretation it is false, or it means that only human beings can engage in explicit reasoning, in which case it is true, but it is then very doubtful whether it *explains* man's success.

The fact is that man is just more intelligent than any animal and that his present technology is *highly* dependent upon his use of language in storing and communicating information. But whatever the combination of mutations and environmental stresses that led the strain of tree shrews that are our ancestors to develop that intelligence faster than the competing strains that led to the contemporary monkeys, all that developed was a neural network that is somewhat superior for problem solving. The problem of communicating is one of the problems at which it has done slightly better than the bees. The use of fire, clothes, and tools to widen man's survival range presents other examples of problem-solving pay-off.

The effects are impressive but deceptive. If man were returned to the jungle today without memories, records, or artifacts, it might well take him longer to climb back, if indeed he could. We are not as jungle-fit as the dawn men. So our success is due to the tiny contributions of the few innovators, hoarded in our language and records, and the rest of us are freeloaders on those men and that device. We *have* done well, but we have earned very little of our present fortune. We, individually, are not very impressive specimens in the evolutionary scrapbook. And we only show up on one page thus far. Our chances of forming a chapter depend on surviving not only the attacks of wolves and plague but also, unfortunately, those of Homo sapiens. In the eyes of evolution it is of little consequence whether a species dies by natural disaster, the attack of a foe, or its own hand. Our intellectual adaptiveness is coupled with, and is perhaps even dependent on, a short-fused hostility toward others of our own species that may well prove powerful enough to terminate our little epoch in biological history before it is one-fiftieth as long as the age of those classroom paradigms of maladaptiveness, the dinosaurs. The unparalleled viciousness of the shrews may be a far more important factor in our survival and its termination than all their other legacies. The irony of our demise would be that the first terrestrial species to understand the mechanism of evolution, and the first to have it within its power to conquer every other form of life on the planet, should be the first to wipe itself out. But we are still an *exceedingly* primitive tribe. If the word "animal" should ever be used in a pejorative way, it could probably be most appropriately used of a creature which wages war with radiation bombs and napalm, uses torture to obtain information and deliberately slaughters those who do not directly threaten it, the women and children and the sick and the old in their native lands, in villages, churches, and hospitals.

There are three leading candidates as successor to man in the evolutionary chronicle of this planet. If he exterminates himself, it would be plausible to nominate an ant (on the assumption that the two most intelligent species with highly developed social collaboration, the baboons and the rhesus macaques would die from any poisons fatal to man). If he does not exterminate himself, the probabilities favor either an invading alien race or a race which man himself creates. There are other interesting but less likely possibilities, including combinations of the three already mentioned. Man's own animal creations are currently best illustrated by the entries in any large dog show, and presumably similar attention could escalate apes into demimen, or men into supermen. In this and the next section, however, we shall be concerned with creations that do not begin with animate raw material. In the biochemical laboratory there has yet been little coverage of the long gap between the inorganic and the animate realms. But the first steps have been taken, and even they demonstrate something important, for they show us that the first steps toward life on earth could occur naturally on continental shelves of the primordial ocean. The development of complex organisms from inorganic materials in the laboratory, however, may never prove possible within the limited time scale that is practically feasible. It is nevertheless perfectly possible in principle.

5. MAN VERSUS SUPERMAN

If life is developed in this way, it will doubtless be possible to tailor it to our needs, either as a food substance or, at a later stage, as a domestic creature. We might succeed in developing some intelligent strain of living entities, as our ancestor *Australopithecus* might conceivably have been a development in and a transplant from the laboratories of an alien race. If we do this or in any other way develop a strain of thinking organisms, we shall have to face the possibility that our creatures may eventually get the best of us.

It is probable that the early days of the relationship between our creatures and our own race would be accompanied by some rearguard disputes over the legitimacy of treating the newcomers as if they were sentient beings or deserving of moral rights. It should be clear that the overwhelming likelihood that the human race itself originated from inorganic chemicals would make the argument rather one-sided. What happened naturally can sometimes be arranged artificially; synthetic diamonds are not intrinsically distinguishable from the natural stones, so pseudomen could certainly feel. Even if we kept pseudomen out of the best preparatory schools and country clubs "because they are, after all, rather different from us," they might soon build better ones or appeal to the Supreme Court for equal treatment. Even a new amendment to the Constitution cannot stave off all the forces of natural selection. Our creatures may become our masters, by merit if not by force. The prospect is one that frightens many people when first they hear it described. And yet they do not admit to being appalled by the possibility that their own children may be better and brighter than they. The process of procreation is merely the use of an ambulatory incubator to provide for the early development of a ravenous combination of complex proteins, and the near replication of this in a laboratory is not so different that a man could not feel as much pride in the creations he produces without the use of a female as in his natural children. If our creations are better than us, the world will be a better place. If not, we should try to make them better. In one way or another our custody of this sphere will probably not be for very long, and perhaps the greatest aspiration we can have is to get ourselves replaced by something that does the job better.

To view this conclusion as satisfying requires a break with the outdated anthropocentrism that still characterizes most popular thought. But the possibility just described is more pleasant than likely. The figures are against us in every direction of calculation. There are sure to be alien races, and there are sure to be a vast number that are more powerful than us; and some of them are sure to treat us as we treated the original inhabitants of what we quaintly call "our land" and continue to treat the inhabitants of other lands with whose rulers we disagree. Contact with aliens may occur this year or next, a hundred years from now or a hundred thousand, without in any way affecting this conclusion. Few of us can think in terms of that time scale, however, and if the passing years yield only fruitless sweeps by the big radioscopes, many will come to think that they have grounds for supposing themselves the great or one of the great races of the galaxy. And perhaps, if enough years pass and we are still around to look, the fact that we have not killed *ourselves* may give us some grounds for that belief. For it may be that the balance of aggressiveness and intelligence that is necessary to generate a technology is doomed by its very nature. It may be that the hostility inherent in the required degree of competitiveness is always more than enough to generate a war of annihilation within ten thousand years of tapping the atom's power. Or it may be that nature itself is booby-trapped and the next step in nuclear research from where we now stand, obvious to any race intelligent enough to get this far, generates the chain reaction which starts in a supernova. So we *may* be the only great technology in the galaxy—for a little while. Our intelligence may be our downfall, just as it has been our path to power. Yet to stop even nuclear research because there may be booby traps would be absurd, for it is just as likely that our discoveries will enable us to fend off the first attacking aliens or provide the power to protect the poor from misery. Caution should not make cowards of us all, any more than boldness should become recklessness.

But of all the creatures we can contemplate, whether made in us or by us or without us, the one form which we can learn the most about ourselves is the machine. For it is the most like us and the most unlike us, the most our own and the most alien.

6. MAN VERSUS MACHINE

In an earlier decade, an approach to the primary problems about man would have had to spend much time on the "life-force" or *élan vital* theory, the idea that life is distinguished by the presence in it of a nonphysical substance. The hypothesis now lacks interest because every attempt to give it content, like the attempts to identify a physical life-substance, failed: "the presence of the life-force" just meant being alive. The life-force theory, vitalism, used to be contrasted with mechanism, the idea that life was a purely physical phenomenon, that all the phenomena of life could be explained in terms of the properties of the physical components of living organisms.

Now this definition of mechanism allows two importantly different interpretations. The demise of vitalism actually leaves open the more interesting choice between these two theories about human nature. We could call one of these *wild mechanism*; it would maintain that if physical components are assembled in such a way as to duplicate overt human behavior, they will, simply on the basis of their properties in ordinary inanimate contexts, necessarily produce an entity which will have sensations, thoughts, and perceptions in the same general way that human beings do. Indeed, an exponent of this theory says, one can only properly understand mental processes as aspects of the human data-processing machinery. *Mild mechanism* would claim that the physical components of human beings exhibit further special properties when combined in the particular way that makes a human being, which are, or account for, at least some of the special "mental events" mentioned. One would not expect these properties to appear in the process of making a mechanical man, however closely it duplicated human behavior. These properties were never manifested prior to the appearance of the higher primates on the Earth's surface, just as (and here the illustrative examples vary from author to author) the wetness of water at normal temperature would never have been manifested on a planet whose surface was at a temperature of several hundred degrees Centigrade. They can only be understood properly by direct study, since they are not foreseeable consequences of any other properties. Of course the components always had this *potentiality* of producing special phenomena when combined in a particular way, but this does not mean that really new properties have not appeared for the first time. In fact, they showed up at some rather recent stage in evolutionary history, probably not more than two or three million years ago.

Both positions are mechanistic (some might prefer to call them physicalistic) because both deny the presence of anything except ordinary physical substances in living organisms. The importance of the distinction between them is that wild mechanism does not have to invoke any special combinatorial properties for biochemicals, hence denies the need for a special study of these, and hence demolishes the last stronghold of anthropocentrism. But even the mild mechanist is retaining very little for the higher animals: a property or two that appear only when a very complex arrangement of components has been set up. In a sense, however, he is the descendant of the vitalist (though he draws his distinction between two groups of living organisms and not between the living and the inanimate) because he does claim that the higher organisms are very importantly different from other physical entities in having certain very special properties.

To put it bluntly, there is surely one very important difference between man and machine, namely, that men have feelings and machines, like rocks, do not. It seems incredible that anyone should want to deny this, and it looks as if the wild mechanist is denying it. And yet variants of the position have consistently attracted some of the boldest and most brilliant psychologists and philosophers of the last 100 years and still do. We shall try to show that (1) there is very good reason for the attraction of wild mechanism, although (2) the mild mechanist is more nearly correct about one most important point, and also (3) that the two positions can be reconciled very substantially though not completely.

The discussion will be couched in terms of the wild and mild theories about the differences between men and machines because this provides the most tangible and challenging residual form of the mind-body problem, much of which has been whittled away by the sharp edge of scientific progress. Nonetheless, a good case could be made for the view that the residue provides the most difficult primary problem of philosophy.

How special, unique, peculiar, or irreducible are the human being's mental activities? In particular, are they just what we would expect and get if we made up a robot to perform human functions? And can we make up such a robot? We shall approach these questions in reverse order, first looking at alleged superiorities of human achievements over those of any possible robot and then at the consequences of success, where success is possible, in duplicating these.

We shall call pseudohuman robots "androids," following a long tradition in science fiction. It is worth noting that the same literature provides an almost essential education for a philosopher wishing to discuss the present issue, because it is only from extensive exposure to casual discussion and description of androids and their activities that one can overcome the tendency to produce shock reactions to the idea of a machine's doing something we normally associate only with human beings. Everyday familiarity with mere clocks and calculators provides a poor basis for insights or disclaimers about the ultimate capacities of machines. In the same way those not familiar with clinical descriptions of and recorded testimony by psychopaths and drug addicts are in an absurdly handicapped position with respect to pronouncements about the nature of psychological compulsion. There may well be conceptual confusions in the way a great science-fiction writer describes an android culture, as in the way a psychiatrist working with addicts describes their condition. But the only way to achieve enough familiarity with the data by appeal to which this condition could be established is by exposure to it; and when the data are about entities that do not yet exist (on our planet), this means exposure to the most comprehensive and realistic accounts of the alternatives by men familiar with the technicalities, men like H. G. Wells in his day and Isaac Asimov in this. The same kind of remark applies to the need for examination of spiritualistic literature before concluding that disembodied existence is a self-contradictory notion. The philosopher can justify living in *his* ivory tower only after careful examination of the ivory towers of others.

Of course, the easy way to show that androids can do something is to exhibit an existing machine that already does it, or at least the plans for one. Almost all the traditional objections to the equality of androids have by now been met in this way, and a book of the second half of the twentieth century no longer has to recapitulate the details. If there are still people who think goal seeking is a human prerogative, we must reply that of course it is possible to make (because it has been made) a machine that will perform some task until its batteries get low and then go off into a strange room, hunt a power outlet, plug itself in, and recharge its batteries before starting work again. This does not show it "has purposes in mind," but it does show goal-seeking behavior, which is one kind of purposeful behavior. If someone still thinks that reproduction is an impossibility for machines, then we can say, "Of course an automatic factory can be built that will manufacture and site-assemble automatic factories to do the same thing." And the factories can be designed to repair themselves. And, if it makes anyone feel better, they can go find and mine the ore from which to smelt the metal from which to machine the parts with which to repair themselves. At that point, they are capable of taking over a planet with their pointless spawning. And we can similarly match the overt human performance with respect to inventing and choosing, socializing and self-criticizing, surprising, learning, and perhaps even understanding. But feeling and perceiving, even understanding in depth, thinking deeply, long-range planning, and introspecting are not so readily matched. And one reason they are not is that they are closer to pure thought or pure sensation, which seem to be essentially internal states and hence not proved present by any external performance.

Now there is something unsatisfactory about the whole procedure we have just employed to show the capacity of the machines for humanlike behavior, and we must discuss it first. We have been suggesting that some machine can do something that, if done by a human being would correctly be called, for example, "recognizing North's signature" or "checking the truth of a mathematical claim." But does that show we should so describe the machine? After all, human beings (1) can do *all* the things mentioned in the last paragraph, whereas each of the machines usually does only *one*; and (2) can do a very wide variety of similar things under each heading, whereas the machines have a quite limited range (one plays chess but not checkers, bridge, blackjack, craps, and so on). So it might be the case that human beings are essentially superior to machines because of their versatility and not because of any particular skill. Although the point is perfectly sound, even an antimechanist might hesitate to claim victory on this ground. After all, once skills have been matched separately, they can surely be combined into one package, monstrous though it might be at first. It seems too trivial to award man the philosophically important prize just because he is a good all-rounder. It seems like saying, in the manner of a nagging parent, that if one's interests are too narrow, one won't have any personality. At any rate, it certainly seems implausible to suppose that this versatility is the key to the possession of sensations, which appears to be the really striking candidate for a property that distinguishes man from machine. In fact, however, the versatility *is* the key to the possession of sensations, and because it is in principle possible to combine all the skills in one supermachine, it is possible to produce a fully conscious android. We shall return to examine this claim later. First, we need to examine three extremely important but fallacious arguments that must be cleared out of the way. Two are attempts to prove that a suitably versatile machine is conscious, and the other is an attempt to show it cannot be. Each makes a good point but not the point it tries to make.

How do we tell whether other human beings are in pain, seeing colors, remembering sad events? By observing their behavior and listening to what they say. Hence, it might be argued (and often is), we can conclude that any android which matches human output of the appropriate kind (yelps when kicked by a horse, composes sorrowful sonnets when frustrated) is really conscious. And there seem no important difficulties in the behavior-matching enterprise. This argument is plainly unsound, because the inference to the sensations of others employs a premise that does not apply to androids. The premise is the fact that others are constitutively very like us and we *know* that we are conscious. Unless we beg the question or give a special proof, we do *not* know that machines can be conscious, and so we cannot infer the inner states from the outer signs. The wild mechanist thinks the special proof can be given; the mild man denies it. Neither commits the fallacy, in this argument, of assuming it is unnecessary.

The outer signs are not just accidentally connected with the inner states, of course. It is not just a matter of fact that people have a natural tendency to avoid painful sensations and increase pleasurable ones. It is partly a matter of definition, though not a *simple* definition. And this forms the basis for the second fallacious argument for the consciousness of androids. If they did not tend to react adversely to a sensation, this would normally show it was not painful. The term "being in pain" refers to a state whose very meaning involves *both* external behavior (and potential behavior) *and* inner sensations in much the same way that the concept of life involves a number of characteristics.

It is arguable that the sensation is *absolutely* necessary before one can say that someone is in pain, though certain examples make this implausible. (If you forget a toothache for a few minutes while someone tells a good joke, is it correct to say you didn't have the toothache then? Aren't there subliminal pains?) Certainly the behavior is only probabilisticly connected, but it must *normally* be present; i.e., if absent, there must be a special explanation or we begin to doubt whether the subject really was in pain, even if that is what he says and believes to be the case.

When we see someone "writhing in pain," as we say, it is not simply a factually sound bet that he is feeling pain; it is an inference from one element in a defining cluster to another. But, unfortunately for the argument, the home location of this cluster is in human beings, and we are not entitled to assume that the outer signs cannot exist by themselves in other kinds of entity. So the fact that there is a connection of meaning with respect to human beings does not make the connection in androids indisputable.

If we are to establish the consciousness of androids, it cannot be done in these ways. On the other hand, to do so at all we must meet another argument, which is really the strongest version of the argument about the impossibility of a robot's doing anything original. The weaker arguments of this family can be met by exhibiting robots with built-in randomizers that control their selection between several possible moves in chess or theorem-proving programs or by a complex interaction of these with associative vocabularies to produce poetry, music, and paintings. Slightly stronger complaints, implying that the preceding gadgets are just fancy kaleidoscopes, run into another kind of difficulty, that of showing how human beings engaged in these activities are, in respect of that activity, behaving any differently from such kaleidoscopes. Critics cannot reliably identify the work of chimpanzees in art shows—indeed, they award prizes to them—and the same is true of randomly created free verse (the *Angry Penguins* case). In the more objective realms, the originality of new and successful computer-produced strategies in checkers and warfare and of new and more elegant proofs in mathematical logic is hard to deny and has already been demonstrated. To say that these were "put into" the computer by the designer is to use that phrase metaphorically and in *exactly* the same metaphorical sense that we put into our children everything they come up with in their adult life. Certainly this includes the originality that is being called spurious in the computer because of the designer's role. Indeed, our children's originality very rarely includes discovering new proofs or strategies. So the dilemma is that novelty, originality, and unpredictability are easily matched, and any respect in which the matching performance appears not to be really the performance of the machine itself but of its designer is a respect in which the performance of a human being is derivative. The versatility point arises here, in muted form, in that one feels more sympathetic to calling a performance creative if it is presented by a person, an entity which, as well as being like us in constitution, produces the performance from a vast repertoire rather than from some narrowly schooled skill.

The limit version of this sequence of arguments about originality is of particular importance, for it attempts to show that consciousness *cannot* be inferred from android behavior. Using the same premises as the argument from the analogy with human behavior, it in fact comes to the opposite conclusion. No matter how well an android simulates human pain behavior, the argument runs, we cannot legitimately infer the presence of sensations because we have a perfectly good alternative explanation of the behavior. We know *exactly* why it behaves as it does, not because it is in pain but because we made it to react in that way, to a violent blow or electric shock or whatever external stimulus produced the reaction. We have the wiring diagram, and that does not include conscious states.

This argument is not a direct disproof of consciousness in the android, but it is, if sound, a disproof of a proof of it, indeed, of any proof beginning with behavioral similarities between human being and android. If no other proof can be found, it would appear to be irrational to believe in the consciousness of the android (compare the atheism-agnosticism discussion in the *God* chapter). The argument supports mild mechanism, of course, in suggesting that consciousness, while a possible accessory to the human type of behavior, is certainly not a prerequisite for it. It may be that in constructing the perfectly behaving robot we are building consciousness in, but it looks as if that possibility is remote and unprovable. Wild mechanism, on the other hand, maintains that if we read the wiring diagram for an android correctly, we shall see that consciousness must be present in the relation and functioning of its components.

At this point we notice a small hypothetical advantage of wild mechanism, by comparison with its mild sibling, as a theory which will decide whether androids are conscious. Whether or not the wild theory can pull off the trick, at least it indicates that it is intending to establish consciousness in the human being and the android in a particular way, viz., from the extraorganismic properties of the components. The mild version claims that consciousness cannot be established by appealing to independently known properties, and it gives us no idea how else we could establish it. Even if a telepath announced that he was getting precisely similar "readings" from an android and a human being, we could not conclude that he was actually reacting to the mental state of the android rather than its brain state. We could not tell this when a telepath was reading a human "mind"; so we certainly cannot tell it with respect to an android.

So, failing the discovery of a proof of wild mechanism, we shall never know whether androids are conscious, for our knowledge that consciousness occurs in the human being does not prove it will occur in a creature of inorganic parts. It may be a bonus property of neural networks, as the mild theory maintains, but not of computer networks. If we are to decide between these two theories, it becomes crucial to examine the exact extent to and sense in which the conscious states are "added on" to, or are an aspect of, the ordinary physical properties of the organism. A most important distinction must be made immediately. Mild mechanism can be construed simply as the claim that human beings are mechanisms which *happen* to have certain feelings under certain circumstances or as the claim that the new property of consciousness is a *functioning part* of the human mechanism. The first view, that states of consciousness are just a by-product of the components of organisms, has been called epiphenomenalism; the second, interactionism.

An even milder view of the relation of mind to body is called parallelism, which not only denies that conscious states affect behavior but also that bodily happenings affect conscious states. But, by any defensible test of causation, being hit can hurt; so bodily events can cause mental ones, and parallelism is out.

The weakest view of all would maintain that there is not even a parallelism between mental and physical events, that mental events may occur without any corresponding change in the physical states. (Nobody denies that there can be brain changes without corresponding mental changes, as in sleep.) Today this is simply philosophical mythology, first propounded for unsound philosophical reasons, and the exact contrary of a presently very well-supported scientific hypothesis. (The philosophical reasons for this position are criticized in the *Responsibility* chapter, which follows this one.)

We have just argued from a simple example to the falsehood of parallelism. Can we similarly exclude one or the other of the two views epiphenomenalism and interactionism? Doesn't a well-thought-out plan or pain cause certain bodily behavior: a series of actions or a visit to the doctor? If so, epiphenomenalism would be false, and interactionism true. But, unfortunately for any simple solution, a counterhypothesis is possible here. It might be that the real cause of the action is the preceding physical state and that the planning or the pain is just a shadow on the screen of the mind, reflecting but not contributing to the action behind the screen. (This is the wiring-diagram argument as applied to human beings.) Apparently the only way to decide betweeen these hypotheses would be to arrange for the presence of the preceding physical state without the preceding mental state and to see if the same effect occurred, or to arrange for the mental state without the physical state. But such arrangements are not possible, in either the epiphenomenalist or the interactionist view, since the mind and body states always occur together. So we seem to have an insoluble dispute at the very heart of the mind-body problem.

In fact the problem is worse than at first appears. Even if one could perform *both* the experiments which we have just described as providing the information needed to decide between the two positions, the decision would not be clear-cut. It may be that one factor (the mental or the physical) produces the effect by itself and that the other does not; and yet it may still be true that when both occur together, the reverse is the case. Such interaction effects are known to occur with the use of inhibitors and facilitators in industrial chemistry, for example. Thus even our impossible experiment would not necessarily settle the issue. Because of the experimental impossibility of manipulating the variables, many problems about causal relationships can be settled only by a theoretical analysis of the events and processes involved, and that is what will have to be done here if any solution is to be achieved.

Is there some way in which we can tell, from an examination of the intrinsic properties or relationships of the mental and physical events themselves, whether the mental events cause the physical events? There seem to be some grounds for thinking so. Suppose that we had been able to bring about the physical state (in particular, the brain state) which accompanies deciding on and planning a picnic for this afternoon, without the associated conscious state. What will happen later? Either we do not start the series of actions involved in the picnic (preparing the food, packing the car, driving to the site) or we do. If we do not, we have surely proved the causal necessity and hence the efficacy of the mental state. If we do, then, since we have not lost our sight, we notice what we are doing. Since we have not lost our reason, we stop doing it until we can work out why we are doing it, and we do not proceed until we have worked through the appropriate mental planning. Hence the planning is necessary: it is not redundant, a mere by-product, an epiphenomenon. The same kind of argument can be constructed with respect to the toothache that causes a visit to the dentist. Hence interactionism is true and epiphenomenalism false, and whether mild or wild mechanism wins, it has to be an interactionist mechanism.

The argument we have just used to demonstrate the involvement of mental processes in human functioning contains a hint which appears to count against wild mechanism. For it envisages a state in which someone "finds himself doing something" without knowing why. This suggests the conceptual possibility that someone might *never* "wake up" in this way, that he might simply go through life, as we say, "like an automaton." This is not in fact the case with human beings because (1) it is not the case for oneself, (2) there are no reasons for supposing anyone else is different from oneself, and (3) there are many reasons for supposing oneself and others to be the same, insofar as such a fundamental matter goes. But it surely might have been the case with human beings and might easily happen with automata themselves. It does not look as if the mere fact that a human being does what he does guarantees that he feels what he feels. If true, this would kill wild mechanism and hence any hope of establishing the consciousness of androids.

At this stage our counterpoint between the robot and human problems again becomes useful. The problem about the android is *whether* it is conscious; the problem about the man is *why* he is conscious (because of an odd bonus property of a certain arrangement of organic compounds or as an essential consequence of what he does). We shall have to think rather carefully about certain aspects of the information-handling arrangements in the construction of an android, for too often one thinks of an android's use of language and sensory input on the model of a phonograph or a fire-detecting system. We shall show how important the versatility point is. Then we shall argue for the truth of wild mechanism and hence for the consciousness of a fully versatile robot, i.e., an android. It follows that wild mechanism must be true for man, whose versatility is the standard by which we judge the robot. That answers the question of the origin and nature of consciousness. The important truth in the mild theory will then be stated, and the compromise between the two theories worked out.

Now clearly an android has to be able to *recognize* words; otherwise it will not be able to pass the simplest behavioral tests for understanding language and things (or use language as we do). This "recognition" will require matching the "perceptual" characteristics of the perceived word or thing to a stored sample to which the appropriate definition or name is attached. In particular, the android cannot be said to be (matching the behavior of) recognizing *its* master or *its* home or *its* servants unless certain important differentiating properties of these entities are automatically "keyed in" by the sight or mention of them. This keying in involves more than merely producing the correct instantaneous responses. It also involves the process by which a familiar word or sight is said to evoke or conjure up associations for us. This means that the android must bring these associations up to its immediate-access vocabulary and be able to produce them as reflex responses when certain other stimuli are presented: recognizing a friend means not only identifying his face as one you have seen before but preferably recalling his name and such data as the last time you saw him, the way you met him, and so on. Many of these facts may have no effect on actual behavior, but the process of recognition involves putting them in a short-order status. Moreover, it is good design to have these immediate associations actively scanned by the android (on an idling basis, not to the exclusion of ordinary sensory processes) in case it comes across something which is useful in the present context, e.g., in order to make polite conversation or pass on stored messages and news. The scanning consists in working through the list of facts, words, etc., associated with a particular stimulus and checking for especially significant correlations with features of the immediate environment, including the present weather, the present appearance of the android's master or slaves, the remarks just made by the other conversationalist, and so on. This double level of activity is not merely an important part of duplicating the human data-handling machinery; it is of very great survival value. And obviously the android, like the human being, is in possession of the information that it is doing both these things at the same time (perceiving and scanning its memory) and is able to report on the present input from each channel, as well as to integrate this input when appropriate. Clearly the material associated with the appearance of the house in which an android lives or with the word "home" would be much richer than that associated with other houses of possibly identical appearance. And understanding the word "home" as used by others involves knowing that this word will have many similar associations for them, of whose exact details one may be ignorant. In short, it requires some understanding of the fact that others exist for whom the language has a similar structural meaning but different particular associations. This rather sophisticated distinction between the common meaning and individual associations must be *implicitly* understood by even the child who learns to use and understand terms like "my home" or "my brother." Unless he grows up to be a logician or a linguist, he may never have more than an implicit understanding of the point, and certainly an android can be programmed to match this. Thus, comprehension of language involves not only the capacity to discriminate different words and their associated meanings but also the capacity to treat other language-using entities as analogues to oneself, acquiring their own associations to words as well as acquiring their common meaning.

Now some of these associations are not simply verbal; they are keyed to behavior or behavioral tendencies of various kinds, including avoidance and gratification behavior. Nor are these behavioral associations mere sentimentality; they are efficient short cuts to producing the appropriate reaction or decision when necessary. We have noted that the word "home" does not produce instantaneous output of *all* the associated data but does lift this list from deep storage into the fast-access region and typically initiates some sequential scanning of it. This activity puts the organism into a different state of readiness with respect to possibly forthcoming stimuli. In the same way, the associated attitudes, behavioral tendencies, and so on are not all manifested when the word appears; but symbols which represent them are part of the associated material, and when scanned they quite properly stimulate certain tensings or relaxings of the physical structure as part of the efficient preparation of the organism for language or nonlanguage action that may later become appropriate. The android *must* stir uneasily as it hears talk of rusting machinery or mention of the date of the First Android Pogrom; otherwise it is not just insensitive but uncomprehending.

It is clear that this wide range of effects that are appropriately induced by verbal and nonverbal stimuli goes well beyond the contents of a dictionary or even an encyclopedia and reaches far into the learning history of the entity. And here too, as, implicitly, in the preceding performances, we find that the need for versatility is part of the need for comprehension of behavior or of language and hence a necessity if even the verbal performance of human beings is to be matched. This is not to say that the chess player has to be a tennis player or an automobile purchaser in order to understand talk about chess as a game, but he must know about the existence of other games of very different kinds and about activities that are not games (for most people) if he is to be said to understand what he is doing and be able to answer some of the simplest questions about it. Meaning resides only in the contrast between what is and what might have been said. Similarly, he must know what it is like to be made to stir uneasily by discussions of death and dismembering if he is to know what it is to be relieved by a reprieve.

Now haven't we begun to cheat by using these words suggesting feelings of various kinds when we are talking about androids? Indeed, isn't it because they cannot have feelings that they cannot understand, rather than that they must have feelings because they do understand? Isn't there a difference, indeed the crucial difference, between stirring *as it were* uneasily and actually *feeling* uneasy, between *flinching* and *flinching from pain?*

This difference is crucial, but what we have been describing are the reasons why an entity that understands the world around it well enough to react to it exactly as we do *cannot* just be stirring as it were uneasily, or flinching as if it were in pain, or acting as if home really meant something to it whereas it really does not at all. It must have an inner state from which these reactions proceed spontaneously, a state which itself is a spontaneous reaction to the circumstances, and it must recognize that inner state as what it is by contrast with all the others that might obtain. And that is what it is to have feelings, to have real feelings. And it is surely true that an entity which does not really feel the appropriate feeling will eventually be caught off guard by a question or a new situation and give itself away. Actors are good imitators of feelings just because they do not have to face unexpected situations, demands for real sacrifices, etc. If an android is equipped with the internal generators that produce exactly the right set of behavioral responses and dispositions for "being in pain," *and* the capacity to associate these with the right kind of stimuli (that is, damaging or disturbing stimuli), *and* the capacity to observe and describe itself as being in this state, *and* the knowledge of the alternative kinds of state to which this one is in marked contrast, *and* drives to do some things and avoid others, including pain, then it appears to itself to be in the state you appear to yourself to be in when you say you are in pain. The *immediacy* of the responses associated with this condition is very important with pain (not with love), and it is the *immediacy* with which the condition itself is produced, the *type* of response and stimulus, and the *immediate* recognition of being in this condition that constitutes—in the crucial sense—being in pain.

Still, the skeptic might say, isn't being in pain just being in pain, not all this apparatus of response mechanisms, and isn't it just the *feeling* that the android lacks?

Thus far we have not made any distinctions between the various kinds of consciousness that have been ascribed to man and denied to robots. Such distinctions may provide us with a slippery slope down which we can slide the skeptic. Consciousness in the sense of possessing a concept of self is fairly easily achieved by an android when he has the capacity to detect the limits of his physical body and has acquired the concept of others like himself. These others are detectable as bodies with a built-in control mechanism using the same language but having different associations with certain words in it because of their different histories and so on. Consciousness in the sense of the capacity for thought, for having thoughts which pass through one's mind in a "stream of consciousness," is a combination of the capacity for directive or associative thinking with the capacity to recognize (in the sense analyzed above) that this is what one is doing—again, it presents no problem for a cognitively versatile robot. Consciousness in the sense of the capacity for perception, e.g., for seeing the color red, is again a combination of a particular skill, viz., an optical-system radiation sensitivity (the capacity to discriminate red) plus the ability to identify one's state as that of responding in a way that is characteristically caused by the external presentation of objects with certain physical properties. "Seeing red" is simply recognizing something as being of a kind to which we have learned to apply the word "red." Our inner state when seeing red is, naturally, highly specific and immediately recognized by us as being that of seeing red. As we argued in the *Knowledge* chapter, however, there is nothing in this event that guarantees we all have exactly the same internal state corresponding to seeing red. The brain cells used by one person for red perception might perfectly well be those used by another for blue perception (though the evidence is against this happening naturally). All that is necessary is that whatever brain cells are used, their stimulation be associated with the appropriate external objects. There are no special states of consciousness floating around that get hooked up to red-object seeing. Most of us *develop* associations and reactions that give this state a little individual flavor, but its main component is still "being in the state which we know is the state produced by receiving visual stimulation from something which belongs to a class to which we have learned to apply the term 'red.'" This is the sense in which there is nothing to consciousness except bodily events, but it is not incompatible with the claim that consciousness is not just brain events; i.e., it is not just the brain events themselves but what they are to the brain's owner.

Consciousness in the sense of having feelings provides the hardest case to make for the robots. But it, too, is essentially the capacity for recognition in the self of certain states which have become or are hereditarily loaded with highly idiosyncratic action potentials and associations. We have elaborated on the skills involved in feeling, and it can now perhaps be seen as a simple extension of the other types of consciousness. But there is a further peculiarity about our reaction to this type of consciousness, which we should take up.

A special barrier to clear thinking about the possibility of robots with feelings is our instinctive recognition that there is no *need* for robots to have any feelings, that they could easily be made so as not to feel any pain or any love. Now, *our* feelings are spontaneous, inescapable, the masters of our heart and reason. We feel toward the robot, in an exaggerated way, as we feel toward someone who is cold, calculating, someone of whom we say, "He has no feelings." But, familiar as these forms of speech are, appropriate as they are to the crude "mechanical men" of science side shows today, tempting as is the picture of a robot as the paradigm of an emotionless creature, the fact is that it is just as easy to make a gushy, overemotional, heart-on-the-sleeve robot as one of the other kind. It just happens to be inefficient for most of the purposes for which androids would be useful. But an android public relations man for a disabled veterans' lobby or a door-to-door salesman for a cosmetics firm might well do best if its emotional associations were on a very short fuse. Of course, we can easily make one which trots out its emotional words like a tape recorder, not hypocritically but just mechanically. Even though there are many human beings who act just like this, it would be thought quite inhuman and repellent in a robot. But there is not the least necessity for the emotions to be "mechanical": we can have a *genuinely* weepy or overhappy android whose feelings really are close to the surface. It is simply a matter of adjusting the sensitivity of the emotional behavior or language outputs to the emotional inputs. This very way of talking makes one feel the emotions are spurious, because one is overinfluenced by the spontaneity and uncontrollability of our natural emotions. But that spontaneity is not immutable; we change a great deal as we grow up or alter the company we keep. More significantly, we change the "emotional indices" of our children very substantially by the way we treat them. We can thus hardly complain that an android's emotion is not real on the ground that the extent of its manifestation is determined, at some stage, by others. We think of emotion in too emotional a way; we know full well why a good android designer would put strong constraints on its manifestation, for these are just the reasons that lead us to attempt control of it in ourselves. And yet we think that to be able to control it shows it really is not there at all.

But it is, or it can be if we want to design a feeling android; and there are good reasons for doing so. Desirable though it is to make an android prospector on the Moon's surface more impervious to damage than a human being, it is equally important that its central control be informed of any damage from radiation or heat that does occur. And the more serious the damage becomes, the more important it is that the android take immediate aversive action. Technically this means that a progressive override must be built in to cut out routine activities and pour more resources into evasion or counterattack. The override must preempt the important energy-conserving drives and organ-protective drives in order that the integrity of the entity itself be preserved. Efficiency of course requires that the override short-circuit the central control, since working via the evaluative and deliberative processes is simply too slow for emergencies. But the central control is in charge in the early stages, when mere discomfort is involved, and of course continues to be informed as the built-in reflexes take over its responses when the emergency becomes more serious. The associations of this occurrence with previously experienced or described emergencies and their often fatal outcome will simultaneously assist in mobilizing all intellectual and energy resources to devise the most effective solution to the emergency problem.

In this state of total commitment to survival, what will happen if the android's human partner calls in on the intercommunication system to ask where the cans of baked beans have been stored? Will the robot patiently answer the question? Will he carefully explain his emergency situation? Not a chance; he'll say, "Later," and flip the switch off. He will be short with people who apply for his time, and if they persist, he will be shorter, indeed, *rude.* And what will his reaction be to further interference when he has already made his preoccupation plain? It will be *irritation, annoyance,* and eventually a justified *anger,* because all these are important and efficient gradations in the scale of motivational states in which decreasing courtesy is appropriate. Whatever the mechanisms in the android, however different from the human being he may be in constitution, he *must have* inner states corresponding to these stages of disregard for the finer feelings of others that are justified by emergency plus thoughtlessness, and he must know that he has them and be able to recognize them even if they build up when he does not intend that they should. What he *does not have to have* is an uncontrollable temper or an overirritable or overlethargic disposition. For many purposes, he might not even need anger, the limit case on the scale of defensible reaction states. But if the android is a close match to human beings in its powers, it will need to conserve the additional resources released by deep emotions, having them triggered only by especially threatening circumstances. Within limits, emotions are efficient, and feeelings are necessary.

In short, while it is not a self-contradiction to say that an entity exhibits anger behavior without feeling angry, it *is* an impossibility to construct an entity which will exhibit anger behavior on appropriate occasions *and* the behavior appropriate to the other human emotions on appropriate occasions *and* do so in a way that stems from a state of the entity which it can recognize as instrumental in producing the outer signs *and* which it can contrast with the other states by reference to the behavior and associations they engender in it and in other language users, and not feel anger.

The moral is that versatility pays, or having the right connections is all it takes to be in the mental swim. This is the case for wild mechanism. It means that androids are conscious and that humans' consciousness springs from what they do and how they do it and is not a bonus property of organic compounds of a certain complexity and organization. We have not, however, quite eliminated mild mechanism. For let us suppose the mild theory drops any suggestion that *just* organic compounds exhibit consciousness and accepts the view that it is a product of certain organizational properties of an entity rather than of constitutive properties. This is to give up one of the distinguishing properties of the position. But a proponent might still argue that consciousness is a new property of the higher organisms, not one of their suborganismic properties. After all, he might say, when the Earth was molten, there wasn't any consciousness around and now there is; so a new family of properties has emerged. There is no basis for the claim that they are nonphysical in any very exciting sense—for example, that they obey different laws and are not related by laws to physical states —but of course they are very different from many, perhaps most, ordinary physical properties. A feeling of pain, for example, does not have mass or spatial location or electric charge. (But compare shadows, and electrons, and field potentials.) It is certainly true that having a feeling, or feeling a pain, is something that can happen only to an entity which has a certain degree of complexity and which exhibits certain kinds of behavior. Of course, almost any very complicated kind of entity has peculiarities associated with it. Sap never rose in a tree until there were trees, arches were never locked on a keystone before Gothic architecture began, and hexaflexagons with their extraordinary properties never existed before the mid-twentieth century. Purposive behavior originated with the simplest forms of life, and pain was never felt until sentient beings existed. To the extent that mild mechanism stresses the existence of something novel appearing, it is correct; to the extent that wild mechanism denies this, it is wrong. But the stress of the wild theory on the natural way in which conciousness emerges and reflection on the natural fact that new systems will have new systemic properties take much of the punch out of the novelty claim.

If we think of the contemporary scales of life from fetus to adult and from the virus to man and the evolutionary scale from the protein molecule to man, we see that they provide considerable support for, though not proof of, two ideas. The first idea is that consciousness in man is not sharply distinct from the capacities of a very wide range of entities: the jellyfish may not have feelings, but snakes and sharks, sea gulls and seals, are harder to dismiss. The second is that consciousness is achieved through a process of increasing complexity, sensitivity, and versatility rather than through the addition of some mysterious ingredient. The wild theory's position is particularly strengthened by consideration of these scales, for it seems far more plausible to think of consciousness as a graduated aspect of the gradually increasing complexity in the brain processes than to think of it as suddenly appearing at some point, as the wetness of water suddenly appears when the temperature-pressure conditions are favorable. The suggestion of a qualitative change at some point is too reminiscent of (indeed, is almost a version of) the dispute over the point in the descent of man from the pre-apes at which he acquired a soul.

There may well *be* bonus properties of the human brain in the original sense of the mild theory. It may be the case that it is capable of extrasensory perception, whereas behaviorally similar androids are not. But consciousness is *not* one of these properties. The gradualist view is also supported by our discussion of the multiplicity of the phenomena of consciousness. Perhaps a snake in some sense feels pain when cut, but it certainly does not have the capacity for sustained thought and a sophisticated self-concept, which are important parts of the essentially multistranded concept of consciousness. A computer with a moderately sophisticated talent for strategic planning may have a self-concept and think but have no capacity for feeling pain. The complex view is surely the correct one here: consciousness is not a simple property, not even several properties, but it is a single name for several capacities which occur in greater and less degree among human beings, animals, plants, and machines. As these entities vary in complexity, they vary in the extent and types of consciousness they manifest, and these degrees and types are no more than the special capacities we have described. This is a parsimonious view but an adequate one, and once more it stresses the affinities between us and the creatures or devices that we eat or use or endure. Man is not just an animal or a machine, but yet he is an animal and a machine. And he will sometime be replaced by one or the other, just as he has sometimes replaced the one by the other.

7. MAN VERSUS GOD

The history of discussion on the nature and significance of man is the history of arguments and discoveries that show man to be less and less like a real God and God to be less and less real than man. In this and the previous chapter we have examined this combined elevation and denigration of man, an elevation obtained by the discovery that his Superior does not exist and a denigration consisting in the recognition that his own superiority to the order of nature is limited and temporary. He is doomed to defeat by his own hand, or by that of invaders who behave as he has always behaved, or by his own maternal or mechanical creations. The tiny chance this will not occur is no loophole at which to aim one's life. The point of life and of man is the point man gives it, *each* man during *his* life. It is not to be found outside man, and this realization is the beginning of wisdom, the beginning of true humility and true pride.

VI

RESPONSIBILITY

0. THE PROBLEMS

If all our behavior can be explained scientifically or is, in principle, completely predictable, how could we possibly have done otherwise? If we could not have done otherwise, how can we be blamed or praised for what we did? Is the drug addict responsible? Is the alcoholic? The delinquent? The man in a fit of temper? Is anybody really responsible for anything? Does punishment or praise have any rational function if people cannot help what they are doing? Can a parent train children to be responsible?

1. INTRODUCTION

The problem of responsibility is caused largely by the apparent conflict between the discovery of scientific explanations of our actions and the "old-fashioned" view that our actions result from our own decisions. If only one of these two kinds of explanations can be true, the scientific evidence seems to favor the first; but the second appears to be the only basis for ascribing to individuals any responsibility for their actions. So scientific progress appears to undercut the doctrine that human beings are responsible for their actions.

But the history of many theoretical disputes in the sciences, as in philosophy and politics, strikingly demonstrates how two positions that at first appear completely incompatible may upon sustained analysis and under the pressure of mutual criticism turn out to be or become no more than differences of emphasis. The conservative versus liberal or Republican versus Democrat disputes in politics lack long-term doctrinal content today, although they still reflect a difference of emphasis or orientation and a difference of policy at a given moment; the positivist versus metaphysician fight in philosophy and the gestalter versus behaviorist division in psychology illustrate the same point. It will be suggested here that the present issue is also resolvable into a difference of emphasis, both emphases being valuable but not entirely incompatible with each other.

2. THE ROOTS OF THE CONFLICT

Scientists have often maintained that our actions, like the behavior of all other objects in the world, are ultimately determined by factors beyond our individual control, specifically our heredity and our environment. This is the claim of determinism; we shall call it D1. It is thought to be a consequence of this view that our feeling that our future actions depend on our own choices (and thus that we are responsible for our choices) is an illusion (D2). *This* is usually thought to be supported by the claim that, given enough knowledge, our "choices" would be predictable long in advance (D3). For many centuries a similar argument was proposed by and puzzled theologians: if God is omnipotent, then He is responsible for everything that occurs and it must be His will that determines (or permits) every human action and not we ourselves; so our free will is illusory (D4). (A related view follows from His omniscience.) In both the scientific and the theological cases there appears to be a clash between determinism and human freedom, with the force, or knowledge, of science or God obliterating man's freedom.

Yet, as other scientists and theologians have argued, that freedom seems well founded. Surely we cannot be mistaken in our belief that our decisions really do determine our actions (F1), that our decisions are not determined until we determine them and hence are not predictable (F2). Surely the whole conception of responsibility and that large part of ethics which depends on it is justified and is not built on sand (F3). Moreover, is it not the case that modern physics is not itself deterministic, so that the scientific case against freedom is now unsupported (F4)?

These conflicting positions present one of the most important and persistently irritating problems of philosophy. A resolution of this dispute is required before any system of law or penology or any way of life or set of human values can be known to be well founded. Such a resolution now appears possible and involves only a middling degree of difficulty, although it has taken several centuries to patch the last few holes in the basic structure of the answer.

3. OUTLINE OF AN ANSWER

Determinism, in the sense in which it has scientific support, is entirely compatible with moral and predictive freedom. The premises of almost every argument on both sides are essentially (though not precisely) sound: the error lies in the conclusion of each side that the other position is untenable. The essential points of support for this reconciliation are now to be set out in a rather concise and systematic way, dispensing with elaborate persuasion for each point, because the strength of the "compatibility claim" is more easily appreciated if it can be quickly grasped as a whole. We shall then turn to a few of the usual problem cases about responsibility, as a way of investigating the consequences and adequacy of the present claim.

We may take determinism to be the doctrine that every event in and every state of the world are wholly governed by precise laws. It is usually assumed, incorrectly, that this is equivalent to the predictability in principle of every feature of the world. This error is unimportant in the present context, but we shall discuss it later. Let us begin the reconciliation process with an examination of the present situation of the doctrine of determinism.[1]

4. THE SCIENTIFIC STATUS OF DETERMINISM

Total determinism is almost certainly false (as F4 claims),[2] but this is irrelevant to the freewill problem and in the greater part of science may be disregarded (hence D1 is effectively true).

4.1 The Uncertainty Principle alone does not guarantee indeterminism, but, conjoined with the quantum theories of measurement and atomic struc-

[1] The technical subsection on the scientific status of determinism, which immediately follows, should be skipped by those made nervous by technical talk; it is included for completeness and for the interest of the scientifically minded, and its validity is not essential to the main argument.
[2] Reference will be made in parentheses to the viewpoints which are being reconciled: the reader will find checking back worth-while only when some obscurity may thereby be clarified.

ture, it certainly implies the essential unpredictability (and, as far as can be seen, the inexplicability) of certain measurable properties of microlevel events, e.g., the time of emission of an electron by a radioactive atom.

4.2 The behavior of very large numbers of particles is very highly predictable, but this does not show that determinism is unqualifiedly true for large objects such as brains and people. For there will be a very few occasions when the indeterminate element in the behavior of a single particle by chance will (and can readily be arranged to) precipitate a chain reaction or cascade effect with marked gross consequences of exactly equal indeterminacy, e.g., the detonation of a bomb or the firing of a synapse.

4.3 The occurrence of such gross nondetermined effects will be exceedingly rare in nature, although they can easily be arranged experimentally. In general, the pervasive effects of measurement errors will swamp their tiny domain and preclude positive identification, though we can be sure they sometimes occur. Hence the study of the natural behavior of large objects should, for practical purposes, proceed as if determinism were true (so D1's claim is pragmatically sound).

4.4 In particular, the minute number of nondetermined "large" events that we have reason to believe occur (see section 4.2) do not coincide in either frequency or location with the decisions we call free (or with the exact brain states associated with those decisions). So free will is not "explained by" or even made possible by the indeterminacy that does exist, since that indeterminacy is not even present in most cases of decisions. (The denial of D1 does not justify belief in F1.)

5. THE ROLE OF DECISIONS

Our decisions are often essential factors in the determination of our actions; nevertheless, they may themselves be regarded as determined in turn by other factors (D1, alternative version) and, *typically,* as predictable (D1, D3).

5.1 The internal mechanical behavior of a coin-operated machine dispensing cigarettes certainly determines what comes out; equally certainly, this activity is or was itself determined by the designer and constructor of the machine and also, on a particular occasion, by the user. They are *indispensable* [3] even though only *intermediate* links in several causal chains. We

---

[3] This claim is *slightly* exaggerated and is corrected in section 5.7.

correctly recognize the indispensability of our decisions (F1) for our actions, in many cases, and incorrectly suppose this means they cannot themselves be caused (D2).

5.2   But the decisions are indispensable *even though* intermediate links in a causal chain. There *are* cases in which our decisions are entirely dispensable, indeed, irrelevant: immediately after deciding to do something, we are swept away in a flood, thrown from a horse, or shot in the arm, and as a result our decision is nullified. These are cases in which the course of events by-passes our processes of decision, just as an automobile thief by-passes the ignition lock when he shorts it out of the circuit. But this does not show it is silly to turn the ignition key on normal occasions. Determinism does not imply fatalism.

5.3   There are other cases in which decisions are irrelevant. A man who is pushed into another man, thereby knocking him down, might be said to be totally compelled or to have no choice about doing what he did, but it would be better to say that knocking the other down was not even an *action* of his. Responsibility does not apply to the case at all. This is an instance of being propelled, not merely compelled. But a man who is threatened with a gun or blackmail and consequently opens a safe or gives away secrets has acted and has chosen: he did just what he meant to do, although he did not *wish* to do it. We may well say he was *compelled* or *made* to open the safe, or did it *against his will*, or *had no choice*; but such language is then being used to mark the contrast with cases in which a decision is made without *undue* pressure or *moral* compulsion. It does *not* mean the agent was incapable of acting otherwise. "He had no choice" here means "There was no *rational* alternative choice open"; it does not mean "He did not make a choice at all" or that the choice was irrelevant. The man with the gun may say to him, "Well, make up your mind—is it worth being shot?" When we say that he had no choice here, we are contrasting it with cases in which he might just as well do one thing as another, e.g., pick one orange from a bowl, rather than another. No overwhelming balance of reasons exists in those circumstances; but, of course, there is probably, in view of the evidence for determinism, some explanation at some level.

The language of choice, of possibility, of alternatives, of compulsion and freedom is highly dependent on the context. It is used to draw contrasts of a certain kind, but precisely *which* contrasts it draws depend on the issues at stake in the particular context: it may contrast rationally loaded with rationally well-balanced open choices, effective with frustrated ones, compelled with free ones. Most of the freewill controversy arises because the opponents assume there is only one possible context for these terms.

5.4   There are some cases in which the role of the decision is not so clear. These include a type of case which we unhesitatingly identify as compulsion, though there are some differences from the one described above. For example, a victim decides not to talk but is then *made* to talk by the use of torture. Suppose he holds out a remarkably long time, but in the end his will is sapped and he talks. This is just like being compelled by force to crawl a half mile over gravel as a punishment in a prison camp; it is done against the will, by or because of force. In cases of compulsion like this, it is not just that one's actions are affected by an external agency; it is that one's choice is irrelevant. *Then* responsibility is abrogated. Determinism claims universal causation, not universal compulsion. The difference from the case of threat or blackmail is that here one tries very hard to avoid doing what one eventually does: one attempts the alternative and suffers for the attempt. Yet, unlike the cases of section 5.2, both of these cases are still cases of actions by the agent.

5.5   The role of reasoning is important. Someone who cannot reason can still make choices (a child can pick out candies); but such a person cannot properly assess complex alternatives and their consequences and hence (although he may choose one of them) cannot be held responsible for the choice, because he did not (and could not) know what it was that he chose. We might deny that he chose *it,* because it is defined by those of its characteristics that should affect a rational choice. But since it is easy to show that most people can sometimes reason enough to understand the alternatives fully, the determinist cannot be denying that this is ever possible.

5.6   Sometimes the determinist is denying that any of the reasons we *think* are our reasons are really our reasons—a superextrapolation of the discovery that we do sometimes (indeed, often) rationalize. But it is simply false to say that we are *always* rationalizing, as we can see from the fact that people often give their reasons for choosing, e.g., a particular route, restaurant, or school and thereafter demonstrate by their behavior that it was just these considerations that did influence them.

5.7   In judging whether someone is responsible for an action which he seems to have chosen to carry out, there is a very close connection between the reasoning involved and the question of the irrelevance of the decision to the action. Suppose that someone chooses, so he thinks, between several alternatives, of which *we* happen to know only one is actually possible for him. It happens that he picks the very one he can do.[4] Now, is he responsible

---

[4] This example and its threat to simple analyses of compulsion have been stressed by Paul Dietl.

for this course of action? At first sight, it would seem not, for his choice is irrelevant in the sense that he would have finished by doing the same thing no matter what alternative he originally chose. Yet we would ordinarily say he is just as responsible for this as he would have been if one of the other alternatives *was* a live option. It seems odd to say his responsibility depends on the way things he did not try would have turned out. His *decision* and his *action* were just the same as they would have been if the alternatives had been possible, and it is these for which we hold him responsible. So the test of irrelevance has to be refined. The crucial criterion is whether the decision or choice is relevant in the sense that it determines the action. It is too crude to take this as meaning that if the choice had been different, the result would have been different.

This apparently puzzling distinction arises from study of cases of over-determination, common enough in ordinary life: a man may correctly be said to die of a heart attack even if he has fatal cancer which would bring about death anyway. A cause is not "a factor without which the effect would not have occurred." It might even have occurred at the same time. A man can be said to do X because he chose to, even though it would have come about that he did X anyway. Whenever he does something *because* he chose to do it, we say he is responsible for it. And now we understand "because he chose to" to mean that his selection of the alternative was the cause of (determined) his performing the action involved. Typically, this implies that he has *good reasons* to believe he could have done otherwise, even when this is false.

5.8 Two further refinements are necessary. Sometimes the selection of (decision in favor of) an alternative is not distinguishable from the associated action, and this is true for actions that are part of one's normal pattern of behavior, such as reaching for a cigarette, as well as for arbitrary choices. As an example of the second kind, in picking a peach from a bowl of peaches there is often no preliminary deliberation or decision—one just reaches out one's hand and picks one. Yet one would surely be said to be responsible for one's choice here. This is one of the cases like the posthypnotic examples (see section 5.9), in which it is by accepting an alternative that one becomes responsible for it. One uses one's arm as a choosing-at-random device, just as one might toss a coin or ask a friend to choose. These cases of *passive responsibility* are still cases of responsibility because one consciously recognizes the selection that has been made for one and accepts it. To say that one decides to accept it is a little exaggerated; one has already decided to accept the outcome when one decides to use this method of selection. One's responsibility stems from *that moment,* because at that moment one's decision does determine one's actions and at that moment one knows and is willing to accept the range of possible outcomes.

5.9 Sometimes the determinist is impressed by post-hypnotic phenomena, or brainwashing, or neural manipulation and suggests that our supposed free choices may all be illusory in this way. But the victims in these cases are still responsible for most of their everyday actions, and the particular area of behavior that has been affected is readily identifiable as one in which their decisions are not really "their own" but are due to someone else's interference. There is simply no significant possibility that all our actions are in this sense due to someone else's manipulation of us.

Might our actions not be *like* this in that they are due to manipulation by our environment, parents, and so on? Of course they might, but "manipulation" is now used in a metaphorical sense and in no way reduces our responsibility for the acts: only if there is someone else who is responsible for manipulating us—diverting us from our natural path—can we pass any responsibility along. If there is no such person, we are acting as our nature leads us to act in the circumstances, in the light of whatever reasons and with as much intelligence as we can muster, and it is just such actions which are our own and our own responsibility. We can perform cosmetic surgery on a person, but this does not show that the face he had before we began was not his own and that he was not responsible for retaining it as long as he did, even though it was molded by factors over which he had no control and thus was not responsible for acquiring it. It should therefore be stressed that with regard to many of the phenomena cited the agent is still responsible, not for the initiation of the act or the inclination to act in such and such a way, but for the performance of the action itself, since he could still restrain himself from the complete action. Suggestion, hypnotic or otherwise, is not compulsion, and current evidence makes it clear that hypnotic suggestion, for example, is rarely, if ever, compelling. The fact that the outsider can produce certain acts by hypnotic suggestion makes him feel as if the actor was "just a puppet," but the actor is really just a person to whom the hypnotist has made a suggestion whose external source the actor has then forgotten.

5.10 It is clear that the question of responsibility is closely connected with the question whether one knows what one is doing. If one agrees to abide by the spin of a coin in settling the evening's plans, one knows what one may be committed to and can reasonably be held to it and held responsible for it. When decisions are made in this way, however, there is a moment when one *may* (perhaps unjustly or unreasonably) still reject the alternative which the coin "selects." In other cases the connection between the selection device and the outcome is automatic or is made without the opportunity for further deliberation. One example is Russian roulette; the revolver's magazine is spun (which makes the selection), and the trigger then pulled without further inspection. Someone who kills himself while playing this game from choice is not deliberately committing suicide, but he is still fully responsible for his death. We say, "He knew what he was doing," or "He knew the risk he was taking," in this case and in the more familiar forms of the same game, such as driving a car after the brake pedal has started to need pumping and concealing embarrassing symptoms from one's physician.

So when we say that knowing what one is doing is closely connected with being responsible for what one does, we do not mean that an agent has to know the *exact* outcome of his choices to be responsible for them. It is certainly enough that he know which outcomes are possible and commit himself to all these possible outcomes via some selection procedure. And it goes without saying that what we have to know about the alternatives is only their choice-affecting properties.

Many of our actions have consequences which we could not have *definitely* foreseen but which were obviously possible and hence are part of our responsibility. When something happens as a result of our actions that was entirely unforeseeable, we are not held responsible for it. But sometimes we talk here of *causal responsibility* (since we did bring it about) as opposed to *moral responsibility.* "Don't blame yourself," we say, "you couldn't have known the child would teach himself to pick locks in order to get into the gun cabinet," although of course it was your leaving the guns and ammunition in the cabinet that "made" the disaster possible.

When someone makes a choice that involves a very slight risk of a bad outcome, where the alternatives involve a worse risk of a worse outcome, and he is unlucky, we should probably say that he is responsible for what happens, though not to blame. Perhaps because we so often operate in a context where responsibility is in question simply because blame is to be apportioned, the allocation (or withholding) of responsibility becomes identified with the allocation (or withholding) of blame and in such cases we often say, "He can't be held responsible for what happened." It is not necessarily misleading to talk this way, as long as we note that the foreseeable consequences of an alternative, whether definite, likely, or just possible, are in some sense part, and rationally certainly should be determinants, of our choice when we choose one particular alternative. (We are thus not merely causal agents in bringing the consequences about but agents who were conscious that our actions might have these consequences, and we can be influenced by this fact.) The narrower conception of responsibility restricts it to those outcomes which one could reasonably have expected or which were so important that their mere probability should have controlled one's decision. On either account the man who continues to drink knows that he may pass the point of no return without realizing it and so is responsible for drunken violence and, in the long time scale, for becoming an alcoholic, although this is not part of his conscious intention.

6. PREDICTABILITY

It is possible that most of an agent's "free decisions" could in principle be predicted by an observer with enough facts and laws (D3), but this in no way makes the decisions dispensable or pointless.

6.1   Our decisions require *our* deliberation; we are their makers *even when* they are predictable. Moreover, we retain possession over them and can reassert ownership if challenged. Often, indeed, others could not tell us what our decisions would be before we made them without being wrong. There are many occasions (e.g., in a poker game) on which no matter what prediction a competitor makes to us about our decision (e.g., to bluff or not to bluff) we would immediately prove him wrong. Thus the decision has not already been determined in the sense that all can know it in advance. Our going through the process of making the decision is therefore most relevant: the decision hangs on that process. It can be changed by interference in that process, and it will be changed if we want to alter others' predictions of the process. This in no way denies that the decision and the preliminaries to it are all intermediate events in a causal chain, whose still earlier members may provide a basis for prediction of the latest ones. It merely affirms the indispensability of the decision in the chain and thereby stresses the difference from the strong compulsion case. (But "indispensability" is, as we shall see, somewhat too strong a term.)

6.2   Just as there are many decisions which we will change as soon as we think them to be predicted, so there are others which are easily predicted by someone with some knowledge of our character and are not in the least affected by our knowledge of their foreknowledge. We proceed with our course of action without any feeling that it is any the less ours because it is known to them in advance. We know, as we put it, that we could change our minds and do otherwise; but there is no reason to do so. To say we could do otherwise is roughly to say that we are not mentally or physically crippled or compelled with regard to the alternative choice but merely lack any sufficient reasons for making it. It is within our powers at this moment. It is just like saying that we have the *strength* to (i.e., that we could) lift the chair on which we are at the moment sitting (though we do not actually do it). It is like saying that the chair *could* support a 250-lb man, though it probably never will. These remarks enable us to infer what would happen if the circumstances were different. But they are not directly about those alternatives; they are about the present state, even though they imply something about "what would happen if. . . ." Capacity claims like this are not undercut by pointing out that the circumstances *are not* different or even that they *could not* be different, given the previous history of the situation.

It is entirely predictable that a teacher will fail a certain student who has averaged less than 25 per cent on the examinations in a course for which 40 per cent is the minimum passing mark. It is predictable that a friend, known for his generosity, will contribute something to a fund for a suddenly deceased colleague's impoverished widow. This in no way conflicts with the claims that they decided to do what they did, were not compelled to do it, could have done otherwise, were entirely responsible for their actions, etc. Thus the regularities on which we base predictions do not prescribe all that is morally possible.

The essential difference between predictability and possibility is reflected in our usual distinction between the nature or character of things and people and the course of events. It is of the nature of copper to dissolve in sulfuric acid, though the course of events brings this fate to only a tiny proportion of the copper on this planet. To say of someone that he can multiply any pairs of three-digit numbers in his head entitles you to expect that he will succeed with a particular sample under suitable motivational conditions, but it does not absolutely guarantee his success, and it certainly does not guarantee that the suitable conditions will ever arise. To say that a man could have done other than he did is thus not strictly translatable into an account of what he would do if circumstances were different, but it normally has some implications for such circumstances and is therefore to some extent assessed by the results of tests under such different circumstances. But "could have" refers to him *now*, just as "soluble" does to copper in the example given above, and their connection with the present physical structure (of brain or molecular bonds) is often as strong as with responses to alternative stimuli.

The difference between nature and circumstances is not just the difference between grounds for drawing conclusions about possibility and about predictability, respectively. We often rely on a man's generous nature or his reasonableness when we are making predictions. We may even say that someone *couldn't* refuse a request like this: he "doesn't have it in him" to turn down such a deserving cause. But this use of "couldn't" is not the one relevant to moral responsibility and is perfectly compatible with a remark of the apparently contradictory form, "Of course, he didn't *have* to give you anything; it's just that he's so generous (or, was touched by your plight, etc.)." The contrasts that are being drawn are quite different. When we say, "He couldn't refuse to help," we mean he (having the kind heart he has, unlike other people) will naturally help. When we say, "He didn't have to help," we mean that he was under no external compulsion to help and did it out of his generous nature. The crucial question in deciding what a man can do, in the sense of "can" that is relevant to responsibility, is the question what alternatives are within his power, i.e. (roughly), are such that under favorable circumstances he would succeed in doing them if he tried. It is not relevant that his nature is such that he would not try to do them, any more than that the circumstances were such that he did not so wish.

It is perfectly proper, in suitable contexts, to say that such facts about a man's nature or the circumstances made any alternative outcome impossible. It is no less proper and not inconsistent, when assessing moral responsibility, to say the opposite. For a crucial difference still exists between the man whose kindly nature makes him "incapable" of meanness and the man whose poor skills in mental arithmetic make him incapable of multiplying 276 by 189 in his head; in one and only one of these cases is intention properly irrelevant. A man is responsible for an act even when trying to do otherwise goes against his nature, if doing otherwise clearly would be possible for him if he tried it (in normal circumstances, not necessarily in those of the particular occasion). We need some careful elaboration of these guidelines to cover cases in which a real argument for the *pathological* incapacity to try any alternatives can be given. It is this which is thought to characterize someone with a compulsion.

7. IMMEDIATE RESPONSIBILITY

We are thus immediately responsible for at least those actions and consequences which we do or bring about intentionally (do from choice), i.e., do while knowing what we are doing and being able to do otherwise (F3). These actions are nevertheless as determined as any other events (D1, but not D2). We now bring some of the earlier conclusions to bear on the concept of responsibility.

7.1 The actions for which we are immediately responsible are simply those which occur under certain special conditions. They are not distinguished by the *absence* of causes but by the *presence* (and effectiveness) of a particular kind of cause, which in the simplest cases is our decision or wish to perform or allow them. To say our decision is the cause of these free actions is not to say that the decision ensures the action of itself but that the decision, together with the physical ability to perform it and favorable circumstances, in this case brings it about. The suggestion that free actions are not caused is generally based on a mistaken analysis of a cause (e.g., as a guarantee in itself, "compelling circumstance," or a non-self-conscious state) or an action (e.g., as something which is essentially unpredictable).

7.2 The ability to do or not to do something, e.g., run a mile in five minutes, or to multiply 274 by 896 in one's head, or to refrain from annoying Republicans at a cocktail party, is of course demonstrated by doing it (where luck is ruled out), but it can usually also be inferred from other performances and states. The absence of the ability is likewise inferable from the failure of serious attempts but not from one such attempt. For example, we may say that a certain baseball player is perfectly capable of hitting a homer on his next turn at bat, and the claim is not disproved by his failure to do so when he tries. But of course if he *never* succeeds, we should not be able to maintain the claim that he *could*. Favorable circumstances are not just the same as luck, for luck does not indicate ability, whereas doing something, even if it is done in favorable circumstances, is taken to show ability.

7.3   Whether or not someone actually tries to do something that he can do if he tries is itself determined by his previous experience and inherited characteristics, but this in no way counts against his responsibility. To say he is responsible is not to say his actions or his wishes are uncaused or that they might just as soon happen one way as another; it is to say his actions were dependent on and not independent of his wishes, intentions, etc. That his wishes (and hence his decision) are "already determined" by previous wishes, learning, intelligence, etc., only means that these are the factors in his personality which explain what he does; it does not mean that the decision has already been made, that it is irrelevant, or that it is not made by him, i.e., that he is not responsible for it.

7.4   It is not true *in every sense* that everyone can "perfectly well wish" for either of any two alternatives open to him. In one clear sense he cannot, because it is (generally) determined that he will wish for (prefer, choose) only one of these ways. Hence one is very tempted to conclude, since his wishes determine his actions, that he cannot act other than as he does. And there is a sense in which this is true, the sense in which we contrast his future with that of a wholly undetermined system. For the latter may behave in any way at all; *he* will definitely act in a way that is usually predetermined. We could put this by saying, "It can do anything, but he can only do one thing." But the sense of "can" in "can do otherwise" which is the one relevant to responsibility is entirely different, as sections 7.1 and 7.2 demonstrate. That sense stresses the difference between actions stemming from choice or intention and those not under the control of the agent's intention at all, and it has no reference to the source of the intention. Of course, if the intention itself is under *compulsion* as opposed to mere *causation*, then further investigations are needed; we shall discuss one of the supposed cases of this, addiction.

8. *MEDIATE RESPONSIBILITY*

An inescapable consequence of this doctrine of responsibility, one worth stressing since a great deal of the domain of responsibility is ruled by it, is the notion of indirect or mediate responsibility. A general formulation of this idea is somewhat cumbrous but worth having in one place for later reference. We are responsible for actions (and consequences) which we could not avoid doing *at the time* or avoid causing, or whose nature we did not recognize, or whose consequences we did not foresee, when there was an earlier time at which we could have acted so as to avoid the later action (or consequence or lack of insight or foresight), at which earlier time we did or should have known that the later result might occur and could reasonably be expected to act so as to avoid its occurrence. We can call this *mediate responsibility,* in contrast with the *immediate responsibility* of section 7. For example, we might say that a husband could not excuse his failure to return home one night on the ground that the main road was blocked if a known or easily discoverable alternative route was open. We now turn to some detailed consideration of applications of these doctrines.

8.1 *Temporary loss of control: drunkenness and anger* A *drunken driver* is responsible for the accident he causes, not because he could have avoided it *at the time when it occurred* (he tried and failed, his reflexes having deteriorated), but because (1) he could have called a taxi to take him home, refrained from drinking, etc. (2) he knew or should have known [5] that by failing to do so he made such an accident possible; and (3) avoiding a significant increase in the likelihood of manslaughter could reasonably be expected of him.

For the same reasons, "uncontrollable fury" is not, as such, a good excuse for manslaughter, since one may reasonably be held to be capable of learning, and be obliged to learn, to control oneself. Frenchmen believe that any reasonable man will (perhaps should) become homicidally angry upon finding his wife in bed with another man, and so they treat this kind of murder (at least of the lover) rather leniently. (Murder of the wife is regarded as wasteful.) This certainly provides a social deterrent against the seduction of married women but is equally obviously open to exploitation by the vindictive or proud though emotionally calm husband.

---

[5] "Should have known" is approximately equivalent to "It was possible for him to find out, and good reasons and means for finding out were known to him, at some earlier time."

8.2 *Semipermanent loss of control: alcoholism, addiction, and bad habits* An alcoholic is typically responsible for continuing to drink to excess, not because he can now by a direct effort of his own unaided will turn down a second drink once he has taken the first, but because either (1) he can turn down or avoid being in a position where he is tempted by the first drink; or (2) if not this, he certainly can call on friends or the Alcoholics Anonymous (AA) emergency crew to stop him from getting drunk; or (3) if not this, he can certainly turn himself in to an alcoholics ward or clinic for treatment, rehabilitation, and so on. If he does not *wish* to avoid drinking to excess, then he may simply be someone whose tastes and interests are different from those of the ordinary person. He is then not necessarily sick or incompetent, though he may be if further conditions apply. We need to look much more closely at his situation before we can assess his responsibility.

Alcoholism or addiction in general is a very complex phenomenon: different individuals have quite different degrees of responsibility and culpability for quite different aspects of their condition. We must avoid the extreme conventional attitudes toward alcoholism, the view that it is an illness for and in which the victim is in no way responsible and the opposing view that it is an example of moral turpitude. Each is an oversimplified response to a complex range of individuals with different needs, obligations, and abilities. An objective observer must surely concede that for some alcoholics, alcoholism (like suicide for others) is a perfectly defensible route to escape a drab and lonely world. It is, after all, a relatively slow poison, not unlike overeating in its effect on life expectancy; and it is an extremely effective short-term antidepressant (in the nontechnical sense of this term). For many others, it is indefensible only because they have contractual obligations to others, e.g., spouses and children, which are of greater importance than their own welfare. Ignoring these may be merely a sign of moral turpitude and not of sickness: one can hardly assume the two are the same.

The most interesting case is that of the alcoholic who is torn between the attractions of drunkenness and its drawbacks, gives in to the former frequently, and with equal frequency regrets it afterward. Much recent "enlightened opinion" has encouraged us to think of him as in the grip of a disease and hence as not responsible. While this attitude has the solitary commendable consequence of encouraging sympathy rather than condemnation,[6] it has little intrinsic justification. In the first place, people are often to blame both for contracting and for continuing to have diseases, e.g., tetanus, venereal disease. The "disease–therefore not responsible–therefore not culpable–therefore sympathy" sequence of inferences is simply unsound. Furthermore there is no good evidence that alcoholism is in any useful medical sense a

---

[6] Sympathy presupposes only misfortune, not responsibility.

disease entity rather than an acquired habit with certain physiological concomitants, very like smoking or chewing betel nut.

In the case mentioned, before we draw any conclusions at all, we need to judge whether the regrets would be almost equally frequent, though in the opposite direction, if the individual suddenly found himself removed from any access to alcohol. If this seems likely, he may simply be a chronic regretter, which is a minor character disorder. Or he may thereby demonstrate low superego strength ("moral character") if it is also clear that, whether he enjoys it or not, his obligations imply that he should not be drinking. If, on the other hand, it becomes clear that the postdrinking regrets are genuine, the pleasure is ephemeral, and a life of alcoholic abstinence is really his ideal and would be enjoyed with few regrets, we are up against what is rather unexcitingly but properly identified as a bad habit. Like smoking, unpunctuality, nose picking, nail biting, overeating, watching the late, late show to its conclusion (however bad it is), and the inability to keep secrets, the *badness of the habit* is dependent on the circumstances of those who manifest the behavior in question; indeed, these circumstances may in some cases make the same behavior a *good habit*. Bad habits are part of nearly all of us, while diseases are alien invaders; we should see the alcoholic as one of us, slightly more out of adjustment in one direction, not as an unluckily infected victim of a strange disease. He is in worse shape than some patients and better than others. Some alcoholics deserve sympathy far less than some smokers; others, far more than most drug addicts or sufferers from diseases known to be ultimately fatal.

Not all bad habits are recognized as such by those who have them, and alcohol and the narcotics are notorious for their alleged corrupting effect on the judgment of their users. This contributes to the picture of "being in the grip of a compulsion," which is commonly thought of as the enlightened view of addiction. It is overdone. There is indeed a natural tendency in man to deny that he is weak or wicked, which may explain why some alcoholics and addicts defend their way of life as theirs by choice. But there is also a natural tendency in man to condemn the sensual tastes he does not share, which partly explains the critic's tendency to suppose that the alcoholic is doing something he should not be doing or cannot help doing and that his defense is merely a rationalization. The alcoholic or addict has discovered a pleasure-giving device of great power, and we who judge it from without are as likely to underestimate its attractions as he is to dismiss its disadvantages. It is worth remembering that most alcoholics who voluntarily undergo treatment cannot bear the thought of total abstinence and do not want it, although achieving the level of moderate drinking is the one impossibility for them. The alcoholic has very different tastes from the moderate drinker, and this alters what must be judged as rational behavior for him. He is not very different from the man who chronically beggars himself at the race track, or on the stock market, or on suburban status symbols. Doing this will be rational and moral or not, depending entirely on his pleasure in it, his regrets about it, and his other values and obligations.

In a society like the United States (in this decade), which savagely punishes drug addicts while practically pampering alcoholics, addiction is probably less advisable than alcoholism; but physiologically and socially it is almost certainly less objectionable than the other habit. Drug addiction (involving the opium derivatives and marijuana) appears to have less tendency to produce pathological conditions (cirrhosis of the liver, brain damage, etc.) than alcoholism, and it appears to inhibit rather than accentuate antisocial behavior: it acts as a sexual and aggression inhibitor rather than stimulator. Of course, where drugs are illegal, they become expensive and the addict will steal to get them; but then even the nonaddicted drinkers of alcohol cheerfully broke the law in the prohibition era and still do in every "dry" area of the country, and in so doing support the crime syndicates. The evils of drugs are largely (not entirely) the product of an absurdly inappropriate approach to them in our society, as the reports of the Joint Committee of the American Bar Association and the American Medical Association make clear.[7] Socially speaking, indeed, drug addiction is a serious problem mainly in urban America, unlike several that the contemporary society encourages, such as the escapist use of early marriage and pregnancy, political and religious conformism, and conspicuous consumption. It has served the scapegoat function long enough and, like alcoholism, deserves to be retired to a more appropriate role in the retinue of man's indulgences. Possibly the more tolerant view of alcoholism impedes tolerance toward drug addiction, for the tolerance masks both guilt and hostility which currently may find their permissible outlet in viciousness toward narcotics users.

Despite the preceding qualifications, it is still true that a process of gradual "enslavement" to alcohol and drugs can be identified and so described with some justice. This process often does proceed contrary to the balance of the wishes of the sufferer and is thus reminiscent of the progress of a debilitating disease. It is still entirely mistaken to put this in the same category as cancer or progressive paralysis, for a very simple reason: deterioration of health in the addict continues only because the subject allows it, indeed, produces it. His feelings are certainly mixed, but when he begins another bout, he does so because he chooses to do so on balance at the time, i.e., despite forebodings of hangover, premonitions of regret, feelings of desperation, etc. If we wish to say he suffers from a disease and if we can *prove* that it really is possible for him to have a better life by staying off alcohol, then it is a disease or debility of motivation and we have an older and excellent phrase for it: he is weak-willed, in this respect. He "can't resist" a temptation that he knows to be a snare: he "has a weakness for" alcohol, as our supposedly unenlightened grandparents used to put it.

The fancy fairy tales about the alcoholic's supersensitivity to some substance in alcohol reduce guilt but are as irrelevant to responsibility as are the withdrawal symptoms: it is not *easy* to kick habits, but it is only a lack of willpower that "prevents" it. The idea that some inherited physiological peculiarity is the key factor in alcoholism is best seen to be irrelevant by looking at the compulsive overeater and the compulsive gambler or the cultural differences in alcoholism rates. The other compulsives are obviously exhibiting the same behavior pattern as the alcoholic, but they can hardly be said to be physiologically "hooked" by food and dice—only psychologically.[8] Does this view make an addict's responsibility any greater? Certainly, for there are ways to break these habits which are *still* within his power (compare the insomniac, the allergic, etc.). It is not now possible for him to resist the full temptation head on and alone, but not only could he have stopped himself before getting hooked (retrospective responsibility), he can still take steps to prevent the temptation from being presented, to arrange aid to help refusal, and otherwise to increase his resistance to indirect opportunities to succumb. But to say he is to be *blamed* implies that he *should* not continue to be an alcoholic, and that is always a further claim and not always a defensible one.

We must conclude that the alcoholic is entirely responsible, though not always culpable, for (1) getting into [9] and (2) continuing in his condition; but we cannot conclude that assistance and sympathy are always inappropriate, for a habit is not made easy to break by recognizing that it is possible to break it. If we wish to call such serious habits compulsions or diseases, we must clearly realize that many compulsions and diseases, including these, are the (mediate) responsibility of those who have them.

Contemporary authorities often, but not always, use definitions of alcoholism which refer to it as if it were a simple condition for which the addict has total lack of responsibility, e.g., ". . . an uncontrollable craving for alcohol"; ". . . has not the power to resist his craving"; and ". . . cannot face reality without alcohol." These are elisions; taken literally, they are convenient falsehoods. They are true only with respect to immediate control, but

---

[8] Some people have a natural *aversion* to alcohol, which may be physiological. But the absence of this does not make one incapable of moderate drinking, i.e., an alcoholic; it just makes one *capable* of becoming an alcoholic. One actually becomes an addict for some specific psychological reasons. And the same appplies to a natural *liking* for alcohol.

[9] In this respect, he is typically different from *some* drug addicts who get hooked while under medical care without realizing it. Alcoholics are virtually all aware of the possibility of alcoholic addiction at many points on the downhill road at which they can still turn back.

mediate control of course exists since alcoholism is not incurable. At least, this is true in the usual sense of alcoholism. The very term "alcoholism" itself, however, is used in contradictory ways: sometimes it is taken to be incompatible with abstinence, sometimes not; the latter usage, which is AA's, is not being discussed here. (Members of AA are abstemious alcoholics, in their terminology; ex-alcoholics, in the usual terminology.)

These unsettled definitions exhibit the philosophical confusions in the area. As long as an alcoholic can lift a telephone, he can prevent himself from excessive drinking; and he rarely, if ever, loses that power. He may lose the *desire* to avoid drunkenness, he may lose the chance to avoid it *easily,* he may lose the capacity to stop *after* a few drinks, but he never loses the *power* to give up drink. It might be better therapeutically and socially speaking to stress this fact rather than the illness-helplessness interpretation. The evidence on the therapeutic effects of the two emphases is not clear. It *is* clear that mediate responsibility for alcoholism is a fact, whether or not it is a therapeutically useful story. At worst an intermediate position should be adopted. The definitions of alcoholism used by the World Health Organization, English and English, and some others avoid the fallacies built into the examples quoted above by referring only to chronic and damaging, not uncontrollable, drinking.

The problem in *curing* addiction is the problem of retraining people to the point at which they exercise their mediate control over this particular aspect of their behavior. It cannot always be done to the point at which *immediate* control is achieved. The key to *exercising* control is motivation, and the reason why addiction is hard to cure is that cure requires remotivation, not that the iron grip of a reflex has to be broken. When there is no overall motivation to abstinence, there are usually no grounds for saying the individual *cannot* stay off the addictive substance. He just does not want to. In such cases, there may be grounds for saying he *should* be "cured," even though he does not see it that way. For example, it may be clear that other values which he espouses more highly than the pleasures of addiction objectively require that he abandon addiction, although he does not realize that they do. We may be able to show that he has lost the capacity to reason about the fact of his addiction, or there may be social reasons, such as criminal tendencies when he is high, why he should be got off the stuff. These cases in which the motivation has to be imposed from outside are, as one would expect, the toughest cases of all, and success is minimal. Mere "drying out" virtually never works because it only eliminates the physiological "need," and this is not the key feature of addiction. The failure of this procedure supports the emphasis in the present account on the entirely subsidiary role of the physiological variables. The use of Antabuse to induce an artificial allergy to alcohol will work only if it is maintained forcibly: it will not produce autonomous abstinence. Of course, this is no problem where the

ADDICTION

GENERAL FACTORS AFFECTING RESPONSIBILITY ASSESSMENT	PARTICULAR FACTORS AFFECTING RESPONSIBILITY ASSESSMENT	TREATMENT	PHYSIOLOGICAL FACTORS	PSYCHOLOGICAL AND SOCIOLOGICAL FACTORS
Type of "addiction" 1. Chronic and damaging use 2. Virtual unavoidability of continuance of bout once started 3. Corruption of judgment (vs. change of tastes) 4. Unavoidability of starting bouts although undesired Origin of addiction 1. training 2. genetic 3. accidental, etc. Associated withdrawal syndrome 1. severity 2. type 3. eliminability	Circumstances and background of individual addict	Possibility Availability Cost	Typically correlative rather than causative	Explanatory as well as correlative

alcoholic's motivation is in the right direction; the diabetic's life is saved, even if inconveniently, by his dependence on insulin. But where the therapeutic drug simply destroys what is still treated as a pleasure, only an extreme form of brainwashing, restructuring the man's dependency system and the prospective environment, is likely to work reliably. Obviously we have got to provide a substitute for an addictive substance (or activity) for someone who has built his needs around this substance, if we want him to live. Prisoners do not all give up sex or sublimate just because they are in jail; they adopt homosexual or autoerotic practices. But it is much easier to sublimate or sacrifice sex than to substitute candy for heroin.

There is certainly *some* physiological dependence of the addict on certain drugs and on alcohol, as on tobacco or masturbation; the difference is only a matter of degree, and this dependence is not the reason for the addiction, or the essence of it. And it is relatively easy to handle, by tapering off or by the use of substitutes. The attempt to *define* addiction in terms of the withdrawal syndrome fails because (1) marijuana and other drugs have none; (2) tobacco, insulin, sex, and a rice diet produce it; and (3) the syndrome can be eliminated without having any effect on the psychological commitment to addition, which immediately manifests itself again at the first opportunity. It is the role of the particular kind of *gratification* in the psychic economy, not the physical substance in the physiological economy, that cannot be handled by making the substance poisonous or by withholding it until tolerance for its absence has been developed. Remotivating requires finding an alternative, not just abandoning the forbidden one. That is what makes it so hard to give an addiction up, just as it is hard for a society to give up its belief in magic or slavery. The difficulty of renunciation does not show it is impossible or even impossible without help; if it is wanted, it can certainly be done, and even if it is not wanted it can possibly be done. But we need to be very sure that we are right and that we can do it, before we try restructuring a man or a culture that does not want to be restructured.

The diagram on page 217 summarizes the complexity of the subject, though not our comments.

Any simple account, any simple definition of addiction, which treats it as analogous to a simple affliction, like an allergy or a brain lesion, must be gravely misleading. At a particular stage of thought it may be salutary to stress one oversimplification rather than another; this is one defense of the emphasis on the bad-habit analysis supported in this section. We acquire habits and addictions, and in doing so we lose some of our rational control over ourselves. We must now ask, How do we acquire that control in the first place?

8.3 Acquiring responsibility   A child acquires a modicum of responsibility in different areas of behavior at different times and in all areas gradually. The process is as follows: initially the child is conditioned by positive and negative reinforcement without comprehension, e.g., for toilet or crying behavior. He learns *that* something is associated with reward or punishment, not *why*. He has no reasoning capacity as yet. He gradually acquires verbal skills and then is able to understand (and give) symbolic representation of the action-reward connections; i.e., he understands as reasons for action or inaction the assertion that some action will lead to reward or punishment of himself. We can say that he now has *prudential* reasons why he should or should not do something.

His training may be extended, still on a reward-punishment basis, so as to make him behave according to moral rules, or it may merely refine the skill with which he acts according to his self-interest. Natural rewards for foresight, care, etc., will tend to condition him to awareness of the second kind; but training by the parents can deliberately attach rewards to what they regard as moral behavior, or to mixed behavior, or to immoral behavior of some kind and thus convey to him a set of additional goals not necessarily autonomous. That is, he may still be obeying the new rules, whatever they are, for selfish reasons, such as expectation of reward from the parents. He may or may not progress from this stage. If he does, he may develop concern for the welfare of others as rewarding in itself, as an autonomous goal. And he may develop other autonomous goals, as a carry-over either from training or from emotional inspiration by others, or he may find these goals within himself. If he does develop concern for others, his actions will now exhibit some unselfish as well as selfish motivation, since he is swayed by considerations of the welfare of others regardless of the prospective returns for his *other* egocentric interests (see section 8.4).

Should he ever get to the point of evaluating actions on the basis of the welfare of everyone concerned *equally,* he is evaluating from what can be defined as the moral point of view (*Morality* chapter). And if he *acts* on that evaluation, he has presumably achieved an historic peak in human endeavor. This may or may not make him happy. Someone may reach almost this same standard of behavior under the pressure of an authority, human or divine, and its threats and promises or the remembered residue of these. But he is then only *overtly* moral, since the welfare of others is not an independent goal for him; and in circumstances in which he estimates he can escape punishment, he will act selfishly, unlike the genuinely moral person. Moreover, even if he believes he can never escape the eye of the moral supervisor, he still acts without pleasure in the action.

Apart from the gradual development of this concern for the welfare of others, which may or may not occur, the child is developing two other traits that are closely connected with responsibility. First, he is developing his perceptual and inferential skills in analyzing choice situations in what he has been taught to believe are moral terms. He does this, under the environment's pressure, just as he develops his skill in detecting disapproval or lying by his parents and others. And, like those skills, moral appraisal becomes an instinctive response, at least with the simpler kinds of choice; and this instinct, when coupled with some motivational concern, is what we call the con-science. The purely analytical aspect of this skill can be and commonly is quite well developed even in a wholly amoral individual. He learns to distinguish "morally good" from "morally bad," which is very useful for him, since it is often in his best selfish interests to follow what is commonly taken to be the moral path either to avoid penalties or to achieve status. But only in the moral individual is the moral perception *directly* connected with action. Having "a moral sense" or "a sense for what is right" usually means having a behavioral commitment to morality and not just the capacity to recognize what is right.

Second, the child is commonly, but again not always, developing and being taught the capacity to bring his behavior under the control of reason—in particular, under the control of long-run considerations about future gains and losses. He may already have learned that the command "No!" is a sign that doing the prohibited act will mean punishment. Even in that simple case, it takes a long time before he modifies his behavior as fast under the verbal threat as under actual punishment. It is much harder still for him to learn to make and give the proper weight to complex calculations involving the chances that he will probably be caught and punished in the distant future. Calculated or carelessly unanticipated probable punishment is a thin substitute for a direct threat by the punitive agent in person, and at first a poor adversary for prospective pleasure. (Similarly, prospective hangovers for the addict have little weight in the scale against immediate relief from the pains of life.) But learning to give the calculated chance of punishment or promise of reward the same weight as the reality is learning what makes the language-using animal the king of the animals. It is learning to behave rationally.

When we talk of a youth as having reached the age of responsibility, we mean an age by which he should have achieved a considerable degree of control over his behavior with regard to long-term considerations. Of course, this presupposes the capacity to reason. And when we are talking of someone as being responsible for morally assessable action, we also presuppose the capacity for moral analysis, though not for moral feeling.

8.4 *Motivation of moral action* The *hedonistic fallacy* supposes that the fundamental human motive is the desire for selfish pleasure. It is a fallacy because it confuses selfish motivation with self-motivation, i.e., motivation by one's own motives. The unselfish person acts from his own motives, of course, but these include concern for the welfare of others and hence are not purely selfish. It is true that an unselfish act *may* in fact give us pleasure, but the real motivation for the act is by definition the pleasure or reduction of misery it gives another. That this can be the real motive or reason, in some cases, emerges from a study of examples of self-sacrifice—cases in which one abandons one's own personal interests when they are incompatible with those of others, e.g., by agreeing to go to the zoo to please the kids, though the prospect appalls. One's own welfare and the welfare of others are both "one's own interests" in the sense of being goals that one wishes to see attained, but the commitment to another's welfare is the unselfish part of one's own interests and is in an obvious sense the interest of another. That one's own interests may include concern for the interests of another is not a proof that the latter are *not* the interests of another, i.e., that one is only selfish; it is simply a proof that one may have unselfish interests. The pleasure we derive from the happiness of others is our own pleasure but not selfish pleasure. This topic is discussed further in Chapter VII.

8.5 *The immature immoralist* The *juvenile delinquent* is typically (but not always) responsible, even if he is a so-called psychopath; but this in no way diminishes the responsibility of his parents and ultimately of the social environment, any more than man's free will diminishes God's responsibility for the evil we do.

Delinquents are sometimes diagnosed or perhaps explained as having psychopathic personalities, i.e., as being arrested at the immediate-authority-recognizing stage of moral development and as having only selfish and usually mainly short-term selfish motivation. This failure to develop a moral sense and the capacity for responsible behavior is most unlikely to be chiefly hereditary and hence probably represents a deficiency in training, at home or at school, or both. Almost all of us, however, exhibit, if to a lesser degree, the same deficiency, so that elaborate attempts to treat it as a special kind of affliction or condition seem inappropriate. The only interesting question about the delinquent, in terms of judging his responsibility for crime, is the extent to which he is deficient in long-term rational control. The immorality or the disrespect for the law that is common in a delinquent is in itself irrelevant to responsibility, since he and we are well aware of the perfectly sound selfish reasons for him to keep the law, i.e., to avoid punishment. A man does not have to love legality in order to be responsible for breaking the law; he only has to know that illegality is unloved.

Even when we have determined responsibility, however, this is only a preliminary to the questions whether punishment is appropriate and, if so, what kind of punishment is appropriate. In settling those questions, considerations of a criminal's hardships, deficiencies in training and knowledge, and previous record are relevant. The native who commits a ritual murder is entirely responsible for his act, but if he lives in a very primitive society with an elaborate mythology that enjoins ritual murder, there would be little sense in blaming him and no justification for allotting the punishment indicated by our usual code. Again, the "hardened criminal" may require a more severe deterrent than the first-time loser (see section 8.8).

It is perhaps worth discussing at greater length the reasons for a distinct juvenile court with a different approach to the criminal, since this might be thought inconsistent with the very pervasive interpretation of responsibility advocated here. A child, like a chimpanzee or a flatworm, can have its behavior modified directly by suitable systematic reward and punishment of the behavior manifested; the very young child can only be trained in this way. As the child develops the power to reason about its choice of action, we adopt the humane and convenient procedure of telling it what will happen if it does something, instead of waiting until it acts. Now in many households what the child actually learns is that these announcements need not be taken too seriously, that they really reflect what the parent would *like* to see done or thinks *ought* to be done, but that the parent can usually be talked out of actually applying the announced sanctions. In such situations it is manifestly inexcusable for the parent to suppose that he is *justified* in punishing the child, on the occasions when he does carry out his warning, simply because he announced that he would. He (or she) must realize that what has really been taught the child is that authority does not mean what it says about punishment, that attempts at self-gratification, even when contrary to the announced rules, usually pay off. This is the worst possible training for "life," and the child is certain to transfer its successful egocentrism to the school and to the social context. If now the school's often-limited armory of authority is inadequate to retrain the child, we have a *trained delinquent* ready to be turned loose, that is, a youth who has been taught for years that disregard of authority and announced penalties pays off. The society can hardly justify immediate maximum sentences for an individual who has been so extensively trained to believe he can circumvent the "official regulations." While it is true that the youth may clearly understand the law and know that retribution in adult society is considerably more efficient than it was in his earlier groups, this at most establishes responsibility and not the justifiability of severe punishment. And it only establishes responsibility if a considerable degree of intelligence is present.

More typically it establishes a highly confused attitude towards authority, due to the conflict between the implicitly learnt possibility of disregarding it and the explicit knowledge of frequent enforcement. A more merciful and effective course than full adult sentencing is to begin retraining, perhaps at a properly disciplined youth camp, perhaps by applying definite punishments on a clearly stated and increasing scale. If it is not too late, this kind of trained delinquent can thus be brought to a point at which he resolves his ambiguous training: he has been taught that crime does and does not pay, and now he must come to see the matter more clearly in terms of the adult environment where it is a relatively unsatisfactory career choice. This discussion is so far independent of developing any interest in obeying the law because it embodies principles of morality. Graduated and strictly applied sanctions will not usually bridge this crucial motivational lack in the child: they do not (of themselves) develop the kind of respect for the law which will ensure legal behavior even in the absence of the likelihood of retribution. But they will go some way toward protecting the child and others from many serious consequences of further misdemeanors. Correctional institutions should, of course, concern themselves just as much with the remotivating goal as with the retraining goal. Certainly they should embody more explicit discussion of the law and lawlessness, of roles and responsibility, than they do now, not under the guise of psychotherapy but as part of the education for citizenship that children get only in the most superficial way today.

Since one of the factors determining culpability (as opposed to responsibility) is the difficulty of avoiding the action in question, it is appropriate here to add a word about possible genetic determinants of delinquency. Although it is unlikely that adolescents inherit a deficiency of the moral sense, since that appears to be mainly a learned response, they probably do inherit a strong drive to rebel. It is extremely likely that a race in which the post-pubescent breaks away from the family ties to form his own family group will have superior survival expectations to one in which independence is long delayed, in a significant range of environments. Hence it is extremely likely that natural selection has developed a strain of rebellious youth which urgently turns to any alternative way of life in order to slake the thirst for independence. In a highly structured society, with economic and social limits on direct competition against the parents, this must often mean turning to lawlessness. We sowed the wind in the jungles long ago and we reap the whirlwind in the cities today.

8.6 Strength of will   So the crucial training for the child, both from his own and from society's point of view, is development of his willpower, his capacity to accord long-range or moral considerations full weight as determinants of action against pressing considerations of immediate welfare.[10] A vital requirement in this training is rewarding the child for resisting temptation. Such training is undercut equally by parents who fail to come through with promised rewards for long-run good behavior and by those who "forgive" promised punishments. Further study of this definition of willpower shows that children can hardly acquire willpower without undergoing deprivation; so the overkind parent is simply excluding all training in this crucial area, and usually is exhibiting his own lack of willpower. It is much harder to exercise restraint than to recognize that one should, and so it takes the child longer to develop will than reason. It is thus not enough to ask simply, "Did he know it is forbidden to steal?" We must also ask, "Has he been taught (or has he had time and reason enough to teach himself) to refrain from doing what is attractive when it is known to be punishable?" The adult has almost no hope of finding an excuse in these terms, since it is obvious enough to his reason that it is desirable to have willpower and since he has had long enough to train himself to exercise restraint, a kind of training which appears to be possible for most adults, at least to a substantial extent. For the same reason, we should not regard an ungovernable rage as a good excuse for crime, except in the rare cases in which it is due to disease or deterioration of the brain or a strain of wholly unprecedented severity.

[10] The clearest examples of willpower involve resisting temptation, e.g., castaways refusing to drink sea water or prisoners of war refusing to collaborate in order to obtain privileges. But there is a continuum from these cases to cases in which we perhaps more usually talk of courage or guts, although willpower is clearly involved: silence under torture, crawling 10 miles on broken legs, etc.

It has been argued that the adult is no more responsible than the child, since whether he will or will not take account of the good reasons for learning restraint is itself determined. But the determinism can be conceded without in any way conceding that the adult lacks responsibility. For it is what the adult himself does about these reasons that determines whether he acquires a capacity for restraint. He has been given the power to reason and act on reason: he has been given responsibility. His own decisions do matter and so he is responsible. To suppose that these decisions do not matter, that he is not responsible, because other earlier factors also matter, is a *non sequitur,* although one of the most seductive in the whole brothel of fallacies.

Should not our conscience prick us for this stern view—for holding that a man is responsible for not having developed his willpower even though whether he does or not is determined by his own earlier training? Indeed it does at first, for it is a rather crudely wrought instrument. But if we sort out the elements in the situation and accept the fact that the allocation of responsibility does not preclude the award of sympathy and aid, we may see the value in equating someone's responsibility with determinism operating through reasonably competent choice machinery. For the evaluation, the treatment, the stimulation, or the prevention of such events is entirely different from that which is appropriate for events which are not under anyone's control. The concept of an agent's responsibility is precisely designed to select the subclass of his actions and their effects that he can recognize for what they are and does because of or in spite of what they are. The whole analysis of the consequences of actions and their moral nature, that is the whole realm of practical and moral reasoning, has its point because it affects or can usefully affect some of our behavior, viz., the behavior for which we are responsible. The domain of actions over which it is to our advantage that reason should hold sway is roughly the domain of responsibility. So the value of the concept of responsibility in no way depends on opposing it to the domain of the empirically determined; indeed, its value would evaporate if reasons did not determine actions. And the idea that they do so, but not in an empirical way, is simply a product of the mistaken belief that physical determinism precludes the existence of genuine alternative actions for the choosers.

8.7 *Legal responsibility* Insanity is sometimes incompatible with responsibility. In the criminal law, *insanity* is often used to mean "chronic absence of responsibility." The capacity for reason or perception may be seriously damaged without making action impossible, as with insanity due to brain deterioration or certain kinds of poisoning. Blind rage may have the same effect, and in both cases mediate responsibility can apply; so before responsibility can be circumvented, the agent must also be shown to have been incapable of avoiding the condition and incapable of training himself to exercise more restraint or of using others to limit its manifestations. Hence the "irresistible-impulse" criterion for lack of responsibility is not alone adequate.

Insanity may cause delusions with respect to which the appropriate response is the act about which the question of responsibility arises. And sometimes the insane individual either does not know he is insane or cannot get himself cured or restrained. Such a case is like that of a person who is misinformed in a way he could not have recognized: he is causally responsible for the physical act he performs but not morally responsible for it, since this involves knowing all about its morally relevant properties. One aspect of an act's real nature is its moral nature, and this has been made the keystone of the most famous legal definition of insanity. The M'Naghten rule asserts that a man is insane only in the absence, due to "disease of mind," of the capacity "to know the nature and quality of the act—or if he did know it, that he did not know he was doing what was wrong." As it has been interpreted, this is a particularly confusing standard because it is not clear whether knowledge of what is wrong refers to (1) knowledge of what is legally forbidden, (2) knowledge of what is taken to be *justifiably* approved or forbidden, (3) knowledge of what is *really* right or wrong, or (4) the possession of moral feelings with substantial motivational power. Responsibility involves only the first kind of knowledge, for culpability we need the second, for legislating the third, and for good citizens the fourth. Apart from its unclarity, the rule is in error, since a man who knew he did wrong but was incapable of refraining due to mental illness would surely qualify as insane. The justification of the M'Naghten rule has mainly been the weakness of the alternatives, and that is not justification enough.

"Actions caused by a mental disease" is a popular "progressive" substitute for M'Naghten, the Durham rule being one version. Unfortunately this rule includes some actions for which the agent is responsible. For example, a paranoid or a kleptomaniac may attack or steal, something he would not do if normal, but he may still have been able to refrain from so acting by exercising greater restraint or foresight. The existence of insanity in such cases constitutes a mitigating factor but not a complete excuse, and hence this definition will not do for legal insanity which wholly precludes responsibility. The practical difficulties of perceiving the limits of responsibility are very great in such cases but are hardly overcome by using a false criterion. Again. a schizophrenic might, in a lucid moment, go to a psychiatrist for help, an action which is caused by his having a mental disease but for which he is surely responsible, contrary to Durham. Or he might mendaciously state on an insurance form that he is sane; since he is insane, this is a felony and it is his "mental disease" that makes it one; so on this rule he would be excused. And so on. The Durham rule is a serious oversimplification.

"Actions whose nature cannot be recognized, or whose commission cannot be avoided, at the time of the act, because of mental disease"—roughly, the Horton rule, proposed in New York State to replace the M'Naghten rule—is about the best substitute to get near the statute books thus far, but its difficulties are obvious. It is too generous, in that it excuses the alcoholic who develops Korsakoff's psychosis, which might lead to an act of violence, although he foresaw it and its likely consequences and could have avoided it. At the time of certain acts, which might even include murder of a spouse, such a man may have lost the powers which would let him avoid it. He is nevertheless just as responsible for them as the drunken driver for an accident, although the desirability of punishment is of course a different issue. It would almost certainly be better to regard legal definitions of insanity as practical criteria for substituting treatment for punishment rather than for adjudicating responsibility.

There are also great difficulties in applying the Horton criterion. Even proving immediate incapacity is hard, while proving absence of mediate capacity is extremely treacherous: most mentally diseased individuals have periods when they know of their condition and can take steps to have themselves committed or restrained. The wide concept of responsibility which is supported in this chapter does not allow for many genuine exceptions. The framers of the New York statute tackled one important difficulty by separately making clear that mere repetition of criminal and antisocial behavior is not to constitute adequate grounds for diagnosing mental disease. But an awkward problem remains. While criminal behavior is not insane in and of itself, there are certainly some laws the breaking of which is prima-facie evidence of insanity. (These do not include the antisuicide laws despite the frequency of the supposedly charitable verdict "suicide while of an unsound mind.") But constantly breaking laws against the consumption of poisonous or paralyzing chemicals such as the leaded alcohols *is* a sign of deranged judgment, which is a loose definition of insanity where this implies absence of the capacity for responsible action.

There are many cases of mental disorder in which responsibility cannot be wholly refuted but in which very little blame is appropriate. We sometimes talk of such cases as cases of "partial responsibility," but that term seems better reserved for multiple-agency situations. The degree of mental disturbance is relevant to the assessment of punishment, not only to guilt or innocence, and medical evidence must be heard on this point prior to sentencing. The criteria in terms of which punishment can be justified are discussed in the next section.

The general conclusion one must draw about the current legal conceptions is that they are grossly defective and should be replaced by the kind of definition given at the beginning of this section, in which both immediate and mediate responsibility are explicitly recognized.

8.8 Punishment Punishment is the infliction of characteristically un-pleasant conditions on someone for doing something which is identified as undesirable by the punitive agency. It can be justified in four very different ways. It is distinguished from mere revenge by the justifiability of these reasons and of the procedures for administration of the duly determined result; and from revenge or self-defense by its institutionalization.

(*i*) *Reformatory.* The prerational child or imbecile is not responsible for his acts in the sense of knowing what he does, but he can justifiably be punished, *if and when* the opposite procedure of rewarding him for avoiding the forbidden act is inefficacious, to the minimum extent necessary to modify his behavior in some desirable direction. A case might be made for saying this is not punishment or that no act is involved, on the grounds that the child does not know what he has done nor, at first, that it is forbidden. It is merely negative reinforcement of certain responses.

A responsible agent can be justifiably punished, on this basis, only if his behavior in respect of the act is *now* modifiable; that he was responsible at the time of the crime only makes him guilty, not justifiably punishable. Again only the minimum efficacious severity can be justified; and we also prefer that the law broken be justifiable and publicly available with its associated range of punishments (or the possibility of their existence reason-ably inferable by the agent).

(*ii*) *Exemplary.* Punishment of an individual may often be necessary even when it is not essential or useful for reform purposes simply because others must be deterred. This rigidity is sometimes expressed in the slogan "The law must be upheld." The effect of not applying the announced sanc-tions is to create, by example, an entirely different law which does not penal-ize first offenders. (Compare the "law" that is implicitly created in a home where the child is not punished for what he is told is wrong.) Optional leniency toward first offenders is a merciful and desirable provision, but its administration has to be tempered with consideration for the discouraging or encouraging effect on other prospective criminals. The virtual certainty of escape if one promises penitence will greatly increase the prohibited be-havior by criminals as by children.

(*iii*) *Restrictive.* Someone may be justifiably treated or detained in a way that might be said to constitute punishment for them, in order to prevent them from *further* damage to themselves or others where the predictable damage would be socially more serious than the loss of liberty. It is defensible to detain someone who has committed no crime if it is demonstrable that this is the only way to prevent him from committing one in the future. But this is not called punishment, because punishment is a supposedly unpleasant condition allocated to someone *for* a particular infraction of a rule. Thus the incarceration of political *suspects* and the commitment of the insane are not punishment. On the other hand, in deciding on the punishment for a criminal it is entirely appropriate for a judge to design it so as to serve the social-protective purpose.

(iv) *Restitutive.* When the other considerations can still be reasonably accommodated, the extent and nature of a punishment should be determined by the desirability of righting any wrong that has been done. The fruits of a criminal's labor in prison and perhaps when released should be used to support those he has deprived; the murderer should surely be made to support his victim's family at least to the degree involved if the victim had been legally divorced from his or her spouse. When the crime is antisocial, some community service should be performed by the prisoner. Manufacture of license plates and mail bags has been popular in the United States and England. It seems likely that, with the increasing cost of labor and the increasing automation of prison supervision, a prison that pays its way could be devised—a very suitable concept.

(v) *Retributive.* The illegitimate entry in the punishment sweepstakes is vengeance masked as justice, called retribution. There are justifiable elements in most so-called retributive theories, but they are included in the first four criteria above.

It is an obvious consequence of this analysis together with the usual moral concern for life that capital punishment is unjustified. For the evidence shows it has no *net* deterrent effect,[11] and it makes the correction of judicial error and the reform of the criminal as impossible as restitution. Further discussion of capital punishment and the general theory of punishment occurs in the next chapter.

9. CONCLUSION

The aim of this chapter has been to show how "free" choices are distinguished from others and how this (1) leads to a constructive approach to problems about responsibility in the child and the adult, compulsions, and punishments and (2) is in no way incompatible with brain determinism. The emphasis of the approach has been on the extraordinary range of one's responsibility which often becomes relevant in one sense just as soon as its relevance in another can be denied.

---

[11] Or fails to show that it has one, even for convicts already in for life.

VII

MORALITY

0. THE PROBLEMS

Are moral judgments any more than an expression of the attitudes we acquire from the society in which we live? Are they not, therefore, highly relative and subjective—not objective claims at all but just sales talk in Sunday dress? Why should one bother with so-called moral considerations unless they overlap with selfish ones? In particular, how could real self-sacrifice ever be sensible? How do you define "good" or "ought"? Isn't it impossible to do this except by using other moral terms, which makes the definition circular? Should not enlightened self-interest (or perhaps pleasure seeking or self-realization) be the ultimate foundation of morality? Should your conscience be your guide? Are there any exceptions to the Golden Rule? How should one interpret "Thou shalt not kill"? To mean that killing is always wrong, or usually wrong, or wrong unless proved otherwise? To whom or to what do moral standards apply: to infants, morons, animals, nations, robots? Is it realistic to suppose that we shall ever get agreement on moral issues, and if not, isn't that good ground for *practical* skepticism about the existence of absolute moral standards? Is there some kind of ultimate distinction between facts and values? Isn't religion the only possible basis for a morality that will work in this imperfect world? Should we praise people for *effort* or for *achievement*? If a saint finds it easy to behave morally, doesn't that show he is not so deserving as if it were very hard for him? Is it someone's motives that determine whether his actions are virtuous, or is it the consequences of the actions?

1. THE CONCLUSIONS

If we indicate the general nature of the proposed conclusions at the beginning of this chapter, the reader will more easily detect irrelevancy and impropriety in the ensuing arguments, since he will know what they are supposed to achieve. With the arguments of *this* chapter, such assistance is almost essential, for they are themselves complicated and their connections and assumptions are not easily stated. In fact, the only way to get a precise understanding of the conclusions is from a careful study of the course of the arguments. But we can begin with an approximation.

Roughly, then, it will be argued that there is a particular conception of morality which can be shown to be an extension of rationality. This conception is relevant to many decisions about actions and attitudes that affect more than one person, and where it is relevant, we shall see that immorality can be said to be irrational. This does not mean that any immoral act by any person is irrational in terms of that person's current goals; it means that having moral goals is rationally preferable to not having them.

Compare the question, Why be moral? with, Why use statistics? As a first answer to both questions it might be said that morality and statistics are extensions of reason and hence have all the sanctions of reason in the circumstances appropriate for their use. To the follow-up question, When *shouldn't* you be acting morally (or using statistics)? we should, prosaically, answer: (1) When it's irrelevant to what you're doing; and (2) when it's relevant but you aren't sufficiently well trained to be able to benefit from its advantages. Specifically, statistics isn't relevant when you're not trying to analyze complex data, and morality isn't relevant when you are analyzing situations which are of concern only to yourself.[1] But if you are ever likely

[1] This is true in the core conception of morality, with whose defense we are concerned. Mild extensions of it, to include the conception of "moral fibre" (i.e., strength of character), duties to oneself, etc., are plausibly defensible.

to be in the other kind of case, it is rational to train yourself (or get yourself trained) to the point at which doing statistical analysis (or acting morally) comes naturally. One cannot immediately blame a man who does not know statistics (or lacks moral feelings) for not using statistics (or acting morally), but one can sometimes blame him for his lack.

So the general line of argument will be that rational but nonmoral evaluation of different possible attitudes toward other people indicates the superiority of the attitude of regarding them as deserving equal consideration (which we shall identify as the moral attitude). For people in different circumstances, the argument has different force. With regard to the children we are now bringing up it clearly indicates a particular way to do this; for a selfish but highly successful middle-aged man it has less impact; for a government official it fully reinforces the ideology of his profession, and so on. So, in the sense that there are good reasons, from his point of view, for a drug addict to take drugs, there can be good reasons for an immoral man to murder for gain. But this in no way shows that taking drugs or murder for gain is in itself rational, for it is not usually rational to allow oneself to become an addict or an immoralist. In the dominant sense, therefore, addiction and immorality are (typically) irrational.

The moral society is a far greater advance on the premoral in practical terms (e.g., likelihood of survival) than the industrial on the nomadic; but the moral revolution requires us to pull ourselves up by our bootstraps with a different twist, for the maximum gain in this case is for those with, individually, the least material power.[2] Democracy is almost a precondition of the moral revolution but no guarantee of it, for a democracy whose culture has led it to place a very high value on bread and circuses, or beer and television, and whose economy provides these, will not have much interest in pulling at its bootstraps.

Some of the other conclusions to be drawn can be indicated briefly. Our natural wants and needs (a motley crew, *not* consisting of pleasure in many guises), like our beliefs and attitudes, are not automatically or intrinsically good but simply a starting point from which we discover that the most efficient way to resolve disputes and improve the expectations of each of us requires the adoption and enforcement of some rules about distribution, obligation, etc. The concepts of moral goodness, rightness, etc., apply within this system of rules in precisely the way that nonmoral concepts of goodness

---

[2] The significance of this difference in the driving force for moral rather than industrial progress becomes clear if one recalls that the basic insight into morality was certainly formulated 250 years ago (in Richard Cumberland's *De legibus naturae*), if not 2,000 years earlier, in Plato, since which time we have created virtually the whole structure of modern science, transformed technology, and made a fair start on colonization of the Moon and decolonization of the Earth. The charms of morality are more subtle than the delights of power.

and rightness apply in the system of rules we develop for strategy in war, mathematics, or consumer research. In terms of these rules we may have to modify or condemn some of the wants from which we start; so the premoral springs of morality eventually become an object for moral assessment themselves. Thus emerge the acclaim for unselfishness and the condemnation of sadism.

In a complex system of this kind it is as hopeless to produce brief nontrivial definitions of "good," "duty," etc., as it is to attempt the corresponding task in chess or bridge with regard to "good move"; but the system is clearly founded on nonmoral facts and evolves morality from them by the application of reason. Thus the ultimate appeal is to an objective truth and not to our beliefs about it; so conscience is only a secondary guide, and consequently we may be blamed for possessing an inadequate conscience.

Formally, the system is best construed as having one basic moral principle, the principle of equal consideration, from which all other moral principles (justice, etc.) can be developed, the principle itself being justified in terms of a comparative evaluation of the possible alternatives and their effects on a society which embraces them. This moral axiom can be interpreted in two ways, yielding what can be termed *strong* and *weak* morality. Weak morality involves the recognition of the rights of others but no positive interest in furthering their welfare other than by such recognition; strong morality involves identification with the interests of others. The first is the domain of obligation, the second of supererogation; the first of honor and decency, the second of nobility, love, and heroism. We shall be concerned especially with the justification of strong morality.

The objectivity of moral judgments, in terms of the system just described, is exactly that of any very complex solution of an important practical or theoretical problem. Emotions are more deeply involved than in most practical problems, but the total authority of facts and reason applies, and we fail if we fight it.

The chapter first discusses some simple difficulties (sections 2 to 7), then turns to the main arguments for morality (sections 8 to 12), and finally considers a series of refinements and more serious difficulties in the light of the developed argument.

2. MORALITY DISTINGUISHED FROM PRUDENCE

The most striking feature that distinguishes what we usually call moral principles from mere good advice is that they are supposed to be obeyed even when obedience does not seem to be in one's own best interest. That is, they supervene over and may contradict self-interest. Obviously, stealing is foolish if one is likely to be caught; this is not a moral conclusion, and in such circumstances there is no great virtue in not stealing. But if you are justifiably certain of getting away with a theft and the gains are very large and your need very great, your own interests appear to conflict with the recommendation of morality. We shall confine our attention to the questions whether, in what sense, how, and which rules of this kind can be justified. One may use the term "morality" to cover any system of "rules to live by," including purely selfish ones and ones that are entirely relativistic, but the usual systems embody the above-mentioned feature of potential clash with self-interest, and they also share a number of common principles (such as injunctions on stealing, lying, and killing); so it is of particular interest to investigate the possibility of supporting a system of this family. It will be argued here that just one system of this kind can be given direct rational support and that all others of this kind, as well as egocentric or relativistic "morality," are insupportable. Hence the terms "moral" and "ethical" (which are synonymous in most contexts) and their associates will here usually refer to the allegedly defensible system we shall try to construct; but sometimes, where the context makes it clear, they will refer to all systems of rules governing behavior which have been put forward as moralities.

3. UNSOUND BASES FOR MORALITY

First, a word or two to remind the reader of some alternative approaches we have already discussed. It is quite clear that morality cannot be ultimately founded on the ordinances of a God since (1) there is no God; and (2) even if there were one, we would still need *independent* standards of morality by which to tell if God is good. For, if the standards are not independent, it is only a definitional truth that He is good; and it cannot then be a definitional truth that we should do what is good, since neither definition implies the other. In fact we have to choose between the two definitions; and one choice leads to a secular morality, the other to a pointless one. (The argument here follows the lines of the criticism, in Chapter IV, of the ontological argument, whose proponents attempt to ensure that God is perfect by definition and also that He exists by definition. The only cake one can eat and have is imaginary.)

It is also quite clear that no appeal to conscience can be a workable foundation for an objective morality, since (1) consciences are inconsistent (those of different persons and even that of the same person) and if support by conscience were the ultimate basis for morality, both views would be equally true (i.e., there would be no objective moral truth); and (2) even if all persons' consciences were always in agreement, this would not rule out the possibility that all were in error. The conscience is the name of our moral sense, but like all other senses, it can surely be mistaken, and the crucial question is how we decide whether it is. That question obviously calls for standards of morality that are *not* conscience-controlled.

Thus there remain to be considered only the ways of sugar-coating the pill if morality cannot be justified and the possibility of a general justification, i.e., one that will be relevant to anyone, no matter what his interests are.

After considering some preliminary difficulties, we shall embark on the attempt at such a universal justification.

4. DOES MORAL DISAGREEMENT SUPPORT MORAL SKEPTICISM?

However one attempts to justify morality, the morality itself is a subject of the utmost complexity. Certainly a rational morality will involve almost every factual difficulty connected with discovering the facts about human behavior, plus the difficulty of avoiding emotional bias in an area where almost every such bias is most powerful, plus the difficulty of combining the facts objectively in the moral apparatus. These difficulties have made it plausible to claim that objective justification of moral claims is impossible.

Since ethics is a field in which emotions are very close to the surface, it is hardly surprising that moral claims are frequently based on one's wish to defend one's actions or intentions rather than on pure reason. No one enjoys the sanctions of disapproval or punishment or the admission of error. With issues of this kind the difficulty of reaching general agreement is no more a proof of the absence of objective standards than is the difficulty of getting the litigants in a breach-of-promise suit to agree on the facts or a proof that there were no facts. The fact that ethical disputes often involve extremely complicated and subtle reasoning and difficult judgments of fact (e.g., long-range predictions about consequences) provides independent grounds for expecting trouble. In these respects ethical disputes precisely resemble many disputes among established scientists about abstract theoretical matters, such as the interpretation of quantum theory or the utility of phenomenological psychology. Thus, although it will be concluded that there are absolute standards in morals in a way lacking in art, this does not mean that a correct single answer to every moral question is now or will on some date be known. The important conclusion is that the correct answers to some moral questions are now known or discoverable, the correct way to discover the answers to others can be indicated, and the correct interim moral attitude or actions can be determined.

5. IS UNSELFISH BEHAVIOR POSSIBLE?

Before showing that unselfish behavior is rationally defensible, it is important to define it and discuss the view that such behavior is impossible. We each have certain interests, wants, needs, or desires that do not concern other people directly, such as the desire for food or an interest in old clocks or the stock market. We may also have certain interests in the welfare or downfall of other people, such as our children, the President, our parents, certain Hollywood or sports celebrities, and our business partners. Some of this concern with other people's welfare simply arises from interests of the first kind. Replacing a President or a partner satisfactorily would be time-consuming and costly, if possible at all; hence it is better for us if he stays alive and well; so we prefer him to take a break when he feels he needs it rather than have a breakdown. But it is commonly the case that, for whatever reason we first come to value another person, the other person often becomes of some intrinsic value to us (similarly for the opposite feelings). This means that even when there is no prospect of personal gain with respect to our *other* interests, we are willing to make an effort to further his welfare. This willingness is the mark of what we call "genuine affection" for them; and it is the sign that, to some degree and in some direction, we are unselfish.

People have sometimes argued that this is not truly unselfish because in these cases we are still gratifying ourselves, albeit by doing something for other people. But this view confuses self-motivation with selfish motivation. There *is* a sense in which every voluntary act is intended to be self-gratifying: the act involves doing something in order to achieve one's own goals, i.e., is done from one's own motives. It does not follow from this sense that the act is selfish, i.e., that it involves disregard for the welfare of others, except insofar as that welfare contributes to one's interests. The unselfish interest in another is one of a man's *own* interests but not one of his *selfish* interests. The moral significance of unselfish behavior is that it helps others "for their own sake," implying "not for what they or others will do in return"; it is not made less moral by the fact that it gives satisfaction to the doer.

6. IS PLEASURE OR HAPPINESS THE ONLY GOAL?

A very similar argument to the one discussed above has been thought to show that all actions are motivated by considerations of pleasure. This conclusion (hedonism) can be combined with the earlier one (egoism). Everything we do, the argument runs, is done to achieve some end we think desirable. Achieving such an end would surely give us pleasure; hence everything we do is aimed at the goal of pleasure.

The natural reply would seem to be that we sometimes do things because we think we should or must—or because we cannot find the willpower to do otherwise—even when it gives us no pleasure, indeed, the reverse. The call of duty, prudence, or compulsion is often not the call to pleasure. In replying to this, the hedonist might first wish to restrict himself to voluntary action and hence exclude compulsive and compelled behavior. Then, he might say, we must recognize that the holy man's pleasure is the common man's poison; the duty-minded man *says* it isn't a pleasure to do his duty, meaning it isn't the kind of thing that people usually call a pleasure, but in fact it is simply an example of his peculiar taste in pleasures. For he cannot deny that he does his duty because he values the discharge of duty, and surely achieving a valued goal is rewarding, i.e., pleasurable or at least *more* pleasurable than the alternatives. The tangle of jargon here obscures the fallacy, which is simply to confuse doing something because one thinks it the best thing to do (and possibly continuing to feel thereafter that it *was* the best thing to do, from which fact one sometimes derives some satisfaction) with doing something simply *because* of the pleasure it will give us.

The human animal, like the dog, can learn or be trained to regard the welfare of other human beings—or sheep—as a goal, and it can similarly acquire an interest in duty at some expense in felt pleasure. Only if we trivially extend the notion of pleasure to cover the condition resulting from doing anything a human being ever voluntary does will doing one's duty always be enjoyable. Mostly, it is pretty painful. The hedonist claim is thus clearly false if the terms are used in the normal way. One *can* be mistaken about one's own motives, but one can hardly be *always* skeptical about the possibility of distaste for and sadness after severely punishing a child or pet of whom one is fond, or about a judge's feelings in passing a mandatory death sentence when he believes the death penalty is indefensible, or about the pain under torture which fails to make one reveal collaborators in a patriotic revolt.

So it is false, as a simple matter of fact, that all one's actions bring one more pleasure than the alternatives, even when they bring one exactly what one expected. Hence one does not always act solely or mainly to bring pleasure to oneself.

Even if it were true that one always feels some expected satisfaction or pleasure after all one's voluntary acts, as indeed one does after many, it would not be true that one always does them *for the sake* of that pleasure, or even *partly* for this reason. It is sometimes said that one can always derive a little satisfaction from the fact that justice is done, even when it is clear that what is done is on balance extremely distasteful, perhaps nauseating, as was foreseen (*Billy Budd*). But this prospective justification is not what leads one to the action; the motive is simply the urge to do what is right. This is not an incidental aim, a stop on the way to obtain a satisfaction, as buying a ticket to an opera is an incidental aim on the way to obtain the satisfactions of attending the opera. The "pleasure" (a grotesquely distorting term for this kind of satisfaction, at best) may not be the real motive at all, although it is foreseeable and occurs. To give another simple example, a good marksman generally obtains satisfaction from pulling off a very difficult shot, but there will be times when this is in no way part of his motive for making the shot. For example, he may be shooting at an enemy sniper with his last round.

A more complex point can be illustrated by using the last example. It is not even correct to argue that the marksman will even obtain his satisfaction in all cases. Let us suppose he pulls off a very difficult long-range shot when on a deer drive but as the bullet strikes home the target spins around and is seen to be the hunter's best friend. Does the hunter feel a tiny glow of satisfaction which is outshone by the brighter light of grief? No; he feels *no* satisfaction and *only* sorrow. So (1) success does not always bring the satisfactions of success, and (2) the satisfactions of success are not always our reasons for attempting a task at which success might in other circumstances be very satisfying.

Finally, even if pleasure were always the chief outcome and even if that pleasure were in a straightforward sense the purpose of our actions, we could not conclude that pleasure is *the* goal of life in the sense the hedonist suggests. For just as rationality cannot be the only goal a man has (see *Knowledge* chapter), neither can pleasure. Pleasure has to be *in* something; it must arise from doing, possessing, admiring, reflecting on, or striving for something. If what we strive for is good and noble, the satisfaction we may obtain from the struggle in no way degrades our action from nobility to hedonism. Since we also have seen that goals may be goals for other reasons than the pleasurable consequences their attainment provides, we can conclude that maximizing pleasure is neither a necessary nor a sufficient account of human motivation.

7. THE PARADOX OF JUSTIFYING MORALITY

Religious people have long stressed that being moral to escape the wrath of God or to enter Paradise is not being moral in the crucial sense, for it is simply exhibiting prudent self-interest. It is sometimes said that we should be moral from *love* of God, not from *fear* of Him or from *hope* for His rewards. If this is our motivation, it is said that we are then being truly moral. But there is a difficulty.

One might put the difficulty in this way. Why is love of God thought by theologians to be a better motive than love of Paradise or fear of hell-fire? It is commonly because love of God is not selfish like love of ease and avoidance of discomfort. But even though this makes it a better motive than some others, it does not make it a good motive, for unselfish love of a nonexistent entity or of an existent but evil one is undesirable. Hence this chain of justification requires the further step of establishing God's existence and goodness on nontheistic grounds. Such a step is impossible because of the failure of natural theology, not because it requires a definitionally impossible task.

But the rational man appears to face an even more acute difficulty. If a rational justification of morality is to be given, it apparently must show that unselfishness is a rationally superior pattern of behavior by comparison with selfishness. That is, it must show that a selfish man has good reasons for being unselfish—if he can be by choice—for else it preaches only to the converted. But the only reasons that are good reasons *for a selfish man* are, it would seem, selfish reasons, i.e., reasons that relate to his own (selfish) interests. So it appears we are faced with the task of giving selfish reasons for being unselfish, which is surely a plain contradiction. It seems that the very attempt to give a universally valid rational justification of morality must fail. Indeed, even if it succeeded, it would in doing so surely fail, since it would have demonstrated that unselfish behavior is really in the best interests of a selfish person, i.e., is not really unselfish. So a dilemma appears to threaten the very possibility of success, before any substantial move has been made. It is a false dilemma. For it proves possible to show that reasons *can* be given to a selfish man that show it is in his interest to abandon the selfish point of view in favor of an unselfish one, just because this is *not* the same as giving a selfish man reasons for acting unselfishly here and now. In order to build up the case, it is essential to relate it to the arguments for the advantage of a system of morality for a *group*.

THE BASIC CASE FOR MORALITY

8. *AN ILLUSTRATIVE EXAMPLE: ARMY DISCIPLINE*

A citizen is about to be conscripted into the armed forces of his country, which is at war. He realizes that the military training which he will undergo is designed to make him obey orders instinctively, regardless of personal cost or judgment. In particular cases, this will undoubtedly mean that he will have to do things which are not in his own best selfish interests at the time, indeed, may cause his death. And there will probably be cases in which he will have to enforce orders from above on others, contrary to his rational judgment of the best way to employ or expend them. Sometimes his own view will be right, and lives will be lost unnecessarily. Now a thoughtful man realizes that there are excellent reasons for this kind of training, even though the power it gives officers is sometimes misused or unluckily employed. Not only is a democratic procedure unworkable at the field-unit level because of the delay involved in discussion and voting; it is sometimes intrinsically deficient. For sometimes the armed forces as a whole can triumph and the country survive only if some parts of them can be expended, without a chance of survival, to save more crucial parts or to obtain a crucial advantage. Now the doomed elements would normally lack any rational selfish grounds for agreeing to such a sacrifice. Men being what they are, i.e., fairly selfish, this means the maneuver would often not be agreed on by the field units required to sacrifice themselves. So the war would be lost because absolute power had not been accorded to the general staff. This power is most effectively developed by training subordinates to almost unconditional obedience and to unconditional commitment to victory.

For the citizen about to be conscripted, it is clear that his own advantage is served by the fact that the forces are run in this way. His own chances of survival are increased by the efficiency of a disciplined army, and so, of course, are those of his country (and hence his family) as well. He has good reasons to vote for army discipline if it ever became an issue at the polls, even though he knows it has potential risks for himself as a possible draftee. Ideally, perhaps, he would like to have everyone else conditioned but not himself, but that option is not open to him; indeed, it is entirely clear to him that the army should be run in such a way as to preclude avoidance of conditioning by anyone. By participating, even on the less-than-selfishly-ideal terms that are available, he definitely adds to the total power of the army and hence to the probability of victory, and the alternatives of draft dodging or desertion are, of course, considerably less attractive. So there are certainly circumstances in which there are expectations of selfish advantage to be gained by submitting to training that may condition one to sacrifice one's life on command. It is, of course, important that the expectations of this happening be more or less evenly spread and tied to emergency conditions. Volunteering for a kamikaze squadron on the day one enlists is hardly a rationally defensible act for a selfish man. But notice that it may be defensible for him to undertake training which sometimes does lead to such patriotic inspiration and valor as significantly to increase the probability of volunteering for highly hazardous duties. For it is a great advantage to the *force* to have such men available and to *his* advantage that the force have advantages. Of course, if the increased likelihood of death outweighs the disadvantages of any alternative open to him, then he is no longer rational to undergo the training.

It must be stressed that the discipline system reaps its benefits just insofar as the training is effective. If the training gets the trainees only to the point at which they obey orders when they are on the parade ground or when an armed officer is behind them, but not to the point of acceptance of the value of obeying an order just because it is an order or of achieving victory even when one risks death to bring it nearer, then it will lose some of its largest advantages. The occasions when most is to be gained by the country are often those when most is to be lost by the heroes. On the other hand, the system is not dependent for all gains on absolute obedience by everyone; it shows important profits even with some obedience by some.

Now obeying orders in an army at war is not the same as acting morally, but it is closely related and the example is instructive in many ways. In particular, the example illustrates the sense in which a system can increase each citizen's chances of survival by conditioning him to regard survival as *less important* than obedience to orders. Similarly, in the usual circumstances of society, each citizen's chances of a satisfying life for himself are increased by a process of conditioning all citizens *not* to treat their own satisfaction as the most important goal. Specifically, a system which inculcates genuine concern for the welfare of others is, it will be argued, the most effective system for increasing the welfare of each individual. Put paradoxically, there *are* circumstances in which one can give a selfish justification for unselfishness.

There are other reasons for this conclusion and ways of widening the range of circumstances in which it applies. These will be developed in later sections. In discussing each advantage, we shall first examine the benefits for the group and then see how these bear on the decisions of the individual in special circumstances, e.g., when groups of this kind exist only imperfectly or not at all or when they can be joined under false pretenses. For the great difficulty in the justification of morality is the transition from arguments for the group's advantage to arguments for the individual's advantage in following the moral path.

9. THE MORAL COMMUNITY: DEFINITION

We have thus far argued for the possibility of unselfish behavior and for the key role of such behavior in the traditional moralities. This element of concern for others is one of the main distinguishing features of a moral system by contrast with a system of conventions or manners, which refers to the form rather than the motivation of behavior. It is also of great importance that the moral code be the dominant one, and any justification of morality must justify its claim to priority over matters of manners, codes of honor, traditions, and laws. We shall now propose a general principle which has unselfish behavior as one consequence and which we shall regard as the defining principle and basic axiom of a moral system. This principle may be taken to define morality because (1) it generates a system of rules which substantially overlaps and is elsewhere extremely close to the common element in what have traditionally been called moral systems, and it also generates *a* moral conclusion on most issues that have traditionally been regarded as moral; and (2) it can be given a rational justification, whereas none of the alternatives can, and hence deserves the title of morality in the same way that the currently best-supported views about the empirical world deserve to be referred to as science and their contraries as unscientific, whatever their popular support in the past or present. The first consideration justifies calling it *a* moral system, and the second justifies calling it *the* moral system, or just *morality*.

We shall call a community (or an attitude, a system of laws, etc.) moral insofar as it accepts the principle that every person has equal rights (and the rational conclusions from this and the relevant facts). To "have equal rights" is to have an equal *claim* to consideration, and a society with this commitment can justify divergencies of *actual* consideration only when these can be shown to be required in order better to serve the claims of all. This apparently paradoxical notion is best explained by exhibiting practical examples. It may, for example, be thought of in terms of an analogy with the voting rights of the legal partners in a business. These are basically equal rights and are inalienable in that they cannot be bought and sold as such: they must always be exercised by the partner to whom they belong. But of course, the partner may make an informal agreement (it cannot be a legal one) to vote the way one of the others or some outsider indicates, and he may do this for profit or from persuasion that it is the best course of action. Again, he may acquire debts or credits in outside life that affect his voting decision; for example, he may now decide or have to vote for quick profits or long gains. And he may act illegally in previously mentioned or other ways and thus render his rights forfeit. Obviously his voting behavior can be assessed in two ways: (1) as sensible or not in the light of his personal commitments and (2) as in the interests of the business. In particular, we might say that he has the *right* to vote on the decision whether to install a new type of generating plant, but it would not be sensible for him to exercise that right since he has none of the relevant technical knowledge. Indeed, in cases like this, it would be perfectly sensible for all the partners to vote in advance that such an issue be decided by a subcommittee of the experts among them or even by outside consultants. About *this* decision, then, a partner not on that subcommittee would *not* carry equal weight. But there were good reasons for him to give up his immediate power on that issue; and—this is the key point—in making the decision to set up the arrangement which restricted his power, his vote did carry equal weight. "Equal rights" means fundamentally or ultimately equal consideration, not equal consideration on specific issues in which there are good reasons for all to adopt a procedure that takes greater account in the immediate case of some persons' views than others'. (Town-meeting democracy is by no means intrinsically preferable to representative democracy.) The question is always whether the reasons for according *unequal* consideration on a particular occasion are derived from principles which accord *equal* benefits (like "Let the decision be made by those with the relevant knowledge").[3]

The President of the United States has a large secretarial staff, bodyguard, and salary for which all residents in the country pay. This is unequal treatment at first sight; we pay and he receives the benefit. But the staff is used to increase efficiency in handling issues which affect us all; so the long-run effect is beneficial to all. Consequently, this is not a case of inequity, i.e., unjust (morally indefensible) discrimination. Similar arguments apply to

[3] Strictly speaking, one should say that everyone receives equal *consideration* in these situations but not equal *treatment;* for these are cases in which the good of all is best served by differential concern with their opinions about the immediate course of action.

the bodyguard and salary. This shows that not only the views but the welfare of one person might be given preference in a wholly moral society.

A congressman has more say in lawmaking than a citizen, but efficiency in serving the needs of all requires a professional government. The universal franchise is the political embodiment of the equality of rights in a moral community, just as due process is part of the legal embodiment of this principle. As now practiced in the United States, the franchise is by no means ideal, but properly amended and enforced it may well be the best possible way to protect the moral rights of the individual concerned.[4] When the constitution of a country or an organization of countries talks about all people being equal, it does not imply they are equally strong, intelligent, or virtuous, and it does not imply that they should receive equal incomes; it simply means they have equal rights, i.e., they must be given equal consideration in the formulation and application of the law of the land and the actions of its government and people. Nor does this necessitate that they be given equal votes, although any case to the contrary would have to be very strong to carry weight against popular demand for the vote. Indeed, the prima-facie case for an effective equal vote is so strong that the axiom of equal rights, which we have taken to define morality, is often thought of as a definition of democracy. The two are equivalent, however, only when a large number of conditions are met, including defensible franchise restrictions, and adequate range of views among candidates, a certain level of intelligence and incorruptibility among the electorate and the representatives, and so on. The matter is further discussed in a later section.

Now what *are* the advantages of a society committed to morality in the sense defined by the axiom of equal rights?

10. THE EXPECTANCY ADVANTAGE FOR THE MORAL COMMUNITY

Consider two groups of people who are facing an occasionally hazardous environment. One is composed of rational selfish people (i.e., people who are more or less rational in all matters except for the fact of their selfishness, whose rationality is in doubt); the other, of rational moral people, otherwise comparable to the first group in skills, intelligence, etc. We first consider only the expectation of life, which we assume everyone in the two groups values substantially. Morality implies the acceptance of the equality of everyone's right to life.

Morality does not imply that anyone has just as much right to *whatever*

---

[4] Some of the more notable deficiencies of law or practice involve the very poor, the colored, widely scattered minority groups, the disfranchisement—whole or partial—of residents of capital states and cities, the young, ex-criminals, and the differential treatment of taxed permanent residents, natives of the territories, and citizens.

he wants as anyone else does to whatever *he* wants. For some people's wants are totally contrary to the moral axiom (e.g., the sadist who wants to hurt an unwilling victim), and in general such wants are given low or zero weight in the moral scale, particularly when they are under voluntary control or remediable (see below). We begin with a case which involves the right to life just because this must be granted, since it is the essential preliminary to all other wants and needs. It does not preclude the possibility that a man can forfeit this right under a defensible system of law, though attempts to defend such a system (these are discussed later) are commonly defective. For this reason, we might express the present principle more exactly by saying that everyone has a prima-facie equal right to life; i.e., he has one unless it can be shown that he has forfeited it. To begin we shall take the equality of the right to life to imply the simple-majority self-sacrifice principle, which requires a moral agent to give up his own life if he can thereby save two or more others. We make the essential modifications to this principle later.

Exposing the two groups to the same hazards, possibly including war, famine, flood, fire, pestilence, and automobiles, we may expect that occasions will arise when this principle has application. On each such occasion, at least 1 more life will be lost in the selfish group, since the selfish individual will choose to survive and in so doing will ensure the death of at least 2 others. It may be that on the average 1,000 more lives will be lost, but at least 1 more will be.

There will thus be a substantial gain in the expectation of life for the average member of the moral group and hence a considerable selfish advantage in joining it (assuming one has no guarantee that the hazards will pass one by), even though doing so requires that one be conditioned to accept the sacrifice of self when the need of others is greater.

It is true that there will be occasions in the selfish group when a man will be able to save his life, whereas in the other group he would have had to give it up. But these cases, which impinge so strongly on the selfish man's imagination as he contemplates the unselfish life, are completely swamped (at least 2 to 1) by the cases in which he will lose his life in the selfish group because someone else acts selfishly. A man's gain in expectation of life will be directly proportional to the frequency with which such situations involve him and to the size of the average group saved (in proportion to the size of the whole group), and these factors will vary greatly from one environment to another, being very high in war and relatively low in a stable modern peacetime society.

We have thus far considered a very crude case. In reality, the gains are enormously increased by (1) using a weighted rather than a simple-majority self-sacrifice principle, that is, by taking account of the worth *to others* of those at stake (and the worth of those others) and the worth to themselves of people in different states of life and health; (2) including cases in which two persons can save the lives of three, seven the lives of nine, etc.; (3) extending the range of sacrifice to refer not only to life but to other values; and (4) taking account of the difference in the quality of the experience between the loss of life for a wholly selfish man, impotent to save himself, and that of a man who willingly lays his life down to save others. Moreover, the selfish group is far worse off than has appeared thus far, for (5) there will be a wider range of occasions on which it will cost one man not his life but only a little *effort* to save the lives of several others, and he will often not expend that effort.

It will be clear, then, that advantages akin to but greater than those with which a high level of discipline rewards an army may be expected by groups which practice self-sacrifice. And these advantages are in terms of whatever each of them individually desires, over a very wide range of such desires. Whatever a man may desire in life, life is always and health usually necessary to enjoy it, and expectations of just these desires are particularly well preserved and enlarged by the moral society.

It might be retorted that the selfish group is perfectly capable of seeing the point just made and will institute a set of rules and enforcing agencies to ensure that its members do not fiddle while their fellows burn. Such a move, while better than nothing, has four weaknesses compared with the situation in the moral group. The police are not always present, when present they may lack the necessary power, they are corruptible, and they are expensive. (And, morally, it involves a substantial risk in welfare or lives to the police themselves.)

In fact, the police can hardly affect the primary case considered above, since if the group which could make the sacrifice contains only one man, he is either a policeman or not and in neither case is subject to immediate police pressure. So, in all the cases in which reprisals for failing to perform the legally enjoined act of self-sacrifice are either unlikely (through ignorance, lack of evidence, incompetent use of it, bribery, rank pulling, etc.) or less severe than the immediate sacrifice called for, the selfish man will not sacrifice himself, and so the advantage still goes to the moral community. This is a large proportion of cases; and to it we must add the cases in which reprisals *seem* unlikely or less important to the naturally biased agent and those in which there is enough uncertainty about the combination of the likelihood of reprisals together with their size to make the selfish act the better choice. And there are other difficulties, to which we now proceed.

11. THE PRODUCTIVITY ADVANTAGE FOR THE MORAL COMMUNITY

The classical economic argument for the division of labor, i.e., specialization, is very simple. A skilled bricklayer can outperform an amateur by a quantitative factor of from 5 to 20, apart from quality of work; but the amateur might add figures that much faster than the professional bricklayer and more accurately. As a bonus, people frequently prefer to do tasks which they do well or do better than others. An arrangement in which these and others can work at their specialties rather than at everything as the need arises will multiply the group's output by a large factor; and under typical conditions on the currency, mobility, stability, form of government, etc., these advantages may be expected to benefit everyone to a significant extent. Now one of the tasks we have to perform in a predatory but property-based society is that of guarding our property, our lives, and our health. On the division-of-labor basis and for other reasons it will pay a rich man to hire guards or an army to do this, and in a wider range of circumstances it will pay most of us to contribute small sums to a police force and perhaps also to an army. If, moreover, contributions are tailored to the amount of property guarded, almost everyone will benefit.

To some extent a police force and its administrative superstructure, underpinnings, and correlatives in the judiciary, executive, and legislative branches of the government can enforce on a selfish person the practices to which a moral person is inclined, e.g., by requiring payment of graduated taxes, penalizing culpable negligence, and arranging land and pension apportionment systems. But there are many difficulties, of principle as well as of practice, in carrying this procedure through to a man's private actions, some of which were mentioned in the previous section: avoidability, corruptibility, power and speed limitations on enforcement, and cost (the direct cost plus the loss of productive workers). Despite the tremendous cost, an external police force usually offers us a tremendous gain. But there is a better way. An effective conscience is simply an internal policeman—inescapable, incorruptible, immediate, and inexpensive. To the degree that people can be trained to continue to be moral even when not under surveillance, we have the major advantages of the police without their drawbacks.[5] This might be called the labor theory of value intuition or the economic interpretation of morality, and it is certainly clear that the historical support of religion and religious ethics by the rich is not without its rewards on this earth.

Thus, there is another way in which "instinctive" unselfishness or moral sensitivity (i.e., strong or weak morality) is of value to a society, and social evolution has undoubtedly favored societies which have encouraged or inherited these qualities, whatever bad reasons they may have had for doing so. It is important to notice that although we may be sure that perfect moral discipline or unselfish love is unattainable, we also know that striving

[5] The police serve a number of functions for which they would always be valuable, including traffic and crowd regulation, safety, and, to some extent, social and even moral instruction.

to instill it is worthwhile since partial success produces partial rewards. There is therefore no basis for thinking that the social idealization we have discussed is irrelevant; the world is a partly moral place, and to live in it we have to undergo considerable pressure in the direction of morality. There is clearly some advantage for us and our children in having the world like that, even if we and our children have to pay the price of being brainwashed into semimorality. But a crucial question remains: Wouldn't it be better still for the selfish individual if he could avoid this corruption of his noble savage instincts (if selfish desires deserve such a glamorous name) into the milksop standards of the slave? Shouldn't he act morally where necessary and selfishly where possible, while trying to get *everyone else* to act morally so as to benefit from their sacrifices?

12. THE ADAPTABILITY ADVANTAGE FOR THE MORAL COMMUNITY

From the standpoint of a normally selfish person, the whole prospect of the unselfish life appears to involve painful sacrifices; indeed, to most people it appears unrelievedly dreary as well as being entirely pointless as a solitary endeavor. But one cannot judge other ways of life as if they were superimposed upon one's current values; they have their own *values,* as well as their own patterns of behavior. If a selfish person is to be given reasons for the superiority of the unselfish way of life, the reasons must carry weight for him now, but obviously they need not involve the assumption that he will remain selfish, i.e., that his rewards in the unselfish way of life will be confined to the assuaging of selfish desires. We are not considering what it would be like to act like a saint while *wanting* to be a sinner. We are considering what it would be like to *be* unselfish, i.e., to *want* to help someone in need when one can do so usefully and to be *glad* to be able to help. Most of us are that way some of the time, at Christmas or with children. The question is whether one can give good nonmoral reasons for being like that more of the time and with more people.

It is clearly possible to derive real pleasure from doing things for others, and it does not seem irrational to do this if we can. Suppose someone told us we were being irrational in giving Christmas presents to our children when we could spend the money on ourselves. He would be assuming that we did not really enjoy it, that it was just an act or that the pleasure we took in it could be shown to be misguided (compare smoking). But neither assumption has to be true. When we try to evaluate the *unselfish* way of life as a possibility, it is a simple misunderstanding to think that it involves painful deprivations simply because it involves giving away things that a selfish person would want to keep. And, far from there being grounds for supposing unselfish values to be irrational, we are developing a rather extensive argument to the contrary. But we are now talking of an advantage possessed by strong morality, in which unselfish behavior is strongly rewarding, by contrast with weak morality, which merely *recognizes* and obeys the moral requirement, often with something of a struggle. It is clear that progressing to strong morality offers a gain in the reduction of such pangs, although society does not *insist* that this further step be taken (require it, expect it, punish its absence) as we can with weak morality; we can only *advise* it, admire it, reward its presence. The society must have (gains the most from) moral conformity; its best way to get it is to encourage moral enthusiasm, which brings a bonus both to the individual (reduction of conflicts) and the society (better conformity, more supererogation). But one hesitates to punish pupils for not doing their assignments the easiest way compatible with meeting the requirements, partly since to do it a harder way is its own punishment. Our goal in teaching the next generation should of course be strong morality, since it brings more benefits and fewer pangs.[6]

Just as giving away some material possessions to the needy or working for their benefit is not a sign of something unpleasant about the unselfish life, so the typically inexhaustible supply of situations and people in need of help is not a sign of something dreary or draining about it. Indeed, since these situations are simply opportunities to do what one wants to do and enjoys doing, they are in precisely the same category as a trout stream in the garden for a keen angler. Of course, if one supposed that the needs of others *always* had precedence over one's own, one would never have any time for one's own activities; but no such rule follows from the moral axiom.

If cow's milk is hard to get in Kurdistan, it is obviously good rational advice to try cultivating a taste for goat's milk, which is readily available. The unselfish person has the enormous advantage over the selfish one that he derives at least as much pleasure from activities and achievements that are always and easily open to him (and in which others, selfish or not, will encourage him) as the ruthless tycoon, collector, or crook does from the occasions when he successfully defeats his competitors. And this advantage exists whether or not others have selfish views or behavior. Since for every winner there is at least one loser, whereas for every good turn there is at

---

[6] A precise account of the moral attitudes should include some minor points. First, there can be self-denying *hatred*, but this would not normally be and is not here regarded as a form of unselfishness. The latter is directed to positive consideration of others. It is not the same as selflessness or extreme altruism, in which all concern for the self is abandoned; it is committed only to recognition of the *equality* of the worth of others. The common suggestion that zero consideration for all others would be a case of equal consideration is mistaken: it is not a case of consideration at all and certainly not a case of consideration equal to that accorded oneself. A commitment to the equal worth of others does not mean that one has exactly the same obligations to every child in Africa as to one's own children. A rational morality is concerned with *efficient* discharge of the moral commitment (see below).

selfish ≟ amoral?

least one beneficiary, the moral group gains at a rate of more than 2 to 1 over the selfish group. Antecedently, not knowing whether one will be a winner or a loser, the selfish group offers less-than-even odds, and the moral group a guarantee of reward with regard to situations of this species.

Of course, the practices of business and collecting can be undertaken in such a way as to be rewarding to the winner without inflicting more deprivation on the loser than he is sensibly able and willing to risk, and in this form they provide socially productive and personally rewarding activities. Competition is a mighty motive, but it is crude to suppose it can serve only unrestrainedly selfish ends. Of course, business and collecting are activities open to a moral man. Indeed, when indulged in by amoral men they are simply more hazardous and not more rewarding.

So the way of life of a saint, even in the company of sinners, is intrinsically remarkably attractive. The truth in "Virtue is its own reward" is simply that it *can* be. And to the extent that his companions are unselfish and his admission to their company is dependent on his own unselfishness, or to the extent—even slight and occasional—that his example or unhypocritical inducements can persuade them to be so, additional bonuses of expectancy and productivity attach themselves to him from the interacting subgroup. In short, a powerful case can be made for taking what we might call the (strong) morality pill, which immediately and painlessly transforms one's attitudes. We must look further into the questions whether and how a rational selfish man should act in the absence of such an easy means of transformation and whether other pills would be still better.

At this point one might raise the objection that the case presented above for the moral way of life only has merit for the timid, those who can't make it the mean way. The opposing doctrine, for the sturdy citizen, might be nastily summarized, "If you can, do them in; if you can't, preach." But it has a strong attraction: after all, if you are enjoying life the way things are in a competitive and rather selfish world, why rock the boat? There are three reasons for rocking that can be couched in terms of concern to the selfish man. First, there are always great uncertainties about the future, and in any selfish way of life these are magnified because the chief values are the especially variable matters of one's health, wealth, and virility or virginity. The moral community provides not only better old-age security and children's benefits (expectancy gain) but more old and other age, and it does it for lower taxes (productivity gain) and with built-in income-booster and jail-avoider [7] (adaptability gain). It is not spineless for a successful man to take out insurance, and the moral attitude is the best insurance at no charge. Nor does it show weakness of mind any more than weakness of spirit; it is almost a standard example of prudence, i.e., rational farsighted behavior. Second,

community

[7] Except in a society whose laws are so violently immoral as to require martyrdom in protest (this situation is discussed later).

selfish standards have a very strong tendency to run away with the rider: "Keeping up with the Joneses" is often the slogan for an endless quest for ulcers. That tendency has been overcome, by those who have mastered or avoided it in themselves, often because they have seen or luckily inherited the value of finding the work itself rewarding rather than just the gains or the winning: the craftsman replaces the collector or the cutthroat. The crucial insight here is that one can always do good work or good works; but if one's goal is to do work that is better *rewarded* than others, then there is a far greater vulnerability to chance or unjust fluctuations in the scale of rewards and indeed an incentive to bring about the rewards illegitimately with the attendant further risks. The degree of control or insight involved in the orientation toward quality or service is no more than that which can readily and does frequently lead to a more humane view of the Joneses and others, with its considerably wider opportunities for rewarding experiences. In short, ruthless competition, even for the successful, is a lean and stringy diet: it forms a valuable element in a well-balanced menu but is poor fare for total subsistence. It leaves little for the one-third of adult life after retirement, for the one-half of adult life not spent at work, for the family the pure competitor acquires because doing that is a competition too, or for the friendship of equals.

These remarks are not going to be conclusive in every case, and they are certainly not going to convince everyone to whom they apply conclusively. Of course, the question to be answered is not whether they *will* persuade someone living the selfish life and enjoying it but whether he is mistaken not to be convinced. Present pleasure is too often overweighted in our considerations. But it is not being maintained that a rational man necessarily forfeits claim to that title by denying that it would be in his interest to become moral. There could be, and perhaps there has been, a person in whose special circumstances the selfish life really provides the best of all lives that are possible for him. He might really be too old to change or so near death as not to have reason to change. But such special cases are not important for the general question of the best way of life, for we may still say of this man that the unselfish life *would have been* the best of all possible lives for him. The claim that the unselfish and rational, i.e., moral life [8] *is* superior would still be a powerful one if it referred only to men as yet unborn, as yet unmolded, untrained, uncorrupted. When we talk of a certain career as ideal for someone with manipulative skills and high reliability, we do not necessarily mean that it is appropriate for all persons like that to drop their tools or pens and begin training for it now, at their ages. We mean that it appears

---

[8] If the argument of this chapter is correct, the rational life involves unselfishness, but in order to avoid begging the question we here talk (redundantly) of the rational unselfish life, as compared with the rational selfish one (a contradiction in the long run, if the argument of this chapter is sound).

to be more rewarding to those in it than any other; we mean that if we could start all over again and could qualify, it would be the best choice. That is the weakest form of the claim for the moral life; and to it we add that almost anyone can qualify, that most people can still qualify, and hence that everyone should be trained as if he could until it is proved that he cannot.

13. THE MORAL COMPROMISE [9]

An absolute dictator who was absolutely selfish and absolutely incapable of or heedless about future weakening, such as premature death by another's hand, illness, the need for active or passive love, esteem by his peers, etc., would not have any need for morality. These conditions have never been met, as far as we can tell, and the chances are now even more strongly against the possibility that they ever will be. That possibility is entirely remote from the condition of the shortsightedly happy but highly selfish tyrant of the office or classroom enjoying his suburban status in a town where he has a fair chance of being mugged, being run over or into, or being crippled by disease or error, in a country with a substantial chance of a recession which will put him out of work, in a world with a substantial chance of a war that will kill or ruin him. It is still remote from the condition of the ruthless petty dictators whose fall and death or exile is almost as reliable as their failure to believe it can happen to them. Indeed, the conditions probably apply only to the devil in a world without God. But they are conceivable, and it should be said immediately that in such conditions there *is* no reason for that man to take account of the values and rights of others. Morality, Nietzsche said, is for the weak. This is true enough, but in the relevant sense we are all weak. To be precise, we are all less powerful than any significantly probable opposing combination of human and natural forces, and for that reason there is great advantage in the moral compromise for every human being.

A word about the general line of the argument. We are currently talking about ways of life for *a rational man.* We have previously talked about ways of life for *a group of rational men.* We have not yet talked about *the rationality of particular acts* for rational men. The distinction between the devil and

[9] In the course of this section appeal will be made to various moral judgments for illustrative purposes, although proofs will not be given of these judgments. The method for giving such proof has already been indicated—the calculation beginning with equality of rights of those concerned and proceeding by taking account of differences of interest —and more will be said later in connection with specific examples. At this stage it is necessary to elaborate on certain general features of the moral system in order to make a case for its rationality, which we must do to complete the proof of any particular moral judgment.

the dictator suggests that the powers required to make morality irrelevant as a way of life are superhuman, but it does not show that a rational selfish man in the midst of life could not have good grounds for a particular immoral action. We are proving the irrationality of particular immoral acts via the irrationality of the immoral attitude which lies behind them; we are not saying that they fail to serve that immoral attitude effectively.

13.1 *The exploitation ideal* To put it bluntly, the purely selfish man would like all other persons to be his slaves, but he lacks the power to compel them or the salesmanship to persuade them. His natural tendency is to approach this ideal as closely as possible by finding weaker or more stupid groups he can exploit. This crude realization is of course one of the roots of the exploitation of racial and religious minorities and, at certain stages of economic development, of the slave, tenant farmer, and wageworker. Both kinds of examples provide us with excellent demonstrations of the short-sightedness of the exploitation. Exploitation of labor tends to produce the reaction of large-scale nationalization or simple governmental expropriation (depending on whether one thinks of Europe or of South America) or the subgovernmental reactions of rampant unions: featherbedding, work rules, pseudo overtime, intimidation, and plant destruction. Exploitation of racial minorities now brings the lucky exploiter (and those who tolerate him) race riots, a poorer economy due to lowered per capita consumption, and large unsafe areas due to the crime rate of subsistence slums; and the exploiter who pushes his luck collects the Mau-Mau through the back door and the land reformers through the front. Does this happen in the lifetime of a selfish man? Not always; some of the early slavers in Africa made their fortunes and died in bed. Could not a selfish man rationally decide to take the chance? Some chances cannot rationally be taken. A man cannot rationally decide to take a chance on not paying for fire insurance when he can easily afford the premium and cannot afford to replace his house. For anyone with the usual interests in survival and the usual capacity of enjoying different ways of life, it is a foolish chance to take. Prudence, which is long-term rationality, is the process of taking precautions, of taking early steps to guard against unattractive even if unlikely eventualities. The very simplest considerations of prudence have now, though not always, outdated exploitation as a rationally defensible approach, even if the exploiter had no interest in his children's welfare. And a more fundamental kind of prudence, we argue here, requires the prudential modification of the exploiter's attitude.

But cannot the rational man take *any* calculated risks? Of course he can, but not where the stakes are his life and the gains no greater than he can obtain in other ways with less risk. There is not a great deal of difference between the courage of an explorer and the attitude of a ruthless slaver from *their* points of view. Each sees certain risks and decides the prospective rewards are adequate compensation. Now we can hardly argue that all explorers of hazardous terrain or all mountain climbers are irrational. Of course, there are some who incorrectly assess their love of danger and discover their mistake. They were wrong but are not thereby shown to be irrational. The rationality of risk taking depends almost entirely on the exact motivation. A taste for excitement, a love of novelty, and the quest for new knowledge are motives with increasing degrees of rationality and social utility as they stand; it is the extent to which they supersede other values, e.g., consideration for others, that is the hidden part of the iceberg. In some explorers, as in the slavers, the motivation becomes immoral because it chokes off all regard for the welfare of others. And it is *this* aspect of it that tends to make it irrational by decreasing the chance of survival or success. The primary motive is not irrational: it is only irrational to allow this motive to displace certain other motives. In an explorer, for example, the drive to go forward alone can become irrational because it leads to inadequate consideration of provisions for the return journey, and so on. There clearly remain explorers for whom the risks are worthwhile, who operate rationally within their framework of values, and who would be less happy at home than even on an unsuccessful trip. It is nevertheless not absurd for them to consider the fact that their expectations of life would be greater if they had a somewhat different set of attitudes and realized as much enjoyment of life within *that* framework. To the extent that this is true and the alternative within their power, they are still imprudent. But, often enough, the alternatives are not available or the society benefits from their atypical attitude so that we can rejoice rather than reform them, unless we are married to them.

The same initial situation applies with regard to the slavers. There were undoubtedly some for whom this career offered rewards they reasonably assessed as being well worth the risks, whose conscience did not trouble them, and whose community thoroughly supported their activity. For them, the way of life was rationally defensible, given the starting point of an amoral attitude toward Negroes. But it seems clear that starting point was never plausible, even in the absence of facts we now possess; it is quite obviously no longer defensible, as appears later in the discussion of the "moral franchise." Unlike the explorers' values, the slavers' necessarily involved a brutal disregard for others whose differences from the slavers were not clearly greater than the differences between the slavers and their handicapped or subnormal fellow citizens.

It has been thought to be a filial duty and a prudent act to eat one's parents when they become too feeble to gather food, because it is better for the tribe to kill them than to have them starve, because they prefer it, and because we acquire the virtues of what we eat and all right-thinking people believe their parents have great virtues. The decision whether it was rational for that tribe, in subsistence conditions, to commit patriphagy is like the decision about the slavers in that it involves two stages. The first starts by accepting their beliefs and judges their actions in the light of those beliefs. The judgment here must surely be favorable, given the fact that the alternative is the death of all. The second stage involves questioning the rationality of their beliefs (compare the rationality of the slavers' amoral attitude), and here we find it very difficult to make a decision without the most exhaustive research into the habits and knowledge of that time and place. It is clear what kind of data bears on the decision, but we would need to be sure we had a very complete reconstruction of their world picture before we could decide. It is not, of course, essential that we be able to make that decision; the present situation is what chiefly concerns us. Whatever the final decision, the problem exists of a correct decision in the absence of all the data we need. With regard to that, there is an important consideration which makes past successes by exploiters scarcely relevant to the conclusions of the selfish man today. Once the lessons have been learned by the revolutionaries, from successful colonial revolt, unionism, or civil-rights movements, it becomes very clear that even groups with little political power (originally) can successfully develop enormous leverage, given moderate cooperation, ingenuity, and patience. Moreover, it is clear that the explicit adoption of definite though humane reprisal pressures against the leading exploiters, at first by such movements and eventually by law and public custom, could multiply the leverage of moral reform still further. Once the exploited have learned this lesson, the probability of successful long-term exploitation diminishes almost to zero. The days of the Republic of South Africa are obviously numbered.

We may talk here of *moral reform* rather than mere *social reform*, because the direction of most rational long-term compromises between countervailing forces tends to be the same as that of the moral solution. To begin with, there is a temptation for the stronger force to consolidate its advantage by pressing for more favorable contractual consideration. Not only is this shortsighted in that it breeds ill will which eventually becomes vengeance when the balance of power changes, but our long experience with this possibility should lead us quickly to incorporate severe penalties in the explicit moral and legal code for such exploitation of a power advantage, penalties which will make it irrational to take advantage of a balance of power. The retroactive reassessment of profits on defense contracts in the United States, if coupled with substantial fines, would be an excellent example of the institutionalization of reprisals for immoral use of an advantage. There is also an analogy in the use of forced or ill-advised confessions, which recent decisions of the Supreme Court have rendered almost totally useless.

It is not accidental that the social equilibrium should tend toward the moral solution the more carefully the matter is thought out and the longer the term of consideration. For, on the view here proposed, the moral system *is* the optimal long-run system, applied to attitudes as well as to acts and rules based on present attitudes.

This convergence of the moral and the practical in human relations is closely analogous to the budgeting for research in large corporations or for quality control in large manufacturing concerns. These practices almost never pay off in the short run as well as a big advertising campaign or ingenious refinancing, diversification, or depreciation-basis juggling. But in the long run they are, when adopted and advertised sensibly, the safest bet of all. Here, too, there is a gross historical bias in favor of this conclusion, as the consumer becomes increasingly well educated and organized, through the consumers' unions, counsels, and panels, cooperatives, mail and membership buying arrangements, college and extension courses, etc. So improvement and quality in the product become increasingly important. As far as nationally distributed stable-demand products are concerned, it is increasingly difficult to make and maintain large profits from a shoddy product, and in almost no cases is it easier than the alternative approach. Of course, cosmetics, real estate, novelties, unethical drugs, insurance, and many other sections of the market are still in a less desirable state.

The argument here involves no commitment to the inevitability of social progress: it is simply a comment on the existence of *some* desirable trends. The trends may reverse themselves because long-term rationality is by no means the most powerful social force as yet and would have to be more powerful than the combination of all others that operate against it before progress could be guaranteed. The moral solution would still be the moral solution, whatever happens in fact; so we are not saying that what will happen is right, or vice versa. The moral solution is only the best long-term bet, and the best bet does not always win; moreover, people do not always *make* the best bet.

But even if this line of talk is not totally starry-eyed, isn't it still pretty naïve? The suggestion about the rationality of immediate adoption of or progress toward the moral solution sounds like prolabor, prointegration promotion. What would be the other side's view? What might be the reaction of a hardheaded vice-president for labor relations, in the process of negotiating the triennial union contract and thinking specifically about the union's attempt to get guaranteed employment for all employees with ten-year standing? He is likely to say two things: "We may have to give it to them eventually, but that's no reason for giving it to them now," and "I don't operate as a moral reformer. I'm hired to make the company's case—and that's the stockholders' case, which is clearly best served by conserving labor costs." The example and the replies illustrate several points about the moral compromise. First, there is absolutely no way of showing, from the facts given, that guaranteed employment is morally supportable. So the issue may be the entirely nonmoral issue of settling mutually agreeable terms for a contract.

On the other hand, it may have moral elements if the effects of dismissal on long-term employees who are residents of the factory town are extremely severe and avoidable by proper inventory and sales program planning or are insurable by diversification, etc., without disastrous effects on the company. And the moral conclusion would go against the union's claim if labor is in very short supply near the plant and the action required to handle this contractual commitment by the company will seriously jeopardize the research or plant budgets and hence the company's stability. The company negotiator is entirely right in saying that eventual compromises should not be anticipated as long as the demand does not have moral backing. If it does, it is probably shortsighted to think that using his power in a labor buyer's market to overrule *moral* obligations on the employer's part will pay off. There are other ways—most obviously, wage *level,* within limits—in which his economic advantage can legitimately be applied. Insofar as he has some freedom to negotiate terms, the fact that he is an agent of only one of the two interests represented in the dispute does not mean he should ignore moral considerations if he can. Not only will ignoring morality be rightly regarded as reducing any moral and semimoral obligations of the workers to the company (e.g., care of plant, voluntary efficiency improvement, loyalty in market reverses), which can easily amount to ten times the other gain, but the effect on future negotiations when the power balance may be different is likely to be disastrous. Morality takes no sides in the long run; it is universal unionism, but it is also full-scale free enterprise. Its value lies in its neutrality.

Much of what has just been said would apply to violations of a conventionally accepted but rationally insupportable morality. The difference is that a conflict eventually arises between what the evidence suggests as the most efficient solution and that which the local morality indicates. Up to a point, of course, consideration for people's preferences even if they are irrational is a good principle of rational morality; but at some stage it becomes foolish and indeed immoral to insist on an indefensible choice, e.g., to refuse in this day and age to allow a man to till his own fields on Easter Monday.

Again, much of what has been said is relevant enough in many circumstances, but it may seem to lack force when we encounter the extreme case. There surely are some entrepreneurs who would argue that their dominant interest in life is in the successes of the market place and that they would gladly take the risks of detection to pull off a gigantic if slightly shady deal, which perhaps would take a slice from the tax collector's pie or that of the featherbedded union men or the wealthy widows of the world. Can this be said to be irrational? Now such persons have an extremely strong tendency to forget their own freely entered contractual obligations to and affection for wife and children, who would certainly suffer severely from the jail sentence which is a possible consequence of an action about which they were not consulted. These persons are compulsive competitors, disregarding considerations which are of great importance to themselves in the long run. But a *truly* unscrupulous man regards his dependents as merely conveniences for his present life. Such a man spends all his current income rather than put a few dollars a month into a life insurance policy, for, of course, life insurance will only benefit others and he can lie to his wife about the matter without guilt since it is convenient to do so.

About such a man we naturally speak in condemnatory moral language, saying that by his approach he exploits the rest of society in his petty way, analogously to the dictator or the criminal, since society eventually pays the bill for his illicit profits if he succeeds and for his family's support if he fails. It follows that there are good reasons for society to take steps against him by the application of sanctions, legal or prelegal, such as ostracism by the business or consumers' community. Much social pressure to behave properly and support charities is in this way self-protectively allied with the economic advantages of ingroup status. In general, then, in a rational group the risks of extremely unscrupulous behavior are simply made so large as to make it irrational. If a man's peccadilloes are minor, the moral considerations, which are then dominated by the overarching principle of minimizing interference, require only that he be plainly identified as amoral and excluded from the normal trust accorded to the moral man. But his cost to the society in terms of the direct loss of the expectancy advantage and the possible effect of his bad example, which may indirectly lose more expectancy advantage, is still important enough for the application of some mild social pressure, roughly amounting to a continued reminder of the advantages of the moral commitment in terms of both convenience and increased expectations. In sum, his life should be made unattractive to the degree that he represents a serious social harm.

Now, our society has certainly not adjusted its deterrents to the level required for making the predator always mistaken in calculating that crime will probably pay. And at this point we must turn to the fundamental consideration of his attitudes. For even if the risks are not really overwhelming, they still exist and can be avoided by a change of attitude or, if relished as such, enjoyed just as much when attached to a less antisocial form of activity. A man who could prove that no such transfer of motivation was possible for him would avoid the charge of irrationality, but the fact that he is incapable of the best life does not show it is not the best life. It would be at this point, however, that the overlap of morality and rationality would terminate. The man's immoral actions could not be said to be irrational ones for him. It should be noted that no one has ever made a plausible case for his own incapacity for moral redirection.

13.2 *The indoctrination ideal and the retreat to equality* Quite apart from the arguments for self-conversion of full members, it is clear from the earlier discussion that a community will benefit greatly if it can encourage all *future* members of the community to adopt the moral attitude. The new members are mainly the children; so this conclusion implies that all persons have an interest in supporting a system which will ensure that all children, including their own, acquire some moral feelings. For the only feasible way of creating or supporting a school, court, and public opinion system which will apply pressure to *others'* children in this direction involves at least the probability of having *one's own* children indoctrinated. Now the selfish man would ideally prefer to see this training aimed to make everyone else's children serve him, his own children going into the served or servant category depending on whether he has selfish or unselfish love for them. But there is no advantage in this argument for others,[10] and he lacks the virtual monopoly of power that would be necessary to control them in the absence of any prospective benefits for them. Moreover, he still stands to obtain vast advantages even from the moral-compromise indoctrination procedure, which trains all children to view all as deserving equal consideration, and for this compromise procedure everyone else also gains. Thus there is an intrinsic advantage about the moral compromise which is lacking in the exploitation ideal, namely, that it represents the optimally attractive arrangement for all rational participants. Unbalance the principle of equal consideration so as to favor a characteristic such as skin color, when no arguments based on the welfare of each can be given for the discrimination, and the system will fail. For it now incorporates exploitation, will lose the support of those discriminated against as soon as they come to recognize this, and will probably and properly elicit later reprisals. There was a time when one class could use a myth or power to maintain unjust disparities, but mass education is ending that. Recourse to rational ethics is the only alternative to the seesaw of shortsighted separate power struggles, victories, and reprisals, whether in wage negotiations or in international affairs. And rational ethics means the recognition of equality of rights.

Equality of rights is, of course, the only basis with this equilibrium property, and it is for this reason and neither because of some divine dole nor because of an unrealistic assessment of man's equality of intelligence, diligence, or power that rights are correctly said to be equal. Rights must be prima facie equal for the same reason that dollar bills must be prima facie equal; a currency must have a constant unit before it can be used to evalu-

[10] Even if they are unselfish, they have no reason to think selfish Jones has any more need of their time than they do; hence it would not be rewarding. Working for others who want slaves but do not need help is not morality but masochism; and since it destroys the expectancy gain, there is no case for mass conversion to masochism.

ate differences. Once we can show the need for a moral currency, the equality of rights follows as a necessity, for it is the defining property of morality. The problem is to show that in a world of interpersonal *differences* there is sense in introducing an abstract concept by which everyone is said to have an *equal* allotment. The arguments given above are intended to show that the very best system for handling practical problems of interpersonal relations is based on such a concept. The role of equality is that of a base line: it determines the standard from which deviations must be justified. It is not a claim that there are no deviations. A very similar role is served in the sciences by the basic laws and tendency statements. We say, for example, that the natural state of motion is rectilinear, but we may readily agree that in the whole history of the Universe there has never been a single case of rectilinear motion. The importance of the base line is not to describe the usual situation but to lay a foundation for an explanatory edifice which will handle actual cases. The Aristotelian notion of natural motion as tending toward a state of rest is a much better approximation to a general truth about motion as we see it, but it does not prove possible to develop a theory on this foundation which will efficiently handle all cases. Similarly, a theory which gave the rich more rights might be a better description of actual practice, but the most efficient social theory allots everyone equal rights and is not in the least contradicted by gross inequality in the actual distribution of goods and services. In the usual applied moralities, great inequalities are acceptable but great inequities are not. Insofar as his intelligence, diligence, and power are greater, a man may earn more, own more, or increase his status in other ways and rightly regard himself as in many ways a more important figure in the community—but not in the minutest degree more important morally. There are ways in which one can elevate one's moral *worth*, but they certainly preclude regarding oneself as more *deserving*, since to do that is to reject the moral axiom itself. "Moral worth" in this sense, in which it can be increased, means moral merit or virtue and not moral rights. The police and the army will have to spend proportionately more time in protecting a "big man's" interests since he owns proportionately more, and the contribution he has to make to taxes in order to match the widow's mite will appropriately be considerably greater. With regard to taxes that go to other services, e.g., education, insurance, and conservation, which serve the community as a whole, generally returning less to the rich than to the poor, the justification of differential taxation is simply that equality of consideration requires attention to the relative ease or difficulty of a contribution. This is obviously not the same as the number of dollars contributed but depends as well on the number of dollars that are left after the contribution has been made. Tax rates should, of course, also depend on considerations of incentive and the exact use of the revenue. Naturally, taxing a rich man to support a lazy man is as immoral as tax evasion by the rich man to avoid supporting the police;

but as taxes hardly ever go to only one service, the question whether a particular tax system is just is usually very complicated. It is indeed an example of a complex practical moral issue that is almost never discussed in a rational way. Exactly *why* is it fair, if it is fair, for bachelors to pay school taxes, when no one pays them for entertaining their girl friends? The usual answers or lack of answers from a citizen provide a strong case for the need for a rational approach to ethics.

CRITICISMS AND REFINEMENTS

14. ATTITUDE INERTIA AND SELF-SACRIFICE

The whole system of morality for which the arguments presented above hold is based on one moral principle (equality of rights), one argument about attitudes which leads to action according to that principle, and one psychological claim about that attitude. The argument is that the strong moral attitude is an optimal position, i.e., that good arguments support adopting it and no good arguments lead to changing it. As a result it is, and properly should be, persistent. The psychological claim is that people can move toward the moral attitude under appropriate environmental, social, and self-help pressures. The persistence of the attitude when attained, combined with its attainability, is the key to the problems which have usually defeated attempts to give a rational foundation for ethics. We shall refer to them as the assumptions of attitude inertia and attitude control. They will be the subjects of the next two sections.

The expectancy advantage depends on minority sacrifice, and a minority that was committed to self-sacrifice only until its turn came up, whereupon it immediately reevaluated its attitudes and changed them, would hardly provide the community with any advantages. We must decide whether this will or will not occur with regard to the moral attitude.

Attitude inertia is not only a psychological fact about attitudes; it is to some extent built into the concept of an attitude. As long as we have what we now call attitudes, they will by definition have more than moment-to-moment stability. They are the *basis* for moment-to-moment decisions about actions, not actions themselves. Practically speaking, it is difficult to conceive of the mental economy's operating at all efficiently, perhaps even at all, without semiconstant dispositions. On the other hand, it will also be a great gain in efficiency, in the dimension of adaptability, if these dispositions are alterable in the long run.

So it is the nature of the reacting and reasoning process that provides us with the property of attitude inertia. Having acquired, whether by pill or by persuasion, a conception of one's fellow men as intrinsically valuable, one has automatically acquired an immediate reason for doing whatever brings about their welfare, within—as we say—reason. The qualification may conservatively be taken to involve such limitations as "up to the point of (1) helping those who can and will be better helped by others, or (2) helping others where more persons can be helped later if I do not spend time on direct aid now, or (3) treating others *more* favorably than myself even when they have no special merits or needs I do not possess." [11] When a man has something approaching the strong (weak) moral attitude, he will be acting morally because he likes (prefers) to act morally. If someone says to him, "Why not abandon the moral attitude and have more good things for yourself?" he would reply that getting things for himself at the expense of others is *not* getting "good things" and has no attraction for him. Or he might reply, somewhat misleadingly, that he *is* currently getting more good things, e.g., feelings that his life is worthwhile, than he would if he kept some of the good things (i.e., material possessions) to which the bystander is referring. This reply is misleading because it sounds as if every time he does something moral, he really does it for selfish reasons (getting good things); in fact, he does it *because it is moral.* His decision, long past, to accept (or take steps that would eventually lead him to accept) that kind of reason was made for what can be described as selfish reasons, the only ones that counted then. But they do not count any more. It is no good to use the inducement of the "more rewarding way of life for you" to get him back on the straight and narrow path of selfishness, because the argument is not reversible. The moral life is better, from a selfish viewpoint, than the selfish life, but no corresponding arguments show the general superiority of selfishness for a man now moral. A man now moral is not contaminated by his past; he is not now *secretly* amenable to selfish arguments because *once* he was. He is motivationally no different from a man who is moral because he has been brought up that way, and such a man would not be persuaded. However a man *gets* to be moral, he *is* moral if he does what is moral *because* it is moral. So the moral life is a rationally stable solution to the problem of how to live. Still, just as there are odd circumstances in which, e.g., the dictator is rational to

[11] A case might be made for more extreme altruism, but not as a general policy, since it is an unstable solution to the problem of allotting rights. The Christian ethic has been interpreted as recommending extreme altruism and in this version differs from the Jewish. The standard illustration concerns two men in a desert with one cup of water, all of which is needed to get one man to nearest oasis, there being no other chance of survival. Two good Christians hand the cup back and forth until the water evaporates. The Talmud is often taken to recommend that the man who has the water when the facts are discovered should drink it—a very practical solution. A rational morality would require (1) some study of any special claims to preferential treatment, e.g., number of dependents or social value of vocation; or (2), in the absence of these, the toss of a coin. The only general case for altruism would have to be based on the belief that it is necessary as an inspiration, to raise others to the more modest level of morality (compare pacifism).

remain selfish, may there not be cases on the other side in which it would be rational to abandon unselfishness?

In the extreme case, when what a man is called on to sacrifice is his life, is it not a little unrealistic to suppose that he will not at that time see certain extremely tangible advantages in being selfish? For *all* advantages, including the pleasures of charitable works, require continued life.

Obviously giving up his life calls for a higher degree of commitment to the worth of others than giving up some time or money. It should be remembered that even if it were impossible that a human being so love another or his duty that he would die for another person, the arguments for morality of a more limited scope would still be conclusive. The major moral returns arise from more mundane matters than noble suicide. Yet it *is* possible for someone to sacrifice, or be willing to sacrifice, his life for others, simply because they will be saved by his act; indeed, it happens often enough, notably in the case of parents and soldiers. In the most frequent situation (as in drawing fire or distracting a predator) the agent does have some chance of survival but is not greatly affected by this as long as he knows his action is almost certain to save the other person or persons. And there are very many cases in which a man has some motivation from other sources (fear of detection, chance of reward, etc.) and considerations of duty are enough to tip the balance. So morality's advantages are by no means dependent upon the willingness of everyone to go the whole way simply for morality's sake.

But given that people are capable of supreme sacrifice partly or wholly for moral reasons, are they rational to make the sacrifice? Should they not draw back at the last moment?

The devil, tempting, says: "Look, you've had a good life so far, an admirable one as well as a satisfying one. I won't even deny that, in your circumstances, it may have been the best possible kind of life. But your luck wasn't good—no fault of yours, of course—and here you're facing the end of it all. Now, you surely don't want to get carried *too* far on this starry-eyed kick. . . . It's time (as you used to say) for a rational, objective look at the two alternatives. Stay with the suckers and die, or get smart and live; it's as simple as that—something or nothing. As a rational fellow you have to admit that a momentary lapse from grace is a small price for your life, and you can more than repay any damage in the years you'll have ahead. In fact, in the long run, with a little remorse to push you along, it's likely to be a definite *benefit* to society if you take things a little easy now, let up on that moral throttle a bit. And a *notable* benefit to you. . . ."

There is no doubt that this kind of appeal will often succeed, because people are often not fully committed to the moral attitude and are not moved in the same direction by other considerations; after all, this is the moment when they have to weigh their commitment to it against all their selfish values. But for a man who has a substantial commitment or a small commitment that is enough to tip the balance of considerations in a particular case, the devil's appeal gets no more foothold than the suggestion to a moderately decent man that he should steal from a beggar's cup because gaining even a little money for no effort is rational. A moderately decent man does not *want* money stolen from a beggar; it is not a value for him. A reasonably decent man does not in the least want the million dollars he can get by stealing it from a charity for indigent blind or paralyzed children. A moral man does not want a life he can have only at the expense of the death of others. This is what it really means to have the moral attitude; this attitude is the one that brings the group the greatest advantages in expectation, productivity, and adaptability and hence provides the strongest arguments for the general adoption and encouragement of this way of life.[12] Once adopted, to whatever degree (the more thoroughly adopted, the more valuable the adaptability advantage is), it becomes one of a man's actual values, and it cannot be said to be irrational just because it points in a different direction from the others, since the case for it depends on this. And it certainly cannot be said to be irrational in that there were no reasons for adopting it.

What about the possibility that the probable circumstances of a particular person's life might be such as to make it irrational to adopt the moral attitude? Might there not be *some* situations in which it is simply frustrating or unpleasant, and not rewarding, and in which the selfish life would be much more rewarding in its own terms? We begin with the easier cases.

For frustration to occur would require that no one that one could help needed help, that no contributions to the common good by creative work or labor were possible. This is hard to imagine. But the possibility is not a real possibility anyway, for a quite different kind of reason. Morality does not replace all other interests; it is simply a further interest, ideally with the potency to outweigh the others in any conflict situation. If the moral interest cannot be indulged, a man has many others on which to fall back and no sense of loss in doing so. For if no one needs his help, this means that others are well and happy, and from this he directly derives satisfactions if he has the strong moral attitude. If his frustration is supposed to spring from seeing others who need his help but will not accept it directly, there will still be many ways he can work toward changing this impediment to helping them, e.g., by education. Or he may be able to do something constructive otherwise than by doing it for someone who can reject it, e.g., by contributing toward medical research. If the frustration is supposed to come from seeing what needs to be done for others and being unable to achieve it through lack of

[12] One might live up to the highest demands of morality even if one had only what we have called the weak moral attitude. But it is not possible to provide such strong reasons for adopting this attitude, and it is not so powerful a guarantee of moral behavior.

cooperation or resources, it is no different from the frustrations that beset a selfish man in attempting to achieve his goals. In both cases, frustration can serve the good purpose of being a goad to further efforts or, if allowed to develop to excess, it can become a source of neurotic incapacitation. The latter possibility is simply a defect in one's capacity for sensible living, in no way a special hardship of the moral life.

In general, then, the attitudinal change suggested is peculiarly immune to invidious comparison with alternatives as far as likelihood of frustration is concerned. Of course, a society which directly persecuted anyone who tried to help others would be an environment in which the moral attitude would be a handicap, but it is hard to see how the society could survive long enough to develop such penalties. It must be severely antiadaptive to impose sanctions on the saving of lives or the keeping of promises. The most extreme proponents of individualism might argue that only by punishing moral behavior could we get people to stand on their own two feet. But it is *immoral* behavior to coddle when coddling is harmful.

There will certainly be particular occasions or particular issues on which a moral man will take a stand that will cause a society to attack him savagely, as many of the great moral reformers have discovered. But the same risk attends any way of life which involves a leadership role, and the pinnacles are rarely reached by the rear guard. Besides, true explorers regard the heat and the mosquitoes as occupational hazards: no pleasure at all but of far smaller consequence than attaining their goals. The man with no ambition may avoid the mosquitoes, but as a goal in life this provides a prospect somewhat lacking in great moments; and, of course, it is obvious that teaching that kind of ideal is no way for the town to get the swamp drained.

Let us suppose that the prospective convert to the moral life happens to be in circumstances in which it is obvious that an immediate and severe sacrifice will be required of a moral man. In a sufficiently extreme case, this would constitute a good reason against moral conversion (it is a version of the absolute dictator's case, in which a straight loss is guaranteed); but the mere fact that a heavy commitment of material goods or of time would be involved would not show there were good reasons against conversion, since these are resources whose expenditure on behalf of others can be rewarding to a moral person. Only if it could be shown that one's life or one's health would have to be sacrificed could a case be made in terms of the necessity of preserving these for any type of rewarding endeavor. This leads us to consideration of a different kind of counterexample.

We might ask, Is there some other attitude, besides the moral one, which might in a similar way be shown to be even more preferable? In particular, we should look for any way of life that this kind of reasoning identifies as admirable but which is so absurd a consequence of it as to cast doubt on the whole procedure. A most interesting move of this kind originates from a consideration of the kamikaze or suicide pilots used by the Japanese in the last stages of the war against the United States and her allies. These pilots were volunteers who felt that the chance to die for their Emperor by striking a great blow against the Allies was more important than life. Extending the case, might one not argue that the most satisfying possible set of values would be one headed by a peaceful (or glorious, or violent, or painful) death, for this is certainly easy to obtain? [13] For a selfish man, wouldn't this be the perfect answer?

Here the devil of the earlier dialogue comes into his own. If one makes death, in whatever form, an actual goal, one eliminates all possibility of fulfillment of other hopes and interests, apart from the brief moments of glory before death. The possibility of enjoyment of all other kinds is to be wiped out, intentionally, as part of a "way of life"—and for what? Not for the sense of achievement that one can get from actions that one considers worthwhile, for one is never in a position to reflect on a successful suicide, glorious or otherwise. Indeed, the only expectation one has, with death as one's highest ideal, is that of contemplating a failure, since only if one fails will one have any experiences at all. If it is argued that the pleasures are those of anticipation, one must point out that these pleasures then become a good reason for prolonging life and comparable pleasure can surely be obtained from anticipation of goals which are consistent with sustained enjoyment. We are not arguing that given the commitment to a glorious death, the prospective suicide (rationally) should change his mind at the last moment, only that he (rationally) should select another kind of commitment at an earlier stage. Given that his brightest and virtually his only value *is* a glorious death, it is, from that point on, rational to act as he does.

Notice the differences between the death risk here and in the moral life. In the latter case, we argue that the *risk* of self-sacrifice exists but that the *gain* in overall expectations of reward is more than enough to compensate for this possible loss. In terms of long-term expectations, then, suicide is as handicapped as a one-event novel. But can't it gain on guaranteed fulfillability what it loses on probable total returns? Indeed, isn't it possible to adopt an attitude that rejects the long-run altogether? For some temperaments this may be possible, though it could hardly be justified as a life plan to govern the citizen's or the state's child-rearing programs, since one presumably has children at least partly because one likes to have them around or thinks that one can benefit from them. In general, the death ideal lacks appeal simply because, unlike the moral ideal, it requires a virtually complete abandonment of all other values and pleasures instead of a mere commitment to the possibility that one might have to renounce them voluntarily, or modify or augment them slightly. The move to morality offers many gains in the

[13] This example was, I believe, suggested to me by Gilbert Harman.

present state of the world, and there are no good grounds at the moment for urging the harder move to the supremacy of suicide. Until the world is poisoned, the main problem is how best to satisfy or how at least to modify our natural thirsts. Morality is mainly for those who wish to live; for them, it is the best way to live. For some who wish to die, life would be better, though they do not know it. For others, death is best; but life still remains behind and morality improves its chances.

These explorations of the nature of commitment thus do not appear to weaken the case for moral commitment but rather to strengthen it by revealing its function more clearly. The comparison with theistic commitment is worth noting. Moral commitment involves no commitment to untrue or unsupported assertions. It does involve a claim with unusual logical properties, the claim that others are of equal value, which reflects not a discovery about other people so much as a discovery about the relative merits of different ways of regarding them. A man may come to regard others as things to be valued (ends in themselves) for reasons which appealed to him just because he did *not* so regard them, i.e., from the "benefits" the belief brings. The theist may commit himself to theism for exactly the same kind of reason, but in his case it does not make the claim true, because the theistic claim is not simply a claim about a man's best attitude. It is a claim about the existence of a special kind of Being. To say theism is "true for him" simply means he believes it, although it is not, in fact, true; no such abandonment of reason is involved in moral commitment. Nontheistic religious commitment is very like or is a form of moral commitment, and the only difficulty is that there are usually several divergencies of such a position from the moral position we are discussing, for example the Buddhist ban on alcohol, and no way of justifying them.

15. ATTITUDE INERTIA AND SOME MORAL PUZZLE CASES

We have seen that the benefits of morality are essentially connected with the nature and consequences of the moral attitude, not just with the nature and consequences of moral acts or principles, and this general point has specific consequences which provide a basis for treating some famous moral puzzles. We shall begin a discussion of these with an example which is easier than they are but provides us with a useful lead-in to them.

Should a soldier *always* obey the orders of his superior officer? The treatment of war crimes has made clear that common moralities draw a line at *some* point. But it is, of course, extremely important to instill in the soldier a readiness to obey even when he does not understand the reasons for the orders or, indeed, when he strongly disagrees with them. This line of argument is not usually thought to include any duty to perform apparently treacherous acts without explanation or to require the active improvement of methods for murdering prisoners (Nürnberg trials). For the benefits that accrue to the moral group from the commitment to instant obedience will be canceled out by the losses if the area of absolute obedience is extended into the territory of the most terrible crimes. To reap the benefits on which survival depends we take the calculated risk in time of war of instilling obedience which will extend to bad or immoral orders. The mere fact that the inertia of the obedience attitude will undoubtedly carry obedience too far on some occasions (on which it is not obviously wrong to obey but actually turns out to have been wrong) does not show that the attitude is to be abandoned. Indeed it does not even show that *on those occasions* the soldier was wrong to obey: he was right, though a civilian might not have been. It follows that an officer must explain orders which appear absolutely improper, whenever there is time to do so, or not expect obedience. This in no way extends to orders which simply appear tactically wrong or involve sacrifice, for those, it can be seen in advance by all parties, are the domains where training to instant obedience pays off.

Now for the puzzles. You are at the bedside of a wealthy dying friend. He tells you that he has a more recent will than the one at his lawyer's office, and he tells you where it is. He asks you to promise to take it to the lawyer. You promise to do so. He dies happy, and you now discover that the new will transfers his huge estate from a charitable and educational trust to his worthless spendthrift nephew, who had always managed to conceal his defects from his uncle. If you destroy the new will, it seems clear to you that a very great benefit to mankind will ensue; if you keep your promise, only a wastrel will profit. Your friend is dead, and he died happy—you can no longer consider the effect on his feelings or his welfare. Does not the kind of moral position advocated here require that one break one's promise, indeed, make it an obligation or even a duty to do so? And is that not seriously at variance with what a man with some moral sensitivity would feel? For even if your friend was not certain you should keep your promise, he would certainly deny that it was your *duty* to break it.[14]

Several points are involved. First, a considerable number of relevant facts may not be known to you. The nephew may have been bound by documents already signed to act as a trustee for the money, sitting under a responsible board; the estate will thereby provide him with worthwhile employment and still go to good causes. Such a possibility—and there are many others—would

---

[14] The relevance of ordinary moral sensitivity is twofold. First, a rational morality overlaps with many traditional moralities, and hence the finger of a conscience steeped in one of the traditional systems may point the rational way. Second, the moral sense, like the grammatical sense, is immensely more sensitive than any explicitly formulated set of rules thus far devised and so, given the first point, deeply deserves our respect while we are attempting to formulate an adequate set of principles.

alter the whole complexion of your action, and possibilities of this kind form an important part of the reasons why a commitment to keep promises, even when doing so appears not to be for the best, is and should be a consequence of the moral commitment. The utility of this commitment is not for maximizing expected gains but for minimizing possible losses; it is an investment in safety, not for maximum yield. The dead man may have told others of the existence of the will or of other copies of it and merely be using you as additional insurance. Your suppression of it will not prevent its adoption and will probably involve you in serious legal difficulties. (The attempt to consider cases in which all such possibilities are absent is unrealistic and hence not productive of genuine counterexamples.)

The system of morality is designed to operate in this world, not in one where knowledge of all relevant circumstances is complete and the capacity to calculate their consequences and weigh them correctly is perfect. Promise keeping is worthwhile just because it provides us with the greater certainty of a man's control over his future actions to replace our uncertainty as to whether the outcome we want will be obtained in some other way. It is part of a system which maximizes expectations, but such a system must have parts whose justification is that they perform a function necessary to ensure that goal for the whole system, not that they each serve that function themselves. The safety valve on a steam boiler has the aim of reducing pressure, the exact opposite of the aim of the whole system, but it is an essential part of any effective system devoted to providing high pressure. Similarly, the system of moral principles contains many items whose role is crucial to but only contributory to maximizing expected gains,[15] not aimed directly at that goal.

Put from another point of view, the key question does not concern the consequences of one's alternative actions in terms of the welfare of those directly affected but the general utility of being able to trust someone who makes a voluntary promise. Having the institution of the trustworthy promise is very like having the institution of unquestioning obedience in the army. Part of its value is that it can be called on and counted on when there is no time to explain and justify (or when secrecy precludes this) and when it is

---

[15] In all the preceding discussions we have talked crudely of "maximizing gains for all," but the only way in which we can appeal to this criterion as a consideration with impact for each individual requires that we construe it as involving strong protective principles which place safeguards, amounting to almost complete bans, on the extent to which the welfare of individuals may be sacrificed to further the welfare of others. The Pareto restriction, which does insist on the ban, is too extreme in any case, but it is particularly extreme because welfare, for its purposes, is calculated in terms of the present set of utilities of each individual instead of in terms of the most satisfactory of the various alternative sets of utilities to which he can move with an effort that does not outweigh the consequent advantages. The concept of justice emerges partly from these individual-oriented constraints on maximization and partly also from the desirability of protecting useful motivations.

important to ensure that later inconveniences are not to be allowed to inter-
fere with the promised performance. Naturally, one of the results of this
institution is the occasional occurrence of unfortunate consequences, but the
same is true if we eliminate the institution; so it is only a question of which
alternative permits fewer disasters and provides more convenience. It must be
remembered that there is no compulsion to make promises; they are an optional institution. If someone asks you to promise something, he is judging
that on this occasion he wants unquestioning obedience and asks you to bind
yourself to this obedience from your willingness to see his need as important.
His need is to have his wish *obeyed*, not just *promised to be obeyed*. Indeed,
the moment that he cannot count on obedience without explanation, later
justification, etc., much of the value of the institution vanishes. Once it is
clear that being able to count on others to keep verbal promises has considerable value for people in certain circumstances and does not lead to pre-
ponderantly bad consequences, then it is also clear that the moral attitude
which commits you to take account of what others want automatically commits you to carrying out promises.

Up to a point. Just as there must, rationally, be limits to the soldier's
obedience, there must be limits to what a promise commits one to if the value
of promise keeping is not to become a liability. So a great deal depends on
the particular circumstances of the puzzle case. There are *certainly* cases in
which one would have to—indeed, one *should*—break one's promise, for
example, when (1) the lives of several people would obviously be endangered
or lost by keeping it, perhaps because of acts unknown to the dying man;
and (2) a minor whim of dotage appears, on the most careful examination,
to be all that is at stake. The point of this discussion has been to show that
the values involved in promise keeping are not just those which accrue on
a particular occasion but those of the institution itself as a useful device in a
society and that this utility, properly analyzed, plus moral concern, obliges
one to fulfill a promise even when the results appear somewhat contrary to
the welfare of those involved, though not in *all* such cases. Just as the
officer will be wise to explain orders which apparently command treachery
or grossly gratuitous cruelty, so the promisee should try to explain demands
to perform an extremely questionable action. When he does not, the fact
that he is a friend often implies that you know him well enough to have
grounds for believing that a good explanation exists. It is also probably true
that the emotional and contractual commitments between you are stronger
than those between strangers, so that you are more inclined to do what he
asks even when it involves considerable difficulties for you. These factors
are the basis for *trust* and for making it a greater obligation, in an imperfect
world, to obey somewhat questionable promises to friends than to strangers.

Similar considerations apply to the case of the judge who must decide
whether to condemn to death a man he knows to be innocent when the al-

ternative is certain to lead to the lynching of ten others or to the start of a very bloody revolution. The inertial attitude here, analogous to the obedience and promise-keeping commitments in the previous cases, is the commitment to justice. It is clear that the utility of the adjudicative branch of the law is sensitively dependent on the extent to which it applies the law without prejudice, e.g., recognizes the antecedent equality of the rights of the litigants. Any discovery that the law is not being applied justly undercuts the control of lawlessness by opening a loophole through which the criminal may (or may hope) to escape by bribery, the use of an eminent, titled, or Aryan front man, or the selection of Jewish or Negro victims, in short, by exploiting whatever weakness the system of justice has turned out to possess.

Why are such preferences in the administration of the law *weaknesses* in a system of justice, granted that they are often illegal? The reasons are (1) the prima-facie desirability that the law should be applied exactly as it has been passed by the legislature, apart from any inconsistencies with previous legislation, since that is what the legislators intended and for which they presumably had good reasons as well as authority; and (2) the desirability that the law not be held in contempt, as is a law whose application can be evaded by devices. These are separate considerations from those pertinent to the question whether the law itself is unjust. In morality as a whole, the importance of justice is chiefly that it is the procedural embodiment of the principle of equal rights and hence a keystone in the structure of applied morality.

The importance of justice makes it extremely desirable that it be administered by those to whom this importance is an intrinsic value, so that they will be prepared to disregard bribes, threats, and inconveniences. For them to do this requires no more than the moral commitment plus recognition of the necessity for justice in the application of morality. But we need them to go beyond the mere perception of their task as a derived obligation; the attainment of justice must become a commitment in itself for them. We do not employ or appoint them as legislators or moralists. Occasions will arise when their ordinary *moral* judgment will be that the ends of society will be best served if they act *unjustly,* and it is of great importance to the system that in the usual examples of such cases they should stand fast by their duty despite the advantages to others that appear to be gained by abandoning it. One might describe such examples as the moral mirror image of the cases involving selfishly rational but immoral acts; here it is a man's *unselfish* motives that lead him to do other than he should. The need for an autonomous commitment to justice arises because the judges are not well placed, entitled, or supposed to make the difficult long-run evaluation of the cost to the enormously valuable institution of justice of their aberration, and each of these shortcomings leads to bad consequences. This is not merely to say judges may err, though that is an important part of it. In a case described above, it is not in the least obvious that saving the ten men who will be lynched by sacrificing the innocent man will guarantee a long-run gain, for the reaction to the mass lynching may be strong enough to arouse the society to the point of taking drastic action that will save more than ten lives in the future. Even in the case in which a revolution will occur, it is not at all clear that the judge is in a position to be sure a revolution is a long-run loss. Even if the long-run effects appeared most clearly good from this failure to do justice, it does not follow that men would be better served if in such circumstances all judges abandoned their commitment to justice. And that consideration enters into the matter since we are all concerned as to what attitude or values to recommend and adopt. Apart from the fact that judges will often be mistaken, if the practice of spot decisions on the apparent merits became the standard judicial practice, the calculations of miscreants would soon include this fact and could thereby make further inroads into the territory reclaimed by morality from our savage alter egos. Complex and expensive "covers," e.g., a kind of wild extrapolation of the present abuses of psychiatric testimony to induce sympathy, could be arranged to deceive judges into making erroneous decisions on the spot. Worse, the deviations can become cumulative through the pressure from the thin end of the wedge. There may be excellent intrinsic grounds for making a single exception (more to be gained than lost), but if this is done once, then the simple principle of justice requires that it be done for any like case. But if this is done for many "like cases," the law has effectively been changed and the new law may not be arguably better than the old in terms of consequences, because people now begin to act from a new base line of illegality and the losses from this change swamp the small gains from the merciful exception to the old law. Hence an attitude oriented solely to the best calculation of the consequences of particular acts, even on the basis of equal rights, cannot be generally encouraged, hence cannot be the best attitude for judges and thus for men in general, and hence cannot be the moral attitude.[16]

---

[16] The categorical imperative and the generalization theses in ethics, as well as rule utilitarianism, agree on this conclusion but are either wrong or unclear about the reasons for it or deny that there are or should be reasons for it. The bases for the commitment to the intrinsic value of justice, for example, include the peculiar equilibrium property of the principle of equal rights which implies the impropriety of discrimination, the propriety of the obligation to justice, the social necessity and advantages of a common moral training, the practical importance of uniform procedures, the need for overshoot rules to achieve the indispensable minimum, and so on. There are rarely simple or single reasons for basic moral principles. But another weakness characteristic of the traditional utilitarian approaches, oversimplification apart, is the failure to see the difference between the best decision, calculated in terms of the consequences for all involved as they *are* at the time, and the best decision, calculated in terms of that *attitude* which is itself determined as best by calculating in terms of the good of all who *may* be involved in such issues.

The moral attitude, we now see, must include attitudes such as love of justice,

Thus the time for boldness in a judge is when he is threatened in the performance of his duty, not when he contemplates abandoning it. The inertia of his commitment should carry him far into the realm of personal doubt. It must indeed carry him far into the realm of person certainty that a greater number of good consequences would result if he would act otherwise than in the way which justice indicates. Yet he can be rationally sure that what he does in acting justly is *right*. We have argued this despite the fact that the judge's doubts will sometimes be justified and his action not productive of the best results; but we shall also argue that there are extreme cases in which the obligation to justice, even by the judge, must be regarded as overthrown. Justice is not to be replaced by the judgment of the best action in terms of the presently determinable consequences or even the actual consequences, but nevertheless justice is justifiable in terms of its role in the whole structure of morality, which is itself justified by its good consequences.

This apparent paradox has seemed to many philosophers to necessitate a commitment *either* to justice (deontological theories) *or* to justification in terms of consequences (utilitarian theories). But the two can certainly be connected (not combined) in the way indicated in footnote 16. How do we justify denying food to children between meals? By appealing to the fact that by refraining from food they now want, they will in the long run and overall enjoy their food more. No paradox for parents is involved; for justice the case is analogous, not quite the same. The optimum system of moral attitudes, rules, and practices requires a commitment to the just act at the expense of an alternative which would maximize benefits on a *particular* occasion. Morality is an edifice whose superiority over enlightened self-interest springs from the mastery of a break-through in building principles, like the move to the arch which yields far greater strength by a process of developing two pathetically unstable drooping columns until they lock together on the keystone. The judge's temptation is like the temptation to span the half-completed arch with a straight beam; he thereby achieves a gain in strength which is not illusory, is entirely permanent, but is less than optimal. It is with the rights of those not yet involved, as well as those who are, that we must be concerned in defining the moral act and attitude; and those not yet involved are better served by incorruptible justice, whether the corruption be from selfish or unselfish motives.

There are certainly cases in which there is in one way no continuity

---

truth, and promises, which must be added to the basic other-valuing attitude by the discovery that the other-directed consequences of people's having such attitudes are better than the consequences when people lack them (i.e., have *only* the other-valuing attitude). One might argue for amending the initial definition of morality to include reference to this complication, but it is just as satisfactory and simpler to see these other commitments as part of the consequences of moral commitment and hence as part of the moral commitment.

of personnel or influences into the future, in which, perhaps, the judge is deciding his last case before retiring or dying. But still the *decision* affects others, it will itself be known, its inconsistency with the judge's past practice may be uncovered, and so on. When all these possibilities have been conclusively excluded, one suspects that the case becomes pretty unrealistic, but it simultaneously does approach the region where a commitment to justice should not supervene over simple other-directed calculations.

Where is the point at which we can justify injustice? Where is the point at which we can give reasons for acting unreasonably? The point is not marked on a mental road map. It is certain only that it lies far beyond the point which the immediately obvious considerations suggest to the man without moral commitment and well this side of the point at which the whole system of morality would collapse. We have done little systematic thinking on these questions, being content to stand in awe as novelists, playwrights, and philosophers ingeniously and tellingly present the poignancy of the dilemma or the excesses of the extremes. And armchair thinking is not enough; the answer must depend heavily on complex questions of fact about the effect of different inertia levels on societies and on subgroups of different kinds. We can only make an educated guess here, as in so many moral problems. The test question is indeed, What would it be like if everyone in this position acted in this way? but, of course, there are a dozen ways of describing or perceiving "this situation" and "this way," and the real difficulty is to decide which of these ways to follow. But so it is with almost any practical problems today: the rules available will not do all the work. One cannot choose a career or a wife except from a foundation of startling ignorance about the most important facts and from a set of rules all of which are known to be widely honored in the breach. When choices must be made, the extent to which they are guesses is unimportant beside the extent to which intelligent analysis of the alternatives can improve the expectations of success. Improvement of the chance of being right from 1 to 3 per cent is a larger gain than that from 50 to 99 per cent in the sense that matters, for it triples one's chance of success rather than doubles it. The good side of extreme ignorance is that bigger improvements are possible, and rationality offers them.

So the present analysis yields an account which meets the objection that calculations of the consequences usually lead to abandoning justice in favor of expediency, without committing us to the view that justice is unsurpassedly important. (Similar arguments apply to duty, obligation, loyalty, etc.) Moreover, it does so without breaking the chain of arguments leading back to the individual, as do more formalistic theories. Defended and interpreted as above, the commitment to justice (by judge and layman, in their different degrees) is seen as defensible in the same way as, and as an extension of, the commitment to the value of others.

16. EVOLUTIONARY ETHICS

A rational analysis of the consequences of the moral attitude thus leads to allotting a greater weight for justice than would be allotted by a procedure of calculation of immediate consequences, even one guaranteed to be accurate. This valuation is in accordance with the instinctive morality of many cultures, a fact which calls for explanation. One may speculate that certain major features of morality, of which this is one, have sufficient advantage for the group which adopts them to make such instinctive discriminations survival characteristics in the evolutionary process of a social creature such as man. This possibility suggests that we be constantly on the alert for instinctive reactions in the moral area for which no good reasons are explicitly recognized in case they are signs that more careful analysis will uncover an advantage for those who share them.

We may surely suppose that the maternal instinct, which is in one respect just a nonintellectual special instance of the moral attitude, is a survival characteristic for those species in which it occurs. But the survival of the *race* (meaning the interbreeding group), for which evolutionary processes select, is only a goal of morality insofar as it is moral to value posterity. At first, that seems an open option rather than a moral obligation. But, since human beings commonly love or have obligations to their children and their children's future happiness usually involves the welfare of *their* children, there is an automatic commitment to the future of the race even if this were not in itself a matter of some pride and concern to many people, childless or not. Similarly, the childless are chained to children as other human beings and thus to their future needs, including the need for the comfort of their children. But the future generations are not the *only* point of morality. For a suddenly sterile race, morality still has much of its meaning and all its force. Members of this race are indeed just people for whom there is no hereafter in *any* sense, and the absence of a racial hereafter is no more fatal to the point of morality than the absence of a spiritual one. Analogously, the discovery of a pill that would make those who take it happy and content but sterile would, except for special circumstances, such as previous promises to bear children, provide a perfectly moral way of life for all mankind.

We have been talking of what might be called evolutionary ethics, but not in the sense in which it was construed to mean a justification for the exploitation of the weak by the strong. That crude theory attempted to make a value out of what happens often but not universally in the nongregarious animals. Morality creates a higher value, in a nontrivial sense; it creates a very ingenious survival mechanism for individuals that transcends individual survival drives. The use of this mechanism distinguishes man from the animals at the level of efficient social behavior, just as his intellectual powers make that distinction possible at the levels of abstract thought and technological achievement. We have not yet progressed very far in the direction of making the functions and formulations of morality explicit objects of study in the way that led to such great success in the natural sciences and crafts. At the practical level this manifests itself in the extreme crudity of the present level of development of the machinery for international peace keeping. Precisely the same problem presents itself here as led to the formulation of national legal codes, with the stakes substantially increased, i.e., the need to abrogate the right to individual violence in order to increase the chance of individual survival. But our failure to recognize the pragmatic basis for interpersonal morality makes the international problem appear as if it were wholly novel, and the shortsighted kind of discussion that characterizes a group of children squabbling over toys persists.

17. THE FORMULATION AND INTERPRETATION OF MORAL MAXIMS

Even a casual study of man's perceptual and intellectual processes reveals that their operation is far too subtle to be described as the application of any rule formulable in our present language or, indeed, in any extension of it up to the limits imposed on length by the need to comprehend the rule. One can speak good English or play good bridge without being able to state the rules for doing so in a way that will ensure that someone following those rules would speak or play as well. Similarly, one may develop a remarkable sensitivity to the moral distinctions of a particular interpretation of morality without being able to state the rules of the system one may be thought of as applying implicitly. One of the main reasons for this is the enormous complexity of moral situations, i.e., the enormous number of morally different combinations of factors that can bear on many social situations. In areas of our experience where this kind of relevant complexity is found it is still very useful to formulate approximations from which to work as a preliminary guideline, and this is the function of most moral rules. "Thou shalt not kill" is simply a starting point, like "Don't end sentences with a preposition" or "Don't trump your partner's ace." These can alternatively be expressed as "Killing (etc.) is wrong (or bad)." There are many exceptions, but the exceptions have to be justified by *special* considerations. As we have previously remarked, the same analysis applies to the laws of physics. The General Gas Law is a useful approximation and can be appealed to as true (enough) for many purposes. For refinements, we add the van der Waals correction; and where that still yields insufficient precision, we add further corrections. Depending entirely on our need for accuracy on a particular occasion, we may or may not have to make one or several of these additional refinements. The first approximation is both mnemonically and communicatively handy, and often entirely adequate.

The prima-facie justification of the basic rule against killing is very simple: most people value their lives very highly and hence benefit from built-in protection for them in others' attitudes. A consideration of the advantages of radically altering this attitude toward their lives shows no gains, chiefly because of the dependence of other advantages on survival. But minor alterations can be justified; so the rule that killing is wrong must be construed as just a rough guide, not a universal truth. For killing in self-defense when there are no feasible alternatives is an exception, since the love of life is in general stronger than what one stands to gain by taking another person's life. The self-sacrifice rule in turn interjects exceptions to the self-defensive rule in cases in which the other individual's life is at stake *and* his value to others is greater (or in which several other individuals' lives are at stake). In the same way, despite a prima-facie commitment to helping others, or others in need, the moral man in an immoral society is in no way obligated to give a handout to anyone who asks for one even if he needs it. Indeed the reverse is the case, since it is clear that rewarding laziness or making it harmless is normally contrary to the interest of both the individual and the society. So there is an excellent basis for the general higher-level principle that obligations to others begin only when the resources of the recipients have been reduced to a risky level. A society does *not* run better if the industrious (or fortunate) and benevolent men beggar themselves to feed the lazy, and *that* is why it is not part of unselfish morality to do this. It is of the utmost importance to recognize the foundations of moral adages if they are to be interpreted and applied correctly. The most obvious proof of this emerges from an examination of the response to changing conditions. If we are taught moral maxims as undying truths about some abstract realm of moral values, we shall have excessive difficulty in adjusting ourselves to changed circumstances. Inertia is of some value, but it needs to be rationally assessable.

As a case in point we might take a contemporary example. Perhaps the most interesting novel moral problem in mid-twentieth-century America arises over the conflict between the principle of aid only to the needy, which we have just been discussing, and the economic problems of overproduction. It is all too clear that an oversimplified conception of the inviolability of moral principles (that is, excessive attitude inertia with regard to these rules) is leading the rich to imagine themselves to be exploited when their contribution to taxes is used partly for substantial compensation and retraining programs administered without extremely rigorous (and hence much more expensive) investigation into the qualifications of those who are assisted. Shocking tales of able-bodied loafers with TV are passed around with the canapés in Santa Barbara and Greenwich, Connecticut. The other side of the issue might be put crudely by saying that unless the rich are taxed and the money is used to make consumers out of the otherwise indigent, the rich will lose more income (because of the drop in market demand) than they do from paying taxes. Putting it another way, one might say that it's entirely right that the devotedly lazy man should be on relief since otherwise he would be filling a valuable space on a production line and not doing a good job there. It is still an advantage (and is becoming a privilege) to work in this economy, for anyone who does not set great store on laziness, because life on relief is extremely poorly recompensed. It may not be a *duty* to consume and encourage consumption, but it certainly helps a capitalist economy; so apart from the moral consideration, the dole is a better treatment of unemployment than starvation for both the rich and the poor.

To see the necessity for a change in attitude about work, consider the possibility that automation will result in an unemployment rate of 75 per cent. Will the unemployed be "lazy good-for-nothings" or even the "unfortunates"? Clearly not. The slogans, phrases, and attitudes of a labor-poor economy are irrelevant to a consumer-poor one. Suppose that a gradual increase in the level and type of unemployment benefits raises them to the point at which they make possible a way of life that many people find very pleasant. Will that have "corrupted their moral fiber"? It may destroy some of the incentive to get a job, but since there are not nearly enough jobs to be got, is that bad? The revolution toward this eventual state may well take place without being clearly recognized, e.g., by a reduction in the working week, an increase in the normal years of education, and vast developments in the fields of recreation, conservation, and assistance so that more people will find work and play indistinguishable. What matters about people is not what they do to earn their money but what they do, and we shall just have to devise a system of appraising people which makes that criterion less dependent on their employment status than was appropriate a generation or two ago. Even then, too little distinction was made between the money a man earned solely because of his own efforts and that which he earned because of the good start he got in life owing to his parents' wealth or influence or education or because he was one of the lucky ones in the vagaries of the business market. Money derived from luck or from others, whether parents or the government relief funds, is equally irrelevant to merit.

All this has been said from the point of view of the internal state of the United States economy. If we consider the United States as a spottily rich country in a world of poorer ones or take a good look at the poverty spots in the United States or at persons suffering from disease or mental disorder rather than economic handicap, we must concede that there are still many obligations to the community of man that make idle consumption indefensible, by rich or by poor. For there is still much need to do something worthwhile for those who really require help. So, on moral grounds alone, the dole should be safeguarded, the foreign and domestic Peace Corps expanded vastly, and internal and international development and assistance funds increased. And such endeavors can be supported on both a voluntary and a paid basis: to be unemployed does not mean to be incapable of doing worthwhile and rewarding work. Thus we can still find value in the condemnation of laziness as long as it is not identified with unemployment in the strict sense.

The educational system in this country is too much influenced by a wealthy class that imagines itself knowledgeable about economic reality and morality because its members have money, a degree, and no jail record. (One might as well assume that the best-paid professors are the best teachers.) This influence is probably the main reason for the general ignorance about the cruder facts of economics and morality, which presently makes Federal intervention a necessity. Cancel Federal taxes and call for voluntary contributions to support the Armed Forces, education, charity, and economic controls and aids, and the country would be destitute and conquered within a decade, and who really doubts it? Yet there is constant advocacy of this and related measures by eminent politicians of both parties. Even long-term self-interest is beyond the average man's capacity today when fat short-term gains leer invitingly. Couple this lamentable defect of will with gross deficiencies in education about the most fundamental issues of morality and economics, and the result is a nation whose only hope is the capacity of its elected representatives to educate themselves in office, to transcend the offered bribes . . . the pressures of propaganda . . . and the short-term charms of reelection, and to apply rational, long-term unselfish considerations. The prospect is less than promising.

This necessity to switch from the work-as-duty to the work-as-privilege attitude is intended to illustrate the importance of retaining enough flexibility to rethink our attitudes and express them in new moral rules. The changes due to advancing technology and education can undercut a system very fast, and nothing undercuts it faster than a parental generation producing attitudes that were appropriate in an earlier stage of the society, when the children can see perfectly clearly that the facts no longer support such attitudes toward, e.g., gainful employment, premarital intercourse, religion, Negroes, Japanese, etc. So modifiability of attitudes is crucial, but it is also essential that our attitudes be rigid enough to survive under pressure. The tension between these considerations is often the force that drives the moral rack. A balance between them must be struck and somehow be expressed. So there is a double difficulty. For even if the best way of life were known, it would undoubtedly require simplification to be expressed in an easily understood form, and there are always many ways to simplify a truth, some of them contradicting others. But simplification is necessary, not only to make it easier to teach children and to remind ourselves of the truth, as well as to make discussion more effective by providing us with useful approximations of various degrees of refinement, but also because attitudes are somewhat indelicate instruments and the cost of commitment is imprecision. Attitude inertia is desirable, but we pay something for it that the phrases "blind loyalty," "blind faith," and "blind obedience" convey. The commitment to higher values comes hard at first, and to make it possible we must sacrifice some refinement in the analysis of consequences, countervailing considerations, and so on. Sometimes all we can train ourselves and others to do in the way of justification is to appeal to some very simple general principle or value: "It doesn't seem *fair*," we say, or "That would be *stealing*," implying that justice should, and theft should not, be done.

Thus we must regard moral maxims like the Ten Commandments as doubly dubious guides. Of course, they cannot be devastated by pointing out a few of the apparent counterexamples, such as justified stealing. It is of the nature of such principles to state norms (i.e., what is normally or properly or ideally the case), not exceptionless general laws. But they may still be wrong in basic conception, *and* they may be wrong through oversimplification. To decide whether they are right is very difficult just because it requires an exhaustive analysis of the current interpretations of the rule as evidenced in the circumstances in which it is applied and the procedures for justifying exceptions. "Thou shalt not kill" has been interpreted as a prohibition of killing flies, hunting deer for sport, slaughtering cattle for food, suicide, euthanasia, and abortion. Now a moment's thought about the rational justification of the rule shows that there is something very odd about applying it to these cases. The rule is an attempt to preserve what is usually the highest personal value of members of the moral community. But, in the cases described, what is being terminated is something *not* wanted by the only *person* who has any legitimate interest [17] in it. So the assessment of a moral maxim like this will depend very heavily on whether killing is taken to mean "the taking of a person's life against the person's will." And, in addition, there is the problem of acceptable excuses and acceptable degrees of simplification. In assessing existing maxims there is also the problem of confusion due to myths about their source, which may lead to further divergence from any rationally defensible system.

Behind such issues of interpreting and assessing moral maxims there lies a basic issue to which we must now turn. To whom do moral rules apply?

In its basic form this is the problem of the moral franchise. What are the limits of the moral community? Who should heed them or be treated in accordance with them? Who is to be treated as equal? Servants, slaves, morons, infants, unborn babies, juveniles, animals, bankrupts, bankers,

---

[17] *Legitimate interest* here means roughly an interest of such a kind that the attitude of respect toward it offers prospective net benefits for the community in the long run.

kings, extraterrestrials, intelligent robots, Communists, Fascists, sadists, psychotics, criminals?

18. THE MORAL FRANCHISE: WHO IS EQUAL?

The inertia of the moral attitude can obviously carry us into difficulties, and it is of great importance that its blunt ways be refined as far as possible without significant loss of its advantages. No exact rules can be given for weighing the importance of, e.g., the dispensing of what appears to be justice against the importance of the apparent consequences. We can only attempt to teach the right answers from discussion and training based on many examples, as we teach the writing of grammatical English. But there is one task for which rules have seemed more feasible, the task of describing the limits of the moral group. And whether by rule or by training, the limits must be known if morality is to be fully applied. So it is of great interest to examine the problem of the "proper" attitude toward (1) swatting flies, (2) pulling off their wings, and (3) breeding them for the sole purpose of feeding ornamental goldfish, by comparison with analogous treatment of microbes, plants, dogs, adult women, the aged, and other minority groups. It is easy to state, and even to make precise, the rule that only human beings (or white or free or intelligent human beings) should be accorded significant rights. The only problem is to decide whether it is true.

Recalling the arguments for the moral attitude toward others, we notice that some of them depend on the potential gain in contributions from and for prospective members to the group, and others on the advantages for the individual of certain standpoints from which to assess potential experiences. Let us examine one example of the way in which such considerations apply to the franchise question. Why should we feel obligations toward the terminally or lifetime sick and insane (including upon occasion the obligation to kill them)? Certainly not because of the potential contribution of *these* individuals to the group. But the advantages of a certain attitude in a group which will probably exist for several generations include those in which roles are exchanged. It is because of the desirability of Good Samaritan insurance for ourselves or those whom we love (the "immediate" group) that care for the indigent can be defended.[18] Membership of the immediate group, however, is a highly contagious condition. For if you care for North and he cares for South, whom you do not know, you have automatically acquired an interest in South's welfare and similarly in the welfare of South's sons and daughters, friends and colleagues, and *their* friends too. Blood may

[18] The reader must constantly remember that morally grotesque notions such as *defending* care for the sick are a rational necessity when assessing or formulating morality and only an absurdity when, having determined that the move is a sound one, we shift into the moral gear.

not always run thicker than water, but if you add the ties of blood to the bonds of friendship chains, you have a substantial chance of being under an obligation to any stranger you meet on the street. Thus you have some direct or derivative interest in the welfare of most of the people you know, and it is a great benefit for all these people to have Good Samaritan coverage. The only feasible way for this to be arranged is by supporting the pressures toward morality on as many persons as possible, which in the usual circumstances means allowing the same pressures to be put on you (and your immediate group). Doing this, as we have argued, also provides gains of other kinds (adaptability, peer esteem, sanction avoidance, etc.). So, of course, people *should* be kind to the unfortunates.

Unfortunate *people,* that is. But the most reliable sources assure us that our chances of turning into an elephant or a mouse, now or later, are exceedingly remote. So why be nice to mice?

Normal Western mores countenance trapping or poisoning pests, including mice, but draw the line at deliberate or careless cruelty to them. But a substantial minority, perhaps disproportionately female, joins many Asians in regarding even such "defensive killing" as unjustified. Another minority, including the Hopi, thinks wanton cruelty to small animals is not a moral matter at all. Who is right?

The four basic considerations bearing on our attitude toward animals are (1) that preserving the simplicity of the negative moral attitude toward casual infliction of pain and the positive one toward rewarding loyalty and service is important; (2) that the chain of affection can extend into the animal kingdom through people to whom we may be linked even if we are not animal lovers ourselves; (3) that the cost of kindness is in general small or nonexistent, and its benefits in terms of the adaptability advantage, peer esteem, or training efficiency are sometimes considerable; but (4) still a point comes, sooner with mice than with men, at which the cost of equal treatment is too great, since the potential gains from including a mouse in the moral community are simply not comparable with those a man offers. Together, these considerations rule out the extremes implied in a literal interpretation of St. Francis' phrase "little brethren" (which he applied to his lice) and the more recent idiom "treat them like animals," which usually refers to practices that are not defensible even for animals. When it comes down to such pressing practical questions as whether it is really immoral to eat turkeys at Thanksgiving or to use inexpensive neck-breaking mousetraps rather than expensive, slightly less effective live-catching traps (releasing the victims somewhere out in the country), we must concede that a final resolution may not be obtained within these pages. But the lines of thought that must be followed are clear and become more important when we generalize such problems into the issues of vegetarianism, vivisection, and blood sports.

In such cases important but unsettled empirical questions concern (1) the effect of callousness toward animals on interhuman attitudes and (2) the extent to which this effect is unavoidable. The answers to this and associated questions about ease of learning determine the weight we should give to the first factor in the list above. Lacking definite answers, we must use a precautionary strategy (discussed below), but there are other important points. There is the question of consideration for the sensibilities of others (the second factor in the list), which up to a point is relevant even when those sensibilities are misdirected. (A morality that took account only of the preferences of totally reasonable beings would have remarkably little value for us.) There are the adaptability advantages of affection toward animals and birds which are obviously exemplified in the pleasures afforded to many people by their pets. Related to but not identical with this source of reward is the obvious benefit provided by those animals which serve or can serve men directly as carriers, guardians, and hunters and can thus be said to "deserve" consideration and the avoidance of wanton cruelty on almost the same basis as the human servant. But even if the animals do contribute directly to the labor force and, within limits, to the police force, they are certainly limited in their intellectual powers and hence in their general utility when new circumstances arise, calling for intellectual and moral decisions. Indeed, they never become moral agents, only the agents of moral agents; they never have moral duties, though their duties may be moral and we may have moral obligations to them. So the network of moral attitudes binds us to treating animals as having some call on our moral sensibilities.

Does this not mean that killing mice to keep them out of the kitchen is highly immoral? Is not this precisely like the treatment of slaves by the amoral slaveowner: ruthless when convenience dictated, kind when it suited him, that is, recognizing no *rights* at all? (To recognize an entity as having rights implies that one acts more favorably toward it than if one's own convenience were all that was at stake.)

There are important differences. Nothing is held to excuse wanton cruelty even to minor mammals; so they are morally accorded a degree of respect which distinguishes them from slaves regarded as mere objects of convenience, as automata. This distinction is justified partly in terms of the negligible importance of the pleasure and conveniences associated with wanton cruelty compared with the possibility that cruelty once tolerated becomes an increasingly casual matter. There is small loss but some expectation of substantial gain. Now when a substantial practical difficulty arises, such as contamination of food or destruction of the house structure, and *no* alternative except the painless extermination of the pest will suffice, the cost of extending the franchise to animals may be held to outweigh the risk of debasing character (in this case by making killing acceptable), upsetting others, reducing possible gains from affection, etc. Of course, there usually *is* an alternative, like the live traps discussed above, but here the practical inconvenience of carrying it out must be weighed against the small differential in preserving the attitude related to morality that is involved. These are empirical hypotheses that are being weighed, and our present state of knowledge about them is minimal. It has been widely held that the hunter or trapper does become a less moral being toward his fellow men as a result of his occupation, but it has also been widely denied. At the moment, it would be impossible to argue conclusively for either position, let alone its extension to the household-pest level; but ignorance of consequences does not make a moral decision impossible or even more difficult: it simply leads to a different decision.

The attitude toward animals that we have just described is very like the attitude of what used to be called the more *enlightened* type of slave-owner toward his slaves. And it is very like the attitude that many people have toward those who are in their power for emotional rather than political reasons—our "devoted slaves," as they called themselves in earlier centuries. That is: affection to a point, consideration to a point, but beyond that the wasteland of exploitation or disregard. Indeed, it is very close to the attitude of most people to most people, distant aliens, they never see. It is enlightening, if not edifying, to reflect that there should be so much similarity between this attitude and that of small boys and experimentalists toward rats.

The emergence of the concept of universal human rights is not entirely a discovery of what was previously true but unrecognized; it is partly the creation of a new social arrangement better suited to a society in which education has become widespread. For once people begin to understand their own powers and see their long-term interests for what they are, a universal franchise is quite clearly the only workable arrangement. It is the most stable balance of power, although this is neither the only root nor the only flower of the moral system. The lesson that the wolf pack learned has taken man a long time to express linguistically, but once it has been done and as long as memory persists, the system of social relations can never revert to the master-slave stratification. It is the fact the animals lack an inferential language and the intelligence to reason with it, rather than that they lack power, that keeps us from *having* to extend the franchise. "Insects of the world, unite" would be a chilling war cry, in face of the vast disparity of numbers: thousands upon thousands for every man. That a group has learned the lesson of cooperative power is not the only reason for extending the franchise to it, of course (compare the sick), but it is a completely sufficient one. This lesson, which led to the labor unions and to the few political revolutions that have aimed at and achieved freedom, is simply that if all will commit themselves to sacrifice for the common cause, the need for sacrifice will be reduced, and the expectations of other gains vastly increased.

A minority, if it stands together, has enormous power in an industrial society. In the limit, a single totally committed man has the colossal power of a rifle or a bomb. If there were in every generation one politically motivated lunatic exploiting this power in every one million citizens instead of one in one hundred million, this nation could probably not maintain its present form of government.

To what extent is society at the mercy of sane but ruthless members or groups? And to what extent does the universal moral franchise increase this susceptibility? Of course, a single man can selfishly exploit society for his own ends if he is already in a position of great power, such as the Presidency. And he frequently does, in many countries. But the system of checks is moderately effective with regard to most long-term villainy in the United States and can certainly be made so elsewhere. Nonetheless, any two or three committed men could present a desperate threat to the nation if it were not for a couple of practical difficulties which lead to a general point. If each man could count on the others to keep to the bargain, they could draw lots for the role of assassin-elect and blackmail the nation with a promise of Presidential assassination. They could demonstrate their power with a near miss or a success followed by the suicide of the assassin and the repetition of the threat (whether to the same or a later President is unimportant), for it is still, and probably always will be, extremely easy to assassinate the President if the assassin has little concern for his own safety. But exactly the attitude required for willingness to profit from such extortion counts against the trustworthiness of the agent whose lot is drawn. The other practical difficulty with this plot, which would trouble even the survivor, lies in collecting and enjoying the ransom. The bond between the members of a self-interested assassins' group is thus too feeble to be analogous to that bearing on the moral attitude, especially because it is specific to one plan and one period of time. The moment that we shift to a case in which an assassination is motivated by considerations of principle, e.g., as the only way to break the grip of a despot, then it can be seen as a cause that is good in itself, deserving of sacrifice, etc. When benefits for *others* are part of the calculation, the assassin can have a motive that transcends the risk of death; and hence most assassinations are politically rather than selfishly oriented. The assassins' group is too small to exploit the rest of the country; but a small group can do it, at least for a while, like the whites in South Africa or the Roman citizens in the Roman Empire.

The Romans had quite a respectable ingroup morality, which they had no trouble at all in not extending to the slaves. But they were aided in accommodating their consciences to this attitude by the fact that the master-slave arrangement was part of the natural evolution of the social structure. If today one attempts deliberately to set up a basis for discrimination on a foundation of mere advantage, one has a trade association, union, or crime syndicate and not a morality. Synthetic gems are still synthetic, and that knowledge can affect their value even when the stones are the same. We know too much to be innocent exploiters, and those we would exploit know too much to make it easy. And yet we still try hard to cheat, for the use of prisoners of war in labor camps in recent wars is pragmatically hard to distinguish from the Romans' practice.

If slavery today would be immoral, why does it not follow that the use of mousetraps is immoral? Is it just that it is easier to identify mice visually than Negroes? In the first place, in terms of our earlier discussion, the *casual* use of cruel mousetraps is not immune to moral criticism. In the second place, there are certainly intrinsic differences which make swatting flies and crushing microbes considerably less wicked than killing people and thus suggest that killing mice is not so bad as murder.

Let us begin by considering microbes. What does a microbe lose when killed? On the one hand, all that he has; but on the other, very little. A basic consideration must be the extent of an entity's awareness of and feelings about life; otherwise cutting flowers and pruning trees becomes cruelty. It is not true that what you do not know you have you cannot lose; but it is true that if you do not know what it is to have, you cannot know what it is to lose. This argument applies equally to the avoidance of pain, the desire for life, and the more sophisticated values. So we deprive the microbe of nothing of any possible significance to "him." As we move up the hierarchy through the jellyfish to the mollusks and the mammals, the argument becomes less decisive but not insignificant. This does not mean that a snake *values* its life, except metaphorically, but the metaphor comes closer to literal truth as the organisms more clearly exhibit pleasure and pain instead of just reflexes. It is marginally plausible to say that a snake likes sleeping in the sun and dislikes being hit with a stick. Of course it behaves toward the first as a goal, and toward the second as something to be avoided. That is not enough to show it enjoys the first and dislikes the second. The further element in this claim is the capacity of the organism to perceive its own condition (compare the *Man* chapter). It is not accidental that the hierarchy of intelligence is about the same as the hierarchy of sensitivity, for both depend upon the capacity for symbolic representation and discrimination. So the snake may be a marginal case and the snail a submarginal one, but the mouse is surely sensitive to pain and fear and deprivation. Taking life at all may be a little wrong, but taking a full life is more wrong. To stamp on the skull of a small, shrieking mouse without thought or to cheer the choreography of ritualized bull slaughtering is surely to show a lack of the sensitivity to similarities that is an important part of moral reasoning.

We have noticed some significant differences between a compact to engage in crime, or even an organization designed to exploit its power advantages in the long run, and the moral commitment of mankind. An interesting further point emerges from the case in which an assassins' group threatens to kill the President and demands money to refrain from doing so. To pay the sum demanded would encourage repetition of the crime and disregard of other laws as well. Not to pay would probably cost the President's life. There again we have the difference between the immediate-calculation best choice and the long-run best choice. On the small scale, this is why there is such a difference between the viewpoint of the police and those approached for ransom in a kidnaping case. The police are concerned about the long-run frequency of kidnaping, which will be reduced by refusal to pay the ransom. The ransomee is more concerned with the welfare of the kidnaped person, and this will usually be best served by payment. It is not pure selfishness that motivates a distraught parent, but it is certainly an overbalance of affection for his own kin at the expense of the kin of others.

This situation demonstrates one of the substantial benefits possible for the participants in moral subgroups. If any subgroup can make a binding agreement in advance not to pay any ransom and publicize this, it will ensure its safety from kidnapers. Now, simply getting its members to put up a large sum, even their entire fortunes, as a bond on this covenant will certainly not prevent them from cracking under the pressure of the moment. But each member of a group which has absorbed the group point of view (perhaps without commitment to the general moral attitude) will be committed, and the protective system will work as long as would-be kidnapers *believe* members of the group to be men of their word.

Similar agreements with respect to other kinds of threats can be much more widely used than at present; their success in the form of labor unions should be taken more seriously. Returning to the original point, we see that the power of a subgroup to enforce its will on the majority is materially reduced in a society in which considerations of the general welfare are paramount, since attempts to exploit immediate anxieties will be largely unsuccessful. Nevertheless, members of even a very small minority—be it the doctors or the truckers or the filibusterers—have an enormous power if they apply themselves to the problem of maximizing their leverage with intelligence and selfless commitment to their subgroup. Even if two men cannot hold a rational nation to ransom for the life of its President, one small group can threaten to, and often does, use its power to cause billions of dollars of loss to the nation. The careless, ruthless, or disproportionately selfish use of such power cannot be tolerated by a nation any more than the careless or ruthless use of strikebreaking forces. The arbitration of industrial disputes is consequently an extremely difficult and important task, requiring a combination of morality, diplomacy, and technical and legal knowledge that does not generally receive the recognition and rewards it deserves.

An exception which merits more attention is the arbitration court system of a country with compulsory industrial arbitration like Australia. Settlement of strikes by labor-management negotiation simply encourages sacrificing the consumer whenever possible and so is intrinsically deficient. The fact that two disputing parties are represented does not mean that all interested parties are represented. The horrified protests about government intervention in such negotiations are simply rejections of what should be the consumer's representative.

In power terms, then, the minority is vulnerable to persecution but also capable of dictatorship. The only compromise that has any significance beyond mere expediency is the system of social justice in which each man has the right to equal consideration in the making of those arrangements which lead to differential treatment with regard to recompense, security, and the conditions of life for him and his. Thus to the degree that men exercise their votes rationally and knowledgeably, the right to an equal vote will yield greater benefits than any other arrangement. To the degree they do not, they destroy the advantages of the universal franchise, with one important qualification. Contrary to the view of political snobs, commonly heard today, the existence of many voters who are stupid, prejudiced, or shortsighted does not make democracy a foolish system. For the justification of democracy today lies largely in its superiority over any feasible alternative and not in its intrinsic perfection. As a means to the discovery and enforcement of a fair solution, the self-interested election of representatives, even by an imperfect electorate, has a long history of superior performance by comparison with the self-professed disinterest of rulers. When legislators who can demonstrate their own transcendence of self-interest and superiority of understanding appear, then they may have reached an appropriate starting point for discussing the drawbacks of the universal political franchise ensuing from defects in the electorate.

The present states which call themselves democracies are all defective to varying degrees, sometimes to an extent large enough to offset the theoretical advantages of a democratic system over a reform junta, for example. So it is not the deficiencies of the electorate but those of the leaders that are matters for *present* concern. As for the future, the participation of a *well-educated and well-informed electorate* in the selection of its representatives may well engender enough further commitment to outweigh any imperfections in its rationality. But education for citizenship is, of course, an absurdity without education in morality. Any country which does not recognize that morality has no foundation or justification except as a solution to the problems of social living will have great difficulty in generating good citizenship in either its citizens or its leaders. For the alternative accounts of morality are contradictory, inherently implausible, and connected only indirectly to social behavior.

In concluding these arguments for the universal moral franchise among men, it is important to recall the great advantages that automatically accrue from increasing the size of any cooperating group—increased total power, increased specialization possibilities, decreased unit cost of goods, and so on —as well as the special advantages of a larger moral group: increased availability of unselfish help and friendship, decreased likelihood of knavery and unprofitable conflict, etc. The qualified extension of moral consideration into the nonhuman domain is justified in somewhat different terms, greater weight being attached to the benefits of positive reinforcement and less to the advantages of group productivity, apart from the points discussed earlier. A quasi morality is often extended to machines, e.g., by those who love their boats or cars. The case for this as an option is similar to part of the case for the animals: machines do not suffer, but they do respond to loving care and make good pets besides. With *very* complicated machines, not yet existing, full moral equality may be mandatory. Equality of *political* franchise has both moral and practical support, since it provides the individual with a defense of his own interests and the government with a representation of the population's concerns.

We now turn to the problem of the practical consequences of the commitment to equality. Does it imply that one should love others' children as much as one's own, for example? It is often held that the ideal of treating all mankind as equal is self-stultifying, since if we really worried as much about each one of the starving thousands of distant lands as about the indigent poor of our own city, neither would benefit; we would have to send our aid to the far land, since greater numbers with greater needs are there, and for just that reason it would do negligible good.

But there is an excellent moral and practical basis for the adage "Charity begins at home," although it does not support the extension to the conclusion that charity *ends* at home. First, it is absurd to suppose that there is ever an obligation to do something which is demonstrably futile. It is demonstrably futile to spread your little charitable gift among a very large number of the needs because none will benefit significantly. Your obligation is to determine the size of a significant contribution and allot as many of these contributions as you can reasonably afford to the most needy individuals or donate your money to an organization that does exactly this. Second, it is important that there should be the least possible wastage through administrative costs and corruption. This can usually be achieved by purchasing and often by administering the gift yourself, except when certain organizations are given special leverage, e.g., a dollar-for-dollar or a transportation-charges-only call on surplus farm products. Hence, assuming reasonable parity of individual needs, there is a second good reason for local preference. You are in the best position to help your neighbors and hence have the strongest obligation to do so. Third, other emotional and moral springs besides the pure sense of duty can help provide the energy or motivation for giving: local pride, mutual friendship, the pleasure of seeing the good results you have brought about, etc. Less than perfect as we are, it is often sensible of us to employ against our weaker selves all the leverage we can develop from less noble sources. We should strive for the moral attitude, but we are not wrong to amplify the feeble signals of conscience with a feedback circuit of a more mundane kind. Fourth, *some* method of selection of moral tasks must be employed, and there is merit in using one which has a tendency to increase the moral level of the recipient. And gratitude in the recipient can effectively be incubated into tangible moral output later by the presence of the benefactor. Fifth, there is a tiny element of moral sense as well as common sense behind the application of patriotic considerations to this problem. As long as the survival and welfare of one's own national or local group are important or strongly contributory to the furtherance of other good causes, it is morally appropriate to bend one's efforts first toward repairing the group's defects so that it may more effectively proceed, by means of example and practice, to more direct contributions. And apart from that lofty consideration, it is, in the sixth place, simply sensible to protect the welfare of the group which can most effectively protect or assist or tolerate you, and to a small extent this factor is involved in aiding local or national charities. Nor are such considerations immoral, for morality does not deny a man's right to self-protection and his own interests when they do not involve disregard of others. But it *is* obviously immoral to refuse to give foreigners surplus grain that will save them from starvation on the ground that it will lower the world asking price, for basic health or lives are substantially more important than profit. It is indeed indefensible to refuse aid in the form of other goods and services even though they *might* be used at home for relative luxury, although the need abroad is *very* much more acute. For even if one did not defend such a refusal explicitly and immorally by denying the moral equality of foreigners, the long-term effects of single-minded concentration on the lesser hardships of compatriots rather than on the greater hardships abroad constitute an implicit denial of this postulate. Even prudential considerations count against moral isolationism, for the poor grow stronger eventually and do not remember kindly those who ate caviar instead of giving alms. And there are rich rivals to help them get stronger if we do not. In short, the international realm is increasingly indistinguishable from the interpersonal one. When the balance of forces rapidly shifts and many issues are at stake, with some difference in the alliances on each, morality is not far behind prudence.

We normally distinguish three levels of moral performance: (1) refraining from gratuitous immorality; (2) discharging obligations or duties; and (3) acting meritoriously, nobly, etc. ("doing good works"). The distinction is reflected in the combinations of praise and blame that are allotted for doing or not doing these things. No praise is due one for not stealing a raincoat from the racks in the college corridor, and one is blamed for doing otherwise. One deserves some praise for keeping a promise when it has been inconvenient to do so and will be blamed for not doing so. But to exist at the subsistence level in order to support some waifs in Hong Kong is said to be "above and beyond the call of duty," to be a "work of supererogation"; here praise is due, but blame for failure to act thus would not be thought appropriate. Insofar as the distinctions go beyond considerations like those of the discussion on our obligations to neighbors versus strangers, they are essentially a concession to man's limitations. A man who is moral in the strong sense cannot stop short at mere duty; he cannot excuse failure to do more, when he *could* do more, on the ground that it is more than duty requires—at least, this is a very feeble excuse, as all recognize by their embarrassment in turning down direct appeals for charity in worthy cases. Since we would go further if we truly loved others as equals and since there are good grounds for doing so, there really is an obligation to go further, though clearly it is less stringent than the direct obligation to do a clear duty.

When we are training children or attempting to train those not properly trained as children, we praise them for not stealing or lying if something was to be gained by dishonesty, because this abstention represents a considerable achievement *for them*. And praise is not just descriptively appropriate for someone who is overcoming difficulties on the way to acting in a desirable way; it serves as a reward and thus aids learning. For just these reasons, in a company of highly moral men it would be inappropriate to issue praise for what now seem to us quite meritorious works, though their works would be nonetheless *good* works. In that company of men, to do only one's duty would be a sign of moral deficiency; it would seem disappointing, indeed, blameworthy. Hence, in that company, our obligations would be greater. Thus the distinction between acts of obligation and of supererogation is chiefly dependent on the individual's capabilities. Now, we all have some long-run control over our capacity to be moral and clearly have an obligation to increase it. So there is a perfectly good sense in which everyone has an obligation to do all the good that he sensibly can, now, and a long-run obligation to do all that he *could* if he were as much better as he could (and should) be. In practical terms, this means that we are usually acting immorally in purchasing luxuries instead of contributing the money to persons with very great need for the elementary necessities. This is a hard standard to meet but a good one at which to aim. It is no harder to defend in utilitarian terms than in the religious ones which have previously led men to adopt it as an ideal. As long as we are weak, of course, it can perfectly well be argued that we need an occasional luxury to keep up our morale or, in prospect, as an incentive to that productivity which indirectly benefits us all. But our "need" for this is more a product of poor upbringing or of laziness in thinking out an overall attitude to life and implementing it in a program of self-reform than of anything essential to the nature of man.

A certain amount of the political enthusiasm for the right-wing position in the United States, with its low-tax and antiwelfare emphasis, arises from the need for a rationalization of selfishness, just as a certain amount of the enthusiasm for the left, with its welfare legislation and a steeply graduated income tax, arises from the need to rationalize envy of the rich and powerful. The right wing's rationalization attempts to show that a true concern for the individual's rights and welfare would lead to a reduction of the role of centralized government and hence of taxes. It inevitably fails, in those terms, because the left wing is not arguing for the desirability of government as such; it is only arguing for the amount of government that, in the light of the known limits of spontaneous justice and charity, is necessary to safeguard individual interests and rights. Conversely, the left's attack on the right as embodying disregard of human suffering is valueless at that level of generality because the right feels that in the long run human suffering is decreased by emphasis on individual responsibility and obligations, even if *at first* this means more suffering. The debate essentially concerns a matter of fact, the relative effects of two different emphases, about which we have no conclusive evidence. Consequently, it tends to be dominated by the participants' emotional predispositions, and those in turn are markedly affected by their selfish interests. The danger arises when it becomes widely believed by either side that this is an issue of fundamental values with regard to which the opposing position is essentially immoral or, at least, antidemocratic. And who does not prefer to think of himself as a champion of liberty and equality, rather than of one side of a highly uncertain wager? In terms of this picture of the dispute, intemperance seems justified, manifesting itself in vicious attack on or censorship of the seditious doctrine. Indeed, with a little retaliation to aggravate the matter, detention, execution, or assassination of the subversives comes to seem a patriotic duty, and we see replayed the pathetic cycle of almost every new "people's" government, which comes to power as a champion of liberty to become in a few years the new tyranny. After all, communism, anarchism, and conservatism are all identified by their theorists as embodying the goal of the withering away of the state. And governments owing allegiance to each of these ideals have turned out in practice to behave in very similar ways. We *must* consider actual practices far more carefully than self-applied labels.

Power is *extremely* corrosive. Against its corruptive effect there can prevail only the *deepest* moral convictions, and these arise in only two ways: from the fires of actual persecution or from the insights of a profound understanding of the lessons of an objective history and morality, an understanding which in turn can only be attained from an educational experience wholly alien to most of the classrooms of the world's schools today. If we feed the children a *patriotic*—indeed, a chauvinistic—history and a *religious* morality (or, rather, twenty different religious moralities as icing on a crudely materialistic set of values) and if both are taught in terms of slogans, hero worship, and romantic myths, we may expect negligible understanding of either side in the great internal and international disputes and hence little real motivation or capacity for compromise. For to understand the moral positions of most men is to see the extent to which they involve the same values as those of other men; and to understand one's own moral position is to realize how many tentative judgments of fact, how many simplifications, how many compromises it involves. That kind of understanding often provides the motivation for compromise; and to understand the process of moral argument requires that one have some skill in the evaluation, and hence the development, of creative compromise. To understand completely is not to accept completely, but it reduces the likelihood of purely emotional rejection. A morality of abstract platitudes is empty, but a morality of dogmatic positions is full of danger.

Once more, in discussing the problem of our attitude toward our fellow men we travel the route from general considerations through political ones back to the educational process. The case for morality is at its strongest when shorn of the complexities and rigidities we see from a certain station in a well-settled life, at its strongest when we are considering it as a viewpoint for an as yet unmolded individual whose luck and talents are still unclear, in short, for a child. But finally we must come back to the problem of the individual in the midst of life.

19. ATTITUDE CONTROL

Do we really have the power to become moral, apart from the reasons to want that power? Does our incapacity for change restrict the argument for morality to recommendations for the kindergarten curriculum?

We have discussed the main elements in any answer to this question in the *Responsibility* chapter. It is certainly true there are limits on what we can change about ourselves; for example, by the time we are adults, we cannot change our mathematical ability from very bad to very good, no matter how diligently we apply ourselves. But many "mental abilities" can still be radically changed at almost any time; a good example is the ability to remember the names of people we meet or read about. "I have a terrible memory for names" only means "I lack the capacity to remember names, as of now"; it does not mean "I am incapable of learning (how to remember) names." Obviously, "I can't understand French" is in the same way an expression of short-term incapacity (but compare "I can't speak French with a native accent"). Equally obviously, to move nearer morality, *some* individuals (for example, some "habitual criminals") have undergone radical reforms in the morality of their behavior. Can we all do this?

Almost all of us do change ourselves or allow ourselves to be changed morally: in either case we are responsible for the change. We gradually overcome the temptations that lead to the petty thefts and frequent lies of our childhood. We find ourselves able to give to an alumni appeal or even to a remote charity (as opposed to a needy friend) without such difficulty as before and indeed may occasionally start going out of our way to find such causes. Arguing with his children, whose side is often defended by his spouse, sometimes makes a parent more susceptible to appeals in terms of the rights of others, a tendency which has its converse in the tendency toward selfishness among long-time bachelors. Similar results may accrue from interactions with coworkers and not occur in the case of self-employed persons. And many people have found in their religion or their later reading an inspiration which has lead them a long way forward on the moral path.

The task of changing one's character ("mending one's ways") is undoubtedly a formidable one, because the changes are slow and require sustained effort. On the other hand, even a very little effort pays off in a somewhat longer time, which is a very important difference from the situation involved in staying on a diet or exercise regimen or giving up cigarettes. There, the minimum effort is considerable (too great for many people), and not only are there no returns for expending a lesser effort, but the failure probably weakens one's confidence (and hence the likelihood of success) in future efforts. But all such tasks become much easier once they have been thoroughly explained, the difficulties and the devices for handling them made clear, and the fact that progress appears slow offset by stress on the importance of the small steps. In the end, of course, it is obvious that we can change our character because, as Aristotle observed some time ago, it is obvious that our standards are affected by the company we keep and it is obvious that usually we choose our companions. And perhaps it is also obvious that we can improve our characters because it is surely obvious that we can ruin them.

It is rather less obvious what company we *should* keep. There is an unfortunate tendency for the "fine upstanding lad" (as the minister would say) to be the one that gets the minister's daughter pregnant. This is an expectable consequence of a young person's talent for acting the expected role plus the usual parent's and university president's extremely superficial conception of what the moral role amounts to. Nice manners to elderly aunts and a proclivity for Ivy League clothes cost little, pay well, and fool the folks. Sticking with a highly unpopular stand on a clear issue of principle, ignoring grades in a worthless course when it is necessary if one is to do a really good research project in a good course, missing all the basketball games because they are boring, refusing to be fondled by strangers who happen to be old friends of one's parents, insisting on information about contraceptives at age sixteen—these are activities virtually guaranteed to upset the family but showing forty times the merit of the usual organization boy who gets the American Legion prize at graduation.

Nor is it ever too late to change, to take up new friends and new interests that lead to new friends. To put it very simply, if one has not lost the use of one's reason, one must concede there is room for self-improvement; if one has not lost one's intelligence, one can see ways in which it can be, slowly, done; and no one is *incapable* of the small efforts that will bring it about. Many of us are too lazy or self-satisfied to do anything, but these are not excuses, merely culpable deficiencies which themselves can be improved. For someone in this category, the best recourse is the roundabout route: if you do not have the strength to do what you concede you should do, you do have the strength to make a deal with someone who will help you to do it in return for similar favors. This deal is sometimes called marriage; at other times it is part of friendship or the patient-therapist or the citizen-government relationship. In the mildest and most obligatory form the interest in morality and the attempt to improve one's responses to it are manifested in the willingness to discuss moral decisions in good faith. For these exhibit respect for the point of view of others and a willingness to allow one's commitment to rationality to bear on one's moral behavior. The first is itself a mild form of morality, and the second a mild way of improving one's moral performance by indirect aid.

But are the gains from a somewhat more moral life *worth* all this planning and effort if one is happy with the life one already has? Complacency with an immoral life is a sign of either ignorance or irrationality —or laziness, to the extent that that is distinguishable from irrationality. A salaried man who makes no provision for his retirement years may well be happy with his life, but that is simply a sign he is stupid. The long-run gains of morality do not fit so readily into double-entry bookkeeping practice as does retirement income, but there is surely a close analogy between the economically destitute old man and the emotionally destitute old man who has lost the physical capacities for enjoyment of his own life and lacks the mental capacity to enjoy the lives of others or to aid them in the ways still open to him. The ancient crone's cruel gossip provides her with pleasure from the misfortunes of others, though not a moral pleasure. But she cannot share it with the objects of her amusement, cannot aid them even with solace or advice, cannot participate in what entertains her except insofar as she espouses other, moral values. And only the moral values and the eschewal of the others provide her with membership in the moral group with its many advantages. But the moral attitude is not merely old-age insurance, nor is it merely insurance; it offers many advantages, and at no point does its case rest on the claim that one cannot be happy though selfish. It is true that people very often turn to religion through unhappiness, but no priest would argue that religion has nothing to offer the well and happy. The same is true of the defensible element in religion, namely, a rational morality.

Closely related to the general question of whether we can become moral is the problem of distinguishing wants from needs or, more generally, justifiable desires from unjustifiable ones. In discussing many moral problems it is easy to see what most people want and what action would best bring this about. But this is hardly the end of the matter; not only may people, even communally, want incompatibles, such as lower taxes *and* greater social security benefits, the pleasure of smoking *and* longer life, but they may also want what is immoral, such as the sacrifice of more maidens, gladiators, pagans, infidels, atheists, Jews, Christians, capitalists, Communists, or other kinds of animal. Another type of case arises when an extremely spoiled child will obviously be made much unhappier by not having a disputed candy bar than the child from whom he is attempting to wrest it. In such cases we must always ask the long-term question, Is the present desire itself desirable? This is simply a special case of the problem about the selfish versus the unselfish attitude; some attitudes are more desirable than others, either in selfish or, later, in moral terms. Different solutions are appropriate, depending on whether the desire is or is not alterable now or at some future time and whether it was or was not alterable at some earlier time. For example, gratifying the strong desire of the spoiled child in the above-mentioned example is usually undesirable since it encourages an undesirable pattern of behavior and attitude, that of selfish indulgence, a pattern which can be changed by withholding gratification. But if that desire was the desperate expression of an unusual and irremediable physiological need for sugar, we *would* take account of its intensity as against the otherwise better claim of the other disputant. Pilate must protest the mob's lust for crucifixion and cannot merely accept it as an ultimate fact, just as state governors today should disregard polls showing public support for the execution of murderers. The voice of the people is not the voice of morality, and killing a man to satisfy blood lust or mistaken beliefs about the effects is just what governorships are made to be abandoned for. As Harry Truman once said of the Presidency, "The buck stops here." It may be helpful to consider two problems of applied morality that involve these points:

1. How should the sadist be regarded and treated? Let us suppose that sadism is inherited, incurable, and irresistible, none of which is generally true. Is the sadist culpable for beating an unwilling victim for pleasure? Yes, because (*a*) the habit is recognizable and recurrent and the sadist can place himself under restraint; and (*b*) this kind of sadism is a practice which does not regard the rights of others as equal, hence is immoral. Is

there any point to punishing him, since there is no possibility of changing him? Of course; his incurability is with regard to a *disposition:* it does not preclude responsibility for its unbridled manifestation. He could have avoided the crime and did not; so he is responsible for doing what he knew to be, or should have known to be, immoral. He is, in short, not significantly different from the alcoholic who injures someone in a car crash when drunk. Our sympathies are sometimes more easily aroused by the more pathological nature of the case, but usually inappropriately. In fact, sadism is by no means so severe as is here supposed, and hence the sadist is typically also immediately responsible. And even in a mixedly moral society, he is strikingly imprudent if he does not exploit the many ways of reducing the risk of manifestation.

2. Would we be justified in forcibly using brain surgery to convert recalcitrant criminals or psychopaths to morality (supposing we knew how to do this)? There is for most of us something peculiarly repulsive about altering a man's body, especially his brain, against his will. The commitment to respect the rights of others reaches its maximum strength in cases of violation of another's mental integrity against his will, for a strong reason: to change a man's nature is very like killing him. It means the end of the individual as he was and as he preferred to be. The continuance of the physical body may justify us in saying that murder has not been done, but, we feel, the morally significant entity is the personality and to destroy that is to eliminate one of the members of the moral community. (Conversely, it is because the fetus has no personality as yet that the moral case against abortion is complicated.)

Of course, there is another side to the question. Self-protection is, and clearly should be, an adequate justification for damaging someone else against his will. Could we not argue that society is simply protecting itself against the criminal in this way?

But self-defense is not a justification for killing someone when there are more merciful and readily available alternatives. For the recalcitrant criminal, there is always jail, which can be a most effective defense for society. While the prisoner is in jail, it is of course perfectly appropriate, by open reasoning, to try to persuade him to reform. We may also undertake to remove any obstacles to reform, such as lack of a trade or psychological blockages. There is no moral reason not to make the therapy, whether it is talk therapy, work therapy, or surgical therapy, as attractive as possible in terms of remission of sentence and financial help for a fresh start. It is unlikely there would be many holdouts against this kind of argument. But if there were, they would maintain a basic right to continued existence or integrity which is among the most fundamental rights in our set of values. For *that* man there is no difference between a painless death and a radical change of personality with associated amnesia. But, again, the long-run arguments have an easier time, and genetic engineering to prevent the birth of sociopathic or even socioapathetic individuals encounters no such difficulty, though there are others. In the short run, too, the practical questions are crucial, and if the security of prisons became negligible because of changes in the restrictive skills of wardens or the escapist skills of prisoners, it might become necessary to swallow our present feelings in order to prevent more serious consequences. This is one of the moral issues in which the right answer is highly dependent on our feelings and in which these are clearly rather easily modifiable. Related examples concern the reactions to voyeurism and culturally unusual sex practices.

20. PARADOXES OF COMMITMENT

Before giving a brief summary of the conclusions of this chapter, we shall turn to some apparent paradoxes about the key element in the present approach, the concept of a rational attitude. From them we can get a clearer idea of the role of this element and a way to handle some important problems of applied morality.

As a first example, it should now be possible to see how it can be rational to adopt an irrational attitude. If one is undertaking to act as a spy in a foreign dictatorship and if hypnotic techniques make it feasible, one might be well advised to have oneself indoctrinated with an attitude of respect or even reverence toward the dictator. During the interim period when one's task is to work up to a position of authority within the country's armed services, this commitment might be the only possible way of passing the loyalty tests required. If one knew that the process was quickly reversible, that the reversal would be carried out when one's aid was needed, and that the likely losses due to one's behavior in this state would probably be heavily outweighed by the gains, the commitment to this belief would surely be rational, one might say, just *because* the belief itself was irrational. It is possible to give selfish reasons for adopting an unselfish attitude, as we have argued in this chapter. One can certainly describe the first kind of situation less paradoxically: one might say that the attitude adopted is the rational one and that we must simply avoid the assumption that rational attitudes necessarily incorporate the beliefs best supported by the evidence, i.e., those which it would be most rational to adopt if one's dominant concern was being right. That is, beliefs which it is probably best for a particular man to hold may not be the beliefs which are most likely to be true. Similarly, one might handle the moral-attitude paradox by saying that we must distinguish between reasons which are relevant for a rational selfish man and selfish reasons. Then we can say that the basic maneuver in the argument for the moral attitude consists in showing that a rational mortal cannot, ultimately, be purely selfish, that moral considerations are, without qualification, good reasons, etc. Yet the other formulation must be explored before it can be transcended. It is too plausible to be dismissed as a mere confusion, just as the idea that "This statement is not true" must be either true or false needs to be explored before it can be transcended.

There are several related paradoxes. The paradox of conscience is one. One should surely always do whatever seems, on careful reflection, to be the right thing to do; but since we are all fallible, what seems to be right will sometimes turn out to be wrong and so sometimes we should do what is wrong. It should first be noted that our obligation to do what we believe to be right is entirely dependent upon the assumption that our beliefs are reasonably good indications of the truth of the matter. That is, we assume prior success in developing a good analytical moral sense or conscience. For if we know our conscience is very unlikely to be right, we certainly have no obligation to heed it. Conversely, insofar as we have good grounds for thinking it reliable and no grounds for thinking that any other arbiter to which we have access is more reliable, then we have good grounds for doing what our conscience dictates. Hence we have good grounds for doing what will sometimes *turn out* to be wrong, i.e., not to be the ideal action had we been able to foresee everything that actually happened, to calculate correctly, etc. But, of course, this does not show we had good grounds for doing what *we knew* to be wrong. Our commitment to the promptings of our conscience needs both effort and justification; it is neither easy nor unconditional.

This paradox is exactly paralleled by one about belief. We should, it seems reasonable to suggest, believe what we think is best supported by the evidence. But long experience makes it clear this will sometimes mean believing something false. It appears to follow that we should believe some false propositions. But all that really follows is that what we should believe is not guaranteed to be true and that the moment its error appears, our obligation to believe it disappears. We never had any obligation to believe something known to be false, only something which was, among other unknown properties, false. Our obligations are to actions, beliefs, and so on as they appear to us after careful scrutiny, using tested instruments; obligations cannot be determined by unknown properties.

With these cases in mind we can rather easily handle the so-called paradox of democracy. Let us suppose that a long and bitter campaign is fought between a manufacturing group and consumers' representatives over passage of a minimum-standards law which applies to chewing gum and that the manufacturing group wins the referendum because of a very successful and very extensive publicity campaign, although the data clearly indicate to the professional statistician that these substandard sweets are responsible for a serious rise in pre-teen-age stomach ulcers. In such a case, the majority have spoken; so in a democracy the proposed law should not be introduced. But objectively speaking, the reverse is the case. Hence democracy is involved in the paradox of laws which should and should not be passed.

"Democracy" is in the same role here as a man's conscience or judgment in the earlier cases. It is only because we can give grounds for believing that more good decisions are made by a system of popular vote and representative government than by the alternatives [19] that we can even argue that what was voted should be done. It is perfectly clear it will not always turn out to be the best choice, but still *it* ought to be done even though it ought not to have been voted. "It" is not a (known-to-be-) mistaken action but an action which in fact happened to be wrong. The pinch in this case is perhaps a little sharper than in the preceding ones because even at the time of the decision it was objectively determinable that the decision was not the best one, in terms of the merits of the alternatives. But the result is the same: we stay with a commitment or an attitude when (1) having a commitment to *some* decision process is on balance better than any alternative, e.g., deciding each issue by whatever method has the strongest support at the time; and (2) in a particular type of situation we have good grounds for thinking that on balance *the* decision process to which we are committed is the best feasible.

A similar argument led us to the solution of the difficulty about justice for a functional theory of morality, for there too we found an apparent contradiction between the decisons made by a procedure supposedly intended to maximize benefits to those it affects and the direct calculation of those benefits. The same type of reasoning enables us to handle a range of cases from the death of Socrates to the decision whether to evaluate the virtue of acts in terms of intent or in terms of consequences. Socrates had the opportunity to escape the death penalty the law had decreed, but he declined to avail himself of it, expressing the view that his commitment to the laws should not evaporate as soon as they turned against him. The penalty was manifestly unjust, indeed, almost unintended, and so one would think the commitment voided. Socrates rightly saw that the inertia of a commitment must carry us far past the point at which we make the commitment revocable on each occasion, since it cannot otherwise yield its great benefits. Whether we should be carried to accept quite so extreme an injustice is not so clear. Whether Socrates' age or particular "crime" makes the case substantially different would require much discussion, but the point of his position is profound.

The great dilemma of judging the virtue of actions in terms of their

---

[19] The matter is actually somewhat complicated by the possibility that even if fewer good *decisions* are made by a democratic electorate, more good *effects* may occur, e.g., because of the greater pleasure of making its own decisions by comparison with having to follow orders.

motives or in terms of their effects further illustrates the two-stage approach to commitments. We can judge acts to be virtuous only if the motives are good, but a pure intent is not enough. It is a *necessary* condition for virtue, not a sufficient one. The commitment to virtuous motives has justification only insofar as it tends to promote beneficial acts. In someone of great stupidity or with absurd conceptions of what is beneficial for others, the results will be bad, not good; and since this is foreseeable, there has to be a supraordinate obligation on all to use only a demonstrably reliable judgment and otherwise to withhold judgment. To the extent that an agent is responsible for his or her failure to achieve these standards, to that extent virtuous motives do not establish virtue. Conversely and more obviously, good results do not make good actions. Interestingly, even actions done *because of good results which were foreseen* are not necessarily virtuous, for the actor may have been entirely careless or overly optimistic in his calculations so that it was pure luck that the good results eventuated. In each case we are moving the analysis behind the motives and consequences to considerations which arise when the problem of justifying that motive (attitude, commitment, etc.) is seen in full light.

This kind of investigation is an important, perhaps the most important, part of the analytical procedures recommended here. It remains only to summarize the conclusions, trying to use examples and perspectives we have not exhausted.

21. CONCLUSIONS

The Ten Commandments do not tell us whether or when lying is better than stealing, and neither they nor the text in which they are embedded provides us with any good reason for believing them rather than the tenets of Islam. That is, they lack adequate specification of scope, order, and foundation. The argument here has been that a comprehensive and defensible morality can be founded on considerations of its effects on the members of a moral society and in no other way. Long-run practical considerations indicate the desirability of certain attitudes, such as keeping calm or obeying military orders or not acting hastily; similarly, long-run considerations of one's relationships with others indicate the desirability of the moral attitude, which is defined as the acceptance of the equal worth of all: in its passive form this means recognition of equality of rights, and in its active form it involves love of others. Apart from the several direct arguments for the moral attitude, there is a vast back door to morality whose portals can hardly be avoided. Since morality as defined here offers important benefits for any member of a group if the rest of the group adopts it, there are good grounds for encouraging both this and the next generation to have moral training. And the benefits are sufficient, whatever one's initial selfishness quotient, to make support for moral training sensible even if the price is that one's own attitudes and behavior are affected by the sanction system set up. The intermediate case between the direct and the indirect arguments for morality is provided by the smalle group with which one most frequently does or can choose to interact—the family, the circle of friends, the coworkers, colleagues, or business associates—in which the tendency of one's own moral commitment to bring about the same commitment in others is quite significant and in which any shifts toward morality result in more frequent and profound benefits for the group than for strangers. Of course, deliberately to restrict equality of consideration to the small group on the ground that one thereby maximizes gains is simply immoral and irrational for the reasons given in the discussion of the franchise.

If we accept the argument which leads to the basic moral attitude, a related argument leads on to certain associated moral attitudes, such as reverence for justice and for honesty, each being quasi-independent but ultimately secondary values. It is demonstrable that treating these values as independent is in the long run better for the members of the moral community than attempting to make all decisions in terms of the sole criterion of maximizing benefits for the members. Moral problems are then problems of determining the best action, etc., from the moral point of view, that is, the point of view founded on equal consideration of all and hence involving independent appeal to this set of secondary values. Unconscious or conscious perception of the advantages of appeal to such a system explains the common elements in different moralities; emotional and cognitive deficiencies as well as circumstantial variations explain the differences.

Since the account given is of the best long-run attitude and system, it does not guarantee a coincidence between the moral and the rational attitudes for everyone whatever his circumstances and background at a particular moment. Indeed, as we have just noted, even a group may be rational without being moral in the short run, but not a tribe or a nation or mankind, since these are entities with a long time dimension. Invincible power, a short life or immortality, full foreknowledge, or lack of education in the individual can contribute to widening the gap between rationality and morality; and in the limit case of a supremely powerful rational Being caring about other beings is simply a matter of taste, not reason, and thus doing the will of such a Being in no way makes it probable that one is doing good.

So we have provided a rational basis for morality, but for many that will be less than enough to spur them to action. For them there will still be the need for inspiration and above all for inspiration by example. And that is the role the great religious and moral leaders have always served. If we can enlist their inspiration while rejecting much of the moral philosophy of their later followers, we shall have a system of morality with both passions and principles that recommend it. But setting a good example is not the way to teach ethics, for there must be a way for the observer to tell that the example *is* good, i.e., an understanding of the foundations of the system. A sinner who has acquired that understanding is not wholly without merit beside the saint who has not.[20]

[20] A comment in terms of the traditional philosophical positions about ethics may be helpful to some readers. We are here accepting the categorical nature of the moral imperative that Kant stressed and are trying to give rational grounds for adopting, though slightly limiting the range of, that categorical imperative. Accepting the spirit of the Utilitarians, we try to avoid their problems by extending considerations of utility to the underlying attitudes and values with which they began their conclusions of utility, and in so doing we are able both to resolve the ambiguity in their formula and to incorporate the point of view of the deontologist. We avoid the letter of the naturalistic fallacy by avoiding the mistake of thinking that capsule definitions of central concepts in a vast system are possible, the defense which makes the valuable concepts of theoretical physics immune to the ravages of the operationalist. But, of course, we sin in the spirit of naturalism in that we derive moral principles from the facts of social and personal life, as the best strategy with which to handle the dilemmas and exploit the possibilities of life. Yet we need not say that good is a natural property in the sense to which G. E. Moore rightly took exception. Nor do we have to say that what man wants is fundamentally good. It is often evil and more often morally neutral; but still it is the moving power of morality, just as the desire to win, while not good or bad strategy in chess, is presupposed by all strategy and generates the "ought" of good play from the "is" of the pieces' positions. We try to render more plausible and then to connect the Platonic and perhaps the Aristotelian endeavors to show that the good life for the individual is the moral life with their own and the later social-contract theorists' recognition of its advantages for the group. The attempt to rise from the selfish to the unselfish point of view, in the terminology of this chapter, is the counterpart to the theologian's description of the struggle from original sin to the path of grace.

CONCLUSION

This book contains a great many conclusions, and an attempt to summarize them explicitly would only produce superficialities or repetition. Still, it may not be inappropriate to say something of their spirit. It is often possible to convey, in part, the spirit of a set of conclusions by pointing out their presuppositions, their implicit starting points. But it is to be hoped that the present conclusions do not spring from any unexamined or unsupported presuppositions or prejudices, for it is clearly the task of philosophy to examine the presuppositions of all positions and to provide the support or criticisms that convert them from presuppositions into argued conclusions or abandoned ideas. It has been one of the aims of this book to show that the elimination of presuppositions is entirely possible, contrary to one's intuition that such an attempt can only lead to an infinite regress of assumptions beyond assumptions. These "unconditional proofs" ultimately appeal only to definitions or to facts not tainted by the issue at hand. Primary philosophy should depend on no other kind of proof.

In the absence of presuppositions there are other ways of conveying the spirit of a set of conclusions, and perhaps the best is by the method of contrasts, comparing it with other contemporary points of view, from some of which its differences might not otherwise be noticed by those whose emotions are strongly set in a very different direction. The "primary philosophy" of this book is not the philosophy of logical positivism, for it does not deny the meaningfulness of the traditional problems about ethics and theism and aesthetics. On the contrary, it stresses their fundamental importance. And yet it shares with positivism a certain hardheadedness, a stubborn demand for evidence and logic, a demand which is itself defended. It is not doctrinaire materialism, for it attempts to underpin, not dismiss, morality and human responsibility and the domain of the mental. But still it is like materialism in stressing the purely material nature of the substratum of which man is composed, with all his mighty powers and his mightier potentialities. It is not linguistic analysis or "ordinary language philosophy" in the sense in which these positions are taken as abandoning the traditional concerns of philosophy in favor of grammatical studies and as blindly accepting the beliefs of the man in the street. However, if one is concerned with the primary problems, it is just as essential now as in the Socratic dialogs to take time and trouble over analyzing each problem and hence the concepts involved in it, for there is no other way to avoid incomplete, ambiguous, or irrelevant solutions. And the techniques of linguistic analysis are the best we have for that job. The position taken here is far from the irrationalism of existentialism—and yet it shares the vital stress on man's own choice and actions as the ultimate pivot of our life and its meaning. It is still less a religious position, and yet no less involved with the ultimate concerns of religion.

Yet these points of similarity and difference are fairly superficial. Like any complex of conclusions about the primary problems, it is best judged not in its entirety but in its particulars, best evaluated not by attaching an old label to the whole, but by careful analysis of the component parts.

Man has many powers, known and yet unknown, psychological and technological. It is quite certain these include the power to solve the primary problems of philosophy, and to apply the solutions to his life. It is less certain that he has solved them, and still less certain that the solutions will be applied. Least certain of all, if they are not, are the chances his life will last the night.

INDEX